CCH

Introduction to Federal Income Taxation in Canada, *2013-2014*

Study Guide

CCH Canadian Limited
300-90 Sheppard Avenue East
Toronto Ontario
M2N 6X1
1 800 268 4522
www.cch.ca

By
Robert E. Beam, FCA
Professor Emeritus, University of Waterloo
Stanley N. Laiken, Ph.D.
Professor Emeritus, University of Waterloo
James J. Barnett, FCPA, FCA
University of Waterloo

Contributors
Ling Chu, M.Tax, CMA
Wilfrid Laurier University
Christy MacDonald, Ph.D., CPA, CA
Deloitte, Kitchener
Devan Mescall, Ph.D., CPA, CA
University of Saskatchewan
Julie Robson, M.Acc., CPA, CA, CPA (Illinois)
University of Waterloo
Barbara Rockx, M.Acc., CPA, CA
University of Toronto
Michael Zender, B.Comm., LLB
Ernst & Young, Toronto

Published by CCH Canadian Limited

ISBN: 978-1-55496-629-5

Typeset by CCH Canadian Limited.
Printed in the United States of America.

About This Study Guide

The purpose of this study guide is to provide you with an effective tool for finding problem material related to the topic you are studying. The Learning Chart found in each chapter aligns the topics covered in that chapter with example problems, review questions, multiple choice questions, exercises, and assignment problems (which are found in the textbook) so that you can easily find either the commentary or problem material related to a particular tax issue. For example, for the Chapter 1 topic "Determination of Income and Taxable Income" (¶1,260), there are three items related to this topic: an Example Problem, Exercise 2, and Assignment Problem 2.

This study guide also contains the solutions to the following problem material in the textbook:
- Review Questions
- Multiple Choice Questions
- Exercises

The solutions to the Assignment Problems are not provided, as many instructors use them for hand-in assignments for grading. However, the DVD included with the textbook contains over 150 problems that are similar to the Assignment Problems. Solutions are provided for these problems.

Study Tips: Throughout the Study Guide, you will find a number of tips to help you get the most out of your study time.

Study Notes: Space has been provided in the Study Guide for you to write your own notes.

How the Text is Organized

The study of Canadian federal income taxation is made more complex, particularly at the introductory level, not because of the lack of good interpretive materials to guide the student, but, in the authors' opinion, because of the lack of organization in the presentation of these materials for systematic study. While the *Income Tax Act* (the Act), the statute governing the federal taxation of income in Canada, is organized generally by source of income, interpretive material available to students at the introductory level is often organized by topics which may cover elements of several sources.

Since the authors of these materials feel that it is important to the understanding of the Act that the student generally studies the major provisions of the statute in sequence, the chapters of this book generally follow the organization of the Act. The purpose of these materials is to guide the student in the study at the introductory level of the major provisions of the Act and some of the related provisions in the *Excise Tax Act* (the ETA) pertaining to the Goods and Services Tax/Harmonized Sales Tax. A copy of the Act plus the Canada Revenue Agency's (CRA's) Interpretation Bulletins, Information Circulars, and Advance Tax Rulings are considered to be important materials for the course. The purpose is to organize the student's reference to interpretive material in the order of presentation in the Act. This book is designed to encourage students to refer to the Act, case law, and the CRA's publications. CRA publications are available at no charge on the CRA website: www.cra-arc.gc.ca.

The Importance of Problem Material

The commentary presented in this book highlights key areas of the Act. The textbook provides additional interpretation of particularly difficult provisions of the Act or elements of the common law or case law in the area. The basic concepts and principles underlying the rules of the legislation are emphasized throughout these materials. Most important for the study of income taxation, it provides fact situations or example problems which demonstrate the application of the provisions of the Act to realistic situations. In fact, the primary teaching approach used in this commentary is the presentation of example problems and exercises with solutions. These solutions demonstrate various methods of approaching actual problems in income taxation. The solutions also provide explanatory and interpretive notes, which are an important component of these materials, often expanding a topic beyond the confines of the particular facts under discussion.

These materials are designed to present situations which will help students to focus their attention on the reading and understanding of a particular provision or set of provisions with the objective of developing more generalized skills to be used in the interpretation of the Act.

References

References are provided in the outer margin of the text beside the paragraphs to which they pertain. These references are to the following sources:

1. ITA refers to the sections of the *Income Tax Act* to be discussed in the chapter;
2. ITAR refers to the *Income Tax Application Rules, 1971*, which are found in the volume containing the Act immediately following the provisions of the Act;
3. ITR refers to the Income Tax Regulations which are also found in the volume containing the Act;
4. ETA refers to sections of the *Excise Tax Act* in which provisions of the Goods and Services Tax (GST)/ Harmonized Sales Tax (HST) can be found;
5. IT, IC, TR, and ATR refer, respectively, to Interpretation Bulletins, Information Circulars, Tax Rulings, and Advance Tax Rulings — Second Series, and are available in a one-volume softcover edition published by CCH Canadian Limited;
6. ITTN refers to Income Tax Technical News releases that are published by the CRA intermittently to provide current technical interpretations.
7. *Folios* refers to *Income Tax Folios* which are being published by the CRA in chapters by topic to update and replace ITs and ITTNs.
8. Cda-U.S. TT refers to the *Canada-United States Income Tax Convention (1980)*; and
9. Doc refers to documents released by the federal government under *Access to Information* legislation and contained in the Tax Window Files of CCH Canadian's Tax Library.

An explanation of these references is provided in Chapter 1. References to sections of the Act are provided for exercises and assignment problems. It should also be understood that in the course of their use within the paragraph of the text, all references preceded by such specific terms as "section", "subsection", "paragraph", "subparagraph", etc., without any indication of the pertinent statute, refer to the provisions of the *Income Tax Act*. Similarly, the provisions of the Income Tax Regulations are preceded by the term "Regulation" without specifying the relevant legislation. In the margin, these references are preceded by "ITA" and "ITR", respectively.

References to the *Excise Tax Act* are usually confined to the GST/HST part of a chapter and are specifically indicated as being to that legislation. References in the margin are preceded by "ETA". An attempt has been made to integrate GST/HST with relevant transactions discussed under the *Income Tax Act* in the chapters where these transactions are discussed.

Acronyms

An alphabetical list of acronyms used in the book appears in the first section of this Study Guide, immediately following the Table of Contents. The list provides the meaning of the acronym and paragraph references where the term is used in the textbook.

Knowledge Reference List

A mapping of the Knowledge Reference List (KRL) to the book is provided in the next section of this Study Guide. Paragraph references and titles in the textbook are shown for each line of the KRL. Students who are interested in reviewing problems and questions on those topics can follow a paragraph listing in the KRL map to the Learning Charts for each chapter in this Study Guide.

Review Questions

A set of review questions is provided at the end of each chapter. These short-answer questions attempt to review key points made in the text or points that are not integrated into the example problems, multiple choice questions, exercises, or assignment problems in the chapter. Discussion notes on the review questions are provided in the Study Guide.

Multiple Choice Question

Since multiple choice questions are common in professional examinations, this textbook provides six or seven such questions covering the material in each chapter, starting with Chapter 2, for a total of over 100 questions. Annotated solutions are provided in the Study Guide to enhance learning through self-study.

Exercises

Exercises have been provided at the end of each chapter. These usually consist of short problems to highlight particular areas of the chapter. They are designed to be fairly narrow in scope, to provide the student with an opportunity to apply the material in the chapter to a specific problem situation. Solutions to these exercises have been provided in the Study Guide.

Assignment Problems

Assignment problems are provided for each chapter of the textbook. These problems are designed to have the student apply the material discussed in each chapter to an actual fact or problem situation. While these problems focus on the key elements of the chapter in much the same way that the solved example problems in the commentary do, the problems are not identical in their coverage or presentation. As a result, it will be necessary for the student to read the assignment problems very carefully in preparing a solution. Solutions to these problems are not available. However, similar additional problems with solutions are provided on the DVD that accompanies the textbook, as discussed below.

Additional Problems with Solutions

Students often request additional problems with solutions that they can use on a self-study basis for preparation for tests and examinations. For this purpose, a comprehensive compilation of problems similar to the Assignment Problems in the textbook and multiple choice questions is provided on the DVD accompanying the textbook. There are over 150 problems and solutions on the DVD, classified by coverage of chapters in the textbook. The problems, most of which have previously been used as examination questions, will provide students with an opportunity to deal with problems of a comprehensive nature. Since these supplemental problems may cover material from several chapters, as examination questions often do, they provide an excellent source for review in preparation for examinations.

Suggested Approach

The authors suggest the following approach to the use of these materials. First, the students should identify the issue in an assignment problem that they need to research, then scan the headings of the particular chapter and use them to look for the topics that relate to that issue. Once the relevant parts of the chapter are identified, students should read the commentary, including any referenced material such as sections of the Act or Regulations, Interpretation Bulletins, Information Circulars, and Advance Tax Rulings. Reviewing any example problems to see how the provisions work will also help develop understanding. The solutions provided for these problems will demonstrate the approach that can be taken for the type of example problem under consideration. The solutions can also be used as a check on the student's understanding as well as a means of providing further interpretation and explanation of the material covered. The exercises at the end of the chapter can be used in a similar manner. Once the parts of a chapter have been completed in this manner, the student should be sufficiently prepared to attempt the assignment problems relevant to a particular part or to the whole chapter. When reviewing material for examination or other purposes, the multiple choice questions at the end of each chapter can be attempted. The solutions in the Study Guide can then be checked. As well, the additional problems included on the DVD that accompanies the textbook can be attempted. Review might also focus on the approaches used to address the various types of problems presented.

Learning Goals

To be a successful tax adviser it is not enough to just know the technical material found in the Act and supporting materials. You need to understand the purpose behind the rules so you can explain to others why your tax plan does not violate either the provision as it is written or purpose behind the provision. You also need to be able to blend a number of complex provisions into a comprehensive plan to accomplish the goals of your client or employer. As shown in the learning model below, you need to know the technical provisions and understand them well enough to be able to craft a comprehensive plan. The end goal is the successful application of knowledge and understanding.

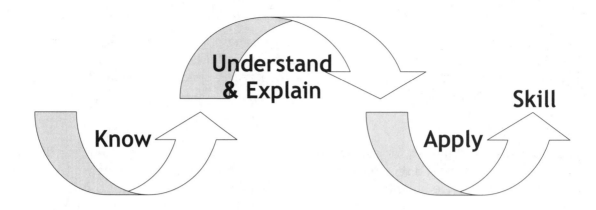

In each chapter of this book we will provide you with what you should Know, Understand & Explain, and Apply as a result of studying that chapter.

Materials at the introductory level on Canadian income tax legislation are not easy to study. A conscientious effort to do the work and, particularly, to do problems and apply what has been read is essential to a good understanding of this material. The authors have attempted to meet the challenge of presenting the material by setting out the work that must be done and by explaining, as best they can, the major provisions of the legislation. The challenge of learning the material is, of course, left to the student.

Robert E. Beam
Stanley N. Laiken
James J. Barnett

July 2013

Table of Contents

Acronyms

Acronym	Meaning	¶
A		
AB	Active business	12,140
ABI	Active business income	12,100
ABIL	Allowable business investment loss	7,720
ACB	Adjusted cost base	7,020; 8,130
ACL	Allowable capital loss	7,020
AII	Aggregate investment income	12,335
AOC	Acquisition of control	11,090
ART	Additional refundable tax	12,335
ATR	Advance Tax Ruling	1,143
B		
BFTC	Business foreign tax credit	10,490; 11,335
Boot (expression)	Non-share/non-partnership interest consideration	16,050
C		
CCA	Capital cost allowance	5,005
CCPC	Canadian-controlled private corporation	11,212
CCTB	Canada child tax benefit	10,460
CDA	Capital dividend account	15,055
CDSB	Canada disability savings bond	9,095.50
CDSG	Canada disability savings grant	9,095.40
CEC	Cumulative eligible capital	5,210
CECA	Cumulative eligible capital amount	5,210
CESG	Canada education savings grant	9,090.20
CG	Capital gain	7,020
CGD	Capital gains deduction	13,370
CGE	Capital gains exemption	13,370
CL	Capital loss	7,020
CLB	Canada learning bond	9,090.30
CNIL	Cumulative net investment loss	13,380
CRA	Canada Revenue Agency	1,350
D		
DBP	Defined benefit pension plan	9,330.10
DPSP	Deferred profit sharing plan	9,330.30
DTC	Dividend tax credit	6,060
E		
ECE	Eligible capital expenditure	5,210
ECP	Eligible capital property	5,210
ETA	*Excise Tax Act*	
F		
FCA	Federal Court of Appeal	1,335
FMV	Fair market value	4,045; 16,155
FTC	Foreign tax credit	10,490; 11,335
G		
GIS	Guaranteed income supplement	
GRIP	General-rate income pool	12,040
GST	Goods and Services Tax	1,400

Acronym	Meaning	¶
H		
HBP	Home buyers' plan	9,395
HST	Harmonized Sales Tax	1,400
I		
IC	Information Circulars	1,143
IT	Interpretation Bulletins	1,143
ITA	*Income Tax Act*	1,020
ITAR	Income Tax Application Rules	1,134
ITC	Investment Tax Credit	11,350; 11,355
ITC	Input Tax Credit	1,440
ITR	Income Tax Regulations	1,136
L		
LLP	Lifelong learning plan	9,400
LLP	Limited liability partnership	18,040
LOCP	Lower of cost or proceeds	5,015.20
LPP	Listed personal property	7,015
LSC	Legal stated capital	15,055; 16,145
M		
M&P	Manufacturing and processing	11,910
MPP	Money-purchase pension plan	9,330.20
N		
NBFTC	Non-business foreign tax credit	10,490; 11,330
NCL	Net capital loss	10,040; 11,075
N-CL	Non-capital loss	10,035; 11,065
O		
OAS	Old Age Security	9,460
P		
PA	Pension adjustment	9,355
PE	Permanent establishment	11,260
PI	Partnership interest	18,060
POD	Proceeds of disposition	7,020
PRE	Principal residence exemption	7,230
PSB	Personal services business	12,155
PSBI	Personal services business income	12,155
PUC	Paid-up capital	15,025
PUP	Personal-use property	7,014
Q		
QSBCS	Qualifying small business corporation shares	13,340
R		
RDSP	Registered disability saving plan	9,095
RDTOH	Refundable dividend tax on hand	12,345
REOP	Reasonable expectation of profit	4,237
RESP	Registered education savings plan	9,090

Acronym   Meaning   ¶

R (cont'd)

Acronym	Meaning	¶
RRIF	Registered retirement income fund	9,410
RRSP	Registered retirement savings plan	9,300

S

Acronym	Meaning	¶
SBC	Small business corporation	13,345
SBD	Small business deduction	12,140
SCC	Supreme Court of Canada	1,340
SIB	Specified investment business	11,150
SIBI	Specified investment business income	11,150

T

Acronym	Meaning	¶
T1	Personal income tax return	
T2	Corporate income tax return	
T3	Income tax return for a trust	
TCG	Taxable capital gain	7,020
TFSA	Tax-free savings account	9,220
TOP	Tax otherwise payable	11,330; 11,335
TV	Tax value	16,060

U

Acronym	Meaning	¶
UCC	Undepreciated capital cost	5,015
UCCB	Universal child care benefit	9,135

Knowledge Reference List

Mapping of Tax Knowledge Reference List to Textbook Paragraphs

Knowledge Reference List		Textbook Coverage
Area: Income Taxation	**ITA Reference**	
1. General Concepts and Principles of Taxation		
Structure of the *Income Tax Act* in Canada		¶1,001 History and Legislation — Canadian Tax System ¶1,020 Introduction to Income Tax Legislation ¶1,030 Tax Principles and Concepts ¶1,110 The *Income Tax Act* ¶1,115 How do I reference the Act ¶1,120 Structure of the *Income Tax Act* ¶1,122 Special transaction taxes ¶1,124 Administration and interpretation ¶1,150 Interpretation of tax legislation ¶1,185 Why Study Taxation ¶1,190 The Practice of Taxation ¶1,195 The role of the PA in Tax Matters
Reference sources — Interpretation bulletins, information circulars, advance tax rulings, and case law		¶1,130 Related References ¶1,140 Other Interpretive Sources ¶1,450 Note on Organization of Legislation and Availability of Interpretive Sources
Liability for tax	Section 2; subsection 250(4)	¶2,000 Liability of Individuals for Income Tax ¶2,010 Liability of Individual Residents ¶2,020 Full-Time Residence ¶2,040 Part-Year Residence ¶2,055 Liability of Non-Residents ¶2,070 International Tax Treaties and Individuals ¶2,200 Liability of Corporations for Income Tax ¶2,220 Residence of Corporations ¶2,240 Liability of Non-Resident Corporations ¶2,250 International Tax Treaties and Corporations ¶19,010 Residents ¶19,020 Non-Residents
Tax evasion	Sections 238, 239	¶1,360 Tax Evasion, Avoidance, and Planning ¶14,025 Criminal Offenses
Tax avoidance — General anti-avoidance rule	Subsections 245(1), (2), (3), (4), (5); paragraph 246(1)(*a*)	¶13,500 General Anti-Avoidance Rule under the ITA ¶13,510 The Statutory Provision ¶13,515 Purpose ¶13,520 Defined terms ¶13,525 Limitation ¶13,530 Examples in the technical notes ¶13,535 Administration and application ¶13,540 Federal Court of Appeal — *OSFC Holdings Ltd.* ¶13,560 Supreme Court of Canada — *Canada Trustco and Mathew et al.* ¶13,580 The Saga Continues — Decisions Since *Canada Trustco*
Liability of directors	Section 227.1	¶14,322 Liability of directors
Books and records	Section 230	¶14,050 Books and records
Concept of residency, deemed resident, part-year resident	Subsection 250(1); paragraphs 250(4)(*a*), (*c*)	¶1,123 Non-residents ¶2,020 Full-Time Residence ¶2,025 Deemed full-time residence ¶2,030 Common law concept of full-time residence ¶2,035 Administrative practice ¶2,040 Part-Year Residence ¶2,045 Applicable law ¶2,050 Clean break or fresh start: The concept ¶2,060 General determination of liability for non-residents ¶2,075 Services in relation to international tax treaties ¶2,080 Resident and "tie-breaker" rules ¶2,085 Permanent establishment ¶2,090 Summary of the Residence Issue for an Individual ¶2,100 Comprehensive Consideration of the Residence of an Individual ¶2,105 Stages of involvement ¶2,110 Consider both sides ¶2,115 Form of advice ¶2,120 Application

Mapping of Tax Knowledge Reference List to Textbook Paragraphs

Knowledge Reference List		Textbook Coverage
Area: Income Taxation	**ITA Reference**	
Concept of residency, deemed resident, part-year resident — *(cont'd)*	Subsection 250(1); paragraphs 250(4)(*a*), (*c*) — *(cont'd)*	¶2,130 Non-tax factors affecting planning for the residence of an individual ¶2,210 Charging Provision ¶2,220 Residence of Corporations ¶2,225 Deemed residence ¶2,230 Common law concept of corporate residence ¶2,240 Liability of Non-Resident Corporations ¶2,250 International Tax Treaties and Corporations ¶2,260 Comprehensive Consideration of the Residence of a Corporation
Currency used for tax information	Subsections 261(2), (3), (5)	¶14,018 Functional currency tax reporting
Exempt entities	Paragraphs 149 (1)(*c*), (*d*), (*e*), (*f*), (*j*), (*k*), (*l*), (*o*), (*o*.1), (*r*), (*s*), (*u*), (*u*.1), (*u*.2), (*x*); subsection 149(5)	¶9,230 Exempt Entities
Withholding requirements and information returns	Paragraphs 153(1)(*a*), (*b*), (*c*), (*d*), (*d*.1), (*h*), (*j*), (*l*)	¶14,320 Obligations of Other Payers, Trustees, etc. ¶14,330 Payments to non-residents ¶14,335 Foreign reporting requirements ¶19,130 Disposing of taxable Canadian property ¶19,140 Deductions and Credits Allowed a Non-Resident ¶19,160 Withholding Taxes on Canadian Source Income — Part XIII Tax
2. Computation of Income		
Income for taxation year	Section 3	¶1,200 Introduction to Income Tax and Taxable Income ¶1,210 Approaches to Defining Income ¶1,240 Computation of Income ¶1,260 Determination of Income and Taxable Income ¶3,037 Defining the Taxation Year
Source and timing of income or loss	Section 4	Throughout the text, particularly in the first 10 chapters
General limitation — Expenses	Sections 67, 67.1, 67.2, 67.3, 67.5, 67.6	¶3,450 Interest on money borrowed for passenger vehicle ¶3,460 Limitation re cost of leased passenger vehicle ¶13,050 Salaries, Bonuses, and Other Payments to the Shareholder-Manager ¶13,055 General Guidelines ¶13,060 Salaries and Bonuses
Alternative business structures — Sole proprietorship, corporations, joint ventures, and partnerships		¶2,000 Liability of Individuals for Income Tax ¶2,200 Liability of Corporations for Income Tax ¶18,000 Partnership
Types of corporations — Canadian-controlled private corporation, public, private	Subsections 89(1), 125(7), 248(1)	¶11,212 Types of Corporations ¶11,213 Private Corporation ¶11,214 CCPC ¶11,215 Public Corporations ¶11,216 Diagrammatic summary of types of corporations
Taxation year, fiscal period	Subsections 249(1), (3), (3.1), (4); Section 249.1	¶3,037 Defining the Taxation Year
Professional business, work in progress, inventory	Section 34.1	¶4,060 Sole Proprietorship
Partnerships — Elimination of corporation tax deferral	Sections 34.2, 34.3	¶18,035 General rules
3. Income or Loss from an Office or Employment		
Basic rules	Section 5	¶3,000 Basic Rules ¶3,040 Salary, Wages, and Other Remuneration Including Gratuities
Taxable benefits	Paragraph 6(1)(*a*)	¶3,050 Amounts Received ¶3,060 Volunteer Services Exemption ¶3,409 Vehicles Other Than Automobiles

Mapping of Tax Knowledge Reference List to Textbook Paragraphs

Knowledge Reference List			Textbook Coverage
Area: Income Taxation		**ITA Reference**	
Taxable benefits — *(cont'd)*	Travel, personal, or living allowances	Subparagraphs 6(1)(*b*)(i), (v), (vii), (vii.1), (x), (xi)	¶3,155 Allowances Overview ¶3,160 Exception of allowance for travelling expenses of sales/negotiating persons ¶3,165 Exception of allowance for travelling expenses of other employees
	Director's or other fees	Paragraph 6(1)(*c*)	¶3,170 Director's or other fees ¶3,220 Benefit from Employer-Paid GST/HST
	Automobile benefits	Paragraphs 6(1)(*e*), (*k*), (*l*); subsections 6(1.1), (2)	¶3,402 Standby Charge and Operating Cost Benefit for Automobile Provided by Employer ¶3,403 Calculation of the standby charge benefit from the use of the car itself ¶3,404 Determining the operating cost benefit ¶3,406 Application of the rules ¶3,408 Employee-Owned Automobile Operating Expense Benefit ¶3,410 Motor Vehicle Allowances Received from Employers ¶3,420 Allowances for motor vehicles — Other persons ¶3,425 Allowance deemed not to be reasonable
	Other taxable benefits	Paragraph 6(1)(*f*); subsections 6(3), (4), (7), (8), (9), (19), (20), (23)	¶3,100 Specific Inclusions ¶3,110 Value of Board and Lodging ¶3,120 Other Fringe Benefits ¶3,125 General rules ¶3,130 Housing loss and housing cost benefits ¶3,135 Employee loans ¶3,230 Employment Insurance Benefits ¶3,240 Payments by Employer to Employee ¶3,250 Restrictive Covenants ¶3,260 Stock Options ¶3,265 General
	Stock option benefits	Paragraph 7(1)(*a*); subsections 7(1.1), (1.3), (1.31), (8) to (16)	¶3,270 Rules applicable for all types of corporations ¶3,273 Stock option cash outs ¶3,275 Rules applicable to Canadian-controlled private corporations ¶3,280 Rules applicable to public corporations — Deferral [Repealed] ¶3,285 Valuation of shares ¶3,287 Risk factors ¶3,288 Federal Budget 2010 proposed changes — 2010 to 2015 ¶3,290 Summary ¶7,290 Disposition of Shares Acquired Under a Stock Option ¶7,295 Disposition of newly acquired securities ¶7,300 Adjusted cost base of shares acquired under a stock option
Deductions allowed and limitations		Paragraphs 8(1)(*b*), (*f*), (*h*), (*h*.1), (i), (j), (*i*.1), (*m*); subsections 8(2), (4), (6), (6.1), (7), (10), (13)	¶3,310 Sales/Negotiating Person's Expenses ¶3,320 Any Employee's Travelling Expenses Other Than Motor Vehicle Expenses ¶3,325 Overview ¶3,330 Conditions ¶3,335 Limitations ¶3,340 Receipts by part-time employees for travelling expenses ¶3,342 Dues and Other Expenses ¶3,345 Workspace in Home ¶3,352 Legal Expenses ¶3,354 Clergy's residence ¶3,356 Teacher's exchange fund ¶3,358 Railway employees ¶3,360 Transport employees ¶3,362 CPP and EI premiums payable in respect of an assistant ¶3,364 Retirement compensation arrangements ¶3,366 Salary reimbursements

Mapping of Tax Knowledge Reference List to Textbook Paragraphs

Knowledge Reference List		Textbook Coverage
Area: Income Taxation	**ITA Reference**	
Deductions allowed and limitations — *(cont'd)*	Paragraphs 8(1)(*b*), (*f*), (*h*), (*h*.1), (*i*), (*j*), (*i*.1), (*m*); subsections 8(2), (4), (6), (6.1), (7), (10), (13) — *(cont'd)*	¶3,368 Forfeitures ¶3,370 Musical instrument costs ¶3,372 Artist's expenses ¶3,374 Tradesperson's tool expenses ¶3,380 Registered Pension Plans ¶3,385 Overview ¶3,435 Overview of Deductible Expenses ¶3,440 Motor vehicle and aircraft — Interest and CCA ¶3,445 Imputed interest deemed paid ¶3,455 Capital cost for a passenger vehicle ¶4,257 Sales/Negotiating Person's Expenses Revisited ¶9,300 Deductions in computing income
Employee or self-employed; personal services business	Subsections 125(7), 248(1)	¶3,010 Employed Versus Self-Employed or Independent Contractor ¶3,015 Overview ¶3,020 The economic reality or entrepreneur test ¶3,025 Integration or organization test ¶3,030 Specific result test ¶3,035 Other considerations
4. Income or Loss from a Business or Property		
Types of income: active business income, property income, capital gain/loss		¶4,020 Business Income Versus Capital Receipt ¶4,021 Overview ¶4,022 Objective of the analysis ¶4,023 Observable behavioural factors or "badges of trade" ¶4,024 Summary ¶4,025 Damages as a Receipt of Income or Capital ¶4,026 Non-performance of business contracts ¶4,027 Cancellation of agency agreements ¶4,028 Loss of property ¶4,030 Other Receipts or Benefits ¶4,031 Profits from an illegal business ¶4,032 Profits from betting, gambling, and windfalls ¶4,033 Subsidies ¶4,034 Forgiveness of debt rules ¶4,035 Business Income Versus Property Income ¶4,036 General classification of income/loss from using/holding property ¶4,037 Determination by corporations ¶4,038 Determination by partnership ¶4,039 Reasons for distinction between business and property income ¶4,070 Conversion of Accounting Income to Net Business Income for Tax Purposes ¶6,010 Interest Income ¶6,065 Dividends Received from Non-Resident Corporations ¶8,020 Capital Receipt Versus Income Receipt Revisited ¶8,025 Primary intention ¶8,030 Secondary intention ¶8,035 Badges of trade or behavioural factors
Extended meaning of carrying on business	Section 253	¶2,065 The meaning of carrying on business in Canada
Owner-manager tax planning	Incorporation	¶13,310 Use of Holding Companies ¶13,315 An extension of integration ¶13,320 Compensation ¶13,325 Deferral of tax on dividends ¶13,330 Implementing an estate freeze
	Compensation options for owner-manager: employment income versus dividends	¶13,010 Considerations in Choosing Elements of Shareholder-Manager Remuneration ¶13,015 Cash Needs ¶13,020 Individual's tax bracket ¶13,025 25% dividend gross-up and credit

Mapping of Tax Knowledge Reference List to Textbook Paragraphs

Knowledge Reference List			Textbook Coverage
Area: Income Taxation		**ITA Reference**	
Owner manager tax planning — *(cont'd)*	Compensation options for owner-manager: employment income versus dividends — *(cont'd)*		¶13,030 41% dividend gross-up and credit ¶13,035 Availability of tax deferral ¶13,040 Avoid exceeding the business limit for the SBD ¶13,090 Other Planning Considerations for Shareholder-Manager Remuneration ¶13,095 Income splitting ¶13,100 Fringe Benefits ¶13,200 Salary Versus Dividends ¶13,210 The Basic Trade-Off ¶13,220 Approximate Amounts of Taxable Dividends That Can Be Distributed Tax-Free ¶13,230 Distribution out of income taxed at small business rate ¶13,240 Distributions out of income not eligible for the small business deduction ¶13,250 Summary of the Salary Versus Dividends Issue
	Shareholder and employee benefits and loans, deemed interest paid	Subsections 15(1), (1.3), (2), (2.1), (2.3), (2.4), (2.6), (5), (9); Section 80.5; subsections 80.4(1), (2), (3), (4), (6), (7), (8)	¶13,075 Shareholder Benefits ¶13,080 Shareholder loans
Basic rules and principles		Sections 9, 11; subsection 12(2)	¶4,015 Income from a business
Inclusions		Paragraphs 12(1)(*a*), (*b*), (*c*), (*d*), (*e*), (*f*), (*g*), (*i*), (*n*), (*t*), (*v*), (*x*), (*y*); subsections 12(3), (4), (11)	¶4,100 Inclusions ¶4,105 Inclusions in Income for Tax Purposes ¶4,110 Amounts Received and Receivable ¶4,120 Inducement Payments or Reimbursements ¶4,130 Restrictive Covenants ¶4,140 Partnership income ¶4,150 Barter Transactions ¶6,005 Specific Inclusions of Property Income ¶6,015 The meaning of interest ¶6,020 Method of reporting income ¶6,025 Accrual rules for individuals ¶6,030 Other interest income provisions ¶6,032 Purchasing a corporate bond at a discount ¶6,034 Zero-coupon bonds ¶6,035 Timing and recognition of interest income ¶6,040 Payments Based on Production or Use ¶6,045 Concept of the provision
Deductions — Limitations		Paragraphs 18(1)(*a*), (*b*), (*e*), (*f*), (*h*), (*j*), (*l*), (*n*), (*p*), (*q*), (*r*), (*t*), (*u*)	¶4,206 Disallowed or restricted deductions ¶4,210 Deductibility of Expenditures ¶4,215 General test — To gain or produce income ¶4,220 Expenditure of a capital nature ¶4,222 Personal or living expenses ¶4,225 Other Prohibited Deductions ¶4,226 Reserves ¶4,227 Payments on discounted bonds ¶4,228 Use of recreational facilities and club dues ¶4,229 Political contributions ¶4,230 Automobile expenses ¶4,231 Payments under the Act ¶4,232 Prepaid expenses ¶4,233 Expenses of investing in sheltered plans ¶4,234 Workspace in home ¶4,235 Deductibility of provincial capital and payroll taxes ¶4,236 Limitation on accrued expenses ¶4,237 Reasonable Expectation of Profit (REOP)

Mapping of Tax Knowledge Reference List to Textbook Paragraphs

Knowledge Reference List		Textbook Coverage
Area: Income Taxation	**ITA Reference**	
Deductions — Limitations — *(cont'd)*	Paragraphs 18(1)(*a*), (*b*), (*e*), (*f*), (*h*), (*j*), (*l*), (*n*), (*p*), (*q*), (*r*), (*t*), (*u*) — *(cont'd)*	¶4,239 Limitation on Amount of Deductions for Deductible Expenditures ¶4,265 Office in the home
Limitations on certain interest, property tax, and construction costs	Paragraphs 18(2)(*a*), (*b*), (*c*), (*d*), (*e*); subsections 18(3), (3.1), (3.2), (3.3)	¶6,215 Limitation on deduction — Vacant land ¶6,220 "Soft Costs" relating to constructions of buildings or ownership of land
Limitations on other items	Subsections 18(9), (11), (12)	¶4,234 Work space in home ¶4,232 Prepaid expenses ¶4,265 Office in the home
Inventory valuation	Subsections 10(1), (1.1), (2), (2.1), (3)	¶4,045 Basis of Valuation ¶4,050 Adjustment for amortization allocation to inventory: Absorption accounting ¶11,105 Accrued or unrealized losses on inventory
Amounts to be included — Dividends	Paragraphs 12(1)(*j*), (*k*), (*l*), (*m*); 82(1)(*a*), (*a.*1), (*b*); subsections 84(1), (2), (3), (4), (4.1), (6), (7), (9); section 90	¶6,050 Dividends from Corporations Resident in Canada ¶6,052 Overview ¶6,055 The issue ¶6,060 Overview of the Canadian dividend taxation system ¶6,065 Dividends Received from Non-Resident Corporations ¶15,035 The effect of corporate law ¶15,040 Effect of PUC in a redemption of shares ¶15,045 Effect of PUC in other corporate distribution ¶15,155 Deemed dividend on increase in PUC ¶15,160 Deemed dividend on winding-up ¶15,165 Deemed dividend on redemption, acquisition, or cancellation of shares ¶15,170 Deemed dividend on reduction of PUC ¶16,095 The issue in concept ¶16,100 The technical solution ¶16,105 Illustration of application ¶16,110 The effect
Deductions permitted	Paragraphs 20(1)(*a*), (*b*), (*e.*1), (*e.*2), (*f*), (*g*), (*j*), (*l*), (*m*), (*m.*2), (*n*), (*p*), (*q*), (*s*), (*y*), (*z*), (*z*1), (*aa*), (*bb*), (*cc*), (*dd*), (*ee*), (*hh*), (*hh.*1), (*ii*), (*qq*), (rr); subsection 20(9); Section 20.01; subparagraphs 20(1)(*e*)(i), (ii), (iii), (iv), (v)	¶4,240 Deductions specifically permitted ¶4,241 Write-offs of capital expenditures ¶4,242 Interest ¶4,243 Expenses of issuing shares or borrowing money ¶4,244 Premiums on life insurance used as collateral ¶4,245 Discount on debt obligations ¶4,246 The system for reserves under the Act ¶4,247 Employer's contribution to RPP ¶4,248 Employer's contribution under a deferred profit sharing plan ¶4,249 Cancellation of a lease ¶4,250 Landscaping of grounds ¶4,251 Expenses of representation ¶4,252 Investigation of site ¶4,253 Utilities service connection ¶4,254 Disability-related modifications and equipment ¶4,255 Convention expenses ¶4,256 Application of the Rules for Deduction ¶5,150 Franchises and Similar Property ¶6,230 Rental Properties ¶6,235 Separate classes — Rental property costing over $50,000 ¶6,240 Losses from rental property ¶6,315 Investment counsel fees ¶6,410 Applicable to Business Income Only ¶6,420 Applicable to Property Income Only

Mapping of Tax Knowledge Reference List to Textbook Paragraphs

Knowledge Reference List		Textbook Coverage
Area: Income Taxation	**ITA Reference**	
Deductibility of interest expense	Subparagraph 20(1)(*c*)(i); subsections 20(3), 20.1(1), (2), (6); 21(1), (3)	¶5,057 Interest Expense ¶6,260 Interest Deduction ¶6,265 Proposed legislation ¶6,270 Loss of the source of income ¶6,275 Capitalization of interest ¶6,290 Personal Loan Planning and Interest Deductibility ¶6,295 Deductibility of interest expenses ¶6,300 Commentary on two Supreme Court decisions on interest deductibility — *Singleton* and *Ludco* ¶6,305 Tax planning ¶6,310 Carrying charges
Split income	Paragraph 20(1)(*ww*)	¶6,115 Tax on split income earned by persons under 18 years of age (the "kiddie tax")
Reserves	Subsection 20(6); paragraph 20(8)(*b*)	¶8,110 Reserves
Convention expenses	Subsections 20(10), 67.1(3)	¶4,255 Convention Expenses
Foreign taxes	Subsections 20(11), (12)	¶6,325 Foreign non-business income tax
Accrued bond interest	Subsection 20(14)	¶6,036 Purchasing an accrued interest bond
Ceasing to carry on business	Sections 22, 23, 24, 25	¶4,285 Sale of accounts receivable in relation to ceasing to carry on business ¶4,290 Sale of inventory
Professional business, work in progress, inventory	Section 34; subsections 10(4), (5)	¶4,300 Professional Business
Scientific research and development (SR&ED)	Section 37	¶4,310 Scientific Research and Experimental Development ¶4,315 Meaning of scientific research and experimental development ¶4,320 General deduction of expenditures ¶4,325 Election method to determine deduction ¶11,355 Qualified scientific research expenditure
5. Capital Cost Allowance		
General principles and definitions	Subsection 13(21)	¶5,000 The Capital Cost Allowance System ¶5,005 Basic Rules ¶5,006 Introduction ¶5,007 Types of capital property ¶5,008 CCA and neutrality ¶5,009 CCA and tax planning ¶5,012 Eligibility for CCA ¶5,040 Comparison of CCA and accounting amortization ¶5,058 Capital cost reduction for cost assistance ¶5,090 Involuntary and Voluntary Dispositions ¶5,054 Example of CCA over time
Recaptured capital cost allowance	Subsections 13(1), (2), (3), (11)	¶5,015 Classes of assets for tangible capital property
Terminal loss	Subsections 20(16), (16.1), (16.3)	¶5,015 Classes of assets for tangible capital property
Special Rules		¶5,080 Insurance proceeds expended on damaged depreciable property
Exchanges of property	Subsections 13(4), (4.1)	¶5,095 Involuntary dispositions ¶5,100 Voluntary dispositions
Change in use, non-arm's length	Paragraphs 13(7)(*a*), (*b*), (*c*), (*d*), (*e*), (*f*)	¶5,110 Change in Use and Part Disposition Rules ¶5,115 Change from income-producing to other purposes ¶5,120 Change from non-income-producing to income-producing purpose ¶5,125 Property acquired for multiple purposes ¶5,130 Change in proportion of use for producing income and other purposes ¶8,135 Non-arm's length transfer of depreciable property

Mapping of Tax Knowledge Reference List to Textbook Paragraphs

Knowledge Reference List			Textbook Coverage
Area: Income Taxation		**ITA Reference**	
Special Rules — *(cont'd)*	Passenger vehicle	Paragraphs 13(7)(*g*), (*h*)	¶4,258 Automobiles ¶4,260 Automobile allowances ¶5,035 Automobiles used in employment or business
	Deemed capital cost — Inducement	Subsection 13(7.4); paragraph 12(1)(*x*)	¶5,059 Inducement Payments
	Expenses of representation	Subsection 13(12)	¶4,251 Representation Expenses
	Disposition of a building	Subsection 13(21.1)	¶5,025 Ownership of property ¶5,030 Disposition of property ¶8,160 Part Disposition ¶8,170 Replacement Property ¶8,175 The basic deferral ¶8,180 Election for additional deferral ¶8,190 Proceeds on Disposition of Building ¶8,200 Disposition of Depreciable Property
	Loss on certain transfers	Subsection 13(21.2)	¶5,056 Transfers to another class — Avoiding recapture
	Available for use	Subsections 13(26), (27), (28)	¶5,015 Classes of assets for tangible capital property
	Consideration — FMV rules	Subsection 13(33)	¶5,015 Classes of assets for tangible capital property
	Half-year rule and short taxation year	Regulations 1100(2), (3)	¶5,020 Taxation year less than 12 months ¶5,060 Exceptions to the declining balance method ¶5,065 Leasehold improvements ¶5,070 Class 14 limited-life intangibles ¶5,075 Manufacturing and processing machinery and equipment
Capital cost allowances classes		Schedules II and III, Classes 1, 8, 10, 10.1, 12, 13, 14, 17, 43, 44, 45, 50	¶5,015 Classes of assets for tangible capital property ¶5,045 Separate class rule of electronic office equipment
6. Cumulative Eligible Capital			
General rules		Subsections 14(1), (2), (4), (5), (6), (7), (10)	¶5,200 Eligible Capital Property ¶5,210 Basic Rules ¶5,220 Comparison to the CCA system ¶5,240 Non-arm's length transactions ¶5,250 Election re: Capital Gain ¶5,210 Basic Rules ¶5,230 Illustration of the Rules ¶5,235 Common aspects
Acquisition — Non-arm's length		Subsection 14(3)	¶5,240 Non-arm's length transactions ¶7,400 Non-Arm's Length Transfers and the Attribution Rules Revised
Dispositions of eligible capital property		Subsections 14 (1.01), (12), (13)	¶15,065 Example of disposition of eligible capital property
7. Taxable Capital Gains and Allowable Capital Losses			
General rules, definitions, and computation		Sections 38, 54; subsections 39(1), 40(*l*)	¶7,010 History ¶7,013 General considerations ¶7,016 Other capital property ¶7,017 Schematic classification ¶7,018 Restrictions ¶7,020 Terminology ¶7,110 Computation of Capital Gains and Capital Losses ¶7,720 Allowable Business Investment Losses ¶7,115 Proceeds of Disposition ¶7,120 Adjusted Cost base ¶7,125 Mutual Funds and DRIPs ¶7,380 Certain shares deemed to be capital property ¶7,710 Section 3 Revisited ¶7,720 Allowable Business Investment Losses

Mapping of Tax Knowledge Reference List to Textbook Paragraphs

Knowledge Reference List		Textbook Coverage
Area: Income Taxation	**ITA Reference**	
General rules, definitions, and computation — *(cont'd)*	Sections 38, 54; subsections 39(1), 40(*l*) — *(cont'd)*	¶8,130 Adjusted Cost Base and Capital Cost ¶8,140 Foreign Exchange Gains and Losses ¶11,070 Treatment of allowable business investment loss
Proceeds of disposition — Allocation	Section 68	¶7,115 Proceeds of Disposition
Inadequate considerations, gifting	Subsections 69(1), (4)	¶7,400 Non-Arm's Length Transfers and the Attribution Rules Revised
Election — Disposition of Canadian securities	Subsections 39(4), (4.1), (5), (6)	¶7,040 Election re: Disposition of Canadian Securities ¶8,150 Debts Established to be Bad Debts
Business investment loss	Subsections 39(9), (12); 50(*l*), (*l.*1)	¶7,720 Allowable Business Investment Losses
Limitations re reserves	Subparagraph 40(2)(*a*)(ii)	¶8,110 Reserves
Principal residence	Paragraph 40(2)(*b*); subsection 40(4); section 54.1	¶7,230 Principal Residence Exemption ¶7,240 Change in Use of a Principal Residence ¶7,255 Section 54.1 — Extended Designation ¶7,260 Subsection 40(4) — Transfer between spouses
Listed personal property	Section 41	¶7,015 Listed personal property ¶7,220 Listed Personal Property
Small business share rollover	Subsections 44.1(1), (2), (11), (12)	¶7,370 Capital Gains Deferral
Personal-use property	Subsections 46(1), (2), (3)	¶7,014 Personal-use property ¶7,210 Personal-Use Property
Special rules	Paragraphs 40(2)(*e*), (*g*); subsections 40(3), (3.1); paragraph 44(7)(*b*); subsections 44(1), (2), (4), (5), 52(3); sections 43, 45, 47, 48.1	¶7,245 Application of the change-in-use elections ¶7,250 Interpretation Bulletin IT-120R6 — Principal residence ¶7,280 Pooling of Identical Assets Purchased after 1971 ¶7,285 Identical properties exempt from cost-averaging rule ¶7,305 Tax deferred election repealed ¶7,306 Special relief for tax deferred elections made prior to March 4, 2010 ¶7,310 Cost of Certain Properties ¶7,315 General Considerations ¶7,320 Dividends in Kind ¶7,325 Stock dividends ¶7,340 Transfer of Property to an RRSP ¶8,210 Election on Change in Use ¶9,370 Contributions of Property ¶15,130 Cash or Stock Dividends ¶15,140 Dividends in Kind
Dispositions to affiliated persons	Subsections 40(3.3), (3.4), (3.5), (3.6)	¶16,130 Transfer of non-depreciable capital property with unrealized capital losses to affiliated persons
Options and convertible property	Subsections 49(1), (3), (3.1), (4); section 51	¶7,350 Options ¶7,352 Call option ¶7,354 Put option ¶7,356 Summary ¶7,360 Convertible Properties ¶17,210 Convertible Properties ¶17,935 Convertible Properties

Mapping of Tax Knowledge Reference List to Textbook Paragraphs

Knowledge Reference List		Textbook Coverage
Area: Income Taxation	**ITA Reference**	
Adjusted cost base — Inclusions	Paragraphs 53(1)(*a*), (*b*), (*f*), (*f*.2), (*h*), (*j*), (*n*); subparagraphs 53(1)(*e*)(i), (ii), (iv), (vi), (x)	¶7,300 Adjusted cost base of shares acquired under a stock option ¶7,330 Superficial Losses
Adjusted cost base — Deductions	Subparagraphs 53(2)(*a*)(ii), (v), (*c*)(i), (ii), (iii), (iv), (v); paragraphs 53(2)(*b*.2), (*d*), (*g*), (*k*), (*l*), (*s*); subsection 52(2.1)	¶18,070 Adjusted cost base (ACB)
Corporate dividend — Transfer of property	Section 55	¶16,240 Sale of shares by a corporation to an unrelated person ¶16,245 Situation addressed by section 55 ¶16,250 Illustration of the effect of section 55 ¶16,255 Exception to the application of section 55
8. Other Sources of Income Inclusions and Deductions		
Inclusions	Subparagraphs 56(1)(*a*), (i), (ii), (iii), (iv); paragraphs 56(1)(*a*.2), (*b*), (*c*.2), (*d*), (*d*.2), (*h*), (*i*), (*l*), (*l*.1), (*n*), (*n*.1), (*o*), (*q*), (*q*.1), (*t*), (*u*), (*v*), (*z*.2); subsections 56(3), (3.1), (6), (6.1)	¶6,320 Legal and accounting fees ¶9,010 Benefits in the Nature of Pensions ¶9,030 Retiring Allowances and Other Payments on Termination of Employment ¶9,040 Support Receipts and Payments ¶9,045 Overview ¶9,050 Spousal support ¶9,055 Child Support ¶9,060 Legal fees in connection with support payments ¶9,070 Annuity Payments ¶9,100 Education Assistance Payments ¶9,110 Other Inclusions ¶9,135 Child Care Benefit ¶9,140 Restrictive Covenants [Proposed] ¶9,145 Inclusion ¶9,150 Exclusion ¶9,155 Schematic of the system for restrictive covenants ¶9,200 Amounts not included in computing income and exempt entities ¶9,210 Specific examples
Indirect payments	Subsections 56(2), (4)	¶9,120 Indirect Payments ¶9,125 Overview ¶9,130 Conditions
Interest-free or low-interest loans	Subsections 56(4.1), (4.2)	¶13,070 Shareholder Benefits and Loans
Maintenance	Section 56.1	¶13,070 Shareholder Benefits and Loans
Deductions	Paragraphs 60(*a*), (*b*), (*c*), (*c*.2), (*i*), (*j*.1), (*j*.2), (*l*), (*o*), (*o*.1), (*p*), (*q*), (*v*.1), (*w*), (*y*); subsections 60.02(1), (2); sections 60.03, 60.1, 62, 63, 64	¶9,310 Capital Element of Annuity ¶9,445 Overpayments included in income ¶9,450 Objections and appeals ¶9,455 Legal fees to establish a right ¶9,460 OAS clawback ¶9,470 Moving Expenses ¶9,475 Deductible Expenditures under Moving Expenses ¶9,480 Flat-rate deductions by administrative practice ¶9,485 Eligible relocation ¶9,490 Child Care Expenses ¶9,495 Eligibility ¶9,500 Limitations ¶9,505 Deduction Calculation for Child Care Expenses

Mapping of Tax Knowledge Reference List to Textbook Paragraphs

Knowledge Reference List		Textbook Coverage
Area: Income Taxation	**ITA Reference**	
Deductions — *(cont'd)*	Paragraphs 60(*a*), (*b*), (*c*.2), (*i*), (*j*.1), (*j*.2), (*l*), (*o*), (*o*.1), (*p*), (*q*), (*v*.1), (*w*), (*y*); sections 60.03, 60.1, 62, 63, 64 — *(cont'd)*	¶9,510 Encouragement for parent to attend school ¶9,515 Application ¶9,520 Disability Support Deduction ¶9,530 Expenses of residents absent from Canada
9. Estate Planning and Introduction to Tax Planning		
Death of a taxpayer — Basic rules	Subsections 69(1.1), 70(2), (3), (3.1), (4), (5), (5.1), (6), (6.2); paragraph 70(1)(*a*)	¶7,500 Death of a Taxpayer ¶7,510 Deemed Disposition on Death ¶14,350 Rights or things
Reserves for year of death	Section 72	
Charitable donations	Subsections 118.1(1), 118.1(4), 118.1(5)	¶10,245 Total Charitable Gifts
Inter vivos transfers — Spouse	Subsections 73(1), (2)	¶17,220 Interspousal Transfer ¶17,250 Summary of Rollovers Covered
Income splitting — Income attribution rules		¶6,075 The reason for attribution rules ¶6,080 Definition of related persons ¶6,085 Transactions subject to income attribution ¶6,090 Avoiding income attributions ¶6,095 Anti-avoidance rules relating to attribution ¶6,100 More types of income subject to attribution ¶6,102 "Second generation" income from property ¶6,105 Loans or transfers to a non-arm's length individuals who are 18 years of age or older ¶6,110 Summary of income attribution rules ¶7,430 Attribution Rules ¶7,435 Capital gains on spousal transfers or loans ¶7,440 Recapture ¶7,445 Summary of provisions ¶9,015 Income Splitting — Canada Pension Plan ¶9,020 Income Splitting — Pension Income
	Transfers or loans to a spouse	Section 74.2; subsections 74.1(1), 82(2)	¶6,070 Income Attribution
	Transfers or loans to a minor	Subsection 74.1(2)	¶6,070 Income Attribution
	Repayment of existing indebtedness	Subsection 74.1(3)	¶6,070 Income Attribution
	Transfers or loans to a trust or corporation	Section 74.3; subsections 74.4(1), (2), (3)	¶13,390 Attribution through a corporation ¶13,395 Imputed interest
	Spouses living apart	Subsections 74.5(3), (4)	¶6,070 Income Attribution
	Exceptions to attribution rules	Subsections 74.5(1), (2), (13); paragraph 74.5(12)(*a*)	¶6,070 Income Attribution
Tax on split income ("kiddie tax")	Section 120.4	¶6,115 Tax on split income earned by persons under 18 years of age ("kiddie tax") ¶13,400 Income-Splitting Tax ("kiddie tax")
Arm's length and affiliated persons	Subsections 251(1), (2), (3), (4), (6); section 251.1	¶7,400 Non-Arm's Length Transfers and the Attribution Rules Revisited ¶7,410 Non-arm's length transfers ¶7,415 Who does not deal at arm's length ¶7,420 Transactions with non-arm's length individuals
Extended meanings — "Child", "parent", "spouse", "former spouse"	Section 252	¶7,400 Non-Arm's Length Transfers and the Attribution Rules Revisited
10. Financially Troubled Businesses		
Unpaid amounts	Subsections 78(1), (3), (4), (5)	¶13,065 Accrued bonuses and other amounts
General rules for debt forgiveness	Section 80	¶4,034 Forgiveness of Debt Rules

Mapping of Tax Knowledge Reference List to Textbook Paragraphs

Knowledge Reference List			Textbook Coverage
Area: Income Taxation		**ITA Reference**	
11. Business Combinations and Corporate Reorganizations			
Sale of a business — Assets or shares			¶15,310 Assets Versus Shares ¶15,315 Allocation of Amounts in Consideration for Disposition of Property ¶15,320 Analysis for the Decision ¶15,330 Summary of Steps for the Sale of an Incorporated Business
Non-arm's length sale of shares — Deemed dividend		Subsection 84.1(1), (2.2); subparagraph 84.1(2)(a.1)(ii), paragraph 84.1(2)(b)	¶15,150 Deemed Dividends ¶16,210 Non-Arm's Length Sale of Shares ¶16,215 The situation: QSBC shares ¶16,220 Conditions for section 84.1 to apply ¶16,225 The basic rules formulated ¶16,230 Application of rules
Transfer of property to corporation		Paragraphs 85(1)(a), (b), (c), (c.1), (c.2), (d), (d.1), (e), (e.1), (e.2), (e.3), (f), (g), (h), (i); subsections 85(1.1), (2), (2.1), (5)	¶16,010 The basic concepts ¶16,015 Situation one ¶16,020 Situation two ¶16,025 Situation three ¶16,030 Basic Technical Rules on the Transfer ¶16,035 Use of the rollover ¶16,040 Conditions for the rollover to apply ¶16,045 Elected transfer price ¶16,050 Non-share consideration or boot ¶16,060 Application of the Basic Rules ¶16,070 The Corporation's Position ¶16,080 The Shareholder's Position ¶16,125 Depreciable capital property ¶16,130 Transfer of non-depreciable capital property with unrealized capital losses to affiliated persons ¶16,135 Summary of stop-loss rules ¶16,140 Benefits conferred on shareholders and related persons ¶16,145 Conceptual example ¶16,150 Benefit conferred on a related persons — Technical rules ¶16,155 Subsection 15(1) benefit conferred on a shareholder — Technical rules ¶16,160 Summary of Rules ¶16,170 Fair Market Value ¶16,180 Section 22 Election ¶16,190 Application ¶17,300 Use of Rollovers in Estate Planning ¶17,310 Objectives ¶17,320 Holdco Freeze ¶17,330 Internal Freeze ¶17,340 Reverse or Asset Freeze
Mergers, divestitures, and acquisitions — Basic rules and planning opportunities	Share-for-share exchange	Subsections 85.1(1), (2), (2.1)	¶17,010 Share-for-Share Exchange ¶17,015 The concept ¶17,020 The conditions ¶17,025 The consequences ¶17,030 Other issues ¶17,915 Share-for-share exchange
	Section 86 reorganization	Subsections 86(1), (2), (2.1), (3)	¶17,040 Reorganization of Capital ¶17,045 Overview ¶17,050 Conditions ¶17,055 A conceptual view of the rollover for a reorganization of capital ¶17,060 Benefit Rule ¶17,920 Reorganizations
	Amalgamations	Subsections 87(1), (1.4), (2)	¶17,070 Statutory Amalgamations ¶17,075 Overview ¶17,080 Conditions ¶17,085 Two levels of rollover ¶17,090 Income tax consequences ¶17,095 Availability of a "bump" on vertical amalgamation ¶17,100 Planning opportunities ¶17,105 Effects of the rollover at the shareholder level ¶17,925 Statutory amalgamations

Mapping of Tax Knowledge Reference List to Textbook Paragraphs

Knowledge Reference List		Textbook Coverage
Area: Income Taxation	**ITA Reference**	
Winding up a subsidiary	Subsections 88(1), (1.1), (1.2)	¶17,110 Winding Up a Subsidiary ¶17,115 Overview ¶17,120 Availability of a "bump" and other effects on the parent ¶17,125 Illustration ¶17,130 Loss utilization ¶17,135 Planning opportunities ¶17,140 Disposition by parent of subsidiary's shares ¶17,930 Winding up a subsidiary
Winding up other companies	Paragraphs 88(2)(*a*), (*b*); subsection 69(5)	¶15,200 Winding up of a Canadian Corporation ¶15,210 Disposition of Net Assets of the Corporation ¶15,225 Timing of winding-up ¶15,230 Components of the winding-up distribution ¶15,240 Application of the winding-up rules ¶15,400 GST/HST and the winding-up of a Canadian corporation
Planning opportunities — Capital gains deduction	Subsection 110.6(1)	¶7,030 Capital Gains Deduction ¶10,060 Capital Gains Deduction ¶10,061 Historical overview ¶10,065 The qualified farm property CGD ¶10,066 The qualified fishing property CGD ¶13,340 Qualified Small Business Corporation Share (QSBCS) ¶13,345 Small business corporation (SBC) ¶13,350 Basic QSBCS rules applied to a single corporation ¶13,355 Modification of the asset test (stacking rule)
12. Partnerships and Their Members		
Partnerships — General rules	Paragraphs 96(1)(*a*), (*b*), (*c*), (*f*); subparagraph 96(1)(*g*)(i)	¶18,015 What is a partnership ¶18,020 Partnership versus joint income ¶18,035 General Rules ¶18,040 Limitation on deduction of partnership losses ¶18,045 Partnership allocations: Anti-avoidance ¶18,050 Computation of taxable income ¶18,055 Personal tax credits generated by the partnership ¶18,060 Partnership Interest ¶18,065 The concept ¶18,070 Adjusted cost base (ACB) ¶18,080 Reorganizations of Partnerships ¶18,085 Transfer of partnership property to a corporation ¶18,090 Transfer of property to a partnership ¶18,100 Fiscal Period of Terminated Partnership ¶18,910 Partnerships ¶18,915 Corporate Partnerships ¶18,920 Transfer of property from a partnership ¶18,950 GST/HST and Partnerships ¶18,955 Treatment of partnerships under the *Excise Tax Act* ¶18,960 The partnership interest ¶18,965 Transfer of property to a partnership ¶18,970 Transfer of property from a partnership ¶18,975 Joint and several liability ¶18,980 Continuation of partnership
Limited partnerships — At-risk rules	Subsections 96(2.1), (2.2)	¶6,250 Depreciation-Based or Similar Tax Shelters
Contribution of property	Section 97	¶18,060 Partnership Interest
Terminated partnership	Subsections 99(1), (2)	¶18,080 Reorganizations of Partnerships
Information returns	Section 233.1	¶14,335 Foreign reporting requirements ¶19,600 Information reporting

Mapping of Tax Knowledge Reference List to Textbook Paragraphs

Knowledge Reference List		Textbook Coverage
Area: Income Taxation	**ITA Reference**	
13. Introduction to Trusts		
General definitions and liability	Subsections 104(1), (2)	¶18,275 Fiscal years ¶18,280 Tax rate ¶18,285 Tax credits ¶18,290 Minimum tax
Types of trusts — Testamentary, *inter vivos*	Subsections 108(1), 122(1.1)	¶18,210 Nature of Trust ¶18,215 General ¶18,220 Types of Trust
Income determination for trusts	Subsections 104(12), (13.1), (13.2), (14), (18), (19), (21), (21.3), (23), (24); paragraphs 104(6)(*b*), 104(13)(*a*)	¶18,230 Settlement of a Trust ¶18,240 Income payable to beneficiary ¶18,250 Computation of Income ¶18,255 Attribution ¶18,260 Tax on split income or "kiddie tax" ¶18,265 Accumulating income and preferred beneficiary election ¶18,300 Family Planning Uses of a Trust ¶18,305 Uses of a trust for income tax advantages ¶18,310 Uses of a trust for non-tax advantages ¶18,930 Disposition from a Trust ¶18,935 Disposition of capital property ¶18,940 Disposition of income interest ¶18,945 Disposition of capital interest
14. Computation of Taxable Income Deductions		
Employee stock options	Paragraphs 110(1)(*d*), (*d*.1), (*d*.01); subsection 110(2.1)	¶10,015 Employee Stock Options
Worker's compensation, social assistance, etc.	Paragraph 110(1)(*f*)	¶10,020 Deduction for certain receipts
Home relocation loan	Paragraph 110(1)(*j*); subsection 110(1.4)	¶10,025 Home relocation loan
Lump-sum payments	Sections 110.2, 120.31	¶10,520 Tax Reduction on Retroactive Lump-Sum Payments
Charitable gifts	Paragraph 110.1(1)(*a*); subsections 110.1(1.1), (2)	¶10,245 Total Charitable Gifts ¶11,050 Charitable Donations ¶11,140 Unused charitable contributions
Gifts of capital property	Subsection 110.1(3)	¶8,135 Non-arm's length transfer of depreciable property
Gifts made by partnership	Subsection 110.1(4)	¶18,055 Personal tax credits generated by the partnership
Capital gains deduction	Subsections 110.6(1), (2.1), (4)	¶13,360 Capital Gains Deduction ¶13,365 Overview ¶13,370 Computation of deduction ¶13,375 Allowable business investment losses ¶13,380 Cumulative net investment loss (CNIL) ¶13,385 Other related provisions
Losses deductible	Paragraphs 111(1)(*a*), (*b*), (*c*), (*d*), (*e*); subsection 111(8); section 111.1	¶7,270 Capital Losses — General ¶10,030 Loss Carryovers ¶10,032 Legislative intent and government policy ¶10,035 Non-capital loss carryovers ¶10,045 Farm loss ¶10,070 Ordering of Division C Deductions ¶10,075 General ordering rules for Division C ¶10,080 Ordering of section 111 loss carryovers ¶11,060 Loss Carryovers ¶11,065 Non-capital loss ¶11,085 Choice to deduct net capital losses to preserve non-capital losses
Net capital losses	Subparagraph 111(1.1)(*a*)(i); paragraph 111(1.1)(*b*)	¶10,040 Net capital loss carryovers ¶11,075 Net capital losses
Net capital losses in year of death	Subsection 111(2)	¶7,500 Death of a Taxpayer

Mapping of Tax Knowledge Reference List to Textbook Paragraphs

Knowledge Reference List			Textbook Coverage
Area: Income Taxation		**ITA Reference**	
Limitations on deductibility and change in control		Subsections 111(3), (4), (5), (5.1), (5.2), (5.3), (5.5); paragraphs 249(4)(*a*), (*b*), (*d*)	¶7,500 Death of a Taxpayer ¶11,080 Restrictions and ordering of deductions ¶11,090 Acquisition of Control of a Corporation and Its Effect on Losses ¶11,095 Conceptual overview ¶11,100 Deemed year-end ¶11,110 Accrued or unrealized losses on accounts receivable ¶11,115 Accrued or unrealized losses on depreciable capital property ¶11,120 Accrued or unrealized losses on eligible capital property ¶11,125 Accrued or unrealized losses on non-depreciable capital property ¶11,130 Elective capital gains and recapture ¶11,135 Allowable business investment losses and losses from property ¶11,145 Deductibility of non-capital losses after an acquisition of control ¶11,150 Loss carryback rules ¶11,155 Summary and application
Taxable dividend received by corporation resident in Canada		Paragraph 112(1)(*a*)	¶11,020 Deduction of Taxable Dividends ¶11,025 Purpose ¶11,030 Dividends paid from untaxed income ¶11,035 "After-tax financing" ¶11,040 Dividends paid on shares subsequently sold for a loss
15. Rules Applicable to Individuals			
Tax payable under Part I		Sections 114, 117 Subsection 115(1)	¶10,135 Marginal Tax Rates ¶10,410 Ordering of Credits ¶10,090 Taxable Income of Non-Residents ¶10,100 Computation of Tax for Individuals ¶10,110 Basic Computation of Tax ¶10,115 Tax rates ¶10,120 Annual indexing adjustment ¶10,125 Overview of tax credit and tax calculation system ¶10,130 Provincial and territorial tax ¶19,140 Deductions and Credits Allowed a Non-Resident
Non-refundable tax credits	Personal, age, pension, and other credits	Section 118	¶10,140 Section 118 Tax Credits ¶10,145 Married or common-law partnership credit ¶10,155 Child amount ¶10,160 Single status — Basic personal tax credit ¶10,165 Caregiver credit for in-home care of relative ¶10,170 Infirm dependant credit ¶10,180 Age credit ¶10,185 Pension income amount ¶10,190 Canada employment credit ¶10,195 Summary of personal tax credits ¶14,360 Personal tax credits
	Other tax credits	Sections 118.01, 118.02, 118.03, 118.031, 118.06; subsections 118.1(1), (2), (3), (5.1), (5.2), (5.3), (6), (7), (7.1), 118.2 (1), (2), (2.1); sections 118.3, 118.4; paragraphs 118.5(1)(*a*), (*b*), (*d*); subsections 118.5(1.1), 118.6(1), (2), (2.1); sections 118.61, 118.62, 118.7	¶10,150 Equivalent-to-married status for wholly dependent person credit ¶10,200 Adoption Expense Tax Credit ¶10,210 Public Transit Passes Credit ¶10,220 Children's Fitness Credit ¶10,222 Children's Arts Tax Credit ¶10,225 First-Time Home Buyers' Credit and Disability Home Purchase Credit ¶10,227 Volunteer Firefighters Tax Credit ¶10,230 Charitable Gifts Credit ¶10,235 Basic Rules ¶10,240 Income limit and carryforward ¶10,250 Gifts of publicly traded securities ¶10,255 Total cultural gifts ¶10,260 Tickets to events ¶10,265 Total Crown gifts ¶10,270 Total ecological gifts ¶10,280 Medical Expense Credit ¶10,285 Calculation of the credit ¶10,290 Medical expenses

Mapping of Tax Knowledge Reference List to Textbook Paragraphs

Knowledge Reference List			Textbook Coverage
Area: Income Taxation		**ITA Reference**	
Non-refundable tax credits — (*cont'd*)	Other tax credits — (*cont'd*)		¶10,295 Notch provision for dependants ¶10,300 Credit for Mental or Physical Impairment (Disability Credit) ¶10,320 Tuition, Education, and Textbook Credits ¶10,325 Tuition Fees ¶10,330 Education credit ¶10,335 Textbook credit ¶10,340 Carryforward ¶10,350 Credit for interest on student loans ¶10,360 Credit for Employment Insurance Premiums and CPP Contributions
	Transfer of unused credits	Sections 118.8, 118.81, 118.9	¶10,370 Transfer of Unused Credits to Spouse or Common-Law Partner ¶10,400 Credits for Part-Year and Non-Residents ¶19,200 Part-Year Residents
	Part-year and non-resident	Sections 118.91, 118.94	¶19,210 Income, Deductions, and Credits ¶19,220 Deemed Acquisition on Entering Canada ¶19,230 Deemed Disposition on Leaving Canada
	Ordering of credits	Section 118.92	¶1,260 Ordering Rules
	Credits in separate returns	Section 118.93	¶1,260 Ordering Rules
	Income for the year	Subsections 120(1), (3), (4)	¶10,005 Calculation of Taxable Income ¶10,420 Income not earned in a province
	Minimum tax carry-over	Section 120.2	¶10,340 Carryforward
	Dividend tax credit	Section 121	¶10,385 Dividend Tax Credit ¶10,390 Election to transfer dividends to spouse
	Overseas employment tax credit	Subsection 122.3	¶10,430 Credit for Employment Outside Canada
Refundable tax credits	Goods and services tax credit	Section 122.5	¶10,440 Refundable GST/HST Credit
	Refundable medical expense supplement	Section 122.51	¶10,450 Refundable Medical Expense Supplement
	Child tax benefit	Section 122.6, 122.61	¶10,460 Refundable Canada Child Tax Benefit
	Working income tax benefit	Subsections 122.7(1), (2), (3), (6)	¶10,470 Working Income Tax Benefit (WITB) ¶10,475 Overview ¶10,480 WITB supplement for persons with disabilities ¶10,485 WITB prepayment
Minimum tax		Sections 127.5, 127.51, 127.52, 127.53, 127.54, 127.55	¶10,540 Minimum Tax ¶10,545 Minimum Amount ¶10,550 Adjusted taxable income ¶10,555 Basic exemption ¶10,560 Basic minimum tax credit ¶10,565 Minimum tax carryforward ¶10,570 Impact of the minimum tax
Changes in residence		Subsections 128.1(1), (4)	¶7,600 Leaving and Entering Canada
16. Rules Applicable to Corporations			
Basic rate for corporations		Section 123	¶11,160 Taxable Income of a Corporation in General ¶11,210 Objectives of Provisions Affecting Taxation of Corporations ¶11,220 General Rates for Corporations ¶11,225 Overview of rates and credits ¶11,235 Effect of provincial corporate tax rates ¶11,240 Effect of corporation type ¶11,245 General rate reduction ¶12,000 Issues Addressed by Integration ¶12,020 Objectives of Integration ¶12,030 The Major Tool for Integration in the ITA ¶12,035 The concept ¶12,040 Application of the concept in theory ¶12,275 Corporate tax rate incentives to incorporate in general ¶12,280 Specific tax savings (cost) and deferral (prepayment) possibilities ¶12,500 Comprehensive Summary of Types of Corporate Income and Federal Corporate Income Tax Rates

Mapping of Tax Knowledge Reference List to Textbook Paragraphs

Knowledge Reference List		Textbook Coverage
Area: Income Taxation	**ITA Reference**	
Refundable tax on CCPC's investment income	Section 123.3	¶12,330 Special Refundable Taxes in respect of Investments in CCPCs ¶12,335 Aggregate investment income ¶12,340 Additional refundable tax (ART) ¶12,345 "Refundable dividend tax on hand" (RDTOH) ¶12,350 "Deeming Rules" ¶12,355 Part IV tax on portfolio and other dividends ¶12,360 Dividend Refund ¶12,365 Anti-avoidance rule ¶12,370 Summary of conditions for Part IV tax ¶12,375 Application of non-capital losses ¶12,380 Actual Application of the Scheme ¶12,390 Imperfections in the integration system for income from investments of a CCPC ¶12,395 Tax deferral at higher tax rates on personal income ¶12,400 Permanent tax savings or costs ¶12,405 Summary of advantages and disadvantages of incorporating investment income eligible for refundable tax
Corporate tax reduction	Section 123.4	¶12,250 The ITC rate for CCPCs
Federal abatement	Subsections 124(1), (4)	¶11,255 Purpose of the provision ¶11,260 Applicable income tax regulations ¶11,265 Cases on the meaning of permanent establishment ¶11,270 Taxable income earned in a province or territory ¶11,310 Manufacturing and Processing Profits Deduction
Small business deduction	Subparagraphs 125(1)(a)(i), (iii); paragraphs 125(1)(b), (c); subsections 125(1.1), (2), (3), (4); paragraph 125(5)(b); subsections 125(5.1), 125(7)	¶12,110 Introduction to the Small Business Deduction ¶12,120 Mechanics of Calculation of Small Business Deduction ¶12,125 The basic limits ¶12,130 Elimination of small business deduction for large CCPCs ¶12,140 Definition of "Active Business" ¶12,145 The "default" definition ¶12,150 Specified investment business ¶12,155 Personal services business ¶12,160 Income incidental to an active business ¶12,230 Manufacturing and Processing Profits and the Small Business Deduction ¶12,270 Incorporated Business Income and Integration ¶12,285 Summary of advantages and disadvantages of incorporating active business income
Private corporations — Dividend refund	Subsections 129(1), (2)	¶12,360 Dividend Refund
Eligible dividends, general rate, and low rate income pool	Subsection 89(1)	¶15,020 Paid-Up Capital of Shares ¶15,025 The tax concept ¶15,030 Technical tax aspects ¶15,055 Components of the account ¶15,060 "The Period" ¶15,065 Example of disposition of eligible capital property ¶15,110 Income Tax Treatment of Taxable Dividends Received or Deemed to be Received ¶15,115 Treatment of taxable dividends ¶15,120 Source of taxable dividends
Capital dividend — General rules	Subsections 83(2), 83(3), (3.1), (4), (5)	¶15,000 Corporate Surplus Balances ¶15,010 Overview ¶15,050 Capital Dividend Account ¶15,180 Capital Dividend
Refundable dividend tax on hand	Paragraphs 129(3)(a), (b), (c)	¶12,345 "Refundable dividend tax on hand" (RDTOH)
Definitions of Canadian and foreign investment income	Subsection 129(4)	¶12,315 Investment Income ¶12,330 Special Refundable Taxes in Respect of Income from Investments of a CCPC

Mapping of Tax Knowledge Reference List to Textbook Paragraphs

Knowledge Reference List		Textbook Coverage
Area: Income Taxation	**ITA Reference**	
Investment income from associated corporation deemed to be active business income	Subsection 129(6)	¶12,210 Deemed Association
Associated corporations	Section 256	¶12,170 Associated companies ¶12,175 Overview ¶12,180 Related persons ¶12,185 Basic association rules ¶12,190 Concept of control ¶12,195 Extended meaning of control ¶12,200 Ownership of shares ¶12,205 Association with third corporation ¶12,220 Corporate Partnerships
17. Rules Applicable to All Taxpayers		
Foreign tax credit	Subsections 126(1), (2), (2.1), (2.3), (6), (7)	¶10,490 Foreign Tax Credit ¶11,320 Foreign Tax Deduction ¶11,325 Purpose and approach ¶11,330 Non-business income tax deduction ¶11,335 Business income tax deduction ¶19,510 Active Business Income Earned in a Foreign Jurisdiction ¶19,515 Unincorporated foreign branch operations ¶19,520 Individuals receiving dividends from foreign corporations ¶19,525 Corporations receiving dividends from non-foreign affiliates ¶19,530 Corporations receiving dividends from foreign affiliates
Political contributions credit	Subsection 127(3)	¶10,500 Federal Political Contribution Tax Credit ¶11,337 Federal Political Tax Credit
Investment tax credit — Basic rules	Subsections 127(5), (9), (9.01), (9.02), (10.1), (10.2), 248(19)	¶11,340 Investment Tax Credit ¶11,345 Overview ¶11,350 Qualified property ¶11,360 ITC for Apprenticeship Expenditures ¶11,370 ITC for Child Care Spaces ¶12,240 Investment Tax Credit Revisited ¶12,245 Overview ¶12,250 The ITC rate for CCPCs ¶12,260 Prescribed proxy amount ¶12,265 Capital expenditures
Refundable investment tax credit	Section 127.1	¶12,255 Refundable investment tax credit
18. Deferred Income Plans		
Definitions	Subsections 146(1), 146.01(1), 146.02(1), 146.1(1), 146.3(1), 147(1), 147.1(1)	¶9,085 Inclusion provisions ¶9,095 Registered disability savings plan (RDSP) ¶9,325 Objectives of pension reform of 1990 ¶9,330 Types of tax-assisted retirement plans ¶9,335 Types of RRSPs ¶9,375 Application
Registered Retirement Savings Plans	Subsections 146(2), (4), (5), (5.1), (8), (8.3), (8.8), (8.9), (8.91), (8.92), (8.93)	¶9,320 Registered Savings Plans ¶9,340 Integration Limits ¶9,345 Contribution Limits for RRSPs ¶9,350 Definition of earned income for RRSPs ¶9,360 RRSP contribution room carried forward ¶9,365 Excess contribution ¶9,380 Contributions to spousal RRSP ¶9,385 Attribution on spousal RRSPs ¶9,390 Withdrawals before retirement ¶9,405 Retirement options
Home Buyers' Plan	Subsections 146.01 (2), (3), (4)	¶9,395 Home Buyers' Plan
Lifelong Learning Plan	Subsections 146.02(2), (3), (4)	¶9,400 Tax-free RRSP withdrawals for lifelong learning plan

Mapping of Tax Knowledge Reference List to Textbook Paragraphs

Knowledge Reference List			Textbook Coverage
Area: Income Taxation		**ITA Reference**	
Registered Education Savings Plan		Subsections 146.1(5), (6), (7)	¶9,090 Registered education savings plan (RESP)
Tax-Free Savings Account (TFSA)		Subsections 146.2(1), (6), (7), (12)	¶9,220 Tax-Free Savings Account
Registered Retirement Income Funds		Subsections 146.3(3), (5), (5.1), (5.4), (6.3), (6.4)	¶9,410 Registered retirement income fund (RRIFs) ¶9,415 Treatment of RRSPs and RRIFs on death
Registered Disability Savings Plan		Subsections 146.4(1), (5), (6), (7)	¶9,095 Registered disability savings plan
Transfers between plans		Paragraphs 146.3(2)(*e*),(*e*.1); subsections 146(16), 146.3(14), 147(19), (20), 147.3(1)	¶9,420 Transfers of Retirement Income and Sheltered Amounts ¶9,425 Direct Transfer ¶9,430 Retiring Allowances
Deferred Profit Sharing Plans		Subsections 147(5.1), (7), (8), (9), (10)	¶9,330.30 Deferred Profit Sharing Plans
Registered Pension Plans		Subsections 147.2(1), (2); paragraph 147.2(4)(*a*)	¶9,355 Calculation of the pension adjustment (PA)
19. Administration, Returns, Assessments, Payments, and Appeals			
Basic returns		Paragraphs 150(1)(*a*), (*d*); subsection 150(2)	¶14,010 Returns, Penalties and Criminal Offences ¶14,015 Returns ¶14,018 Functional currency tax reporting ¶14,020 Penalties ¶14,025 Criminal Offences
Other returns		Paragraphs 150(1)(*b*), (*c*); subsections 150(3), (4)	¶14,220 Amended Returns ¶14,340 Deceased Taxpayers ¶14,345 Tax Returns ¶14,355 Other Return
Electronic filing of returns		Section 150.1	
Payment of tax	Estimate of tax	Section 151	¶14,030 Payments and Interest ¶14,325 Payments to residents of Canada ¶14,330 Payments to non-residents
	Instalments for individuals	Subsections 156(1), (3); section 156.1	¶14,035 Individuals
	Instalments for corporations	Subsections 157(1), (1.1), (1.2), (1.3), (1.4), (1.5), (2.1), (4); paragraphs 157(3)(*a*), (*b*)	¶14,040 Corporations
	Payment of remainder	Section 158	
Assessment — Important dates		Subsections 152(3.1), (4), (4.2), (5); paragraphs 152(6)(*b*), (*c*), (*d*), (*f*)	¶14,110 Assessments and Reassessments ¶14,365 Summary of filing deadlines
Notice of assessment		Subsections 152(1), (1.1), (2), (3)	¶14,110 Assessments and Reassessments
Taxpayer's representative		Subsections 159(2), (3)	¶14,300 Obligations of Payers and Other Persons ¶14,310 Employers ¶14,324 Taxpayer's legal representative
Joint liability for tax-split income		Subsection 160(1.2), (1.3)	¶13,095 Income Splitting
Interest and penalties, failures, and omissions		Subsections 161(1), (2), (2.2), (4.1), (9), 162(1), (2); section 163.1; subsections 163(1), (2)	¶14,020 Penalties ¶14,025 Criminal Offences
Misrepresentation by third party		Section 163.2	¶14,910 Penalties
Refunds and interest		Subsections 164(1), (1.5), (2), (3), (3.2)	¶14,120 Refunds and Interest
Objections to assessments and appeal process		Subsections 165(1), (2), (3)	¶14,210 Objections and Appeals

Mapping of Tax Knowledge Reference List to Textbook Paragraphs

Knowledge Reference List		Textbook Coverage
Area: Income Taxation	**ITA Reference**	
20. Other Taxes		
Tax on old age security benefits	Subsections 180.2(1), (2)	¶1,121 Parts 1 and 1.2 — Income tax and tax on OAS benefits ¶10,510 Tax on Old Age Security Benefits
Tax on certain taxable dividends	Subsections 186(1), (2), (4)	¶6,060 Overview of the Canadian Dividend Taxation System
Non-resident — Tax on income from Canada: interest, rents or royalties, alimony, dividends	Paragraphs 212(1)(*a*), (*b*), (*d*), (*h*), (*j*.1), (*l*), (*q*); subsections 212(2), (3), (4)	¶19,110 Income Earned in Canada by Non-Residents ¶19,115 Employment Income ¶19,120 Business Income ¶19,123 Regulation 105 withholding requirements ¶19,125 Branch tax ¶19,130 Disposing of taxable Canadian property ¶19,145 Tax credits available to non-residents ¶19,150 Provincial/Territorial Income Tax Obligation ¶19,160 Withholding Taxes on Canadian-Source Income — Part XIII Tax ¶19,165 Rental income alternative — Section 216 elections ¶19,170 Canadian benefits alternative — Section 217 election ¶19,300 Impact of Canada — Foreign Country Tax Treaties ¶19,310 Application of the treaties ¶19,420 Thin Capitalization — Inbound Loans ¶19,430 Corporate Debt Owed by a Non-Resident — Outbound Loans ¶19,435 Cross-border shareholder loans/balances ¶19,440 Low interest cross-border loans/balances ¶19,540 Passive Income Earned in a Foreign Jurisdiction ¶19,545 Controlled foreign affiliates

Mapping of Tax Knowledge Reference List to Textbook Paragraphs

Knowledge Reference List		Textbook Coverage
Area: Goods and Services Taxation — *Excise Tax Act*	**ETA Reference, Part IX, Division I–VIII**	
1. General Rules		
Definitions — "Taxable supply"; "zero-rated supply"; "exempt supply"; "person"; "property"; "recipient"; "service"; "registrant"	Subsection 123(1)	¶1,400 Introduction to the Goods and Services Tax (GST)/Harmonized Sales Tax (HST) ¶1,410 Overview and Basic Concepts ¶1,420 Supplies ¶1,435 Point-of-Sales Rebates ¶2,310 Liability for GST/HST ¶2,315 Supplies in Canada ¶2,317 Supplies in an HST province ¶2,320 Supplies by non-residents ¶4,400 The GST/HST Impact on Business Activity ¶4,410 Commercial Activity ¶4,415 Carrying on business ¶4,420 Adventure or concern in the nature of trade ¶4,425 Exclusions from the definition of commercial activity ¶5,300 Capital Personal Property and the Input Tax Credit System under GST/HST ¶6,510 Interest and Dividends ¶6,520 "Soft Costs"
Small suppliers	Section 148	¶1,420 Suppliers
Consideration	Section 152	¶1,420 Suppliers
Imposition of tax	Subsections 165(1), (3); section 166; subsection 167(1)	¶4,430 Value for Tax
When tax is payable	Subsection 168(1)	¶4,435 When GST/HST is payable
Input tax credits	Subsections 169(1), 170 (1) (2); paragraph 169(4)(*a*)	¶1,440 Input Tax Credits ¶1,445 Restricted Input Tax Credits ¶4,450 Input Tax Credits ¶4,455 General rules ¶4,460 Restrictions
Taxable benefits	Subsections 173(1), (2)	¶4,440 Automobile operating cost benefits paid by employer
Passenger vehicles	Section 201; subsections 235(1), 253(1)	¶4,490 Lease of passenger vehicles ¶5,320 Passenger Vehicles and Aircraft ¶5,325 Passenger vehicles owned by registrants other than individuals and partnerships ¶5,330 Passenger vehicles and aircraft owned by registrants who are individuals or partnerships
Importation of goods and services	Sections 212, 213, 215	¶2,380 Imports
2. Collections and Remittances		
Collection of tax	Subsections 221(1), 222(1), (2); section 223	¶14,410 Collection and Remittance of tax ¶14,420 Disclosure of tax
Remittance of tax	Subsections 225(1), (2),(3), (4), 228(1), (2),(3), 229(1), (2),(3), 231(1), (3), 232(1), (3), 237(1)	¶4,475 Excess charges ¶4,480 Price reductions ¶4,485 Bad debts ¶14,440 Remittance of Tax ¶14,620 Amended Returns and GST/HST Adjustments
Meals and entertainment	Subsections 236(1), (1.1)	¶4,270 Meals and entertainment ¶4,495 Food, beverages, and entertainment expenses
3. Returns, Administration, and Reporting Requirements		
Returns	Subsections 238(1), 239(1)	¶14,430 Returns and Reporting Periods
Registration	Subsection 240(1)	¶2,330 Registration Requirements for Residents ¶2,335 Test for registration ¶2,340 Definition of commercial activity ¶2,345 Exclusions from commercial activity ¶2,350 Exceptions from the registration requirements ¶2,360 Registration and Collection Requirements for Non-Residents

Knowledge Reference List			Textbook Coverage
Area: Goods and Services Taxation — *Excise Tax Act*		**ETA Reference, Part IX, Division I–VIII**	
Registration — (*cont'd*)		Subsection 240(1) — (*cont'd*)	¶2,365 Meaning of non-resident ¶2,370 Mandatory registration ¶2,375 Voluntary registration
Fiscal and reporting periods		Subsections 243(1), (2); 244(1); 245(2); 247(1); 248(1)	¶5,310 Basic Rules ¶8,010 Avoidance ¶19,410 Transfer Pricing
Administration and enforcement	Books and records	Subsection 286(1)	¶14,450 Books and Records
	Assessments	Subsection 296(1)	¶14,510 Assessments and Reassessments ¶14,520 Refunds and Interest
	Objections and appeals	Subsection 301(1.1); section 302	¶1,300 General Background on Administration and Enforcement of the Act ¶1,310 Onus of Proof ¶1,320 Appeals ¶1,350 Administration and Enforcement ¶1,360 Tax Evasion, Avoidance, and Planning ¶14,610 Objections and Appeals

Chapter 1
Introduction

LEARNING GOALS

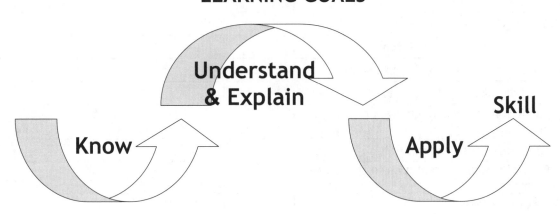

Know

By the end of this chapter you should know some of the history and policy principles of income tax in Canada and how the *Income Tax Act* and the *Excise Tax Act* (pertaining to the goods and services tax) are structured, interpreted, and administered.

Understand and Explain

You should understand and be able to explain how to find what you need in the Act and how to put together the calculation of income for tax purposes, taxable income, and federal income tax for individuals. In addition, you should be able to explain how to interpret tax legislation. Completing the Exercises (¶1,850) is a good way to deepen your understanding of the material.

Apply

You should be able to use your general knowledge and understanding of the calculation of income and the interpretation of tax laws to put together the calculation of income, taxable income, and federal income tax for individuals and to find the meaning of certain words and phrases in the *Income Tax Act*. Completing the Assignment Problems (¶1,875) is an excellent way to develop your ability to apply the material in increasingly complex situations.

Chapter 1 – Learning Chart

Topic	Example Problem (✓)	Review Questions (N/A)	Multiple Choice (N/A)	Exercises (¶1,850)	Assignment Problems (¶1,875)
¶1,000 BACKGROUND AND INTRODUCTION					
¶1,001 History and Legislation — Canadian Tax System					
¶1,010 Brief history of the Income Tax Act					
¶1,015 Constitutional basis for income taxation					
¶1,020 Introduction to Income Tax Legislation					
¶1,021 The federal budgetary process					
¶1,022 Public submissions for change or amendment					
¶1,023 Adoption of specific proposals					
¶1,024 Federal Budget presentation to the House of Commons					
¶1,025 Passage of law					
¶1,030 Tax Principles and Concepts					
¶1,035 Classification of taxes					
¶1,040 Desirable characteristics of an income tax					
¶1,045 Tax reform guidelines					
¶1,100 STRUCTURE OF THE INCOME TAX ACT AND INTERPRETATION					
¶1,110 The Income Tax Act					
¶1,115 How do I reference the Act?					
¶1,120 Structure of the Income Tax Act				1	1
¶1,121 Parts I and I.2 — Income tax and tax on OAS benefits					
¶1,122 Special transaction taxes					
¶1,123 Non-residents					
¶1,124 Administration and interpretation					
¶1,130 Related References					
¶1,131 Historical footnotes					
¶1,132 Related matters					
¶1,133 Draft legislation: Pending amendments					
¶1,134 Income Tax Application Rules					
¶1,135 International tax conventions or treaties					
¶1,136 Income Tax Regulations					
¶1,140 Other Interpretive Sources					
¶1,141 Judicial decisions (common law)					
¶1,142 Forms					
¶1,143 CRA publications					
¶1,144 Technical notes and explanations					
¶1,145 Generally accepted accounting principles					
¶1,150 Interpretation of tax legislation					3
¶1,151 Precision					

Study Guide: Chapter 1

Topic	Example Problem (✓)	Review Questions (N/A)	Multiple Choice (N/A)	Exercises (¶1,850)	Assignment Problems (¶1,875)
¶1,152 Plain and obvious meaning					
¶1,153 Intention of Parliament					
¶1,154 Remission orders					
¶1,155 Contextual approach					
¶1,156 Form versus substance					
¶1,157 Exceptions override general					
¶1,158 Specific words followed by general					
¶1,159 Precedents					
¶1,160 Interpretation Act					
¶1,180 AREAS OF PRACTICE AND THE ROLE OF THE PROFESSIONAL ACCOUNTANT					
¶1,185 Why Study Taxation?					
¶1,190 The Practice of Taxation					
¶1,191 Compliance					
¶1,192 Legal interpretation					
¶1,193 Tax appeals and tax litigation					
¶1,194 Tax planning					
¶1,195 The Role of the Professional Accountant in Tax Matters					
¶1,200 INTRODUCTION TO INCOME TAX AND TAXABLE INCOME					
¶1,210 Approaches to Defining Income					
¶1,212 Income versus capital					
¶1,215 The economist's perspective					
¶1,220 The role of generally accepted accounting principles					
¶1,225 The doctrine of constructive receipt					
¶1,240 Computation of Income					
¶1,245 Aggregation formula					
¶1,250 Sourcing or tracing of income					
¶1,260 Determination of Income, Taxable Income, and Federal Income Tax for Individuals	✓			2	2
¶1,300 GENERAL BACKGROUND ON ADMINISTRATION AND ENFORCEMENT OF THE ACT					
¶1,310 Onus of Proof					
¶1,320 Appeals					
¶1,325 Initial steps					
¶1,330 Tax Court of Canada					
¶1,335 Federal Court of Appeal					
¶1,340 Supreme Court of Canada					
¶1,350 Administration and Enforcement					
¶1,360 Tax Evasion, Avoidance, and Planning					
¶1,400 INTRODUCTION TO THE GOODS AND SERVICES TAX (GST)/HARMONIZED SALES TAX (HST)					
¶1,410 Overview and Basic Concepts					

Topic	Example Problem (✓)	Review Questions (N/A)	Multiple Choice (N/A)	Exercises (¶1,850)	Assignment Problems (¶1,875)
¶1,420 Supplies					
¶1,425 Zero-rated supplies					
¶1,430 Exempt supplies					
¶1,435 Point of Sale Rebates					
¶1,440 Input Tax Credits					
¶1,445 Restricted Input Tax Credits					
¶1,450 Note on Organization of Legislation and Availability of Interpretive Sources					
¶1,455 Excise Tax Act structure — Parts					
¶1,460 Structure of Part IX of the Excise Tax Act — GST/HST legislation					
¶1,465 Schedules to the Excise Tax Act					

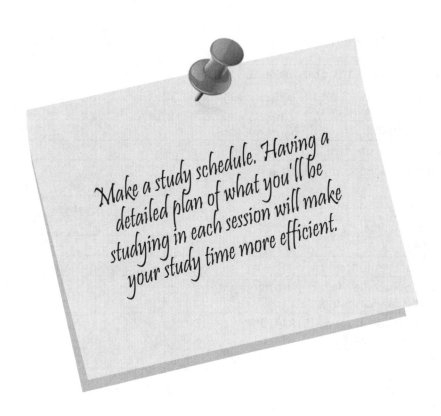

Make a study schedule. Having a detailed plan of what you'll be studying in each session will make your study time more efficient.

Study Notes

Chapter 1 – Solutions to Exercises

CHAPTER 1
Introduction

Exercise 1

The following summary is discussed in more detail below:

Case	Topic	Part	Division	Subdivision	Provision
(A)	Taxable capital gain	I	B	c	paragraph 38(*a*)
(B)	Membership dues	I	B	a	subparagraph 8(1)(*i*)(i)
(C)	Personal injury award	I	B	g	paragraph 81(1)(*g*.1)
(D)	Expense limit	I	B	f	section 67
(E)	Parent.................	XVII	—	—	subsection 252(2)
(F)	*Inter vivos* trust	I	B	k	subsection 108(1)
(G)	Filing deadline	I	I	—	paragraph 150(1)(*b*)
(H)	Shareholder benefit	I	B	b	subsection 15(1)
(I)	Non-arm's length	I	B	f	paragraph 69(1)(*b*)
(J)	Investment fees	I	B	b	paragraph 20(1)(*bb*)

(A) Part I, Division B, Subdivision c, paragraph 38(*a*): — Most definitions applicable to the Taxable Capital Gains and Allowable Capital Losses subdivision of Part I, Division B are found in section 54. However, this definition is set out at the beginning of Subdivision c. Definitions of terms used throughout the Act are found in subsection 248(1). If a term is not specifically defined in subsection 248(1) or in a section elsewhere in the Act, judicial precedents should be consulted for the meaning of the word.

(B) Part I, Division B, Subdivision a, subparagraph 8(1)(*i*)(i): — Employment income and deductions are set out in sections 5 to 8 of Part I, Division B, Subdivision a of the Act. All deductions from this source appear in section 8 with the major list of deductions occurring in subsection 8(1) and further explanation or restriction of these deductions appearing in subsections 8(2) to 8(11).

(C) Part I, Division B, Subdivision g, paragraph 81(1)(*g*.1): — Income from property acquired as personal injury award is one in a limited list of items found in section 81 which are not included in computing income.

(D) Part I, Division B, Subdivision f, section 67: — Inclusions and deductions in the computation of income are generally found in Part I, Division B, Subdivisions a, b, c, d or e. In this case, however, the rule is found in Subdivision f dealing with general rules relating to the computation of income from all sources.

(E) Part XVII, subsection 252(2): — The word "parent" appears throughout the Act, so the definition is most likely to be in Part XVII on "Interpretation."

(F) Part I, Division B, Subdivision k, subsection 108(1): — Trusts and their beneficiaries are dealt with in Subdivision k of Part I, Division B. The definitions section for this subdivision is section 108.

(G) Part I, Division I, paragraph 150(1)(*b*): This is a procedural matter generally handled in Division I of Part I of the Act dealing with Returns, Assessments, Payment and Appeals.

(H) Part I, Division B, Subdivision b, subsection 15(1): — A benefit received by a shareholder, if it is to be taxed, would likely be income from property which is handled in Subdivision b of Division B of Part I. Inclusions from that source are generally listed in sections 12 to 17.

(I) Part I, Division B, Subdivision f, paragraph 69(1)(*b*): — This provision can be found in the set of general rules pertaining to the computation of income in Subdivision f of Division B of Part I because it affects the computation of income from a variety of sources.

(J) Part I, Division B, Subdivision b, paragraph 20(1)(*bb*): — Investments provide income from property and deductions from such income are generally listed in subsection 20(1).

Exercise 2

DIVISION B

Par. 3(*a*)	*Subdivision a*			
	Sec. 5, 6, 7, 8	Employment income		$ 60,000
	Subdivision b			
	Sec. 9	Business income	$ 10,000	
	Sec. 9	Property income	3,000	13,000

Subdivision d			
Par. 56(1)(*a*)	Retiring allowance		20,000
	Total par. 3(*a*) income		$ 93,000
Par. 3(*b*) *Subdivision c*			
Par. 38	Taxable capital gain (net of allowable capital loss)		20,000
			$113,000
Par. 3(*d*) *Subdivision b*			
Ssec. 9(2):	Rental property loss		(4,000)

Division B income			$109,000
Par. 111(1)(*a*)	Non-capital loss	$ 4,000	
Par. 111(1)(*b*)	Net capital loss	5,000	(9,000)
	Taxable income		$100,000

Federal tax after credits			
Tax before credits			$ 19,464
Sec. 118(1)	Personal credits		(3,312)
Sec. 118(10)	Canada employment credit		(168)
Sec. 118.7	CPP contributions credit		(353)
Sec. 118.7	EI premium credit		(134)
Sec. 118.5	Tuition credit		(68)
Sec. 118.6	Education and textbook credit transfer		(80)
Sec. 118.1	Charitable donation credit		(550)
Basic federal tax			$ 14,799

Exercise 3

Subsection 212(1) is a "charging provision" because it charges someone with the responsibility for paying a tax.

The components of subsection 212(1) are as follows.

(A) the person who is the subject of the provision

- "every non-resident person"

(B) the activity, event or condition that must be met for the provision to apply

- "on every amount that a person resident in Canada pays or credits or is deemed by Part I to pay or credit to the non-resident person as . . ." [followed by paragraphs (*a*) to (*w*) that list types of payments, such as a management fee, interest, rent, etc.]

(C) the consequences of the activity or event to the person who is the subject of the provision

- "*shall* pay an income tax at 25% on every amount . . ."

- note the use of the word "shall", indicating a mandatory payment

- note that the 25% rate can be reduced by a tax treaty which overrides the Canadian *Income Tax Act*

(D) the time frame for the application of the provision

- in the year that the amount is paid or credited is implied

Chapter 2
Liability for Tax

LEARNING GOALS

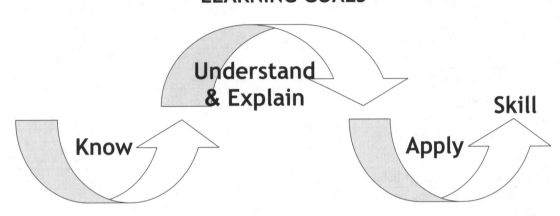

Understand & Explain · Know · Apply · Skill

Know

By the end of this chapter you should know the basic provisions of the *Income Tax Act*, *Excise Tax Act*, and case law that relate to liability for tax and residency. Completing the Review Questions (¶2,800) and Multiple Choice Questions (¶2,825) is a good way to learn the technical provisions.

Understand and Explain

You should understand and be able to explain when an individual or a corporation is resident in Canada and whether they are liable for income tax or GST/HST. Completing the Exercises (¶2,850) is a good way to deepen your understanding of the material.

Apply

You should be able to use your knowledge and understanding of residency and liability for income tax in a practical fact situation to determine whether a person is or is not liable for income tax. Completing the Assignment Problems (¶2,875) and the Advisory Case (¶2,880) is an excellent way to develop your ability to apply the material in increasingly complex situations.

Chapter 2 — Learning Chart

Topic	Example Problem (✓)	Review Questions (¶2,800)	Multiple Choice (¶2,825)	Exercises (¶2,850)	Assignment Problems (¶2,875)
¶2,000 LIABILITY OF INDIVIDUALS FOR INCOME TAX		1			
¶2,010 Liability of Individual Residents					
¶2,020 Full-Time Resident		3			
¶2,025 Deemed full-time resident					
¶2,030 Common law concept of full-time resident			2, 5	1, 2	1, 2, 3, 4
¶2,035 Administrative practice					
¶2,040 Part-Year Resident		2, 5			
¶2,045 Applicable law					
¶2,050 Clean break or fresh start: The concept			4		
¶2,055 Liability of Non-Residents					
¶2,060 General determination of liability		9	3		
¶2,065 The meaning of carrying on business in Canada		4, 10, 11, 12			
¶2,070 International Tax Treaties and Individuals					
¶2,075 Services		15			
¶2,080 Resident and "tie-breaker" rules		13			
¶2,085 Permanent establishment					
¶2,090 Summary of the Residence Issue for an Individual					
¶2,100 Comprehensive Consideration of the Residence of an Individual					
¶2,105 Stages of involvement					
¶2,110 Consider both sides					
¶2,115 Form of advice					
¶2,120 Application	✓				
¶2,130 Non-Tax Factors Affecting Planning for the Residence of an Individual					
¶2,200 LIABILITY OF CORPORATIONS FOR INCOME TAX					
¶2,210 Charging Provision					
¶2,220 Residence of Corporations		6, 7, 8, 14	1	3	5
¶2,225 Deemed residence					
¶2,230 Common law concept of corporate residence					
¶2,240 Liability of Non-Resident Corporations				4	6, 7, 8
¶2,250 International Tax Treaties and Corporations					
¶2,260 Comprehensive Consideration of the Residence of a Corporation	✓				
¶2,300 REGISTRATION REQUIREMENTS AND LIABILITY FOR THE GOODS AND SERVICES TAX AND HARMONIZED SALES TAX					
¶2,310 Liability for GST/HST			6		
¶2,315 Supplies in Canada					
¶2,317 Supplies in an HST province					

Topic	Example Problem (✓)	Review Questions (¶2,800)	Multiple Choice (¶2,825)	Exercises (¶2,850)	Assignment Problems (¶2,875)
¶2,320 Supplies by non-residents					
¶2,330 Registration Requirements for Residents					
¶2,335 Test for registration					
¶2,340 Definition of commercial activity					
¶2,345 Exclusions from commercial activity					
¶2,350 Exceptions from the registration requirements					
¶2,360 Registration and Collection Requirements for Non-Residents					
¶2,365 Meaning of non-resident					
¶2,370 Mandatory registration					
¶2,375 Voluntary registration					
¶2,380 Imports					

CHAPTER 2

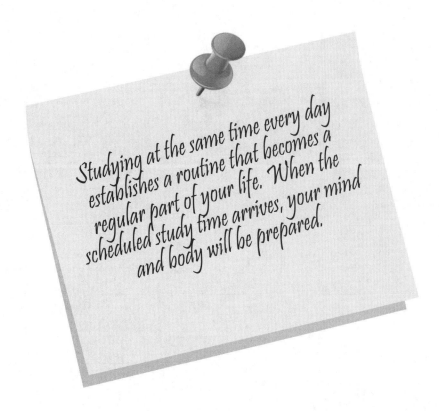

Studying at the same time every day establishes a routine that becomes a regular part of your life. When the scheduled study time arrives, your mind and body will be prepared.

Study Notes

Chapter 2 —
Discussion Notes for Review Questions

(1) Canadian individuals are taxed based on residency and not their citizenship. Canadian residents are taxed on their world income.

ITA: 2(1)

(2) He or she will be deemed to be a resident only if he or she sojourned in Canada for 183 or more days during the year.

ITA: 250(1)

(3) You need to look at other factors to determine where they have a "continuing state of relationship", such as family and social ties and other personal property. The Interpretation Bulletin categorizes the type of facts that can be used to establish residential ties.

Income Tax Folio S5-F1-C1 — Determining an Individual's Residence Status

(4) He or she would be considered to be a non-resident of Canada throughout the year. However, since he or she carried on business in Canada during the year while a non-resident, he or she would be taxable in Canada on his or her Canadian business profits for the year.

ITA: 2(3)

(5) If he or she is establishing a "fresh start" in Canada on March 31 then he or she becomes resident on that date and is taxed in Canada on his or her world income from that date. The sojourning rules would not apply since they only apply to non-residents who are in Canada on a temporary basis.

(6) The residency of a corporation is either determined by the common law test of "central management and control", or a corporation is deemed to be a Canadian resident if it is incorporated in Canada after April 26, 1965, or it meets the tests outlined in the Act if it was incorporated before that date.

ITA: 250(4)

(7) A corporation is deemed to be resident in Canada if it was incorporated in Canada after April 26, 1965. Reference to the tax treaty would be the next step but Canada does not have a tax treaty with Bermuda. Therefore, it would be resident in Canada and taxable in Canada on its world income.

ITA: 250(4)(a)

(8) Any company which was incorporated in Canada before April 27, 1965 and which carried on business in Canada in any year after that date is deemed to be resident in Canada. An extended meaning of carrying on business includes soliciting orders in Canada. The facts fit the meaning because of the continuity of the order solicitation over a period of years. Therefore, the company would be resident in Canada and taxable in Canada on its world income.

ITA: 250(4)(a)
ITA: 253(b)

(9) Subsection 2(3) refers to "employed in Canada in the year or a previous year". Therefore, section 115 of Division D requires the income from an office or employment to be taxed in Canada.

ITA: 115(2)(c)

(10) The U.S. company is soliciting orders in Canada and, therefore, is carrying on business in Canada. The corporation is, thus, taxable in Canada on the profits related to these sales.

ITA: 2(3), 115, 253

(11) Under the extended meaning of carrying on business, the U.S. company would be a non-resident carrying on business in Canada and liable for tax on its earning in Canada. However, under the Canada–U.S. tax treaty, the U.S. company would probably not be taxable in Canada because its profits are not earned from a permanent establishment in Canada.

ITA: 253

(12) Yes, a person can be a resident of more than one country since residency is determined under the laws of each country. Article IV of the Canada–U.S. tax treaty provides rules for resolving who collects the tax where a person is a resident of both the United States and Canada.

(13) Under Article VII of the Canada–U.S. tax treaty, it will only be subject to tax on the income attributable to that permanent establishment.

(14) Article XIV of the Canada–U.S. tax treaty will cause him to be taxed in the United States only if he has a "fixed base regularly available to him" in the United States Therefore, he will only pay tax in Canada on this income.

Chapter 2 —
Solutions to Multiple Choice Questions

Question 1

(B) is correct. Since X Ltd. is not incorporated in Canada, it is not deemed to be resident in Canada. Since the directors are not resident in Canada, X Ltd. is not resident in Canada under the common law "central management and control" rule.   ITA: 250(4)

(A) is incorrect because X Ltd. is deemed to be resident.   ITA: 250(4)(*a*)

(C) is incorrect because X Ltd. is resident under the common law "central management and control" rule.

(D) is incorrect because X Ltd. is deemed to be resident; the common law "central management and control" rule would also apply.   ITA: 250(4)(*c*)

Question 2

(C) is correct. Generally, the CRA will consider the individual not to have severed residential ties within Canada if he has a dwelling available for occupancy.   Income Tax Folio S5-F1-C1 — Determining an Individual's Residence Status

(A) is incorrect, because taking his wife and children with him to Germany is not feasible, since the couple is legally separated and the children are not dependent on him for support.   Income Tax Folio S5-F1-C1 — Determining an Individual's Residence Status

(B) is incorrect, because giving up Canadian citizenship has little relevance in determining residency.

(D) is incorrect. Although putting all his household furniture and personal effects into storage in Canada is a residential tie, the tie is a weaker one than that cited in (C).   Income Tax Folio S5-F1-C1 — Determining an Individual's Residence Status

Question 3

(B) is correct. Only the $50,000 of employment income earned in Canada would be reported on Mr. Ng's Canadian personal income tax return for the year.   ITA: 2(3), 115

(A) is incorrect. The $10,000 interest, earned by the non-resident, is not taxable under either Part I (ssec. 2(3)) or Part XIII (ssec. 212(3), "fully exempt interest").

(C) is incorrect for the same reason as (A).

(D) is incorrect, because only residents of Canada are subject to Canadian income tax on their worldwide income.   ITA: 2(1)

Question 4

(C) is correct. Because Jay ceased to be a resident of Canada on April 30 of the year, only his worldwide income during the first four months of the year ($26,000 = $25,000 + $1,000) is subject to tax in Canada under Part I and would be reported on his Canadian personal income tax return for the year.   ITA: 2(1), 114

(A) includes income earned while not a resident of Canada: $58,000 = $25,000 + $1,000 + $30,000 + $2,000. The $30,000 of employment income earned in New Zealand and the $2,000 of Canadian interest earned from May 1 to December 31 of the year are not subject to Part I tax because Jay is not resident in Canada at that time. The $2,000 of Canadian interest is exempt from withholding tax under Part XIII.   ITA: 2(1), 114

(B) includes the salary earned in New Zealand: $56,000 = $25,000 + $1,000 + $30,000. As in (A), above, the $30,000 of employment income earned in New Zealand is not subject to tax in Canada.

(D) excludes the worldwide income earned while Jay was a resident in Canada. As discussed in (A), above, this would be reported on his Canadian personal income tax return for the year.   ITA: 2(1), 114

Question 5

(B) is correct. Judy is a non-resident. She seems to have severed her residential ties to Canada (moving her belongings) and established new ties to London, England (buying a house).

(A) is incorrect. James is still a resident of Canada. There is no indication that James has severed his residential ties to Canada or established ties to London, England.

(C) is incorrect. Since ERT Limited was incorporated in Canada after April 26, 1965, it is deemed to be a resident of Canada.   ITA: 250(4)(*a*)

(D) is incorrect. Doug is deemed to be a resident of Canada because he is a member of the Canadian armed forces.   ITA: 250(1)(*b*)

Question 6

(C) is correct.

Sales (taxable at 13%) $250,000
Purchase of supplies from a registrant   30,000
$220,000 × 13% = $28,600.

(A) incorrectly takes a deduction for salaries which is an exempt supply: $250,000 − $30,000 − $70,000 = $150,000. $150,000 × 13% = $19,500.

(B) incorrectly takes a deduction for interest expense: $250,000 − $30,000 − $20,000 = $200,000. $200,000 × 13% = $26,000.

(D) incorrectly includes exports (which are zero-rated) and takes a deduction for interest expense (an exempt supply): $250,000 + $100,000 − $30,000 − $20,000 = $300,000. $300,000 × 13% = $39,000.

Chapter 2 – Solutions to Exercises

Exercise 1

(A) Alpha is a part-year resident of Canada in the year. He would be a resident until August 27 of the year when he appears to have made a "clean break" with Canada. While in Canada he would not have been sojourning, so the deeming rule would not apply.

ITA: 250(1)(*a*)

(B) Beta has no residential ties with Canada. Citizenship is not a determining factor in establishing such ties.

(C) Gamma is a non-resident of Canada and is taxable only on employment income earned in Canada.

ITA: 2(3)(*a*), 115(1)(*a*)(i)

(D) Delta is either a part-year resident of Canada or a non-resident employed in Canada, depending on the facts of his stay in Canada. He is also taxable under paragraph 2(3)(*c*) because the shares are taxable Canadian property.

ITA: 115(1)(*b*)(iv)

(E) Epsilon is deemed a resident of Canada because of his relationship to his mother.

ITA: 250(1)(*c*)(i), 250(1)(*f*)

(F) Mu is not deemed to be a resident of Canada by any of the deeming rules. She has never been resident in Canada. Therefore, she is not a resident of Canada.

ITA: 250(1)

Exercise 2

[See: *MacDonald v. M.N.R.*, 68 DTC 433 (T.A.B.).]

(A) The resident option → taxed in Canada on worldwide income for full year:

ITA: 2(1)

Criterion: residence is a question of fact dependent on the degree of permanency in the relationship between a person and a place;

Evidence:

(i) factors indicating this relationship between the appellant and Canada,

1. he sold his house in the United States and paid an American capital gains tax for not buying another residence,

2. his wife, upon arriving in Canada, rented premises pending the purchase of a house,

3. she and the children, whom the appellant was supporting to the extent of $600 per month, stayed in Canada all year-round,

4. he stayed in Canada when he was off-duty to the extent of 166 out of 180 days in 1964,

— full-time presence is not necessary,

5. other non-determining factors,

— joint account in Canada where pay cheques were deposited during his vacations,

— joint ownership of a car with New Brunswick registry,

— citizenship irrelevant;

(ii) factors detracting from a relationship with Canada,

1. a few rooms, without exclusive use, made available for him at his sister's house in the United States,

— not a permanent abode,

— an individual can have more than one residence,

2. U.S. citizen and previously and subsequently resided in the United States with a stated intention to return,

— but only 1964 in question on the facts,

— stated intention must be supported by behavioural facts,

— worked for a U.S. company and paid in U.S. currency,

— but not determining because a Canadian resident can be involved in such a situation, providing employment services abroad for a non-Canadian company,

— memberships and investments including bank accounts, securities and pension plan in United States,

   — factors may indicate U.S. residence, but not determining and also possible for a person resident in Canada,

— no Canadian memberships or investments and no application for family allowances,

   — not determining factors and also possible of a Canadian resident,

— children living in United States,

   — married and apparently not dependent,

— phone in wife's name in Canada,

   — a factor, but hardly determining,

— neither employed in Canada nor carrying on business in Canada,

   — not necessary condition for full-time residence.

(This list of factors is longer but there is more substance for full-time residence.)

(B) The deemed resident option → taxed in Canada on worldwide income for full year: ITA: 2(1)

Criterion: the condition of sojourning an aggregate of 183 days or more;   ITA: 250(1)

Evidence: his total stay in Canada in the year was only for 166 days; therefore, the condition is not met.

(C) The part-year resident option → taxed in Canada on worldwide income for part of the year   ITA: 2(1), 114, 118.91
resident in Canada with deductions applicable to the period of part-year residence and non-refundable tax credits either prorated for or applicable to the period of part-year residence (as long as not resident in Canada during some other part of the year);

Criterion: clean break or fresh start during 1964;

Evidence: neither occurred.

(D) The non-resident option → taxed in Canada on income earned in Canada: ITA: 2(3)

Criteria: employed in Canada, carried on business in Canada or disposed of taxable Canadian property in the year;

Evidence: none of these conditions occurred in the year.   ITA: 2(3)

(E) Conclusion: if the taxpayer is to be found a resident it must be as a full-time resident:

   — the major factors indicate a relationship with Canada which would warrant a conclusion of such resident status.

Exercise 3

(A) Inch Incorporated is resident in Canada by virtue of the common law principle of central   ITA: 250(4)
management and control. The corporation cannot be deemed resident in Canada because it was not incorporated in Canada.

(B) Foot Limited is deemed resident in Canada because it was incorporated in Canada after   ITA: 250(4)(a)
April 26, 1965.

(C) Yard Incorporated is not resident this year by virtue of the common law principle of central
management and control. Furthermore, the corporation cannot be deemed resident in Canada because it was not incorporated in Canada.

(D) Mile Limited is resident in Canada. The corporation was incorporated in Canada before   ITA: 250(4)(c)
April 27, 1965 and after that time it was resident by virtue of the central management and control rule.

Exercise 4

Canada levies tax on non-residents who carry on business in Canada. Carrying on business in   ITA: 2(3)
Canada is distinguishable from carrying on business with Canada. While Samson solicits sales from Canadians, it does not have a permanent establishment in Canada, nor does it employ a Canadian salesperson or agent. Given these facts, Samson is not liable for Canadian income taxes on the $76,000 profit originating from within Canada.

Chapter 3
Employment Income

LEARNING GOALS

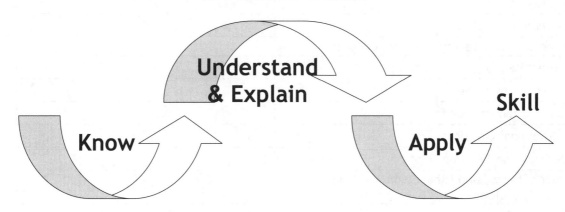

Understand & Explain

Skill

Know

Apply

Know

By the end of this chapter you should know the basic provisions of the *Income Tax Act* that relate to employment income and expenses. You should be able to calculate employment income and distinguish between a self-employed independent contractor and an employee. Completing the Review Questions (¶3,800) and Multiple Choice Questions (¶3,825) is a good way to learn the technical provisions.

Understand and Explain

You should understand and be able to explain how employment income and expenses are calculated and why the provisions are designed the way they are. Completing the Exercises (¶3,850) is a good way to deepen your understanding of the material.

Apply

You should be able to apply your knowledge and understanding of employment income and expenses to real life situations. Completing the Assignment Problems (¶3,875) is an excellent way to develop your ability to apply the material in increasingly complex situations.

CHAPTER 3

Chapter 3 — Learning Chart

Topic	Example Problem (✓)	Review Questions (¶3,800)	Multiple Choice (¶3,825)	Exercises (¶3,850)	Assignment Problems (¶3,875)
¶3,000 BASIC RULES		1, 9			
¶3,010 Employed Versus Self-Employed or Independent Contractor	✓	2, 3		1, 2	1
¶3,015 Overview					
¶3,020 The economic reality or entrepreneur test		4			
¶3,025 Integration or organization test		5			
¶3,030 Specific result test		6			
¶3,032 Conclusion—No one test					
¶3,035 Other considerations					
¶3,037 Defining the Taxation Year					
¶3,040 Salary, Wages, and Other Remuneration Including Gratuities					
¶3,050 Amounts Received		7, 8			3
¶3,060 Volunteer Services Exemption					
¶3,100 SPECIFIC INCLUSIONS		18			
¶3,110 Value of Board and Lodging					15
¶3,120 Other Fringe Benefits				5	
¶3,125 General rules				3, 7, 11	2, 3, 4, 10, 13, 15, 16
¶3,130 Housing loss and housing cost benefits				6	16
¶3,135 Employee loans	✓	11	4	8	2, 5, 8, 11, 15
¶3,150 Allowances					
¶3,155 Overview		12			2, 14, 15, 16
¶3,160 Exception of allowance for travelling expenses of sales/negotiating persons			2	14	
¶3,165 Exception of allowance for travelling expenses of other employees					16
¶3,170 Director's or Other Fees					8
¶3,220 Benefit from Employer-Paid GST/HST				15	
¶3,230 Employment Insurance Benefits	✓	10			8, 10, 15
¶3,240 Payments by Employer to Employee	✓				9
¶3,250 Restrictive Covenants					
¶3,260 Stock Options					
¶3,265 General					
¶3,268 Stock options—Withholding tax					
¶3,270 Rules applicable for all types of corporations					3, 4, 5, 10, 12, 14
¶3,273 Stock option cash outs					
¶3,275 Rules applicable to Canadian-controlled private corporations				9	16

Topic	Example Problem (✓)	Review Questions (¶3,800)	Multiple Choice (¶3,825)	Exercises (¶3,850)	Assignment Problems (¶3,875)
¶3,280 Rules applicable to public corporations	✓		5		3, 4, 5, 10, 12, 14
¶3,285 Valuation of shares					
¶3,287 Risk factors					
¶3,288 Employment Income and Capital Loss—2010 to 2015					
¶3,290 Summary	✓				
¶3,300 DEDUCTIONS FROM EMPLOYMENT INCOME					
¶3,310 Sales/Negotiating Person's Expenses		14	6	11, 13, 14	11, 12, 13, 14, 15
¶3,320 Any Employee's Travelling Expenses Other Than Motor Vehicle Expenses					
¶3,325 Overview					16
¶3,330 Conditions		15		14	16
¶3,335 Limitations				11, 13	12, 13, 14
¶3,340 Receipts by part-time employees for travelling expenses		16			
¶3,342 Dues and Other Expenses					10, 12, 14, 15
¶3,345 Work Space in Home		17	3	12	14
¶3,350 Other Expenses					
¶3,352 Legal expenses				4	
¶3,354 Clergy's residence					
¶3,356 Teacher's exchange fund					
¶3,358 Railway employees					
¶3,360 Transport employees					
¶3,362 CPP and EI premiums payable in respect of an assistant					
¶3,364 Retirement compensation arrangements					
¶3,366 Salary reimbursements					
¶3,368 Forfeitures					
¶3,370 Musical instrument costs					
¶3,372 Artist's expenses					
¶3,374 Tradesperson's tool expenses					
¶3,380 Registered Pension Plans					3, 10, 12, 13, 15, 16
¶3,385 Overview					
¶3,400 AUTOMOBILE BENEFITS, CAR ALLOWANCES, AND CAR EXPENSES					
¶3,402 Standby Charge and Operating Cost Benefit for Automobile Provided by Employer					
¶3,403 Calculation of the standby charge benefit from the use of the car itself		13	1	10	3, 6, 8, 13
¶3,404 Determining the operating cost benefit			1	10	3, 6, 8, 13

Topic	Example Problem (✓)	Review Questions (¶3,800)	Multiple Choice (¶3,825)	Exercises (¶3,850)	Assignment Problems (¶3,875)
¶3,405 Summary of employer-provided automobile benefits					
¶3,406 Application of the rules	✓				6
¶3,408 Employee-Owned Automobile Operating Expense Benefit					
¶3,409 Vehicles Other Than Automobiles					
¶3,410 Motor Vehicle Allowances Received from Employers					14
¶3,415 Overview					
¶3,420 Allowances for motor vehicles — Other persons					7, 8
¶3,425 Allowance deemed not to be reasonable			2		7, 8, 14
¶3,430 Expenses					
¶3,435 Overview				11	11, 14, 15, 16
¶3,440 Motor vehicle and aircraft — Interest and CCA				11, 14	11, 14, 15
¶3,445 Imputed interest deemed paid				8	11, 15
¶3,450 Interest on money borrowed for passenger vehicle					11, 14, 15
¶3,455 Capital cost for passenger vehicle				14	14, 15
¶3,460 Limitation re cost of leased passenger vehicle					14, 15, 16
¶3,470 Application of Rules	✓				
¶3,500 GST/HST REBATE ON EMPLOYEE DEDUCTIONS	✓				16
¶3,600 APPLICATION OF RULES UNDER SUBDIVISION "A"	✓				

CHAPTER 3

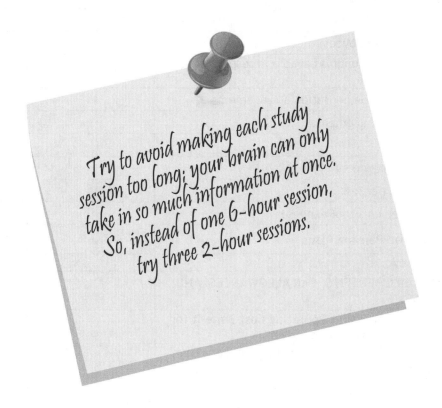

Try to avoid making each study session too long; your brain can only take in so much information at once. So, instead of one 6-hour session, try three 2-hour sessions.

Study Notes

Chapter 3 —
Discussion Notes for Review Questions

(1) The personal tax return (T1 General) does not include RPP contributions, union and professional dues and other paragraph 8(1)(*i*) deductions in the calculation of employment income. These are included under the heading "Net Income" in the personal tax return. It would be misleading to use the personal tax return format for this specific purpose, because certain deductions are limited to the amount of employment income in the year, such as the home office expense deduction.

(2) An employee can only deduct those expenses that are specifically allowed under section 8 whereas a self-employed individual may deduct all expenses incurred to earn business and property income as permitted by Subdivision b. Both the employee and the self-employed individual are subject to the reasonableness test.

ITA: 67

(3) No one test is conclusive in itself. All tests should be considered together before a conclusion is reached.

(4) The control subtest in the economic reality or entrepreneur test determines whether one person is in a position to order or require not only what is to be done but how it is to be done. Where such control, by the business over the individual, does exist, an employer–employee relationship is implied.

(5) The integration or organization test examines the degree of economic dependence of the individual on the organization. Where the individual is financially dependent on the organization, then an employer-employee relationship is implied.

(6) The specific result test looks at the expected results of the work performed. An employee–employer relationship usually contemplates the employee putting his or her personal services at the disposal of his or her employer during a given period of time without reference to a specified result and, generally, envisages the accomplishment of work on an ongoing basis. On the other hand, where a party agrees that certain specified work will be done for the other, it may be inferred that an independent contractor relationship exists.

(7) The Act uses the word "received" to determine the timing of the taxation of employment income. In this case, she will be considered to have received her bonus in the year she received the cheque. Just because she chose not to cash the cheque does not change the timing of when she received the payment.

ITA: 5

(8) The Act uses the word "received" to determine the timing of the taxation of employment income. The voluntary deferment of an unconditional right to receive the bonus is not an acceptable method of deferring income.

ITA: 5
Blenkarn v. M.N.R., 63 DTC 581 (T.A.B.)

(9) Employers cannot deduct all of the taxable benefits reported on the employee's T4. Items such as deemed interest benefits and standby charges for automobiles are not deductible to the employer since they are not expenses that are incurred for the purpose of earning income.

ITA: 80.4

(10) If the employer makes *any* of the premium payments then the benefit payments received will likely be taxable.

ITA: 6(1)(*f*); IT-428

(11) The CRA follows normal commercial practice such that the first day of the contract is counted and the last day is excluded for purposes of determining the number of days of interest. In this case the number of days from June 2 to June 29 inclusive will be used to determine the benefit, that is, 28 days.

(12) A reimbursement is a payment by an employer to an employee for expenses of the employer which have been paid by the employee and which are substantiated by receipts. This is normally accomplished by submitting an expense report. An allowance is a fixed amount which is paid to an employee in excess of his or her salary without the requirement that the employee be accountable for the amount expended.

IT-522R, pars. 40, 50

(13) The standby charge is calculated as follows:

$$\frac{20,004}{20,004} \times 2\% \times 12 \times (\$40,000 + \$5,200) = \$10,848.$$

(14) The five conditions that a salesperson must meet in order to be able to deduct expenses are:

ITA: 8(1)(*f*)

(a) he or she must be employed in the year in connection with the selling of property or negotiating of contracts for his or her employer;

(b) under the terms of his or her contract of employment he or she must be required to pay his or her own expenses;

(c) he or she must be ordinarily required to carry on his or her duties away from his or her employer's place of business;

(d) he or she is remunerated in whole or in part by commissions or other similar amounts fixed by reference to the volume of the sales made or the contracts negotiated; and

(e) he or she was not in receipt of a reasonable allowance for travelling expenses in respect of the taxation year that was not included in computing his or her income.

ITA: 6(1)(*b*)(v)

(15) The four conditions that must be met to allow an employee to deduct travelling expenses, other than car expenses, are:

ITA: 8(1)(*h*)

(a) he or she is ordinarily required to carry on his or her duties away from his or her employer's place of business or in different places;

(b) under his or her employment contract, he or she is required to pay the travelling expenses incurred by him or her in the performance of his or her duties;

(c) he or she was not in receipt of a reasonable allowance for travelling expenses that was not included in computing his or her income; and

ITA: 6(1)(*b*)(v), 6(1)(*b*)(vi), 6(1)(*b*)(vii)

(d) he or she did not claim any deduction for railway company employees, salespersons, or transport company employees.

ITA: 8(1)(*e*), 8(1)(*f*), 8(1)(*g*)

(16) There is nothing in paragraph 6(1)(*b*) that would exclude this allowance from income. However, another rule would apply to cause this receipt to be exempt from tax. In order to be exempt under this provision, the allowance must meet the following tests:

ITA: 81(3.1)

(a) he must deal at arm's length with his employer;

(b) he must have other employment or business income (not necessary in this case, since he is employed as a professor or teacher at a designated educational institution);

(c) the amount received must be reasonable and must relate only to travel to and from part-time employment; and

(d) the part-time location must be at least 80 km away from both the employee's ordinary place of residence and his principal place of employment or business.

(17) Neither word is defined in the Act. However, an Interpretation Bulletin interprets the word "principally" as more than 50%. Therefore, as long as the employment-use of the workspace is its main or chief purpose, the test is met. "Exclusively" is not defined in the tax law, so reference is made to other sources. *Webster's English Dictionary* defines "exclusively" as "to the exclusion of all others" which is a much more onerous test.

IT-352R2, par. 2

(18) The Act deems that taxes withheld have been received at the time the bonus was paid. Therefore, even though the company still had the government's portion of the bonus, tax cannot be deferred on it. In addition, if the amount withheld in respect of the tax was not deemed to have been received by Ms. Smith, then she would not have received credit for the payment of this tax on her personal tax return.

ITA: 153(3)

Chapter 3 —
Solutions to Multiple Choice Questions

Question 1

(A) is correct: $12 \times 2\% \times \$34,500 = \$8,280$.

ITA: 6(2)

(B) and (C) are wrong because the operating cost benefit is computed as: 27 cents × 15,000 personal-use kilometres = $4,050. Part (B) incorrectly computes the operating cost benefit as: 15,000/20,000 × $3,600 = $2,700. Part (C) incorrectly computes the operating cost benefit as: 26 cents × 15,000 personal-use kilometres = $3,900.

ITA: 6(1)(*k*); ITR: 7305.1

(D) is wrong because he does not have more than 50% employment use.

ITA: 6(1)(*k*)(iv)

Question 2

(B) is correct: $50,000 salary + $3,500 allowance – $3,000 automobile expenses = $50,500. The car allowance is taxable because it is not based solely on kilometres driven. Since the car allowance is taxable, the automobile expenses can be deducted. The entertainment expenses are not deductible because she has no commission income.

ITA: 6(1)(*b*)(x), 8(1)(*f*), 8(1)(*h*.1)(iii)

(A) incorrectly excludes a deduction for automobile expenses: $53,500 = $50,000 salary + $3,500 allowance. The automobile expenses are deductible because the allowance is included in income.

ITA: 8(1)(*h*.1)
ITA: 6(1)(*b*)

(C) incorrectly includes a deduction for entertainment expenses: $49,500 = $50,000 salary + $3,500 allowance – $3,000 automobile expenses – $1,000 entertainment expenses. The entertainment expenses (50% × $2,000) are not deductible because she has no commission income or income from negotiating contracts.

ITA: 8(1)(*f*)

(D) incorrectly excludes the car allowance and the deduction for automobile expenses and incorrectly includes a deduction for entertainment expenses: $49,000 = $50,000 salary – $1,000 entertainment expenses.

Question 3

(A) is correct. Susanne Denholm can claim home office expenses because she is required by contract to maintain an office in her home and she works principally in her home (i.e., "most of the time"). The $500 correct amount of deductible home office expenses is calculated as follows:

ITA: 8(1)(*i*)(iii), 8(13)(*a*)(i)

Heat, hydro & maintenance: $5,000 × 10% = $500

Subsection 8(13) allows deductions under paragraphs 8(1)(*f*) or 8(1)(*i*). Since Susanne does not have any commission income, she can only deduct items under paragraph 8(1)(*i*). The distinction between (*f*) and (*i*) is that under (*f*) the expenses are fixed in nature and under (*i*) they are variable in nature (like supplies deductible under (*i*)). Since the only expenses that are variable with use are the heat, hydro, and maintenance, they are the only ones deductible. The mortgage interest is not deductible under either (*f*) or (*i*), since the only interest that is deductible as an employment expense is for automobiles and aircraft.

ITA: 8(1)(*j*), 8(2)

(B) incorrectly includes a deduction for property taxes and insurance: $1,100 = $500 + $200 insurance + $400 property taxes. The insurance (10% × $2,000) and property taxes (10% × $4,000) are not considered to be supplies. However, if Susanne had commission income, 10% of her insurance and property taxes would be deductible.

IT-352R2, par. 6
ITA: 8(1)(*i*)(iii)
ITA: 8(1)(*f*)

(C) incorrectly includes deductions for insurance, property taxes and the general telephone line: $1,400 = $500 + $200 insurance + $400 property taxes + $300 general telephone line. The insurance, property taxes and the cost of the general telephone line (50% × $600) are not deductible. If Susanne had commission income, the cost of the general telephone line would still not be deductible — only long-distance calls would be deductible.

IT-352R2, pars. 6, 10(a)
ITA: 8(1)(*i*)(iii)

(D) incorrectly includes insurance, property taxes, the general telephone line and mortgage interest: $3,800 = $500 + $200 insurance + $400 property taxes + $300 general telephone + $2,400 mortgage interest. The insurance, property taxes, the cost of the general telephone line and mortgage interest (10% × $24,000) are not considered to be supplies. If Susanne had commission income, the mortgage interest would still not be deductible since the Act limits interest expense of an employee to interest on automobiles and planes.

IT-352R2
ITA: 8(1)(*i*)(iii)
ITA: 8(1)(*j*)

Question 4

(A) is correct. The loan qualifies as a home relocation loan. The benefit is computed using the lower of the prescribed interest rate at the time of the loan (4%) and the prescribed interest rate during the year (3%). Therefore the employment benefit is $1,000 (3% × $100,000 – 2% × $100,000 interest paid). ITA: 6(9), 80.4(1), 80.4(4)

(B) incorrectly computes the employment benefit using 4%: $2,000 = 4% × $100,000 – 2% × $100,000.

(C) incorrectly ignores the 2% interest paid in the computation of the interest benefit: $3,000 = 3% × $100,000.

(D) incorrectly computes the employment benefit using 4% rather than 3%. The 2% interest paid is not deducted: 4% × $100,000.

Question 5

(D) is correct. The stock option benefit is ($40 – $30) × 1,000 shares = $10,000 in 2012.

(A) incorrectly subtracts a deduction (½ × $10,000) in computing the benefit ($10,000 – $5,000). This deduction is a Division C deduction. ITA: 110(1)(*d*)

(B) incorrectly computes the benefit based on the sales price of $48,000 ($48,000 – $30,000 = $18,000) rather than the price of the stock at the time of purchase.

(C) incorrectly includes the taxable capital gain in the employee benefit (($48,000 – $40,000) × ½ + ($40,000 – $30,000) = $14,000).

Question 6

(B) is correct.

Meals and entertainment (50% × $14,000) .... $ 7,000
Driving costs (90% × $10,000) 9,000
Expenses eligible for deduction $16,000

ITA: 8(1)(*f*)

Tim can either claim a deduction for these amounts to the extent of his commission income ($5,000) or he can claim a deduction for his automobile costs ($9,000) alone, without the commission limitation. The maximum deduction is therefore $9,000. ITA: 8(1)(*f*) 8(1)(*h*.1)

(A) is incorrect because it is the commission-limited amount. ITA: 8(1)(*f*)

(C) is incorrect because it is the full meals and entertainment amount ($14,000) and ignores the $5,000 commission limitation. ITA: 67.1

(D) is incorrect because it represents the expenses eligible as a salesperson ($16,000) but ignores the $5,000 commission limitation. ITA: 8(1)(*f*)

Chapter 3 — Solutions to Exercises

Exercise 1

[See: *Isaac v. M.N.R.*, 70 DTC 1285 (T.A.B.)]

The following tests are applied to determine whether R.N. is an employee or an independent contractor.

Economic Reality or Entrepreneur Test

In applying the control subtest, the question is whether Canadian Forces Hospital, Halifax controlled not only what was done by R.N. but how it was done. In this case the Hospital exercised control over R.N. in connection with dividing up the patients to be cared for among the available nurses and imposing routine rules and regulations with regard to the administration of drugs and other medications. On the other hand, the Hospital did not exercise any control over the method in which R.N. did her work, which requires special knowledge, skill, and judgment. Accordingly, it does not appear that the Hospital exercised sufficient control to conclude that R.N. was an employee on the basis of this test alone.

However, the application of the other subtests is particularly revealing. R.N. does not run the risk of financing the equipment, supplying other assistants necessary to carry out her duties in the Hospital or seeking out clients. R.N. used the equipment and supplies furnished by the Hospital. She neither hired nor fired any of the nursing assistants who worked under her. She could only request that the Hospital hire additional staff to assist her. The clients were patients of the Hospital. R.N. was not in a position to substitute the services of another nurse if she was unable to perform her duties. All this evidence tends to establish that from an economic reality point of view R.N. was an employee, but this test may not be definitive in this case.

Integration or Organization Test

The Hospital deducted Canada Pension Plan contributions from her pay as they did with the nurses who were employed full-time by the Hospital. R.N. appeared to be economically dependent on the hospital, although she was not precluded from offering her services elsewhere. R.N. was subject to co-ordinational control of the hospital in terms of where to perform her services and when to do so. On the other hand, R.N. was not eligible for the regular benefits of a full-time nurse such as holidays, sick pay, retirement plan, etc. She was hired on a day-to-day basis at a *per diem* rate of pay. Her services could be terminated on 24 hours notice if full-time nurses became available. On the weight of the evidence it can be argued that R.N. is an employee of the Hospital based on the integration test.

Specific Result Test

On the one hand, it was R.N.'s personal services that were at the disposal of the Hospital. Her work was done on a continuous day-to-day basis without there being any limited or specified amount of work that she had, by contract, to accomplish. She could not substitute another person to perform her duties if she was unable to do so. On the other hand, R.N. was not a full-time nurse for any specified period of time. Her time was made up on a weekly basis in advance. She could be laid off on 24 hours notice. On balance, it appears that the evidence leads to the conclusion that, by applying the specific result test, R.N. was an employee. This conclusion is consistent with that for the integration or organization test.

Conclusion

The application of the control subtest of the economic reality or entrepreneur test leads to the conclusion that R.N was not an employee of the Hospital. The application of the other subtests of the economic reality test, the integration test and the specific result test leads to the inference that R.N. was an employee of the Hospital. (Your own conclusion after weighing all of these tests.)

Exercise 2

The courts generally rely on three tests to determine whether or not an individual is an independent contractor or an employee. Applying these tests should therefore help us determine the status of Ms. Capwell in relation to the architectural firm of Davies Ltd.

ITA: 248(1); *Wiebe Door Services Ltd. v. M.N.R.*, 87 DTC 5025 (F.C.A.)

(1) Economic Reality or Entrepreneur Test

(a) Control Test

The first test examines the day-to-day time commitment that is expected of an individual and the accountability of the individual to the corporation. In this instance, Ms. Capwell must work at least 14 days a month on the project (but the specific days appear flexible); however, she appears to be able to work under her own direction and on other projects on her days off. It does not seem to be conclusive as to whether or not Ms. Capwell is an employee given this test, but the evidence supports that she would be an independent contractor given the circumstances.

(b) Ownership of Tools

It is not clear, but Ms. Capwell appears to provide her own car, equipment, and technical expertise. We might also conclude that since she is working on the premises, many of her expenses, such as supplies and her place of work, will be covered by Davies Ltd. This test appears to support contractor status.

(c) Chance of Profit, Risk of Loss

This test assesses whether the individual incurs her own business risk, legal liability, and expenses. In this case, she is getting paid a flat fee of $4,000 per month, which we must assume is directly related to billable hours of work. She estimates that 30% of her contracting revenues will come from other sources, which is not entirely insignificant. This test is also not conclusive, and depending on the details, could go either way.

(2) Integration or Organization Test

This test determines whether or not the individual is economically dependent on the payer organization and is an integral part of the corporation. In this case, Ms. Capwell is not completely dependent on Davies for all of her income, but she retains an office on the premises and also receives some employee benefits in the form of underground parking. However, it's possible that the nature of the work demands she attend the company's offices. This test is inconclusive, but depending on the circumstances, slightly favours her being viewed as an employee.

(3) Specific Results Test

As the name suggests, the object of this test is to determine whether the individual's services were acquired to complete a specific task. In this case, there is no doubt that Ms. Capwell was taken on to complete a specific project, after which the contract will be fulfilled. Given this, she would appear to be an independent contractor.

Conclusion

The tests would seem to favour independent contract status, principally because of the flat fee for one specific project.

The results of the tests do not always provide us with a definitive answer as to whether or not an individual should be viewed as an employee. However, they can help guide us to make that determination. In this case, the facts lead toward the independent contractor conclusion. Given that the contract was drafted for a specific project, and that Ms. Capwell seems to be working independently, the courts would probably allow the designation of independent contractor status.

Exercise 3

(A) Specifically exempted.

ITA: 6(1)(a)

(B) Exempted; provincial employer health tax.

ITA: 6(1)(a)

(C) and (D) Exempted, since the premium was paid to a private medical plan.

ITA: 6(1)(a)

(E) Taxable. The Interpretation Bulletin only exempts tuition fees where the course is primarily for the benefit of the employer.

ITA: 6(1)(a), IT-470R, par. 18, 19

(F) Normally, taxable, but since the payment meets the conditions, namely that the Christmas gift is under $500 and is not cash or near cash, the CRA's position is that the gift is not a taxable benefit.

ITA: 6(1)(a)

(G) Partly taxable: The CRA takes the position that there will be no benefit if William had reimbursed the company the actual cost ($420). Since William did not completely reimburse the company for the actual costs, then the benefit would be calculated by taking the difference between the actual costs ($420) and the amount paid by William ($200) for a taxable benefit of $220.

ITA: 6(1)(a); IT-470R, par. 28

(H) Taxable, but the CRA takes the position that the amount would not be taxable if the membership was principally for the employer's advantage rather than the employee's.

ITA: 6(1)(a); IT-470R, par. 34

(I) Taxable unless the financial counselling was in respect of re-employment or retirement.

ITA: 6(1)(a), 6(1)(a)(iv)(B)

Exercise 4

Paragraph 8(1)(*b*) allows for the deduction of legal expenses against employment income in the year, on account of legal expenses incurred by the taxpayer to collect or establish a right to salary or wages owed to the taxpayer that, if received by the taxpayer, would be required by this subdivision to be included in computing the taxpayer's employment income. *ITA: 6, 8*

Paragraph 6(1)(*j*) requires any reimbursement to either be included in income or reduce the expense being claimed.

Legal expenses may also be deductible for other purposes such as to earn income from business or property or as another deduction [ITA 60(*o*), (*o*.1)], but only those expenses specifically listed in section 8 can be deducted from employment income [ITA 8(2)].

Other resources — IT-99R5, Legal and Accounting Fees; CRA Guide T4044, Employment Expenses

Exercise 5

The $6,000 merchandise discount is a taxable benefit. Administrative practice reflected in the Interpretation Bulletin does exempt discounts on merchandise, but they must be offered to all employees and not to just select groups. If there was an overall discount of 10% to all employees, it would seem reasonable in the circumstances to include only 25% in income; however, the Interpretation Bulletin is silent on this point. *IT-470R* *IT-470R, par. 27*

Exercise 6

None of the $7,500 is a taxable benefit. The exclusion for an eligible housing loss applies because the loss was incurred in an eligible relocation. The Interpretation Bulletin statement no longer reflects the law, according to a 2011 Tax Court of Canada decision. *ITA: 6(1)(a), 6(19), 6(20), 248(1) "eligible relocation"; Wunderlich v. The Queen, 2011 TCC 539; IT-470R, par. 35*

Note that on the sale of the house, the loss cannot be greater than the actual loss to the employee, calculated as the amount by which the cost of the house exceeds the net selling price received. A reimbursement of actual moving costs is not a taxable benefit. *IT-470R, par. 37*

Exercise 7

Premiums paid:

(A) Group term life insurance premiums paid by an employer are a taxable benefit. *ITA: 6(1)(a), 6(4)*

(B) and (C) The extended health care and dental care plans are private medical plans; hence, the premiums paid by the employer are not employment income. *ITA: 6(1)(a)*

(D) Since the sickness or accident income protection plan is a group plan, premiums paid by the employer are exempt from employment income. *ITA: 6(1)(a)*

Conclusion:

The following rearrangement would result in a lower tax cost:

(A) Company should pay for 100% of the extended health care and dental plan.

(B) Employees should pay the provincial medical plan premiums since company payments would be taxable benefits.

(C) Employees should consider paying the sickness or accident income protection premium themselves.

When an employer pays *any* portion of the premium for this type of plan, amounts that are paid out of the plan are taxable as employment income, less the employee's contribution to date. Conversely, if the employee pays all of the premiums, none of the amounts paid out of the plan are taxable. Since this particular plan has benefits of only 50% of the wages, the employee would be in a relatively poor cash position. The imposition of tax, even though at a lower rate, would certainly result in extreme hardship if the illness is prolonged. *ITA: 6(1)(f)*

Exercise 8

Benefit would be the sum of: *ITA: 6(9), 80.4*

(A) Car loan — prescribed rates

1st quarter	7% × $15,000 × 90/365	= $259
2nd quarter	6% × $15,000 × 91/365	= 224
3rd quarter	8% × $15,000 × 92/365	= 302
4th quarter	7% × $15,000 × 92/365	= 265

$ 1,050

(B) Home purchase loan[1]
  The lesser of the prescribed rate at the time of the loan (i.e., 7%)
  and the prescribed rate per quarter.

$$
\begin{array}{llll}
\text{1st} & 7\% \times \$100,000 \times 90/365 & = \$\ 1,726 \\
\text{2nd} & 6\% \times \$100,000 \times 91/365 & = \ \ \ 1,496 \\
\text{3rd} & 7\% \times \$100,000 \times 92/365 & = \ \ \ 1,764 \\
\text{4th} & 7\% \times \$100,000 \times 92/365 & = \ \ \underline{1,764} & 6,750
\end{array}
$$

(C) Other loan

$$
\begin{array}{llll}
\text{1st} & 7\% \times \$\ 10,000 \times 90/365 & = \$\ \ \ 173 \\
\text{2nd} & 6\% \times \$\ 10,000 \times 91/365 & = \ \ \ \ \ 150 \\
\text{3rd} & 8\% \times \$\ 10,000 \times 92/365 & = \ \ \ \ \ 202 \\
\text{4th} & 7\% \times \$\ 10,000 \times 92/365 & = \ \ \ \ \underline{176} & \underline{\ \ \ 701} \\
& & & \$\ 8,501
\end{array}
$$

Less amounts paid[2]

$$
\begin{array}{lll}
\text{(a)}\ 6\% \times \$\ 15,000 \times 365/365\ldots\ldots\ldots\ldots\ldots & \$\ \ \ 900 \\
\text{(b)}\ 4\% \times \$100,000 \times 365/365\ \ldots\ldots\ldots\ldots & 4,000 \\
\text{(c)}\ 7\% \times \$\ 10,000 \times 365/365\ldots\ldots\ldots\ldots & \underline{\ \ \ 700} & \underline{5,600} \\
& & \$\ 2,901
\end{array}
$$

The Act would deem $150 of the car loan interest ($1,050 – $900) to be paid in the year and, therefore, eligible for an interest deduction, since the interest was deemed to be paid within 30 days of the year-end, as required. | ITA: 80.5 ITA: 8(1)(*j*), 80.4(1)(*c*)

An Interpretation Bulletin indicates that the deemed interest expense must be prorated for employment use. | IT-522R, par. 27

$$\frac{27,000\ \text{km}}{45,000\ \text{km}} \times \$150 = \$90$$

The interest deduction provision would deny a prorated deduction of the $900 paid on January 15 of the following year, since it was not paid in the taxation year in question. However, this amount would be eligible for a deduction in the following taxation year to the extent of the business use. | ITA: 8(1)(*j*)

The interest limitation restricts the interest to the lesser of (a) $90 and (b) $300 × $^{365}/_{30}$ × 27,000/45,000 = $2,190. | ITA: 67.2

— *NOTES TO SOLUTION*

  [1] If this loan had been as a consequence of an employment relocation, Division C of the Act would have provided a deduction for five years, equal to the imputed interest benefit on the first $25,000 of the "home relocation loan", as defined. As a result, in this particular case, the overall benefit on the housing loan would have been reduced by $1,688 (i.e., $25,000/$100,000 of $6,750). See Chapter 10 for a complete discussion of this provision. The "lesser of" comparison is made on a quarter-by-quarter basis. | ITA: 110(1)(*j*), 248(1)

  [2] The interest benefit is calculated on an aggregate basis. Any excess interest payment on one loan effectively reduces the deemed interest benefit on the other loans. | ITA: 80.4

Exercise 9

Year 1 — No tax effect.

Year 4 — No tax effect.

Year 5 — No tax effect, since the employer is a Canadian-controlled private corporation.

Year 6 — Must take into employment income under Division B the following: | ITA: 7(1.1)

$$50,000\ \text{shares} \times (\$3 - \$1) = \underline{\$100,000}$$

  — Will have a capital gain of
$$50,000\ \text{shares} \times (\$6 - \$3) = \underline{\$150,000}$$

— May be eligible for the capital gains deduction for qualifying small business corporation shares.

ITA: 110.6(1), 248(1)

— Since Katrina sold these shares within two years after the date of acquisition, she is not entitled to a deduction of one half of the subsection 7(1.1) inclusion. She is also not entitled to a general deduction since the exercise price of $1.00 was less than fair market value ($1.50) at the date the option was granted.

ITA: 110(1)(d), 110(1)(d.1)

Exercise 10

(a) Car benefit if business-use kilometres are 10,000

Standby charge

ITA: 6(1)(e), 6(2)

$$\frac{20,004 \text{ km}^{(1)}}{20,004 \text{ km}} \times [2\% \times (\$20,000 \times 12)] = \dots \quad \$4,800$$

Operating costs$^{(2)}$ (12,000 km × $0.27)	3,240	$8,040
Less: amount reimbursed		1,800
Total car benefit if business-use kilometres are 10,000		$6,240

ITA: 6(1)(k)(v)

(b) Car benefit if business-use kilometres are 20,000

Standby charge

ITA: 6(1)(e), 6(2)

$$\frac{12,000 \text{ km}^{(3)}}{20,004 \text{ km}} \times [2\% \times (\$20,000 \times 12)] = \dots \quad \$2,879$$

Operating costs$^{(4)}$ (50% × $2,879) =	1,440	$4,319
Less: amount reimbursed		1,800
Total car benefit if business-use kilometres are 20,000		$2,519

ITA: 6(1)(k)(v)

NOTES

$^{(1)}$ The employee does not qualify for the standby charge reduction since the car is not used more than 50% in the performance of employment duties when the business use is only 15,000 km. Therefore, in this outcome, the value of A in the formula (i.e., 12,000 km) is deemed equal to the value of B in the formula (i.e., 1,667 × 12 rounded).

$^{(2)}$ The election method is not available to the employee, since the car is not used more than 50% for business.

ITA: 6(1)(k)(iv)

$^{(3)}$ When the business-use kilometres is 20,000, the employee qualifies for the standby charge reduction and the numerator becomes the lesser of (a) 12,000 km, and (b) 1,667 km × 12 months.

$^{(4)}$ The operating benefit election at 50% of the standby charge is the same as $0.27 × 12,000 km = $3,240. The election method is available since employment kilometres comprise more than 50% of the total.

Exercise 11

Reille is limited in the amount he can claim to the $24,000 he made in commission income. Sales expenses (paragraph 8(1)(f)): Reille is permitted to claim 50% of the entertainment meals, and 50% of the out-of-town meals if he was out-of-town for more than a 12-hour period when he had these meals (subsection 8(4)). Reille may claim the $18,000 spent on hotels and airfare. Professional dues of $250 are deductible under paragraph 8(1)(i).

ITA: 8(1)(f), 8(1)(i), 8(4)

Hotel and airfare	$18,000
Out of town meals (4,000 × 50%)	2,000
Entertainment meals (2,500 × 50%)	1,250
Total sales expenses (paragraph 8(1)(f))	21,250
Professional dues (paragraph 8(1)(i))	250
Total employment expenses allowable	$21,500

The $21,250 is less than the $24,000 made in commissions so it, plus the $250 for professional dues, is deductible as employment expenses.

The cost of the notebook computer is not deductible since it is a capital asset. Also, CCA is not allowed on the computer because the only CCA that can be claimed against employment income is for automobiles and aircraft.

Exercise 12

The Act would appear to deny any deduction in respect of Calvin's workspace in the home. In order for Calvin to avoid the restrictions, one of two conditions must be met, neither of which appear to be adhered to. The first alternative condition is that the work place in the home must be where the individual principally performs the employment duties. The second alternative condition is even more stringent, namely, that the work place must be used exclusively for employment income purposes and that the work place must be used on a regular and continuous basis as a meeting place for employment-connected persons.

ITA: 8(13)

If Calvin had met one of the conditions, then he would be able to deduct some of the expenses indicated as long as he met the conditions of paragraph 8(1)(*i*). First Calvin must have a contract with his employer indicating that he must pay for office rent and supplies and the employer completes and signs a T2200. However, of the expenses indicated, only the maintenance expense, including fuel, electricity, light bulbs, cleaning materials and minor repairs, on a prorated basis will be permitted. The imputed rent of $1,000 is not deductible; this position was confirmed in the *Thompson* case by the Federal Court–Trial Division.

ITA: 8(13)

IT-352R2, par. 2, 3
89 DTC 5439 (F.C.T.D.)

Exercise 13

Since the question refers to meal expenses for employees, you need to refer to subsection 8(4). A deduction for personal meals consumed while travelling is only allowed where the employee is away from the municipality/metropolitan area for a minimum of 12 hours. All meal costs, regardless of their nature and purpose, are also restricted by subsection 67.1(1) to 50% of the actual cost. However, long-haul truck drivers can deduct 80%.

ITA: 8(4), 67.1(1)

Exercise 14

Allowances and related expenses: There are two conditions that must be met in order to permit the allowance to be excluded from income:

ITA: 6(1)(*b*)(vii)

(a) the allowance must relate to travel outside of the municipality in which the employer's office is situated;

(b) the allowance must be a reasonable amount.

The $10,000 accommodation allowance is a taxable allowance, since the amount is an unreasonable amount on the assumption that the incurred expenses of $12,000 were reasonable. Therefore, she is entitled to a deduction, since she meets the other conditions of this paragraph; namely, she ordinarily travels in respect of her employment duties and is required by her employment contract to pay for her own expenses.

ITA: 6(1)(*b*)(vii), 8(1)(*h*)

Total accommodation expenses	$12,000
Less: disallowed meal portion (50% × $4,500)	2,250
	$ 9,750

ITA: 67.1(1)

The car expenses are deductible since she meets the conditions of this paragraph which are quite similar to paragraph 8(1)(*h*), described above, to the extent of the following calculations:

ITA: 8(1)(*h.*1)

Gas	$1,500
Maintenance	500
Capital cost allowance (½ × 30% × $30,000 × 1.13)	5,085
Insurance	1,200
Licences	90

Interest — lesser of:

    (a) $4,000

    (b) $300 × $\dfrac{361 \text{ days}}{30}$ = $3,610

	3,610
	$11,985

Deductible car expenses:

$$\frac{15,000 \text{ km}}{21,000 \text{ km}} \times \$11,985 = \$8,561$$

Exercise 15

13/113 of the sum of:

    (a) Deductible expenses including HST but excluding
        exempt supplies:[1]

Accommodation and meals	$ 9,750
Gas and maintenance	1,429[2]
	$11,179
(b) Capital cost allowance	3,632[3]
	$14,811
(c) Less: any expenses for which a reasonable allowance was received	Nil
	$14,811
Rebate (13/113 of $14,811)	$ 1,704

Par. 6(8)(*c*) Employment income inclusion in year of receipt of rebate:

$$\frac{\$11,179}{\$14,811} \times \$1,704 = \underline{\underline{\$1,286}}$$

Par. 6(8)(*d*) Capital cost reduction under ssec. 13(7.1) in year of receipt:

$$\frac{\$ 3,632}{\$14,811} \times \$1,704 = \underline{\underline{\$418}}$$

— *NOTES TO SOLUTION*

[1] Exempt supplies: insurance, licences and interest in respect of car.

[2] $\frac{15,000 \text{ km}}{21,000 \text{ km}} \times (\$1,500 + \$500) = \underline{\underline{\$1,429}}$

[3] $\frac{15,000 \text{ km}}{21,000 \text{ km}} \times \$5,085 = \underline{\underline{\$3,632}}$

Chapter 4

Income from Business:
General Concepts and Rules

LEARNING GOALS

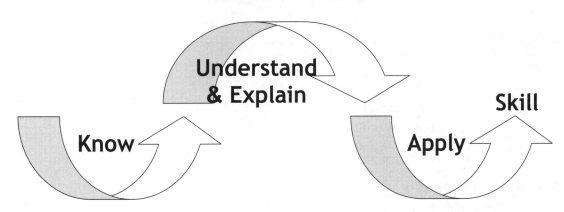

Know

By the end of this chapter you should know the basic provisions of the *Income Tax Act* that relate to the calculation of business income and expenses, and some of the GST/HST implications for business activity. You should be able to start with accounting income and make the necessary adjustments to arrive at business income for tax purposes. Completing the Review Questions (¶4,800) and Multiple Choice Questions (¶4,825) is a good way to learn the technical provisions.

Understand and Explain

You should understand and be able to explain what business income and expenses are, when to recognize them, and why they are treated the way they are for tax purposes. Completing the Exercises (¶4,850) is a good way to deepen your understanding of the material.

Apply

You should be able to use your knowledge and understanding of business income and expenses to identify and resolve practical problems. Completing the Assignment Problems (¶4,875) and Advisory Case (¶4,880) is an excellent way to develop your ability to apply the material in increasingly complex situations.

CHAPTER 4

Chapter 4 – Learning Chart

Topic	Example Problem (✓)	Review Questions (¶4,800)	Multiple Choice (¶4,825)	Exercises (¶4,850)	Assignment Problems (¶4,875)
¶4,000 BASIC RULES					
¶4,010 The Concept of Business Income					
¶4,015 Income from a business		2			
¶4,020 Business Income Versus Capital Receipt		1	5	2, 5	1, 5, 6
¶4,021 Overview					
¶4,022 Objective of the analysis					
¶4,023 Observable behavioural factors or "badges of trade"					
¶4,024 Summary	✓				
¶4,025 Damages as a Receipt of Income or Capital		3, 4		4	2
¶4,026 Non-performance of business contracts					
¶4,027 Cancellation of agency agreements					
¶4,028 Loss of property					
¶4,030 Other Receipts or Benefits		5, 6			8
¶4,031 Profits from an illegal business					
¶4,032 Profits from betting, gambling, and windfalls					
¶4,033 Subsidies					
¶4,034 Forgiveness of debt rules					
¶4,035 Business Income Versus Property Income			6		
¶4,036 General classification of income/loss from using/holding property					
¶4,037 Determination by corporations					
¶4,038 Determination by partnership					
¶4,039 Reasons for distinction between business and property income					
¶4,040 Inventory Valuation					
¶4,045 Basis of valuation	✓			6, 12	10, 11
¶4,050 Adjustment for amortization allocation to inventory: Absorption accounting	✓				
¶4,060 Sole Proprietorship					8
¶4,070 Conversion of Accounting Income to Net Business Income for Tax Purposes					
¶4,100 INCLUSIONS					4
¶4,105 Inclusions in Income for Tax Purposes					
¶4,110 Amounts Received and Receivable					8
¶4,120 Inducement Payments or Reimbursements					
¶4,130 Restrictive Covenants					
¶4,140 Partnership Income					
¶4,150 Barter Transactions and Inducement Payments					2
¶4,200 DEDUCTIONS					
¶4,205 Overview					

Topic	Example Problem (✓)	Review Questions (¶4,800)	Multiple Choice (¶4,825)	Exercises (¶4,850)	Assignment Problems (¶4,875)
¶4,206 Disallowed or restricted deductions		7		1	
¶4,210 Deductibility of Expenditures				7	
¶4,215 General test — To gain or produce income			1, 2	10	7
¶4,220 Expenditure of a capital nature		10			5, 10, 14
¶4,222 Personal and living expenses			6		
¶4,225 Other Prohibited Deductions		8	1, 2, 3	8, 9, 12	5, 6, 7, 8, 10, 14, 16
¶4,226 Reserves					
¶4,227 Payments on discounted bonds					
¶4,228 Use of recreational facilities and club dues					
¶4,229 Political contributions					
¶4,230 Automobile expenses					
¶4,231 Payments under the Act					
¶4,232 Prepaid expenses					
¶4,233 Expenses of investing in sheltered plans					
¶4,234 Work space in home					
¶4,235 Deductibility of provincial capital and payroll taxes					
¶4,236 Limitation on accrued expenses					
¶4,237 Reasonable Expectation of Profit (REOP)					3
¶4,238 Proposed amendments related to REOP					
¶4,239 Limitation on Deductible Expenditures		9, 11	2, 3	1, 3	6, 8, 9, 10, 12, 13, 14, 16
¶4,240 Deductions Specifically Permitted		12, 13	1, 4	10, 11, 12, 13	4, 7, 9, 11, 16
¶4,241 Write-offs of capital expenditures					
¶4,242 Interest					
¶4,243 Expenses of issuing shares or borrowing money					
¶4,244 Premiums on life insurance used as collateral					
¶4,245 Discount on debt obligations					
¶4,246 The system for reserves under the Act	✓				
¶4,247 Employer's contribution to registered pension plan					
¶4,248 Employer's contribution under a deferred profit sharing plan					
¶4,249 Cancellation of lease					
¶4,250 Landscaping of grounds					
¶4,251 Expenses of representation					
¶4,252 Investigation of site					
¶4,253 Utilities service connection					
¶4,254 Disability-related modifications and equipment					
¶4,255 Convention expenses					

Topic	Example Problem (✓)	Review Questions (¶4,800)	Multiple Choice (¶4,825)	Exercises (¶4,850)	Assignment Problems (¶4,875)
¶4,256 Application of the Rules for Deduction	✓				18
¶4,257 Sales/Negotiating Person's Expenses Revisited					13
¶4,258 Automobiles					
¶4,260 Automobile allowances					
¶4,265 Office in the home					12, 13, 14
¶4,270 Meals and entertainment	✓		2, 3		
¶4,275 Summary of Business Income Adjustments					
¶4,280 Ceasing to Carry on Business					
¶4,285 Sale of accounts receivable				14	
¶4,290 Sale of inventory					
¶4,300 Professional Business					
¶4,310 Scientific Research and Experimental Development					15, 16
¶4,315 Meaning of scientific research and experimental development (SR&ED)					
¶4,320 General deduction of expenditures					
¶4,325 Election method to determine deduction					
¶4,400 THE GST/HST IMPACT ON BUSINESS ACTIVITY				15	17
¶4,410 Commercial Activity					
¶4,415 Carrying on business					
¶4,420 Adventure or concern in the nature of trade					
¶4,425 Exclusions from the definition of commercial activity					
¶4,430 Value for tax					
¶4,435 When GST/HST is payable					
¶4,440 Automobile operating cost benefits paid by employer					
¶4,450 Input Tax Credits					
¶4,455 General rules					
¶4,460 Restrictions					
¶4,470 Adjustments to Net Tax					
¶4,475 Excess charges					
¶4,480 Price reductions					
¶4,485 Bad debts					
¶4,490 Lease of passenger vehicles					
¶4,495 Food, beverages, and entertainment expenses					
¶4,500 Application of the Rules	✓				
¶4,900 SUPPLEMENTAL NOTES					
¶4,910 Adjustment for Amortization Allocation in Inventory: An Illustration of the Effect					

CHAPTER 4

Study Notes

Chapter 4 —
Discussion Notes for Review Questions

(1) This type of transaction is commonly referred to as an "adventure in the nature of trade" and would result in business income, if the facts of the situation indicate that it has the "badges of trade". One of the indicators that a transaction is an adventure in the nature of trade is that the taxpayer has specialized knowledge in respect of the transaction. Mr. Fritz is a real estate salesperson and, hence, on the surface appears to meet this test. Since "business" is defined to include "an adventure in the nature of trade", this transaction would be classified as business income.   ITA: 248(1)

(2) There is no requirement in the Act to use GAAP for tax purposes. The courts have, on occasion, rejected conformity between income for accounting and tax purposes, particularly in cases where GAAP is at variance with the court's concept of ordinary commercial trading and business principles and practices or common law principles. However, GAAP profits are usually used as the starting point for the calculation of net income for tax purposes.

(3) No. Since the performance of this contract would have been income to Opco if the customer had completed it, the damages received would also be treated as business income.

(4) The agreement was of such importance to Aco Ltd. that it would constitute a large part of the company's total business structure. As a result, the receipt may be treated as a capital transaction on the sale of eligible capital property with no cost base. Thus, 50% of the receipt is included in business income. (See Chapter 5.)

(5) No. Income from illegal activities is taxable. Subsection 9(1) does not impose conditions on   IT-256R
how the profit is earned. See IT-256R for the CRA's position. See, also, the cases listed in the text on this issue.

(6) The subsidy is taxable as if it were an expense reduction to Opco. Refer to the CRA's position.   IT-273R2

(7) There are a number of limitations that restrict the deductibility of expenses even though they   ITA: 18
may have been incurred to earn income. Expenditures that are not deductible include:

- capital outlay or loss;   ITA: 18(1)(*b*)

- use of recreational facilities and club dues;   ITA: 18(1)(*l*)

- political contributions; and   ITA: 18(1)(*n*)

- limitations on interest and property taxes.   ITA: 18(2), 18(3.1)

(8) A provision specifically prohibits the deduction of any amount paid or payable under the Act.   ITA: 18(1)(*t*)
As a result, the interest paid to the Receiver General will not be deductible.

(9) Not necessarily. The Act also places a limitation on the amount of an outlay or expense. It can   ITA: 67
only be deducted to the extent that it is "reasonable in the circumstances".

(10) If the replacement of the roof served to restore it to its original condition then the cost should be fully deductible in the year incurred. If the replacement roof was superior to the old roof, the cost could be considered capital in nature. This would result in an addition to the undepreciated capital cost pool. Then, the cost would be deductible over a number of years. An Interpretation Bulletin comments   IT-128R
on the issue of income *versus* capital expenditures.

(11) No. Airplane, train, or bus fares are specifically excluded from the 50% limitation.   ITA: 67.1(4)(*a*)

(12) The reserve is only allowed if the company is the manufacturer of the product and pays an   ITA: 20(1)(*m.*1)
arm's length party to take over the obligations of the warranty for the company.

(13) Yes. The deduction of certain expenditures of a capital nature made in Canada that are in   ITA: 37(1)(*b*)
respect of scientific research and experimental development is permitted. These expenditures do not include land.

CHAPTER 4

Chapter 4 —
Solutions to Multiple Choice Questions

Question 1

(D) is correct. A deduction for interest and penalties on late income tax payments is denied.

ITA: 18(1)(*t*)

(A) is a deductible item. A deduction for amounts paid for landscaping business premises is allowed.

ITA: 20(1)(*aa*)

(B) is a deductible item. A deduction for interest on money borrowed to finance the purchase of a factory for use in its business is allowed.

ITA: 20(1)(*c*)

(C) is a deductible item. If the beneficiary of a $100,000 term life insurance policy on an employee is the employee's family, the cost of the insurance premium is part of the cost of the employee's remuneration package. As such, it is not denied as it is incurred for the purpose of earning income.

ITA: 18(1)(*a*)

Question 2

(C) is correct. The entire $15,000 spent on three social events for all employees at a particular location is deductible as long as the number of events does not exceed six.

ITA: 67.1(2)(*f*)

(A) The deduction for $11,000 of accrued legal fees for a pending law suit is not allowed, because it is a contingent liability. There is no legal liability to pay this amount.

ITA: 18(1)(*e*)

(B) The deduction for $4,000 of donations to registered charities is denied because it is not incurred for the purpose of earning income. The donations would be deductible in the computation of taxable income.

ITA: 18(1)(*a*), 110.1(1)(*a*)

(D) The deduction of $1,500 for golf club membership dues for employees is denied.

ITA: 18(1)(*l*)

Question 3

(D) is correct, because the Act provides an exception to the 50% rule for the cost of meals and entertainment relating to a fund-raising event the primary purpose of which is to benefit a registered charity.

ITA: 67.1(2)(*b*)

(A) is incorrect since donations to political parties are not deductible. The federal political donation would be eligible for a tax credit.

ITA: 18(1)(*n*), 127(3)

(B) is incorrect, because accrued bonuses are not deductible if they are unpaid 180 days after year-end.

ITA: 78(4)

(C) is incorrect, because the deduction for a financial accounting reserve for warranty expenses is denied.

ITA: 18(1)(*e*)

Question 4

(A) is the correct answer. The $7,000 deduction is computed as follows:

Legal expenses related to the purchase of an investment in shares.........	$ 0	ITA: 18(1)(*b*)
Legal expenses incurred to dispute a tax assessment	5,000	ITA: 60(*o*)
Legal expenses related to the issuance of debt (¹⁄₅)	1,000	ITA: 20(1)(*e*)
Accounting fees in connection with the preparation of a prospectus (¹⁄₅)	1,000	ITA: 20(1)(*e*)
	$ 7,000	

(B) incorrectly deducts $1,000 for the legal expenses related to the purchase of an investment in shares: $8,000 = $1,000 + $1,000 + $5,000 + $1,000.

(C) incorrectly deducts all of the legal expenses related to the issuance of debt and the accounting fees in connection with the preparation of a prospectus but none of the legal fees for the tax dispute: $15,000 = $5,000 + $5,000 + $5,000.

(D) incorrectly deducts only the $5,000 legal expenses related to disputing the tax assessment.

Question 5

(D) is correct. Most of the facts support capital gains treatment: the nature of the asset (real estate), its use and intended use (rental), the 10-year holding period and the unsolicited offer for sale. As a result, the gain on the sale of the land will likely be treated as a capital gain for income tax purposes.

(A) is incorrect. Because Sam is a real estate agent, the CRA may argue that the gain on the sale of the land is business income (not a capital gain).

(B) is incorrect. The fact that the land has been held for 10 years supports capital gains treatment, not business income treatment.

(C) is incorrect. The unsolicited offer for sale supports capital gains treatment, not business income treatment.

Question 6

(A) is correct. Legal fees to defend a lawsuit brought by a customer would be deductible.   ITA: 18(1)(*a*)

(B) and (C) are incorrect because these items (accounting loss on the sale of capital property and the principal amount of a mortgage) are on account of capital and therefore not deductible.   ITA: 18(1)(*b*)

(D) is incorrect because personal and living expenses are not deductible.   ITA: 18(1)(*h*)

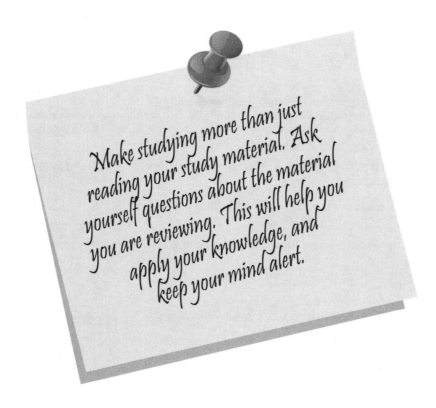

Chapter 4 – Solutions to Exercises

Exercise 1

Employee Perk	Employee Taxable Benefit	Employer Impact	
Tuition fees for the child of employee	$2,800 not a taxable benefit and jurisprudence supports an exempt scholarship for the child.	Deductible as compensation expense	ITA: 9, 11, 18, 20
Out-of-town meals	Not taxable to employee	50% deductible for employment duties	
Entertainment for clients	Not taxable to employee	50% deductible for employment duties	
Professional dues	Not taxable to employee	Deductible for employment duties	
Notebook computer for employment	Not taxable to employee	Deductible CCA for employment duties	
Membership for health club	Not taxable if employment-related	Not deductible for company	
Interest-free loan	$40,000 is subject to an imputed interest taxable benefit of $2,400 (deductible by the executive as was used to invest in company shares)	No impact on employer	
Life insurance premiums	$150 taxable benefit	Deductible as compensation expense	
Reimbursement for supplies	Not taxable to employee	Deductible CCA for employment duties	

Exercise 2

[See *Hiwako Investments Limited v. The Queen*, 78 DTC 6281 (F.C.A.)]

The intention of the taxpayer corporation in this case can only be inferred from the facts of the case. The nature of the asset involved in the transaction is of prime importance in this case. It was an income-producing asset that would have been regarded as a fixed capital asset had it been held longer. Normally, the increase in value on the sale of a capital asset is taxed as a capital gain. The gain represents an enhancement of value by realizing a security in the same sense that a growth stock may be sold for a gain that is regarded as a capital gain. Thus, the prospect of an increase in value does not, by itself, characterize the gain as income from business.

The nature of the activity surrounding the transaction could characterize it as an adventure in the nature of trade. However, it could be argued that an income-producing property was purchased as an investment and circumstances changed such that the investment had to be sold. This would not necessarily be regarded as a gain made in an operation of business in carrying out a scheme for profit-making.

The Court indicated that the concept of "secondary intention" does no more than refer to a practical approach for determining certain questions that arise in connection with "trading cases". If property is acquired where there is no business or the purchaser has not considered how he or she will use it, then the sale may be regarded as an adventure in the nature of trade, supporting a secondary intention to sell at a profit. However, where the property in question is an active, profit-producing property, it may be more difficult to conceive of its having been held as a speculation in the sense of an adventure in the nature of trade.

The fact that the principal shareholder of the corporation had a long history of trading in real estate does not necessarily mean that his intention in the transaction at hand was to trade. That fact could be outweighed by the income-producing capital nature of the particular property in question.

The Court held that the gain was not income from a business, based on the foregoing reasons. However, some believe that the arguments for business income are stronger in this case and that the decision in this case should be limited to its specific facts.

CHAPTER 4

Exercise 3

(a) If the company leased the vehicle and provided it for Samuel, the company would be able to deduct the cost of the lease as a business expense. Samuel would have a taxable benefit that would consist of:

ITA: 9, 11, 18, 20

Standby charge	($400 × 12 × ⅔) =	$3,200
Operating cost benefit	(10,000 × $0.27) =	2,700
Taxable benefit		$5,900

(b) If the company purchased the vehicle, it would claim capital cost allowance using the CCA rate of 30%, thus receiving a tax reduction. This option requires the company to lay out cash and the company should do an analysis of which of the first two options is better for it for the period of time the automobile is needed. Samuel would have a taxable benefit that would consist of:

Standby charge	2% × $22,000 × 12 =	$5,280
Operating cost benefit	10,000 × $0.27 =	2,700
Taxable benefit		$7,980

(c) The allowance would cost the company $3,660, calculated as follows:

$0.54 × 5,000 km =	$2,700
$0.48 × 2,000 km =	960
Total	$3,660

This amount would be deductible as an expense for the employer as it is tied to the CRA's automobile expense deduction limits.

Samuel's operating costs incurred for business purposes = $1,029 ($2,500 × 7,000/17,000) plus depreciation. Samuel would be receiving $3,660 per year, which implies $2,631 ($3,660 – $1,029) for depreciation.

Exercise 4

The $225,000 would be considered a capital receipt based on the *Parsons-Steiner Limited v. M.N.R.* case.

62 DTC 1148 (Ex. Ct.)

The following paraphrased excerpt from that case will help explain the conclusion:

On the whole therefore having regard to the importance of the franchise to Cars' business, the length of time the relationship had subsisted, the extent to which the appellant's business was affected by its loss both in decreased sales and by reason of its inability to replace it with anything equivalent, and the fact that from that time the appellant was in fact out of business, leads to a conclusion that this was a capital transaction. The payment in question was to replace "a capital asset of an enduring nature". It was one which Cars had built up over the years and which on the termination of the franchise they were obliged to relinquish. The payment received in respect of its loss was accordingly a capital receipt.

Exercise 5

Various factors must be examined in the determination of whether the dispositions should be considered income from a business or a capital gain.

ITA: 248(1)

Primary intention

The stated primary intention was to develop the properties into shopping plazas, thus, to earn income from these properties. However, this intention must be supported by objectively observable behavioural factors.

Behavioural factors

Relationship of the transaction to the taxpayer's business

AMC's main business appears to be the development and management of revenue properties. It also frequently engages in the sale of undeveloped properties. The fact that these transactions are closely related to AMC's main business and the fact that its major shareholder is a realtor and, therefore, heavily involved in buying and selling land, points to treatment of the sales as income from a business.

CHAPTER 4

AMC often sells property when it is not feasible to develop and, as such, purchases land with good resale value. This focus on good resale value indicates an underlying intention of selling property for a gain. This indicates a treatment of the dispositions as business income.

Number and frequency of transactions

Transactions of buying and selling undeveloped land are frequently entered into as it is AMC's business to develop land. This frequency indicates treatment as income from a business.

Conclusion

It could be argued that AMC's primary intention was to hold the third parcel of land to develop it and earn income from it; therefore, its sale should be treated as a capital gain. But because of the likely secondary intention of earning a profit on its sale, the frequency of this type of transaction, and the closeness to AMC's primary business, it is likely the court would consider all the dispositions as income from a business. The court could say that AMC held onto the third parcel for six months only in order to get the best price and therefore to make a substantial profit.

Exercise 6

Since actual cost is known it must be used. Therefore, an assumption about cost is not appropriate. Market value is probably best reflected in net realization value for this inventory. The following calculation of inventory values could be used:

Item	Actual cost	Reg. 1801 Market	Ssec. 10(1) Each item at lower of cost or market
Mufflers	$1,120.00	$ 992.00	$ 992.00
Tailpipes	745.75	706.50	706.50
Exhaust system	633.75	604.50	604.50
Shock absorbers	4,979.20	5,056.00	4,979.20
Brackets	1,304.80	1,211.60	1,211.60
Clamps	1,134.90	1,396.80	1,134.90
Total		$9,967.40	$9,628.70

Either the $9,967.40 value can be used or the $9,628.70 value can be used. However, the ending valuation method used in a particular year must be the same as that used for the end of the preceding year.

ITR: 1801
ITA: 10(1), 10(2.1)

Exercise 7

(a) The *income-earning purpose test* is found in paragraph 18(1)(*a*) — the "general limitation" re: an outlay or expense made or incurred for the purpose of gaining or producing income from the business or property. Students can list any of the following related sections, ITs or ICs in their answer:

ITA: 18(1)(*a*), 18(1)(*b*), 18(1)(*c*), 18(1)(*e*), 18(1)(*h*), 67, 248(1)

Related sections: subsections 20(1), 20(16); subsection 21(1); subsection 26(2); section 30

ITs: IT-99R5; IT-185R; IT-211R; IT-261R; IT-357R2; IT-364; IT-467R2; IT-475; IT-487; IT-521R

ICs: IC 77-11; IC 88-2

(b) The *capital test* is found in paragraph 18(1)(*b*) — no deduction is allowed for an outlay, loss, or replacement of capital, a payment on account of capital or an allowance in respect of depreciation, obsolescence or depletion except as expressly permitted by this Part.

Related sections: subsection 14(5); subsections 20(1), (10), (16); subsection 24(1); subsection 26(2); section 30

ITs: IT-187; IT-467R2; IT-475

ICs: none

(c) The *exempt income test* is found in paragraph 18(1)(*c*) — limits an outlay or expense to the extent it may reasonable be regarded as having been made or incurred for the purpose of gaining or producing exempt income.

Related sections: none

ITs: IT-467R2

ICs: none

(d) The *reserve test* is found in paragraph 18(1)(*e*) — no deduction for an amount as, or on account of, a reserve, a contingent liability or amount or a sinking fund except as expressly permitted by this Part.

Related sections: none

ITs: IT-215R (archived); IT-321R (archived); IT-467R2

ICs: none

(e) The *personal expenses test* is found in paragraph 18(1)(*h*) — no deduction for personal or living expenses of the taxpayer, other than travel expenses incurred by the taxpayer while away from home in the course of carrying on the taxpayer's business.

Related sections: subsections 20(1), (16); subsection 248(1) "personal or living expenses"

ITs: no primary ITs

ICs: none

(f) The *reasonableness test* is found in section 67, which states no deduction is allowed for an outlay or expense in respect of which any amount is otherwise deductible under this Act, except to the extent that it was reasonable in the circumstances.

Related sections: subsection 8(9); subsection 248(1) "amount"

ITs: no primary ITs

ICs: none

Exercise 8

(A) The deduction of these costs are prohibited, notwithstanding the argument that the lodge was used to produce income from client business.

ITA: 18(1)(*l*)

(B) The deduction of costs are allowed if they were incurred in the ordinary course of the company's business of providing the property for rent. The facts of this case *may* fit this exception.

ITA: 18(1)(*l*)

Exercise 9

First, it must be determined whether any expense incurred may be deducted in respect of the home office. To make this determination, the specific conditions outlined in subsection 18(12) are that:

ITA: 18(12)

(i) the office is the principal place of business; or

(ii) it is used exclusively for the purpose of earning business income and is used on a regular and continuous basis for meeting clients, customers, or patients in respect to the business.

Since Karim performs only consulting work, the home office qualifies under condition (i). Although Amina teaches in addition to consulting, it is only part-time and her principal business is consulting. Therefore, she also qualifies under condition (i). Amina and Karim are carrying on separate self-employed businesses. Since they also live together, the home office expenses would be split on an agreed basis. Assuming that the split was agreed at 50%, both taxpayers would be permitted to deduct 50% of the eligible home office expenses. Eligible home office expense is equal to 500/2,000 square feet times the total home office costs. Supplies, materials, and software would be considered business expenses, not home office expenses. Therefore, Amina and Karim may **each** deduct the following as their 50% share of the expenses:

Home office expense (subsection 18(12))	$23,600 × 25% × 50% =	$2,950
Supplies and materials	$1,800 × 50% =	900
Computer and software lease	$2,300 × 50% =	1,150
Total		$5,000

Exercise 10

(A) — contribution may be made within 120 days of the end of 2013,

— an employer contribution to a defined benefit RPP is deductible where it is made on the recommendation of an actuary in whose opinion the contribution is required so that the plan will have sufficient assets to provide benefits in accordance with its terms as registered,

— in this case, both the current service contribution and the lump-sum amount based on an actuarial valuation would be deductible in 2013, if they are in accordance with the plan.

(B) A full deduction of an amount paid in the year is permitted — or a taxpayer may elect to write it off in equal amounts over the 10-year period beginning in the current year.

ITA: 20(1)(*cc*)
ITA: 20(9)

(C) The deduction of the full amount of utilities connection costs is permitted. Since the taxpayer does not own the gas lines but the utilities company does, the amount is not eligible for capital cost allowance.

ITA: 20(1)(*ee*)

(D) Salary of an owner-employee's spouse is an allowable deduction to a corporation as long as it is reasonable in the circumstances. While $7,000 per month for full-time secretarial work is probably not reasonable, some lesser, reasonable amount would be deductible in this case. The amount in excess of a reasonable amount will not be deductible to the corporation, but will be included in the recipient's income from employment.

Exercise 11

Only ½ of the discount of $108.10 may be deducted because the bond was issued at less than 97% even though within the ⁴⁄₃ × 9% or 12% yield range.

ITA: 20(1)(*f*)

Given that the discount is paid effectively on maturity when the principal amount is repaid, then the $54.05 is deductible in 2013.

Exercise 12

Net income per financial statements		$150,000
Add: Items deducted in financial statements but not deductible for tax purposes:		
Provision for income taxes — current	25,000	
— future	130,000	
Depreciation expense	40,000	
Non-deductible interest — re interest on late taxes	2,500	
Bond discount	7,500	
Inventory (closing) to FIFO basis	10,000	
		$365,000
Deduct: Items not deducted in financial statements but deductible for tax purposes:		
Landscaping costs	$12,000	
Inventory (opening) to FIFO basis	15,000	(27,000)
Net Income for tax purposes before CCA		$338,000

ITA: 18(1)(*e*)

ITA: 18(1)(*b*)

ITA: 18(1)(*t*)

ITA: 18(1)(*b*), (*e*)

ITA: 10(1)

ITA: 20(1)(*aa*)

ITA: 10(1)

Exercise 13

This transaction would likely involve a receipt of income because the intention is likely to make a profit on the purchase and sale of land. This would be substantiated by the frequency of transactions in land or, at least, the indication of an adventure in the nature of trade. During the year of sale the following income would be computed:

Revenue from the sale of land		$250,000
Less: cost of land	$107,500	
real estate commission	12,500	120,000
Income from the sale of land		$130,000
Less: reserve for amount not due until later year*		
$\frac{\$130,000}{\$250,000} \times (\$250,000 - \$110,000)$		72,800
Income after reserve		$ 57,200

ITA: 9

ITA: 20(1)(*n*)

* The reserve is not available, unless the sale occurred within 36 months of the end of the year in which a reserve is to be taken.

ITA: 20(8)(*b*)

Note that the minimum two-year repayment period does not apply on the sale of land which qualifies for the reserve. In the next year, the reserve of $72,800 would be taken into income.

ITA: 12(1)(*e*)(ii), 20(1)(*n*)(ii)

Exercise 14

Since Mr. Flint has sold substantially all of his business assets to a person who intends to carry on the business, a section 22 election is available. Note that Mr. Flint and Mr. Small must elect jointly in prescribed form [T2022] to have section 22 apply. Mr. Flint must include last year's doubtful debt reserve in income. Then, Mr. Flint may deduct, as a business loss, the difference between the face value of the accounts ($45,000) and the consideration paid by Mr. Small which should be equal to their fair market value ($36,000). Hence, Mr. Flint will have a deduction of $9,000. Mr. Small must include the same $9,000 difference in his business income for the taxation year of the purchase. However, Mr. Small will now be put in a position to deduct an appropriate reserve for doubtful debts at the end of the taxation year or to write off any of the accounts that can be established to have become bad debts, since an amount has been included in income in respect of these receivables.

ITA: 20(1)(*l*)
ITA: 12(1)(*d*)

ITA: 22(1)(*a*), 22(1)(*b*)

ITA: 20(1)(*l*), 20(1)(*p*)
ITA: 22(1)(*c*)

		Income Effect
Mr. Flint		
Last year's reserve		$ 6,500
Loss on sale: Proceeds	$36,000	
Face amount	(45,000)	(9,000)
Net effect		$(2,500)
Mr. Small		
Mr. Flint's loss on sale included in income		$ 9,000
Face amount of receivables		$45,000

If the election is not used, the loss of $9,000 would be a capital loss, only ½ deductible as an allowable capital loss. Furthermore, an allowable capital loss can only be offset against a taxable capital gain.

ITA: 22

Exercise 15

Since the corporation is carrying on business, it is engaged in a commercial activity. Therefore, the corporation is required to register and collect HST on its supplies, i.e., sales of goods, which are "taxable supplies." As a registrant, the corporation is entitled to a full input tax credit (ITC) in respect of HST paid or payable on goods and services that it purchases exclusively for use in its commercial activity. If HST collected or collectible on its sales exceeds its ITCs, the corporation must remit the difference. On the other hand, if ITCs exceed HST collected or collectible, a refund of the excess is available.

ETA: 123(1)

ETA: 169(1)

The following is the appropriate HST treatment of the items listed:

(a) Net income per financial statements would have been increased by HST charged which is included in revenue and reduced by HST paid or payable which is included in costs. HST charged net of ITCs from HST paid or payable must be remitted.

(b) There are no HST implications for the provision for income taxes.

(c) HST paid on the purchase of depreciable property provides an ITC, as discussed in Chapter 5. When the cost of the asset is subsequently written off through depreciation or capital cost allowance, there are no further HST implications.

The following costs would involve payment of GST/HST on taxable supplies and, hence, would give rise to an ITC:

(a) inventory of goods purchased, and

(b) landscaping goods and services.

The following costs would not involve the payment of HST, since they are for exempt supplies:

(a) interest paid on income tax due results from a financial service, and

(b) bond interest also results from a financial service.

Chapter 5
Depreciable Property and Eligible Capital Property

LEARNING GOALS

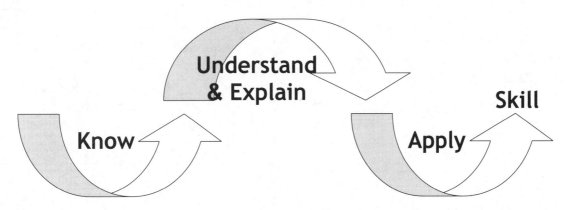

Know

By the end of this chapter you should know the basic provisions of the *Income Tax Act*, and the *Excise Tax Act*, pertaining to the GST/HST, that relate to depreciable and eligible capital property. Completing the Review Questions (¶5,800) and Multiple Choice Questions (¶5,825) is a good way to learn the technical provisions.

Understand and Explain

You should understand and be able to explain how to calculate capital cost allowance and cumulative eligible capital amount, which is the tax equivalent of amortization for capital and intangible property. Completing the Exercises (¶5,850) is a good way to deepen your understanding of the material.

Apply

You should be able to use your knowledge and understanding of depreciable and eligible capital property to advise taxpayers on the tax implications of the purchase of these assets. Completing the Assignment Problems (¶5,875) is an excellent way to develop your ability to apply the material in increasingly complex situations.

Chapter 5 – Learning Chart

Topic	Example Problem (✓)	Review Questions (¶5,800)	Multiple Choice (¶5,825)	Exercises (¶5,850)	Assignment Problems (¶5,875)
¶5,000 THE CAPITAL COST ALLOWANCE SYSTEM					
¶5,005 Basic Rules					
¶5,006 Introduction					
¶5,007 Types of capital property					
¶5,008 CCA and neutrality					
¶5,009 CCA and tax planning	✓				
¶5,012 Eligibility for capital cost allowance					
¶5,015 Classes of assets for tangible capital property	✓	1, 4, 5, 6, 7, 8		4, 8	2, 7, 8, 9
¶5,020 Taxation year less than 12 months	✓	9		6	
¶5,025 Ownership of property				1	
¶5,030 Disposition of property		2, 3		5	2, 6, 7, 8
¶5,035 Automobiles used in employment or business		10	1	2, 3, 8, 9	1, 2, 6
¶5,040 Comparison of capital cost allowance and accounting amortization					
¶5,045 Separate class rule for electronic office equipment					
¶5,054 Example of CCA over time	✓		5	4	2, 7, 8
¶5,056 Transfers to another class – Avoiding recapture					
¶5,057 Interest expense					
¶5,058 Capital cost reduction for cost assistance		11			
¶5,059 Inducement payments					
¶5,060 Exceptions to the Declining Balance Method					
¶5,065 Leasehold improvements			2, 4	4, 6, 8	2, 7, 8
¶5,070 Class 14 limited-life intangibles		12	6	4, 6, 8	2, 7
¶5,075 Manufacturing and processing machinery and equipment					
¶5,080 Insurance Proceeds Expended on Damaged Depreciable Property					
¶5,090 Involuntary and Voluntary Dispositions					
¶5,095 Involuntary dispositions				7	10
¶5,100 Voluntary dispositions	✓				
¶5,110 Change in Use and Part Disposition Rules					
¶5,115 Change from income-producing to other purpose					
¶5,120 Change from non-income-producing to income-producing purpose					3
¶5,125 Property acquired for multiple purposes					
¶5,135 Non-arm's length transfer of depreciable property					
¶5,150 Franchises and Similar Property					
¶5,200 ELIGIBLE CAPITAL PROPERTY					

Topic	Example Problem (✓)	Review Questions (¶5,800)	Multiple Choice (¶5,825)	Exercises (¶5,850)	Assignment Problems (¶5,875)
¶5,210 Basic Rules		13	3	1	
¶5,220 Comparison to the Capital Cost Allowance System					
¶5,230 Illustration of the Rules				10, 11	2, 4, 5
¶5,235 Common aspects		14			
¶5,240 Non-arm's length transactions					
¶5,250 Election re: Capital Gain	✓				
¶5,300 CAPITAL PERSONAL PROPERTY AND THE INPUT TAX CREDIT SYSTEM UNDER GST/HST					
¶5,310 Basic Rules					
¶5,320 Passenger Vehicles and Aircraft					
¶5,325 Passenger vehicles owned by registrants other than individuals and partnerships					
¶5,330 Passenger vehicles and aircraft owned by registrants who are individuals or partnerships					
¶5,900 SUPPLEMENTAL NOTES					
¶5,910 Lease-Option Arrangements	✓				
¶5,920 Leasing Property					
¶5,930 Capital Personal Property for GST/HST Purposes					

CHAPTER 5

Study Notes

Chapter 5 —
Discussion Notes for Review Questions

(1) The full amount of the capital cost is added to the CCA class. The half-year rule makes a separate adjustment for purposes of calculating CCA in the year of acquisition, but this adjustment does not affect the capital cost.
ITR: 1100(2)

(2) A terminal loss is allowed only when the asset sold is the last asset in the class. Otherwise, the proceeds are credited to the UCC of the class under the definition of "undepreciated capital cost" and CCA is claimed on the remaining balance.
ITA: 13(21), 20(16)

(3) "Cost amount" reflects the tax value of an asset at a particular moment in time. With respect to depreciable property, cost amount is that proportion of the UCC that the capital cost of the asset is of the capital cost of all the assets in the class. Capital cost is not defined, but as used here, it means the laid-down cost which includes the actual cost plus all costs of preparing the asset for use.
ITA: 248(1) "cost amount"

ITA: 13(21)

(4) The "capital cost" is the amount that is added to the CCA class when the asset is first acquired [item A in the definition of "undepreciated capital cost"]. See (3) above for a broadly worded definition.
ITA: 13(21)

(5) Certain exceptions to the half-year rule are found in the Regulations. However, regulations for leaseholds and for classes like Classes 24 and 27 provide their own version of the half-year rule.
ITR: 1100(2)
ITR: 1100(1)(b), 1100(1)(t), 1100(1)(ta)

(6) The half-year rule is a simple, arbitrary adjustment that is made to reflect a period of ownership during the year. It is a simpler alternative to prorating CCA for the number of days the asset is owned during the year.

(7) Normally, the statement is true. However, the "available-for-use" rules do not allow CCA to be claimed until the asset is available for use by the taxpayer.
ITA: 13(26)–(32)

(8) An Information Circular provides the CRA's position on when the CCA claim for prior years can be changed. If the change results in a lower taxable income for the year, it must be requested within the normal time limits for appeals (see Chapter 14). If the change does not result in a lower taxable income, as, for example, the case of a loss year, the change will be allowed.
IC 84-1, par. 9, 10

(9) A regulation provides for this daily proration in the case of the short taxation year of a business, as might occur, for example, in the start-up year.
ITR: 1100(3)

(10) Normally, this statement is true. However, a regulation allows a CCA claim equal to one-half the normal CCA in the year of disposition, as compensation for the inability to claim a terminal loss on the disposal of a Class 10.1 automobile. To qualify, the taxpayer must have sold an auto that was in Class 10.1 and that was owned by him or her at the end of the preceding year.
ITR: 1100(2.5)

(11) Your client is correct. The Act reduces the capital cost of depreciable property for grants, subsidies, forgivable loans, deductions from tax, investment allowances or other assistance received on the acquisition of the property.
ITA: 13(7.1)

(12) There are four choices available for the legal costs of obtaining the patent:

    (a) deduct them as expenses of representation;
ITA: 20(1)(cc)

    (b) deduct the costs equally over 10 years;
ITA: 20(9)

    (c) capitalize them in Class 14 by an election not to include them in Class 44 and depreciate them over the life of the patent; or
ITR: 1103(2h)

    (d) capitalize the costs in Class 44 and depreciate them at a 25% declining-balance rate.

Any deduction under paragraph 20(1)(cc) or subsection 20(9) is subject to recapture.
ITA: 13(12); IT-99R5

(13) There is only *one* CEC pool for all eligible capital expenditures for each business. Since Mrs. Smith is only carrying on one business within her corporation, the additions to the company's CEC account in the year will be 75% of $10,800.

(14) He is able to deduct the full CEC balance as a business loss in the year that he ceased to carry on business.
ITA: 24

Chapter 5 —
Solutions to Multiple Choice Questions

Question 1

(C) is correct. The maximum CCA is: $\frac{1}{2} \times 30\% \times \$30,000 = \$4,500$.

ITA: 13(7)(*g*); ITR: 7307(1)

(A) incorrectly uses the $50,000 cost of the vehicle to compute CCA: $\frac{1}{2} \times 30\% \times \$50,000 = \$7,500$.

(B) incorrectly ignores the half-year rule: $30\% \times \$30,000 = \$9,000$.

(D) incorrectly uses the pre-2001 maximum Class 10.1 cost of $27,000: $\frac{1}{2} \times 30\% \times \$27,000 = \$4,050$.

Question 2

(A) is correct. $10,000 is the lesser of $\frac{1}{5} \times \$80,000 = \$16,000$ and $\$80,000/8 = \$10,000$. For 2013, the year the cost was incurred, the maximum CCA = 50% of $10,000 = $5,000.

ITR: 1100(1)(*b*), Sch. III

(B) is incorrect. It is 50% of the $16,000 amount calculated in (A).

(C) is incorrect because the $10,000 figure does not take into account the 50% rule.

ITR: 1100(1)(*b*)

(D) is incorrect for the reasons outlined for (B) and (C) combined.

Question 3

(D) is correct. The maximum CECA claim is: $75\% \times \$100,000 \times 7\% = \$5,250$.

(A) is incorrect: $\$100,000/40 = \$2,500$. Forty years is the maximum period for amortization of goodwill for accounting purposes only.

(B) is incorrect: $\frac{1}{2} \times \$100,000 \times 7\% = \$3,500$. The $\frac{1}{2}$ rate does not apply for purposes of additions to the CEC pool.

(C) is incorrect: $7\% \times \$100,000 = \$7,000$. Only 75% of the cost is used before multiplying by 7%.

Question 4

(B) is correct because the remaining lease term in 2013 is three years and the first renewal period is three years. The maximum CCA claim is $5,000, calculated as follows:

Lesser of: (i) $\frac{1}{5} \times \$60,000$ = $12,000
           (ii) $\$60,000/(3 + 3)$ = $10,000

For 2013, the year the cost was incurred, the maximum CCA is: 50% of $10,000 = $5,000.

ITR: 1100(1)(*b*)

(A) is incorrect, because it uses the initial 5-year term of the lease in the calculation in place of the remaining lease term of three years: $\$60,000/(5 + 3) = \$7,500 \times 50\% = \$3,750$.

(C) is incorrect, because the greater ($12,000), as opposed to the lesser ($10,000), of the two amounts calculated has been used: $\$6,000 = 50\% \times \$12,000$.

(D) is incorrect, because it uses the initial 5-year term of the lease in the calculation in place of the remaining lease term of three years and ignores the 50% rule in Regulation 1100(1)(*b*): $\$60,000/(5 + 3) = \$7,500$.

Question 5

(B) is correct. Under the Regulations, dies and moulds and software are not excepted from the half net-amount rule, but the other Class 12 items are: linens are listed in paragraph (*g*), cutlery and dishes are listed in paragraph (*b*) and kitchen utensils costing less than $500 are listed in paragraph (*c*). $\frac{1}{2} (\$1,200 + \$600) + \$15,000 + \$400 = \$16,300$.

ITR: 1100(2)

(A) is incorrect because it uses the half net-amount rule on all Class 12 assets: ½ ($1,200 + $600 + $15,000 + $400) = $8,600.

(C) is incorrect because it ignores the half net-amount rule on the dies and moulds: $1,200 + ½ × $600 + $15,000 + $400 = $16,900.

(D) is incorrect because it ignores the half net-amount rule on the dies and moulds and software: $1,200 + $600 + $15,000 + $400 = $17,200.

Question 6

(D) is not available, since the property is not eligible capital property.

(A), (B), and (C) are all options for the treatment of patent costs.

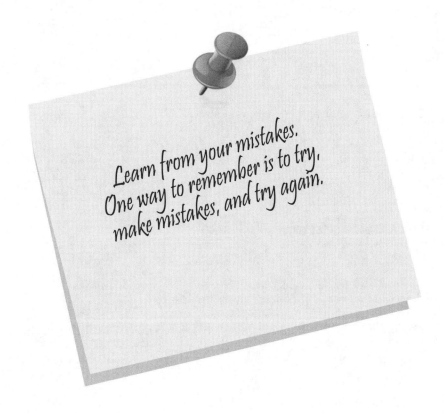

Chapter 5 — Solutions to Exercises

Exercise 1

The overpass is not eligible for capital cost allowance, since the owners have no title to the land on which the footings are placed and capital cost allowance cannot be claimed on assets that are not owned (see *Saskatoon Community Broadcasting Co. Ltd. v. M.N.R.*). The cost of the overpass qualifies as an eligible capital expenditure.

58 DTC 491 (T.A.B.)

Exercise 2

Harrison's automobile is defined as a passenger vehicle for CCA purposes. Passenger vehicles with a cost in excess of $30,000 (2013 amount) must be placed into a separate CCA class, Class 10.1. The depreciation rate for class 10.1 assets is 30%. However, CCA may only be taken on the deemed capital cost of the vehicle up to a maximum of $30,000 (paragraph 13(7)(*a*) and ITR 7307(1)). Harrison's maximum CCA claim for the first and second year of owning the car would be calculated as follows:

ITA: 13(7); ITR: 7307(1)

Year 1

Capital cost of additions	$30,000
Less CCA (30,000 × 30% × 50%*)	4,500
UCC, end of year 1	$25,500

* Half-year rule applied.

Business use CCA (CCA × usage %) = $4,500 × 40% = $1,800

Year 2

UCC, Beginning of Year 2	$25,500
Less CCA @ 30%	7,650
UCC, end of Year 2	$17,850

Business use CCA (CCA × usage %) = $7,650 × 40% = $3,060

Exercise 3

No terminal loss can be deducted for an automobile in Class 10.1. The special "half-year rule" to compute capital cost allowance in the year of disposition applies to Class 10.1.

ITA: 20(16.1); ITR: 1100(2.5)

(A)	Jan.	1/13	UCC (Class 10.1)	$ 18,475
		2013	CCA (½ × .30 × $18,475)	(2,771)[1]
			Proceeds of disposition	(12,000)
			Terminal loss of $3,704 denied	Nil
(B)		2013	Purchase ($36,000) (new Class 10.1) max.	$ 33,900[2]
	Dec.	31/13	UCC before adjustment	$ 33,900
			One-half of net amount (½ × $33,900)	(16,950)
			UCC before CCA	$ 16,950
			CCA @ 30% of $16,950	(5,085)[3]
			Add: ½ net amount	16,950
	Jan.	1/14	UCC	$ 28,815

—NOTES TO SOLUTION

[1] Note that 75% of $2,771 or $2,078 is the deduction based on business use.

[2] Limited to $30,000 plus HST (13%) or $33,900, since it was acquired after 2000.

[3] Note that 75% of $5,085 or $3,814 is deductible, since CCA claimed is not subject to the limitation on sales/negotiating person's expenses.

ITA: 8(1)(*f*), 8(1)(*j*)

Exercise 4

	Cl. 1: 4%	Cl. 8: 20%	Cl. 10: 30%	Cl. 13: S.L.	Cl. 14: S.L.	Cl. 29: 50%
Jan. 1/13						
UCC	$120,000	$75,000	$40,000	$42,000	$54,400	Nil
2013 Purchases:						
— mfg. equip.						$50,000
— off. equip.		10,000				
Disposals:						
— building	(100,000)[1]					
— equip.						
Dec. 31/13						
UCC before adjustment	$ 20,000	$85,000	$40,000	$42,000	$54,400	$50,000
½ net amount	Nil	(5,000)	Nil	Nil	N/A	(25,000)
UCC before CCA	$ 20,000	$80,000	$40,000	$42,000	$54,400	$25,000
CCA..................	(800)	(16,000)	(12,000)	(1,250)[2]	(3,400)[3]	(12,500)
½ net amount	Nil	5,000	Nil	Nil	N/A	25,000
Jan. 1/14						
UCC	$ 19,200	$69,000	$28,000	$40,750	$51,000	$37,500

—*NOTES TO SOLUTION*

[1] Capital gain on disposition of building of $50,000.

[2] Lesser of: (a) ⅕ of $50,000 .... $10,000 ⎫
                                                          ⎬ $1,250
             (b) $50,000/40 (max.) .... $ 1,250 ⎭
        — not reduced by ½ because not first year of ownership.

[3] $\dfrac{\$68,000}{(20 \times 365)} \times 365 = \$3,400$

Exercise 5

The proceeds from the sale of Liam's building are greater than the UCC of the building. This would indicate that, although Liam claimed CCA in previous years, the market value of the building did not decline. Accordingly, CCA claimed in previous years must be recaptured and added to income for tax purposes in the current year. Liam must report recaptured CCA of $15,500, calculated as follows:

ITA: 13

Class 1 — 4%		
UCC, beginning of year		$144,500
Less disposition at lesser of:		
Capital cost	$160,000	
Net proceeds	$180,000	160,000
Recaptured CCA		$(15,500)

Note that no CCA may be claimed in the year of the disposition since the UCC balance in the class after recapture is nil.

Exercise 6

(a)(i) $100,000 × 20% × ½ = $10,000

ITA: 20(1)

   (ii) $100,000 × 20% × ½ × (90/365) = $2,466

In (ii), CCA is prorated because the taxation year is less than 365 days.

(b) Leasehold improvements — CCA is lesser of

   (1) $25,000 × ⅕ × ½ = $2,500

(2) $\$25,000 \times \frac{1}{12} \times \frac{1}{2} = \$1,042$

(Twelve years is the denominator; this includes the initial lease term and the first renewal period.)

(c) The franchise is for a limited term, hence it is a Class 14 asset. The CCA on Class 14 assets is computed on a straight-line basis over the remaining life of the asset. The half-year rule does not apply to Class 14. CCA allowed to July 31 (153 days) is:

$\$25,000 \times \frac{1}{15} \times (153/365) = \$699$

Exercise 7

				Cl. 3: 5%	
Jan. 1, 2012	UCC			$ 221,000	
	Disposal[1]				
	lesser of:				
	(a) capital cost	$300,000			
	(b) proceeds	$295,000		(295,000)	
Dec. 31, 2012	UCC			$ (74,000)	
	Recapture			74,000	
Jan. 1, 2013	UCC			Nil	
Aug. 2013	File an amended return for 2012 as follows:				ITA: 13(4)
Jan. 1, 2012	UCC			$ 221,000	
	Deemed proceeds				ITA: 13(4)(c)
	lesser of:				
	(a) capital cost	$300,000			
	(b) proceeds	$295,000	→ $295,000		
	reduced by lesser of:				
	(a) recapture ($295K – $221K)	$ 74,000	→ $ 74,000		
	(b) replacement cost	$400,000		$(221,000)	
Dec. 31, 2012	UCC			Nil	
	Recapture			Nil	
Jan. 1, 2013	UCC			Nil	
				Cl. 1-NRB: 6%[2]	
2013	Purchase of new building	$400,000			
	Less: reduction above	74,000		$ 326,000	ITA: 13(4)(c)
Dec. 31, 2013	UCC			$ 326,000	
	CCA @ 6% of [$326,000 – (½ × $326,000)]			(9,780)	
Jan. 1, 2014	UCC			$ 316,220	

—*NOTES TO SOLUTION*

    [1] The CRA appears to require that even if a replacement property is purchased before the tax return for the year of disposition must be filed (i.e., within six months of the taxation year-end), the recapture must be reported in the year of disposition. The taxpayer can request a reassessment if and when the replacement is purchased within the specified time limits. In lieu of paying tax initially on the recapture, the CRA will take acceptable security until the final determination of tax is made.

IT-259R3, par. 3

    [2] Note how the rules allow for a replacement with an asset of another class.

ITA: 13(4)

Exercise 8

ITA: 20(1)

a. **Class 1** ($208,895 + \frac{1}{2}$ ($20,000)) × 4% = $ 8,756

b. **Class 13 — Leasehold Improvements**
   Lesser of:
   (i) $\frac{1}{10}$ × $\frac{1}{2}$ × 70,000 $3,500

   (ii) $\frac{1}{5}$ × $\frac{1}{2}$ × 70,000 $7,000

   CCA for the year $ 3,500

c. **Class 50 (Computer equipment)**

UCC, beginning of year	$40,000
Additions	0
	$40,000
CCA 40,000 × 55%	22,000
UCC, end of year	$18,000

d. Class 10 (trucks)

UCC, beginning of year	$25,000
Less dispositions ($10,000 – $1,000)	(9,000)
	$16,000
CCA 30%	4,800
UCC, end of year	$11,200

e. **Class 14 — Licence**
   $30,000 × $\frac{1}{15}$ × (122*/365) $ 668

   * Number of days from June 1 to September 30.

Exercise 9

The change in use rules could be applied as follows:

ITA: 13(7)(d)

			Cl. 10:[(1)] 30%
2011	Purchase (85% of $14,600)		$12,410
Dec. 31, 2011	UCC		$12,410
	CCA @ 30% of [($12,410 – ($\frac{1}{2}$ × $12,410)]		(1,862)
Jan. 1, 2012	UCC		$10,548
2012	Disposal (5% of $12,200)[(2)]		(610)
Dec. 31, 2012	UCC		$ 9,938
	CCA @ 30% of $9,938		(2,981)
Jan. 1, 2013	UCC		$ 6,957
2013	Purchase (10% of $9,800)[(3)]		980
Dec. 31, 2013	UCC		$ 7,937
	CCA @ 30% of [$7,937 – ($\frac{1}{2}$ × $980)]		(2,234)
Jan. 1, 2014	UCC		$ 5,703

In practice, however, the following calculation of capital cost allowance might be made:

		Cl. 10: 30%	Business deduction of CCA
2011	Purchase	$14,600	
Dec. 31, 2011	UCC	$14,600	
	CCA @ 30% of $\frac{1}{2}$ × $14,600	(2,190)	85% of $2,190 = $1,862
Dec. 31, 2012	UCC	$12,410	
	CCA @ 30%	(3,723)	80% of $3,723 = $2,978

		Cl. 10: 30%	*Business deduction of CCA*
Dec. 31, 2013	UCC	$ 8,687	
	CCA @ 30%	(2,606)	[80% + ½ (90% – 80%)][(4)]
			of $2,606 = $2,215
Jan. 1, 2014	UCC	$ 6,081	

— *NOTES TO SOLUTION*

(1) Since the automobile cost less than the prescribed limit, it is placed in Class 10.   ITA: 13(7)(*g*)

(2) Lesser of proceeds at fair market value and capital cost.

(3) Since fair market value is less than cost, the increase in capital cost is based on fair market value.

(4) An increase in use for business represents an addition to the class which is subject to the half-year rule. In practice, the CCA may be computed simply as 90% of $2,606 or $2,345.

Exercise 10

The cumulative eligible capital account would be affected as follows:

Year	*Opening balance*	*Par. 20(1)(b) deduction*(1)	*Ssec. 14(1) business income inclusion*	*Closing balance*
2000	$ 8,100	$ 567		$7,533
2001(2)	7,533	527		7,006
2012	7,006	490		6,516
2013	6,516	—	$18,684(3)	
Total		$1,584		

2013 Opening balance	$ 6,516
Sale (¾ × $45,000)	(33,750)
Negative balance	(27,234)
Minus: previous CECA claims	1,584
Balance	$(25,650)
Income inclusion:	
Previous CECA claims	$ 1,584
⅔ × $25,650	17,100
Total	18,684
Untaxed: ⅓ × ¾ × ($45,000 – $10,800)	8,550
	$ 27,234

— *NOTES TO SOLUTION*

(1) 7% of the declining balance.

(2) No amortization deductions taken in the 2002 – 2011 period because of business losses.   ITA: 20(1)(*b*)

(3) The sale in 2013 would result in $18,684 of business income which is equal to the sum (rounded) of par. 20(1)(*b*) deductions ($1,584) plus ½ of the gain of $34,200 ($45,000 – $10,800).

Exercise 11

Jan. 1, 2005	Purchase of goodwill (¾ × $40,000)	$ 30,000
Dec. 31, 2005	Cumulative eligible capital amount @ 7%	(2,100)
Jan. 1, 2006	Cumulative eligible capital	$ 27,900
Dec. 31, 2006	Cumulative eligible capital amount @ 7%	(1,953)

Jan. 1, 2007	Cumulative eligible capital	$ 25,947
June 1, 2007	Purchase of licence (¾ × $50,000)............	37,500
	Cumulative eligible capital	$ 63,447
Dec. 31, 2007	Cumulative eligible capital amount @ 7%	(4,441)
Jan. 1, 2008	Cumulative eligible capital	$ 59,006
Dec. 31, 2008	Cumulative eligible capital amount @ 7%	(4,130)
Jan. 1, 2009	Cumulative eligible capital	$ 54,876
Mar. 1, 2009	Purchase of trademark (¾ × $20,000)	15,000
	Cumulative eligible capital	$ 69,876
Dec. 31, 2009	Cumulative eligible capital amount @ 7%	(4,891)
Jan. 1, 2010	Cumulative eligible capital	$ 64,985
Nov. 1, 2010	Purchase of goodwill (¾ × $50,000)...........	37,500
	Cumulative eligible capital	$ 102,485
Dec. 31, 2010	Cumulative eligible capital amount @ 7%	(7,174)
Jan. 1, 2011	Cumulative eligible capital	$ 95,311
Sept. 7, 2011	Sale of goodwill (¾ × $100,000)	(75,000)
	Cumulative eligible capital	$ 20,311
Dec. 31, 2011	Cumulative eligible capital amount @ 7%	(1,422)
Jan. 1, 2012	Cumulative eligible capital	$ 18,889
Dec. 31, 2012	Cumulative eligible capital amount @ 7%	(1,322)
Jan. 1, 2013	Cumulative eligible capital	$ 17,567
Aug. 3, 2013	Sale of license (¾ × $150,000)	(112,500)
	Sale of trademark (¾ × $200,000)	(150,000)
Dec. 31, 2013	Cumulative eligible capital	$(244,933)
	Business income	172,433
	Non-taxed ⅓ of "gain" [⅓ × ($244,933 – 27,433)]	72,500
Jan. 1, 2014	Cumulative eligible capital	$ Nil

ITA: 14(1)

The business income in 2013 is calculated as:

The total of:

(a)   the lesser of:

      (i) the negative amount .... $ 244,933

          and

      (ii) the total of: ....

          all cumulative eligible capital deductions ...... $ 27,433

          less: all recaptured deductions in prior years... Nil

                             $ 27,433

          The lesser is .... $ 27,433

and

(b)   ⅔ of (negative amount less recaptured in deductions in
      (a)(ii), above [⅔ × ($244,933 – 27,433)] 145,000*

Business income $172,433

* This is the same as ½ of the economic gain:

Proceeds ($100,000 + $150,000 + $200,000) .... $ 450,000

Cost ($40,000 + $50,000 + $20,000 + $50,000) .... (160,000)

Economic gain .... $ 290,000

½ = ... $ 145,000

Chapter 6
Income from Property

LEARNING GOALS

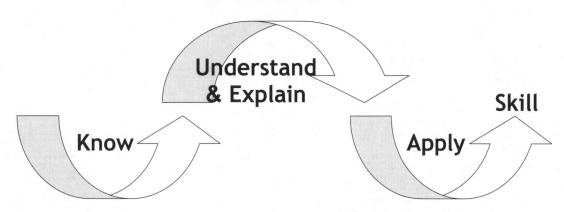

Know

By the end of this chapter you should know the basic provisions of the *Income Tax Act* that relate to property income and the income attribution rules that are uniquely applicable to property income. It is important to know the distinction between property income and business income, since they are two separate sources of income on which different income tax rules may apply. You should also know a little about how the GST affects some property income issues. Completing the Review Questions (¶6,800) and Multiple Choice Questions (¶6,825) is a good way to learn the technical provisions.

Understand and Explain

You should understand and be able to explain the tax treatment of specific types of property income and expenses, including the basic questions of who will pay the tax, and when and how much tax will be paid. You should also understand some basic tax planning strategies that can be utilized in real life to maximize the after-tax return on investment. Completing the Exercises (¶6,850) is a good way to deepen your understanding of the material.

Apply

You should be able to apply your knowledge and understanding of property income to real life situations. Completing the Assignment Problems (¶6,875) is an excellent way to develop your ability to identify tax issues and to apply the material in increasingly complex situations.

Chapter 6 – Learning Chart

Topic	Example Problem (✓)	Review Questions (¶6,800)	Multiple Choice (¶6,825)	Exercises (¶6,850)	Assignment Problems (¶6,875)
¶6,000 INCLUSIONS					
¶6,005 Specific Inclusions of Property Income					
¶6,010 Interest Income		1, 2		1	2, 7, 10
¶6,015 The meaning of interest					
¶6,020 Method of reporting income					
¶6,025 Accrual rules for individuals	✓				
¶6,030 Other interest income provisions					
¶6,032 Purchasing a corporate bond at a discount	✓				
¶6,033 Treasury bills	✓				
¶6,034 Zero-coupon bonds	✓				
¶6,035 Timing and recognition of interest income	✓				
¶6,036 Purchasing an accrued interest bond	✓				11
¶6,040 Payments Based on Production or Use					1
¶6,045 Concept of the provision	✓				
¶6,050 Dividends from Corporations Resident in Canada			1, 5		2, 7, 8, 10
¶6,052 Overview					
¶6,055 The issue					
¶6,060 Overview of the Canadian dividend taxation system	✓				
¶6,065 Dividends Received from Non-Resident Corporations			5		7, 8
¶6,070 Income Attribution		3, 4	3, 6	2	2, 9, 10, 11
¶6,075 The reason for attribution rules					
¶6,080 Definition of related persons					
¶6,085 Transactions subject to income attribution					
¶6,090 Avoiding income attributions	✓				
¶6,095 Anti-avoidance rules relating to attribution					
¶6,100 More types of income subject to attribution					
¶6,102 "Second-generation" income from property					
¶6,105 Loans or transfers to non-arm's length individuals who are 18 years of age or older					
¶6,110 Summary of income attribution rules					
¶6,115 Tax on split income earned by persons under 18 years of age (the "Kiddie Tax")	✓				
¶6,120 What else can be income split?					
¶6,200 DEDUCTIONS					
¶6,210 Carrying Charges on Land					
¶6,215 Limitation on deduction — Vacant land	✓	5		3	3, 11

Topic	Example Problem (✓)	Review Questions (¶6,800)	Multiple Choice (¶6,825)	Exercises (¶6,850)	Assignment Problems (¶6,875)
¶6,220 "Soft Costs" Relating to Construction of Buildings or Ownership of Land					5
¶6,230 Rental Properties		6	2	4, 5, 7	4, 7, 10
¶6,235 Separate classes — Rental property costing over $50,000					
¶6,240 Losses from rental property	✓				
¶6,250 Depreciation-Based or Similar Tax Shelters					
¶6,260 Interest Deduction		7			
¶6,265 Proposed legislation	✓				
¶6,270 Loss of the source of income	✓	10			
¶6,275 Capitalization of interest					
¶6,290 Personal Loan Planning and Interest Deductibility		8, 9	4	6	10, 11, 12
¶6,295 Deductibility of interest expenses					
¶6,300 Commentary on two Supreme Court decisions on interest deductibility — *Singleton* and *Ludco*					
¶6,305 Tax planning	✓				
¶6,310 Carrying charges					
¶6,315 Investment counsel fees					
¶6,320 Legal and accounting fees					
¶6,325 Foreign non-business income tax					
¶6,400 DIFFERENCES BETWEEN BUSINESS AND PROPERTY INCOME					
¶6,410 Applicable to Business Income Only					
¶6,420 Applicable to Property Income Only					
¶6,500 GST/HST AND PROPERTY INCOME					
¶6,510 Interest and Dividends					
¶6,520 "Soft Costs"					6
¶6,900 SUPPLEMENTAL NOTES					
¶6,910 Prescribed Debt Obligations	✓				
¶6,920 Proposed Amendments to Interest Deductibility and REOP					
¶6,930 GST/HST and Property Income					
¶6,935 Payments based on production or use					
¶6,940 Rental properties					

CHAPTER 6

Study Notes

Chapter 6 —
Discussion Notes for Review Questions

(1) The principal would be separated from the accrued interest and cause the interest to be included in Billy's income as interest income. The purchaser can deduct the same amount that the vendor included in income.

ITA: 20(14)(*a*)
ITA: 20(14)(*b*)

(2) Interest accrued annually to the anniversary date of the bond is taxable, requiring tax to be paid from some other source of funds, since no interest will be received on the compound interest bond. Your client may wish to invest in the type of Canada Savings Bonds that pay interest annually. Note that the annual accrual rules may not present a cash flow problem if the holder of the bond is not taxable on the accrued interest due to a low level of total income.

ITA: 12(4)

(3) Attribution would not appear to apply to cause any income allocated to Mrs. Simpson to be reallocated to her husband since there is no attribution of business income. (It should be noted that, if she is not actively involved in the business, then she will not be a specified member of the partnership and the income from the partnership will be deemed to be income from property.)

ITA: 74.1(1)

ITA: 248(1), 96(1.8)

(4) Although the corporation is carrying on a business, Mrs. Smith is not. She will be earning property income (i.e., dividends on the shares), so the exception to the attribution rules for business income does not apply. Attribution as a result of guarantees would only cause the attribution rules to apply if the loan was not at commercial rates. If the bank is charging commercial interest rates, then the attribution rules will not apply.

ITA: 74.5(7)
ITA: 74.5(1)

(5) The interest on the 10 acres would be capitalized since it is not used in business and there is no revenue from the land.

ITA: 18(2)

(6) CCA cannot be claimed to create or increase a loss on rental property. However, those loss limitation rules do not apply to a corporation whose principal business was the leasing, rental, development or sale, or any combination thereof, of real property owned by it. In this case, Rent Co. will be able to claim CCA to create or increase a loss.

ITR: 1100(11)–(14)

(7) No interest is deductible if Ms. Campbell is considered to realize a capital gain on the sale of the gold. Since capital gains are not income from business or property, she does not meet the requirements and cannot deduct the interest. Also, there is no provision that would allow her to capitalize the interest to the cost of the gold. On the other hand, if the gain on the sale of the gold is considered to be income from business or property, the interest would be deductible. Note that the CRA would allow her to choose income treatment for these transactions.

ITA: 9(3)
ITA: 20(1)(*c*)
ITA: 53
IT-346R, par. 8

(8) In the *Attaie* case, the Federal Court–Trial Division agreed that the interest expense was deductible. However, the Federal Court of Appeal reversed this decision and decided that the interest was not deductible, since there was not a direct link between the borrowed funds and the income from property.

87 DTC 5411 (F.C.T.D.)
90 DTC 6413 (F.C.A.)

(9) Under the proposed plan, the interest would not be deductible since the money is not being used to earn income. However, if your client were to borrow from the bank the $100,000 needed to loan to the purchaser in order to complete the sale of his existing house, then at least the interest would be deductible up to 8%. The purchaser would then be in a position to pay the full purchase price for the new residence.

(10) Since the corporation that your client invested in has gone out of business, there is no longer a possibility of earning income from business or property. However, the amount of the lost capital would be deemed to continue to be borrowed for the purpose of earning income and, hence, would allow the interest in this case to continue to be deductible. Refer to IT-533, paragraph 19.

ITA: 20.1(1)

CHAPTER 6

Chapter 6 —
Solutions to Multiple Choice Questions

Question 1

(B) is correct. The calculation is as follows:

Grossed up dividend ($12,000 × 1.18)	$14,160
Combined tax rate	× 46%
	$ 6,514
Dividend tax credit	(2,160)
Net tax	$ 4,354

(A) incorrectly ignores provincial tax: $14,160 × 29% – $2,160 = $1,946.

(C) incorrectly ignores the dividend tax credit:

$$14,160 × 46\% = \$6,514$$

(D) incorrectly ignores the gross-up and the dividend tax credit: $12,000 × 46% = $5,520.

Question 2

(B) is the correct answer. The calculation is as follows:

	Property			
	1	*2*	*3*	*Total*
UCC at Jan. 1st	$100,000	$75,000	$150,000	
Rental revenue for the year	$ 58,000	$22,000	$ 20,000	
Expenses for the year	50,000	20,000	20,000	
Income before CCA	$ 8,000	$ 2,000	(Nil)	$10,000
CCA: 4% × UCC	$ 4,000	$ 3,000	$ 6,000	$13,000
Maximum CCA [Reg. 1100(11)]				$10,000

(A) is incorrect. $13,000 is the CCA calculation ignoring the rental property restriction.   ITR: 1100(11)

(C) is incorrect. $7,000 is the maximum CCA calculation on the first two buildings only. This calculation ignores the fact that the CCA on the third property can be claimed against the net rental income on the first two properties.

(D) is incorrect. It is one-half of the $13,000 calculated in (A) above.

Question 3

(B) is the correct answer. The $12,000 of dividend income will be attributed to Mr. P. Mabel and   ITA: 56(4.1)
Mr. P are related and it can reasonably be considered that one of the main reasons for making the loan was to reduce tax.

(A) is incorrect. The $3,000 of interest income will not be attributed. Peter is not under 18 years of age and, therefore, attribution does not apply. If it had been a loan, instead of a gift, subsection 56(4.1)   ITA: 74.1(2)
would apply and may attribute the income.

(C) is incorrect. Even though an interest-free loan was made to which attribution would apply,   ITA: 56(4.1)
there is no property income from the cottage to attribute.

(D) is incorrect. Even though a gift was made to a spouse to which attribution would apply, there is   ITA: 74.1(1)
no property income from the chequing account to attribute.

Question 4

(B) is correct. The premium paid on a $100,000 term life insurance policy on the taxpayer's life   ITA: 20(1)(e.2)
which is required as collateral for a $100,000 bank loan used to purchase a $100,000 investment in common shares is deductible.

(A) is incorrect because commissions paid on the purchase of an investment in common shares are capitalized as part of the cost of the shares.

ITA: 18(1)(*b*)

(C) is incorrect because the Act does not allow a deduction for interest expense on a loan to invest in a registered retirement savings plan.

ITA: 18(11)(*b*)

(D) is incorrect because commissions paid on the sale of an investment in common shares are a selling cost deducted in computing the capital gain on the sale of the shares. One-half of a capital gain is a taxable capital gain which is computed under Subdivision c of Division B of Part I of the Act, whereas income from business or property is computed under Subdivision b.

Question 5

(D) is correct: $20,000 × 1.18 + $8,500 + $1,500 tax withheld = $33,600.

ITA: 82(1)

(A) is incorrect because it ignores the gross-up on the dividend and the foreign income: $20,000.

(B) is incorrect because it ignores the gross-up on the dividend and the foreign tax withheld: $20,000 + $8,500 = $28,500.

(C) is incorrect because it ignores the gross-up on the dividend: $20,000 + $8,500 + $1,500 = $30,000.

Question 6

(D) is correct.

(A) is incorrect because the tax on split income only applies to taxpayers under age 18 throughout the year. Since Ron is 18, the tax on split income will not apply.

ITA: 120.4 "specified individual"

(B) is incorrect because the only exemption regarding inherited shares is for shares inherited from a parent. If Ron had been under 18 at any time in the year, the tax on split income would have applied to dividends received on the shares.

ITA: 120.4 "excluded amount"

(C) is incorrect because the tax on split income does not apply to capital gains on a disposition to an arm's length person.

ITA: 120.4 "split income"

CHAPTER 6

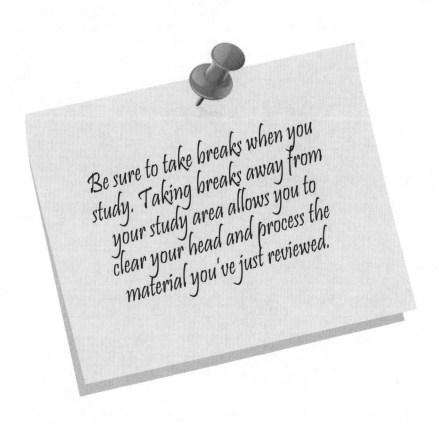

Be sure to take breaks when you study. Taking breaks away from your study area allows you to clear your head and process the material you've just reviewed.

Chapter 6 — Solutions to Exercises

Exercise 1

(A) In its June 30, 2013 taxation year, the corporation would be required to include in income the interest received March 31, 2013 for the period October 1, 2012 to March 31, 2013 plus interest accrued from April 1 to June 30, 2013. Accrued interest from October 1, 2012 to January 1, 2013 (the period prior to acquisition), which was purchased with the bond, would give rise to a deduction.

ITA: 12(3), 20(14)

(B) The Act would require accrued interest from November 1, 2013 to October 31, 2014 to be included in income in 2014.

ITA: 12(4)

(C) The anniversary day would be December 31, 2013. Accrued interest from the date of purchase to December 31, 2013 would be included in 2013 income.

(D) The first anniversary day would occur October 31, 2014 and accrued interest would be included at that time. The CRA has, in the past, administratively allowed Canada Savings Bond interest to be accrued on a "bond year" basis. The Act gives legislative effect to this practice.

IT-396R, par. 25;
ITA: 12(4)

(E) The $80 received each year would be included in income. On November 30, 2013, there will be an anniversary day, but all of the interest accrued to that day will have been included in income as interest received in the year.

ITA: 12(1)(c)

Exercise 2

(A) (i) The Act would attribute the income on the bond to him even though she is legally entitled to receive it, since a gift is considered to be a transfer and is not a fair market value exchange which would be exempt.

ITA: 74.1(1), 74.5(1)

(ii) Since a sale is also considered to be a transfer, attribution would apply except that, in this case, the transfer would be exempt because it was for fair market value consideration, as long as they elect jointly not to have the rollover apply.

ITA: 74.1(1), 74.5(1)(a), 73(1)

(iii) This situation still involves a sale directly between husband and wife and is, therefore, a transfer subject to the attribution of income. A non-interest bearing demand note would not qualify for the exception because a commercial rate of interest was not charged.

ITA: 74.1(1), 74.5(1)(b)

(iv) The loan of funds would result in attribution, because the exception would not apply since a commercial rate of interest was not charged on the loan.

ITA: 74.1(1), 74.5(2)

(B) If the loan was to a non-arm's length minor or a niece or nephew who is also a minor, then attribution would apply to transfers or loans by means of a trust to or for the benefit of a minor in the same way as spousal attribution applied in part (A), above. However, there are special rules pertaining to transfers or loans to a trust which will be discussed in Chapter 18.

ITA: 74.1(2)
ITA: 74.1(1)

(C) Attribution of income does not apply to a transfer involving an individual who is 18 or older. However, another provision might apply to transactions (iii) and (iv) involving loans. The key condition for this rule to apply is that one of the main reasons for the loan was to reduce or avoid tax on income from property or substituted property. A loan bearing a commercial rate of interest would be exempt from attribution.

ITA: 74.1(2)
ITA: 56(4.1)

Exercise 3

(i) The deductibility of carrying charges is not limited because the land is being used in the course of the hotel business.

ITA: 18(2)

(ii) The Act will limit the deductibility of carrying charges to 75% of their total (i.e., to the amount of the net revenues) so as not to create a loss by their deduction, unless the land is owned by a corporation whose principal purpose is the rental of real property (i.e., land and building) owned by it. This is not the principal purpose of a hotel corporation.

ITA: 18(2)(e)

ITA: 18(2)(f)

(iii) The deductibility of carrying charges may be limited in the same manner as in (ii), above, until the property is used in the business.

ITA: 18(2)

Exercise 4

	Class 1: 4%	Class 1: 4%	Class 8: 20%	Total
	Building 1	Building 2[(1)]		
UCC, January 1	$148,000	—	$25,000	
Purchases	—	$137,500	—	
UCC, December 31	$148,000	$137,500	$25,000	
CCA.	5,920	2,750[(2)]	4,350[(3)]	$13,020
UCC, January 1	$142,080	$134,750	$20,650	

— *NOTES TO SOLUTION*

[(1)] Separate class for rental building costing $50,000 or more. ITR: 1101(1ac)

[(2)] 4% of [$137,500 − (½ × $137,500)].

[(3)] Net rental income before CCA ($9,270 + 3,750) $13,020

CCA on rental building and leasing properties (i.e., furniture and fixtures) limited to $13,020 [$13,020 − ($5,920 + $2,750) = $4,350] . . . . (13,020)

Net income from rental properties . . . . Nil

Note that where less than maximum capital cost allowance is taken, the less than maximum amount should be taken in classes with relatively higher CCA rates, so that the UCC carried forward to the following year is eligible for CCA at the higher rate in that subsequent year.

Exercise 5

(A)

	Property A	Property B	Total
UCC, January 1	$330,000	$480,000	
Disposal	(336,000)	—	
UCC, December 31	$ (6,000)	$480,000	
Recapture	6,000	—	
CCA @ 4% (Class 1) — see below	—	(12,000)	
UCC forward	Nil	$468,000	
Revenue	$ 13,500	$ 22,500	$36,000
Recapture	6,000	—	6,000
Expenses before CCA	(11,250)	(18,750)	(30,000)
Net	$ 8,250	$ 3,750	$12,000
CCA (4% of $480,000 = $19,200; limited to net above)			(12,000)
Net income from property			Nil

(B)   The rule to defer recapture applies on a voluntary disposition of a "former business property". A rental property is excluded from the definition and, hence, the deferral rule does not apply. ITA: 13(4), 248(1)

Exercise 6

Interest expense is deductible if there is a reasonable expectation of earning income from property. ITA: 20(1)(c)

Investment	Not deductible	Deductible
Common shares		$20,000[(1)]
Gold bullion	$25,000[(2)]	
Corporate bond		20,000[(3)]

Preferred shares (RRSP)	10,000[4]	
Common shares		30,000[5]
Paintings	15,000[6]	
GICs		20,000[5]
Total	$50,000	$90,000

Deductible interest = $90,000 × 8.5% = $7,650

— *NOTES TO SOLUTION*

[1] As there is an expectation of dividend income on common shares, the interest is deductible.

[2] As capital treatment has been chosen for gains/losses on the gold bullion, the interest is not deductible.

[3] The corporate bond is income-producing and the associated interest would be deductible.

[4] The preferred shares were purchased in an RRSP; deduction of interest is disallowed.

[5] The associated interest on the common shares and GICs would be deductible, as there is the expectation of earning property income.

[6] The paintings from well-known galleries would be considered an investment for earning future capital gains and, therefore, the associated interest would not be deductible.

Exercise 7

Since the rule relates to capital cost allowance, Regulations Part XI, Capital Cost Allowances, would be a starting point. More specifically, ITR 1101(1ac) deals with the separate classes rule related to rental properties having a cost of at least $50,000.

ITR: 1100(11), 1101(1ac)

The other special rule is ITR 1100(11), which states that capital cost allowance on rental properties can only be deducted to the extent that it does not create or increase a net loss from all rental properties combined. Note that Interpretation Bulletin IT-195R4, Rental Property — Capital Cost Allowance Restrictions, provides further details.

Chapter 7
Capital Gains: Personal

LEARNING GOALS

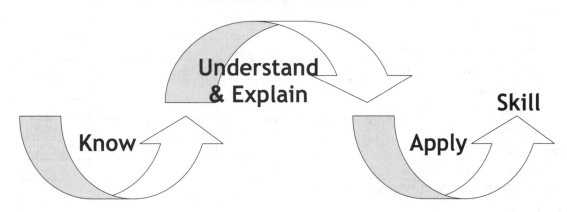

Know

By the end of this chapter you should know the basic provisions of the *Income Tax Act* that relate to capital gains and losses. The focus of the chapter is on provisions that would primarily affect individuals. Completing the Review Questions (¶7,800) and Multiple Choice Questions (¶7,825) is a good way to learn the technical provisions.

Understand and Explain

You should understand and be able to explain

- how to calculate proceeds of disposition and the adjusted cost base to determine the capital gain or loss;
- how capital gains and losses are taxed;
- the special rules for principal residences, personal-use property, and listed personal property;
- the special case of an allowable business investment loss; and
- how capital gains and losses fit in to the calculation of income for tax purposes.

Completing the Exercises (¶7,850) is a good way to deepen your understanding of the material in this chapter.

Apply

You should be able to apply your knowledge and understanding of the rules pertaining to capital gains and losses in a way that accomplishes a client's goals. Completing the Assignment Problems (¶7,875) is an excellent way to develop your ability to apply the material in increasingly complex situations.

Chapter 7 — Learning Chart

Topic	Example Problem (✓)	Review Questions (¶7,800)	Multiple Choice (¶7,825)	Exercises (¶7,850)	Assignment Problems (¶7,875)
¶7,000 OVERVIEW OF THE TAXATION OF CAPITAL GAINS					
¶7,010 History					
¶7,012 Capital Property					
¶7,013 General considerations					
¶7,014 Personal-use property (PUP)					
¶7,015 Listed personal property (LPP)					
¶7,016 Other capital property					
¶7,017 Schematic classification					
¶7,018 Restrictions					
¶7,020 Terminology					
¶7,030 Capital Gains Deduction					
¶7,040 Election re: Disposition of Canadian Securities					
¶7,100 GENERAL RULES					
¶7,110 Computation of Capital Gains and Capital Losses					
¶7,115 Proceeds of disposition		1			
¶7,120 Adjusted cost base		2			
¶7,125 Mutual funds and DRIPs	✓			10	7
¶7,200 SPECIFIC PROVISIONS FOR THE TAXATION OF CAPITAL GAINS					
¶7,210 Personal-Use Property	✓	4, 5	1, 5	4, 5, 8, 17	9, 10
¶7,220 Listed Personal Property	✓	5	5	4, 5, 8, 17	9, 10
¶7,230 Principal Residence Exemption	✓	3	2	1, 2	1, 10
¶7,240 Change in Use of a Principal Residence		10		3	2
¶7,245 Application of the change-in-use elections	✓				
¶7,250 Interpretation Bulletin IT-120R6 — Principal residence					
¶7,255 Section 54.1 — Extended designation		11	3	3	
¶7,260 Principal Residence Exemption — Transfer Between Spouses	✓				
¶7,270 Capital Losses — General					
¶7,280 Pooling of Identical Assets	✓		5, 8	6, 7, 9, 10	3, 4
¶7,285 Identical properties exempt from cost-averaging rule					
¶7,290 Disposition of Shares Acquired Under a Stock Option					6, 8
¶7,295 Disposition of newly acquired securities	✓				
¶7,300 Adjusted cost base of shares acquired under a stock option	✓				7
¶7,310 Cost of Certain Properties		6, 8, 9	4	15	3, 4
¶7,315 General consideration					
¶7,320 Dividends in kind					

Topic	Example Problem (✓)	Review Questions (¶7,800)	Multiple Choice (¶7,825)	Exercises (¶7,850)	Assignment Problems (¶7,875)
¶7,325 Stock dividends	✓	6	4	9	4, 5
¶7,330 Superficial Losses	✓				3, 4
¶7,340 Transfer of Property to an RRSP					
¶7,350 Options		14, 15		11	
¶7,352 Call option					
¶7,354 Put option					
¶7,356 Summary	✓				
¶7,360 Convertible Properties		16			
¶7,370 Capital Gains Deferral	✓				
¶7,380 Certain Shares Deemed to be Capital Property					
¶7,400 NON-ARM'S LENGTH TRANSFERS AND THE ATTRIBUTION RULES REVISITED		17, 18	6, 7, 8	12, 13, 14	5, 6
¶7,410 Non-Arm's Length Transfers					
¶7,415 Who does not deal at arm's length?					
¶7,420 Transactions with non-arm's length individuals					
¶7,430 Attribution Rules					
¶7,435 Capital gains on spousal transfers or loans					
¶7,440 Recapture					
¶7,445 Summary of provisions					
¶7,500 DEATH OF A TAXPAYER					
¶7,510 Deemed Disposition on Death			9	15	8
¶7,600 LEAVING AND ENTERING CANADA		12, 13	10	16	
¶7,700 COMPUTATIONAL RULES					
¶7,710 Section 3 Revisited		7	5	17	7
¶7,720 Allowable Business Investment Losses	✓				7
¶7,900 SUPPLEMENTAL NOTES					
¶7,910 Cost of Assets Owned on December 31, 1971					
¶7,930 Principal Residence on Farm Land					
¶7,940 GST/HST Rules for Dispositions of Residential Property and Used Goods					
¶7,945 Sales of used residential or personal-use real property					
¶7,950 Sales of used goods and acceptance of trade-ins					
¶7,980 Stock Option Benefit—Tax-Deferred Election Repealed					
¶7,985 Special relief for tax-deferred elections made prior to March 4, 2010					

CHAPTER 7

Study Notes

Chapter 7 — Discussion Notes for Review Questions

(1) "Proceeds of disposition" is defined to include the principal amount of the mortgage that is owed to the mortgage company. This transaction may trigger recaptured CCA or a terminal loss.

ITA: 13(1), 13(21.1), 20(16), 54 "proceeds of disposition" (*h*)

(2) Whenever the adjusted cost base becomes negative there will be an immediate capital gain. The only exception to this rule is for a partnership interest in a general partnership (but not a limited partnership).

ITA: 40(3)

(3) Until the end of 1981 each individual could own and claim a principal residence. After that time the principal residence exemption is restricted to one residence per family. The rules provide the framework for deciding which residence should be claimed for which years in order to maximize the exemption. Mr. Chan and his wife must choose one residence or the other for the exemption.

ITA: 54 "principal residence" (*c*)
ITA: 40(2)(*b*)

(4) The cottage is considered to be "personal-use property" (PUP). Any loss on the disposal of PUP cannot be deducted. The losses are considered to arise as a result of normal personal use over time.

ITA: 40(2)(*g*)(iii), 54

(5) For the purpose of calculating the capital gain or loss on any disposal of PUP the taxpayer's cost is deemed to be the greater of the adjusted cost base of the property and $1,000. Similarly, the taxpayer's proceeds of disposition are deemed to be the greater of actual proceeds and $1,000. Listed personal property (LPP) is defined to be a subset of PUP; therefore, the $1,000 rule also applies to LPP.

ITA: 46(1)

ITA: 54

(6) The dividend should be included with the gross-up in income. The amount of the dividend before the gross-up will increase the cost base of the shares and effectively reduces the capital gain or increase the capital loss when the shares are sold.

ITA: 53(2)

(7) The result of the taxable capital gains minus the allowable capital losses cannot be negative. Any negative amount is a "net capital loss" that can be carried back three years or forward indefinitely.

ITA: 3(*b*) of Div. B; 111(1)(*b*), 111(8) of Div. C

(8) You would be deemed to have acquired the prize at a cost equal to its fair market value at the time you received it.

ITA: 52(4)

(9) The car has a cost base equal to the $35,000 benefit included in her income as a shareholder benefit.

ITA: 15(1), 52(1)

(10) If Mrs. Smith did not make any structural changes to the house, then there will not be any change in use. The house will still remain her principal residence. She will have to declare the rental income and can deduct the expenses that relate to it.

Income Tax Folio S1-F3-C2 — Principal Residence

(11) Since she was moved by her employer nine years ago and was still employed by that employer when she moved back this year, the Act modifies paragraph (*d*) of the definition of "principal residence" to allow her to continue to claim her house as her principal residence for more than the 4 years generally allowed on a normal change in use under the definition. All years qualify since she was still resident in Canada, as required. She still has to make the election not to have a change in use in the year they moved. As a result, on the sale of the house, she will be able to claim the full principal residence exemption.

ITA: 45(2), 54, 54.1

ITA: 40(2)(*b*)

(12) The Act causes a deemed disposition on all her property other than certain property and certain items that are subject to withholding tax. In this case the term deposits will be deemed to be disposed of, but since there is no capital gain, there would not be any tax.

ITA: 128.1(4)

(13) Mr. Shiloh will be excepted from the deemed disposition rules on the shares of his U.S. employer since he was in Canada less than 60 months in the past 10 years.

ITA: 128.1(4)

(14) The Act generally treats the sale of this option as a disposition with the cost base being nil. Therefore, the capital gain will be equal to the proceeds and will be taxed in the year the option is sold.

ITA: 49(1)

(15) On the granting of an option there is a disposition and the ACB is deemed to be nil. He does not have the alternative of reducing the cost base.

ITA: 49(1)

(16) A rollover on the exchange of the common shares for the debentures is provided as long as the debenture had the conversion feature built into its terms and no cash was received. The shares will have a cost base of $10 each, so the accrued gain of $10 per share will be deferred until the common shares are sold.

ITA: 51

(17) If a person sells something to someone with whom he or she does not deal at arm's length then the proceeds will be deemed to be the fair market value. Related parties do not deal at arm's length, but in this case the two are not related. However, it is a question of fact whether persons not related to each other are dealing at arm's length. In this case there is no evidence of hard bargaining and the transaction is obviously not at fair market value. Therefore, it would be unlikely that they would be considered to be dealing at arm's length and the proceeds would likely be deemed to be $100,000. Her friend will have a cost base equal to what she paid for the land of $50,000. As a result there will be double taxation.

ITA: 69, 251, 251(1)(*c*)

(18) At the time of the gift, Bill will be deemed to have sold the shares at their fair market value. Scott will be deemed to have received the shares at a cost to him equal to the fair market value at the time of the gift. Since the shares were a gift, the attribution rules applicable to an income-splitting loan will not apply.

ITA: 69(1)(*b*), 69(1)(*c*)

ITA: 56(4.1)

Chapter 7 –
Solutions to Multiple Choice Questions

Question 1

(C) is correct. The loss on the automobile is not allowed since it is personal-use property (PUP). The $1,000 rule means that the gain on the boat (which is PUP) is $500, the gain on the painting (which is listed personal property (LPP)) is $300, and the loss on the jewellery (which is LPP) is $400. Since the deductible portion of the $400 LPP loss is limited to the LPP gain in the year ($300), the capital gain is: $500 + $300 – $300 = $500. The $100 LPP loss can be carried over against LPP gains.

(A) is incorrect, because it ignores the $1,000 rule and computes the gain on the boat (PUP) as $900, the gain on the painting (LPP) as $700, and the loss on the jewellery (LPP) as $1,200. The LPP gain is then offset by a portion of the LPP loss, leaving the $900 gain.

(B) is incorrect, because it does not subtract the deductible portion of the LPP loss from the LPP gain: $500 + $300 = $800.

(D) is incorrect, because it deducts the full LPP loss ($400) against all the gains: $500 + $300 – $400 = $400.

ITA: 2, 41(1), 46(1), 54

Question 2

(B) is the correct answer. Since Amanda had no capital gain on her house, she must have designated it as her principal residence for all but one of the years 2004 to 2012. She therefore has two years to designate in respect of the cottage: one of the years not used on the house (say, 2012) plus 2013. Since she owned the cottage eight years (2006 to 2013), the principal residence exemption for the cottage is: $^3/_8 \times \$80,000 = \$30,000$ (3 = 2 years designated + "one-plus rule"). Therefore, Amanda's taxable capital gain is $25,000 ($^1/_2 \times$ ($80,000 – $30,000 principal residence exemption)).

(A) is incorrect, because $80,000 is the capital gain before the exemption.

(C) is incorrect, because it uses $^2/_8 \times \$80,000 = \$20,000$ as the principal residence exemption: $^1/_2 \times$ ($80,000 – $20,000) = $30,000.

(D) is incorrect, because $50,000 is the capital gain, not the taxable capital gain.

Question 3

(B) is correct. Because Gary made the election to be deemed not to have changed the use in respect of the property, there is deemed to be no change in use in 2007. The only disposition occurs in 2013 on the date of sale. The Act allows Gary to designate the property as his principal residence for up to four years where the election was made. The gain on the property is $500,000 ($850,000 – $350,000) and the total years of ownership were 18 (1996 to 2013) and the maximum number of years that can be designated is 16 (1996 to 2007 plus 4). Therefore, the principal residence exemption is [(16 + 1)/18] $\times$ $500,000 or $472,222. The capital gain is therefore $27,778 ($500,000 – $472,222) and the taxable capital gain is $13,889 ($^1/_2 \times$ $27,778).

ITA: 45(2)

ITA: 54
ITA: 45(2)

(A) is incorrect because there is a taxable capital gain to report in 2013 because not all years of ownership qualify as years eligible for a principal residence. The extension of the four-year rule does not apply, because Gary did not move back into the residence before it was sold.

ITA: 54.1

(C) incorrectly calculates taxable capital gains of $50,000 in 2007 [$^1/_2$ ($550,000 – $350,000)] and 2013 [$^1/_2$ ($850,000 – $550,000)]. The timing is wrong because there is no deemed disposition in 2007 because of the election. The amount is also wrong because 12 years (1996 – 2007) can be designated in respect of the residence.

ITA: 45(2)

(D) correctly calculates the gain in 2013 as $500,000 without claiming any principal residence exemption, resulting in a taxable capital gain of $250,000 ($^1/_2 \times$ $500,000).

Question 4

(B) is correct. The amount of the dividend is $4, the increase in the paid-up capital, and this is also the cost of the shares (ssec. 53(3)). However, the individual's net income would increase by $5.52, since it is a taxable dividend: $4 $\times$ 1.38 gross-up = $5.52.

ITA: 82(1)

(A) is incorrect because although $4 is the amount of the dividend, the amount included in net income is the grossed-up dividend (1.38 $\times$ $4 = $5.52).

(C) is incorrect because the amount of the dividend is not based on the $10 fair market value of the share.

(D) is also incorrect because the amount of the dividend is not based on the $10 fair market value of the share and the amount included in income is the increase in paid-up capital grossed up by 1.38, not the fair market value grossed up by 1.38.

Question 5

(C) is correct.

Shares		$1,600
Personal-use property		700
Listed personal property	$500	
Listed personal property	(140)	
Listed personal property losses of prior year	(100)	260
Shares		(820)
Personal-use property		Nil
Capital gain		$1,740
Taxable capital gain (½)		$ 870

(A) is incorrect because it deducts the $1,000 personal-use property loss: ½ ($1,740 – 1,000) = $370.

(B) is incorrect because it deducts the $1,000 personal-use property loss and does not multiply by the ½ fraction: ($1,740 – $1,000) = $740.

(D) is incorrect because it does not deduct the listed personal property loss of other years: ½ × ($1,740 + $100) = $920.

Question 6

(A) is correct.   ITA: 74.1(2)

(B) is incorrect, because capital gains or losses do not attribute on loans or gifts to minors.

(C) is incorrect, because there will be a capital gain on the gift.   ITA: 69

(D) is incorrect. $100,000 is the capital gain. The taxable capital gain is:

½ × $100,000 = $50,000.

Question 7

(C) is correct. There is a superficial loss because Ms. Y has incurred a loss and an affiliated person   ITA: 40(2)(*g*), 54
(Mr. Y) acquired the shares within 30 days of the disposition.

(A) is incorrect, because it ignores the superficial loss rule and computes the loss as ½ × ($800,000 – $900,000).

(B) is not correct, because Ms. Y elected out of the interspousal rollover.   ITA: 73(1)

(D) is not correct. There is no attribution because she elected out of the subsection 73(1) rollover   ITA: 74.5
and received fair market value consideration (i.e., $800,000 cash).

Question 8

(A) is correct since only the gift to the son will result in a taxable capital gain.

The ACB of Mike's stock is:

100 × $3.11 plus $39 commission (incl. sec. 7 benefit)	$350	
100 × $4 plus $50 commission	450	
200	$800	= $4 ACB per share.

ITA: 47, 53(1)(*i*)

His taxable capital gain on the gift to his son is: ½ ($6 – $4) × 100 = $100.

There is no taxable capital gain on the gift to his wife, because the transfer occurs at his $4 ACB   ITA: 73(1)
since no special election was filed.

(B) incorrectly excluded brokerage commissions from the ACB of his shares as: ½ ($6 – $711/200) × 100 = $122.

(C) incorrectly computes a capital gain on the gift to Mike's wife: ½ ($6 – $4) × 200 shares = $200.

(D) is incorrect, because it incorrectly computes a capital gain on the gift to his wife and does not apply the ½ fraction to compute the taxable portion of the gain: ($6 – $4) × 200 = $400.

Question 9

(C) is correct. The calculation is as follows:

	Division B income
Toronto home (no capital gain; principal residence)	—
Rental property in London, Ontario	
— Land: ½ ($100K – 50K)	$25,000
— Building: recapture = $25K – $2K	23,000
Taxable capital gain = ½ ($35K – $25K)	5,000
Mutual fund units: ½ ($60K – $12K)........................	24,000
Shares of a public company: ½ ($100K – $90K)	5,000
	$82,000

(A) incorrectly ignores recapture: $82,000 – $23,000 = $59,000.

(B) incorrectly multiplies the recapture by the ½ taxable capital gains fraction: $25,000 + ½ × $23,000 + $5,000 + $24,000 + $5,000 = $70,500.

(D) incorrectly includes a capital gain on the principal residence: $82,000 + ½ × ($840,000 – $300,000) = $352,000.

Question 10

(B) is correct, because the taxable capital gain is computed as follows: listed shares of a public corporation resident in Canada (= ½ × ($40,000 – $10,000) = $15,000) + painting (= ½ ($10,000 – $6,000) = $2,000) = $17,000.

The rental real estate in Canada and the registered retirement savings plan are specifically   ITA: 128.1(4)
exempted from the deemed disposition rules.

(A) incorrectly excludes the taxable capital gain on the painting.

(C) incorrectly includes ½ of the gain on the RRSP ($10,000).

(D) incorrectly includes a $25,000 taxable capital gain on the rental real estate in Canada.

Chapter 7 – Solutions to Exercises

Exercise 1

Step 1: Determine gain per year of ownership

	City home	*Cottage*
Par. 40(2)(b) gain		
P of D	$ 517,500	$ 375,000
ACB	(400,000)	(250,000)
Gain	$ 117,500	$ 125,000

Gain per year: $\dfrac{\$117,500}{12 \text{ years}} = \$\ 9,792$　　$\dfrac{\$125,000}{7 \text{ years}} = \$\ 17,857$

Step 2: Assignment of no-option years

In the five taxation years 2002 to 2006, Ms. Amin owned only the Regina home. Therefore, there is no option in those years but to designate the city home as her principal residence.

Step 3: Gain determined under paragraph 40(2)(b)

The gain per year of ownership for the cottage ($17,857) exceeds that for the city home ($9,792). If all seven years are assigned to the cottage, however, one year will be wasted. Hence, the city home should be designated for one of the years 2007 to 2013.

	City home	*Cottage*
Gain	$ 117,500	$ 125,000
Exemption	(68,542)[1]	(125,000)[2]
Capital gain	$ 48,958	Nil
Taxable capital gain	$ 24,479	Nil

— NOTES TO SOLUTION

[1] $\dfrac{1 + 5 + 1}{12} \times \$117,500 = \$68,542$; years designated — 2002 – 2006 and one of 2007 – 2013

[2] $\dfrac{1 + 6}{7} \times \$125,000 = \$125,000$; years designated — all but one of 2007 – 2013

Exercise 2

Step 1: Determine gain per year of ownership

	City home		*Cottage*		
P of D		$ 247,000		$ 164,000	ITA: 40(2)(b)
ACB	$ 180,000		$ 90,000		
SC	12,000	(192,000)	6,000	(96,000)	
Gain		$ 55,000		$ 68,000	

Gain per year . . . .　$\dfrac{\$55,000}{16 \text{ years}} = \$\ 3,438$　　$\dfrac{\$68,000}{11 \text{ years}} = \$\ 6,182$

Step 2: Assignment of no-option years

In the five taxation years 1998 to 2002, Peter owned only the city home. Therefore, there is no option in those years but to designate the city home as his principal residence.

Step 3: Gain determined

ITA: 40(2)(*b*)

The gain per year of ownership for the cottage ($6,182) exceeds that for the city home ($3,438). If all 11 years are assigned to the cottage, however, one year will be wasted. Hence, the city home should be designated for one of the years 2003 to 2013.

	City home	*Cottage*
Gain	$ 55,000	$ 68,000
Exemption	(24,063)[(1)]	(68,000)[(2)]
Capital gain	$ 30,937	Nil

— *NOTES TO SOLUTION*

[(1)] $\frac{1 + 5 + 1}{16} \times \$55,000 = \$24,063$; years designated — 1998 – 2002 and one of 2003 – 2013

[(2)] $\frac{1 + 10}{11} \times \$68,000 = \$68,000$; years designated — all but one of 2003 – 2013

Exercise 3

When Howard rents his home, he is deemed to have changed the use of the home and a capital gain may be triggered. However, Howard can designate the home with the appropriate number of years and should not be taxed on the gain. Under this course of action, Howard would now have a rental property from which he must declare the income less all his expenses. However, a rental loss could not be generated with capital cost allowance on the home and equipment therein.

ITA: 45(1)

ITR: 1100(15))

Alternatively, Howard could elect to defer the gain until he either sells the home or rescinds his election. Note that the CRA normally permits a retroactive election at the time of sale. In this situation, Howard would not be allowed to claim any capital cost allowance on the home or the election to be deemed not to have changed the use would be invalid.

ITA: 45(2)

Income Tax Folio
S1-F3-C2 — Principal
Residence

ITA: 45(2)

The election would permit Howard to designate his Vancouver home as his principal residence for at least four extra years depending upon whether he is self-employed or employed.

ITA: 45(2)

(A) Self-employed

Paragraph (*d*) in the definition of a "principal residence" permits Howard to designate his Vancouver home as his principal residence for four years, while it is being rented, if he elects to be deemed not to have changed the use according to paragraphs (*b*) and (*d*) of the definition.

ITA: 54
ITA: 45(2)

Howard might consider rescinding his election after the fourth year. This course of action would enable Howard to claim capital cost allowance after the fourth year subject to the loss restrictions discussed above.

(B) Employed

The Act waives the four-year restriction discussed above if Howard (or his wife) has moved at least 40 km closer to his new work location. Howard then can designate his Vancouver home as his principal residence during all the rental years if:

ITA: 54.1

(i) Howard subsequently resumes ordinary habitation of his home while employed with the same employer; or

(ii) Howard subsequently resumes ordinary habitation of his home within one year from the end of the year in which he terminates employment with that employer; or

(iii) Howard dies.

Note that "ordinarily inhabited" means any time during the year according to the CRA, but Howard cannot temporarily move back in order to qualify for this exemption.

Income Tax Folio
S1-F3-C2 — Principal
Residence

CHAPTER 7

Exercise 4

	Painting		Antique clock		Outboard motor		Gold coin	
P of D		$2,000		$1,200		$1,000		$1,000
ACB	$1,000		$1,000		$1,000		$1,000	
SC	100	(1,100)	20	(1,020)	15	(1,015)	10	(1,010)
CG (CL)		$ 900		$ 180		$ (15)		$ (10)

Net taxable capital gain:

LPP — Painting.	$ 900	
— Gold coin	(10)[1]	
	$ 890	
— ½	$ 445	
PUP — Antique clock (½ × $180)	90	
	$ 535	

— NOTE TO SOLUTION

[1] Listed personal property losses, whether current or carried-over, are applied at the full capital gain (capital loss) amount.

Exercise 5

	Cost	Proceeds	CG (CL)	Taxable amount
Listed personal property:				
Oil painting	$ 2,500	$ 1,000	$(1,500)	
Rare coin	1,300	1,000	(300)	
Bible	1,000	5,000	4,000	
			$ 2,200	
2010 LPP — CL			(1,200)[3]	
			$ 1,000	$500
Personal-use property:				
Canoe	$ 1,000	$ 1,000	Nil	
Antique car[1]	15,000	10,000	Nil [2]	
Antique chair[1]	1,000	1,200	200	
Antique table[1]	1,500	2,000	500	
			$700	350
				$850

— NOTES TO SOLUTION

[1] Antiques are not listed personal property under the definition in section 54.

[2] Losses on personal-use property assets are not allowed.

[3] Listed personal property loss carryovers are netted against capital gains, not taxable capital gains.

Exercise 6

(A) P of D 200 shares @ $25	$5,000	
ACB 200 shares @ $33[1]	$6,600	
SC	75	(6,675)
CL[2] (Superficial loss of $1,675)		Nil

(B) Adjusted cost base of shares

$$
\begin{array}{ll}
\text{50 shares @ \$33} & = \text{\$1,650} \\
\text{200 shares @ \$26} & = \quad 5,200 \\
\text{superficial loss} & \quad\quad \underline{1,675} \\
& \quad \underline{\$8,525} \div \text{250 shares} = \underline{\$34.10}
\end{array}
$$

— *NOTES TO SOLUTION*

(1)
$$
\begin{array}{ll}
\text{100 shares @ \$30} & = \text{\$3,000} \\
\text{150 shares @ \$35} & = \quad \underline{5,250} \\
& \quad \underline{\$8,250} \div \text{250 shares} = \underline{\$33}
\end{array}
$$

(2) Since Ivan acquired additional shares of Solid Investments within the 30-day period.

Exercise 7

(a) For identical properties acquired after 1971, the weighted "moving average" basis is to be used to calculate the ACB of each individual property (subsection 47(1)).   ITA: 47(1)

High Growth Co.

Date	Shares Purchased	Share Price	Adjusted Cost Base	ACB/Share
Jan. 1/07	1,000	$3.00	$ 3,070	$3.07
Jun. 5/08	3,000	2.80	8,490	
	4,000		11,560	2.89
Aug. 5/08	1,500	3.80	5,770	
	5,500		17,330	3.15
Dec. 3/09	1,000	5.10	5,220	
	6,500		22,550	3.47
May 1/10	(3,000)	3.47	(10,410)	
Nov. 8/11	1,000	5.75	5,880	
	4,500		18,020	4.00
Jan. 9/12	(1,500)	4.00	(6,000)	
	3,000		$12,020	4.00

Note: The disposition of shares has no effect on the moving average cost.

(b)

HIGH GROWTH CO. ACB:

Jan. 10/07	(20,000 × $0.25) + $200 =		$5,200
Jan. 14/07	(4,000 × $0.80) + $75 =		$3,275
Totals	24,000 shares		$8,475
May 20/13	Proceeds	$7,200	
	ACB	(8,475)	
	Broker fees	(150)	
	Capital loss	$(1,425)	
	Allowable capital loss	$(712.50)	

Exercise 8

		With Sale	
Paragraph 3(*a*)	Sources of income		ITA: 3, 5, 6, 7, 8, 9
Sections 5–8	Employment income	$23,000	
Section 9	Business income	10,000	
Paragraph 3(*b*)	Taxable capital gains		
	Sale of antique painting		
	(.50 × (29,000 – 9,000))	10,000	
Section 3	Net income for tax purposes	$43,000	

Exercise 9

Adjusted cost base:

1,000 shares @ $35	$35,000
brokerage	500
2006 — stock dividend — 50 shares (5% × 1,000) × $10	500
2008 — stock dividend — 105 shares (10% × 1,050) × $10	1,050
2010 — stock dividend — 231 shares (20% × 1,155) × $10	2,310
	$39,360

Shares (1000 + 50 + 105 + 231) = 1,386
ACB per share: $39,360 ÷ 1,386 = $28.40

Exercise 10

2012:	Capital gain allocated....................................	$ 96.37
	Taxable capital gain (½ × $96.37)	$ 48.19

The taxable capital gain of $48.19 must be included in her income for 2012.

2013:	P of D (25 units)	$ 718.00
	ACB (25 units @ $27.38[(1)])	(684.50)
	CG...	$ 33.50
	TCG (½ × $33.50)	$ 16.75

— *NOTE TO SOLUTION*

[(1)] Adjusted cost base of units:

72.788	units.......................................	$2,000.00
3.774	units @ $25.535	96.37
76.562	units.......................................	$2,096.37

Weighted average: $2,096.37 ÷ 76.562 = $27.38

Exercise 11

Doctor Wright

July 1, 2012 — acquired an option (capital property) with an adjusted cost base of $5,000.

Feb. 1, 2013 — transaction resulted in a capital loss of $3,000 (i.e., $2,000 – $5,000) and allowable capital loss of $1,500.

Doctor Holmes

Feb. 1, 2013 — acquired an option with an adjusted cost base of $2,000.

May 1, 2013   — acquired a property with an adjusted cost base and a capital cost of $102,000 ($100,000 + $2,000).

Devalued Properties Ltd.

July 1, 2012   — received business income of $5,000; not a capital gain.

May 1, 2013   — received business income of $100,000; not a capital gain. May subtract the cost of property inventory to arrive at income for tax purposes.

         — note that section 49 is not applicable if the gain is not a capital gain.

Exercise 12

(A) Since they are related by marriage, they are not at arm's length.   ITA: 251(2)(*a*), 251(6)(*b*)

(B) Since they are not considered to be related by blood, they are at arm's length.   ITA: 251(6)(*a*)

(C) Since they are still legally married, they are not at arm's length.

(D) The facts of a situation can determine that two unrelated persons are not at arm's length.   ITA: 251(1)(*b*)

Exercise 13

	James *(seller or transferor)*	*Hayden* *(purchaser or transferee)*
(A) sale at $2,000	has proceeds of $2,000 and, hence, a capital gain of $800 (i.e., $2,000 – $1,200)	deemed [par. 69(1)(*a*)] to have acquired at $1,500 resulting in potential double-counting of $500 gain
(B) sale at $1,200	deemed [par. 69(1)(*b*)] to have proceeds of $1,500 and, hence, a capital gain of $300	acquired at $1,200 resulting in potential double-counting of $300 gain
(C) gift	deemed [par. 69(1)(*b*)] to have proceeds of $1,500	deemed [par. 69(1)(*c*)] to have acquired at $1,500

Exercise 14

(A) (i) Since a gift is a transfer, the interspousal rollover would automatically deem that Alice's proceeds of disposition are equal to her adjusted cost base ($12,000), resulting in no capital gain.   ITA: 73

(ii) Alice would be subject to the income attribution rules on any dividends from the shares, because a gift would not meet the exception, since the fair market value of the property transferred exceeded the fair market value of the consideration received and an election out of the interspousal rollover was not made.   ITA: 74.1, 74.5(1)(*a*); ITA: 73(1)

(iii) Alice would also be subject to capital gains attribution for the same reason as discussed in part (A)(ii), above. There would be full capital gains attribution on all substituted property.   ITA: 74.2; IT-511R, par. 27

(B) (i) Since Alice does elect out of the interspousal rollover, the non-arm's length transfer rule, with which the transaction conforms, will apply, since the cash consideration ($15,000) was equal to the fair market value of the property transferred. A capital gain of $3,000 would be triggered.   ITA: 73(1); ITA: 69(1)(*b*)(ii)

(ii) There would be no income or capital gains attribution, because Alice has conformed with the attribution rule exception. The fair market value of the property transferred did not exceed the fair market value of the consideration received and an election out of the interspousal rollover was made.   ITA: 74.5(1)(*a*); ITA: 73(1)

(C) (i) Unless Alice elects not to have the provisions of the interspousal rollover apply, there will be no capital gain triggered on the transfer to her husband.   ITA: 73

(ii) Although Alice has received consideration (debt) with a face value ($15,000) equal to the fair market value of the property transferred, the interest rate must be at least equal to the prescribed rate at the time or a commercial rate. In addition, the Act requires that Alice elect out of the interspousal rollover. Therefore, Alice will be subject to both income and capital gains attribution.   ITA: 74.5(1)(*b*)(i); 74.5(1)(*c*)

CHAPTER 7

(D) The result would be the same as in (A), above, since the shares would be considered substituted property for a transfer of cash for no consideration.

(E) The result would be the same as in (C), above, since the shares would be considered substituted property.

Exercise 15

Capital property A

(A) If Mr. Emerson departs prior to June 1, 2013, there will be no capital gain on the capital asset which he brought from the U.S. by virtue of the 60-month short-term exemption.   ITA: 128.1(4)

(B) If he departs subsequent to June 1, 2013, there will be a taxable capital gain on ½ of the excess of the proceeds of disposition ($12,000) over the fair market value at the time of entry ($5,000), namely, $3,500.

Capital property B

(A) First, it is necessary to determine whether the capital property acquired in Canada is exempt from immediate departure tax but will be taxed on its ultimate disposition.   ITA: 2(3)

(B) If the property is not exempted then the taxpayer will be taxed at the time of exit from Canada.

Exercise 16

			2012	*2013*
Par. 3(*a*)	Income from non-capital sources (non-negative):			
	Employment income		$25,000	$30,000
	Property income		10,000	—
	Business income — other		8,000	—
			$43,000	$30,000
Par. 3(*b*)	Net taxable capital gains (non-negative):			
	Taxable capital gain — personal-use property (½ × $8,000)		$ 4,000	—
	Plus			
	Listed personal property gain	$4,000		
	Less: LPP loss carryforward — 2009	(1,000)		
	LPP loss carryback — 2013	(1,500)		
		$1,500		
	Taxable net gain — ½ thereof	750		
			$ 4,750	
	Public corporation — allowable capital loss	(4,750)	Nil[(1)]	
	— taxable capital gain			$ 4,500[(2)]
			$43,000	$34,500
Par. 3(*d*)	Losses from non-capital sources:			
	Property loss		—	(4,000)
	Business loss		—	(9,000)
	Allowable business investment loss		(3,000)[(3)]	(1,000)[(4)]
	Division B income		$40,000	$20,500

— NOTES TO SOLUTION

[(1)] Of the $6,000 allowable capital loss (½ × $12,000), $1,250 cannot be claimed in 2012 and will be carried back or forward under Division C as a "net capital loss" to be discussed in Chapter 10.

[(2)] ½ × $9,000

[(3)] ½ × $6,000

[(4)] ½ × $2,000

Chapter 8
Capital Gains: Business Related

LEARNING GOALS

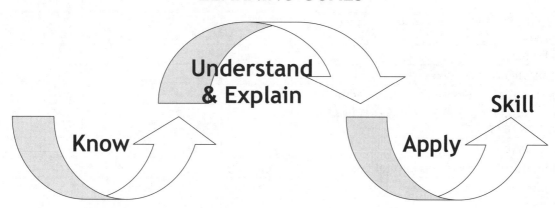

Know

By the end of this chapter you should know some provisions of the *Income Tax Act* that relate to capital gains and losses realized by business. Completing the Review Questions (¶8,800) and Multiple Choice Questions (¶8,825) is a good way to learn the technical provisions.

Understand and Explain

You should understand and be able to explain

- the difference between an income and a capital receipt;
- some of the points related to capital gains as they may arise in a business;
- bad debts on capital property.

Completing the Exercises (¶8,850) is a good way to deepen your understanding of the material.

Apply

You should be able to apply your knowledge and understanding of the rules pertaining to capital gains and losses in a way that accomplishes a client's goals. Completing the Assignment Problems (¶8,875) is an excellent way to develop your ability to apply the material in increasingly complex situations.

Chapter 8 – Learning Chart

Topic	Example Problem (✓)	Review Questions (¶8,800)	Multiple Choice (¶8,825)	Exercises (¶8,850)	Assignment Problems (¶8,875)
¶8,000 OVERVIEW OF CAPITAL GAINS IN A BUSINESS CONTEXT					
¶8,010 Avoidance					
¶8,020 Capital Receipt Versus Income Receipt Revisited		1, 2, 3, 4, 5			1
¶8,025 Primary intention					
¶8,030 Secondary intention					
¶8,035 Badges of trade or behavioural factors					
¶8,100 VARIOUS CAPITAL GAINS PROVISIONS IN A BUSINESS CONTEXT					
¶8,110 Reserves	✓		1		2
¶8,130 Adjusted Cost Base and Capital Cost					
¶8,135 Non-arm's length transfer of depreciable property					
¶8,140 Foreign Exchange Gains and Losses	✓	6		1	
¶8,150 Debts Established to be Bad Debts		12		3	
¶8,160 Part Disposition		7			
¶8,170 Replacement Property		8, 9, 10	2	2	3, 4
¶8,175 The basic deferral	✓				
¶8,180 Election for additional deferral	✓				
¶8,190 Proceeds on Disposition of Building	✓			4	5, 6
¶8,200 Disposition of Depreciable Property	✓				
¶8,210 Election on Change in Use	✓	11			
¶8,300 INCOME RECONCILIATION REVISITED	✓				7

Don't memorize — understand.
Why is the provision there?
How does it work conceptually?

Study Notes

Chapter 8 —
Discussion Notes for Review Questions

(1) The transaction will probably be an income receipt. The partnership appears to have been set up specifically to buy and hold the land. The partnership agreement seems to confirm that their primary intention was to make a profit, since the agreement specifically states how the income is to be split. If, after five years, they still have done nothing to develop the land to earn rental or other income, then it would appear to be a speculation gain and, therefore, income.

(2) The transaction will probably be an income receipt. Rachel has used her specialized knowledge, derived from her normal occupation, to make the large profit. This factor, combined with her trading history, would weigh heavily in favour of income treatment.

(3) Normally, stock market transactions are treated as capital gains or losses. However, his intention seems to be to make a profit in trading shares, thereby indicating an income receipt. He may elect to have these transactions treated as capital gains. However, Winston should be careful that the CRA does not subsequently deem him to be a "trader" and thereby revoke his election. ITA: 39(4), 39(5)

(4) The transaction would probably be an income receipt. Her primary intention is to develop the shopping centre for sale which would be an income transaction. Therefore, the sale of the land prior to development would also be an income transaction.

(5) Capital receipt (not taxable). Doug's $15,000 net winnings should not be treated as income because his actions are more in the nature of a hobby, not making a profit. If this was his business, the profits would be taxable and any losses would be deductible. IT-334R2, par. 10

(6) The loss on foreign currency is a capital loss. However, as an individual, she must deduct $200 from the loss in arriving at her capital loss. In this case her capital loss is $2,300. ITA: 39(2)(b)

(7) One way to approach this question is to assume that the cost was allocated equally to each acre. Therefore, the cost of the three acres sold would be $\frac{1}{2}$ of the original cost of the six acres or $12,000. However, the CRA, in applying the law, may consider that $12,000 is too high an amount to be "reasonably regarded as attributable to that part," since the lake-front portion would usually be more valuable than the non-lake-front property assuming that access is still available to both parcels. This, then, becomes a valuation issue. ITA: 43

(8) He has to replace the land before the end of the second taxation year after the initial year. If they finally agreed to the price in 2013 then he has until December 31, 2015 to replace the property. The initial year is the year that the "amount has become receivable as proceeds of disposition", i.e., 2012 in this case. ITA: 44(1)(c)
ITA: 44(1), 44(2)

(9) Yes. In order for these rules to apply the destroyed equipment must be either property that was stolen, destroyed or expropriated or a "former business property". The definition of former business property only refers to real property which has a common law definition of "land and building". Equipment is not included in that definition. However, if the property is stolen, destroyed or expropriated, it only has to meet the definition of "property". In this case the equipment meets this definition and the replacement property rules can apply. Of course, any potential recapture would be offset, by the normal rules, because the purchase of the new machine was made in the year of loss. ITA: 248(1) "former business property"

(10) Under the definition of "former business property" the advice she received was incorrect. This building qualifies as a former business property, since it is rented to a related corporation and is used in the related corporation's business. ITA: 248(1) "former business property", 251

(11) A change in use does not include a transfer of property from one income-producing use to another. In this case the property is being transferred from earning property income to earning business income. As a result there is no income to report on July 1 of last year when zoning was applied for. However, when the property is eventually sold an assessment will need to be done at July 1 of last year since the increase in value up to that point will be a capital gain and any profit after that date will be business income from the sale of the condominiums. ITA: 13(7), 45(1); IT-218R

(12) Ms. Chung can elect to have disposed of her note when it is established to have become uncollectible. This will result in a capital loss equal to $100,000 and the note will then have a cost equal to nil. All or some of this loss can then be carried back under Division C to be applied against the previous capital gain. If the original property disposed of was personal-use property then the debt would have been "personal-use property". Then the Act allows a capital loss only to the extent of the capital gain on the original disposition. ITA: 50(1), 54 "personal-use property"
ITA: 50(2)

Chapter 8 –
Solutions to Multiple Choice Questions

Question 1

(B) is correct. The gain is: $600,000 – $100,000 = $500,000. The maximum 2013 reserve is computed using the lesser of the percentage of proceeds payable after the end of the year ($510,000/$600,000 or 85%, in this case) and four fifths ($\frac{4}{5}$). Since the lesser amount is four fifths, the reserve is $400,000 ($\frac{4}{5}$ × $500,000) and the capital gain is therefore $100,000 ($500,000 – $400,000). The minimum taxable capital gain is therefore $50,000 ($\frac{1}{2}$).

ITA: 40(1)(*a*)

(A) is incorrect, because the capital gain must be multiplied by $\frac{1}{2}$ to compute the taxable capital gain.

(C) is incorrect, because it uses the 85% figure to compute the reserve and does not multiply the result by $\frac{1}{2}$: $500,000 – 85% × $500,000 = $75,000.

(D) is incorrect, because it uses the 85% figure to compute the reserve: $75,000 × $\frac{1}{2}$.

Question 2

(D) is the correct answer. Since the expropriation is an involuntary disposition, the property must be replaced by the later of two taxation years from the end of the taxation year in which the disposition took place or 24 months from the end of the taxation year in which the disposition took place. Since the relevant taxation year was May 31, 2014, the two-year deadline is May 31, 2016.

ITA: 44(1)(*c*)

(A) incorrectly uses the one-year deadline which is applicable for voluntary dispositions.

(B) incorrectly uses two years from the disposition date as the deadline.

(C) incorrectly uses two years from the end of the calendar year of the disposition as the deadline.

Question 3

(C) is correct

It can be concluded from the facts that Steve's primary intention was to purchase the boat and sell it for a profit. He bought the boat and immediately sold it for a profit the way a person in the boat-sales trade would act. He did not use the boat personally or rent it out for use as a capital asset. The transaction was, in some sense, related to his sporting goods retailing business which would give Steve some insight into the purchase and sale of a boat in this way. Profit from an adventure in the nature of trade is considered to be business income.

(A) incorrectly includes the profit as a taxable capital gain, rather than business income.

(B) incorrectly includes the income as income from property, rather than income from business.

(D) incorrectly includes the profit as a taxable capital gain, rather than business income from an adventure in the nature of trade.

Question 4

(A) is correct

Involuntary disposition: They replaced within the time limit.

Replacement cost	$950,000
Deferred capital gain	(50,000)
Capital cost	$900,000
Deferred recapture	(260,000)
UCC before CCA	$640,000

(B) incorrectly ignores the deferred capital gain.

(C) incorrectly ignores all deferrals.

(D) incorrectly ignores the deferred recapture.

Question 5

(B) is correct

Result	Land	Building	Total
Proceeds	$390,000	$ 360,000	$750,000
Capital cost	$150,000		
UCC		360,000	
Capital gain	$240,000		
Terminal loss		$ 0	

Subsection 13(21.1) would disallow the terminal loss by making the proceeds on the building equal to the UCC with the remaining proceeds allocated to the building.

(A) incorrectly ignores the reallocation of proceeds.

(C) incorrectly ignores the reallocation of proceeds and calculates the taxable capital gain, rather than the capital gain, as required.

(D) incorrectly calculates the taxable capital gain, rather than the required capital gain.

Chapter 8 — Solutions to Exercises

Exercise 1

Sale of asset

P of D — Canadian dollars ($10,000 × $0.99)	$ 9,900
ACB — Canadian dollars	(4,000)
CG	$ 5,900
TCG (50%)	$ 2,950

Currency

P of D — Canadian dollars received	$10,200
ACB — Canadian dollars at time of sale	(9,900)
Gain	$ 300
Exempt portion for an individual taxpayer	(200)
CG	$ 100
TCG (50%)	$ 50

Exercise 2

(A) During the years prior to the settling of the claim, Tax Processing Ltd. is deemed to own the destroyed asset. Hence the company can continue to take capital cost allowance.   ITA: 44(2)

		Class 10: 30%
UCC before the fire		$17,150
CCA — 2011	$ 5,145	
CCA — 2012	3,601	(8,746)
UCC before proceeds received		$ 8,404

(B) In the second year after the fire (2013) when the company received the proceeds, the company would be deemed to have sold the computer for $60,000 with the following tax consequences:

Taxable capital gain:

P of D		$60,000
ACB		(50,000)
CG		$10,000
TCG (½ × $10,000)		$ 5,000

Recapture:

UCC before proceeds received		$ 8,404
Less the lesser of:		
(i) Capital cost	$50,000	
		(50,000)
(ii) P of D	$60,000	
Recapture		$41,596

(C) In the year of purchase of the new computer (2015), which is within the 24-month time limit for an involuntary disposition, Tax Processing Ltd. would file an amended return for the 2013 year in which the taxable capital gain and recapture were recognized.

Taxable capital gain:
   $\frac{1}{2}$ of the lesser of:

(i) capital gain (see above)		$10,000		
(ii) P of D	$60,000			= Nil
less replacement cost	70,000	Nil		

ACB of new computer in 2014: ($70,000 – $10,000) = $60,000   ITA: 44(1)(*f*)

Recapture: ITA: 13(4)

Class 10: 30%

UCC before proceeds received (see above calculation) . . . . $ 8,404

Less deemed disposal: ITA: 13(4)(*c*)
   lesser of (i) cost ($50,000)
             (ii) P of D ($60,000) $50,000

   Less the lesser of:
         (i) the recapture
            ($8,404 – $50,000) $41,596
         (ii) replacement cost 70,000   41,596   8,404

UCC after proceeds received, Dec. 31, 2013 . . . .   Nil

Class 50: 55%

2015 addition:
   Capital cost of replacement property $70,000
   Less reduction for deferred gain 10,000   ITA: 44(1)(*f*)
   Deemed capital cost $60,000
   Less reduction for deferred recapture 41,596   ITA: 13(4)(*d*)
UCC before CCA $18,404
   CCA (55% of $\frac{1}{2}$ × $18,404) . . . . (5,061)
UCC after CCA $13,343

Exercise 3

If section 22 is not used, Mr. Flint must still include in income last year's reserve of $6,500. However, the loss of $9,000 will be regarded as a capital loss which is only fractionally deductible and can be offset only against taxable capital gains. Since Mr. Small has not included any amount as income in respect of these accounts receivable, he will not be allowed a deduction for a reserve or for bad debts because the conditions of the reserve for doubtful debts or the bad debt expense rules will not be met. If Mr. Small collects more than the $36,000 fair market value, the excess will be a capital gain and, if he collects less than $36,000, the difference will be a capital loss.   ITA: 20(1)(*l*), 20(1)(*p*)

Exercise 4

Sienna Research Inc. has what, at first, appears to be a terminal loss on the building and a capital gain on the land. When this occurs, subsection 13(21.1) reallocates the proceeds so that the terminal loss is reduced by the capital gain on the land.   ITA: 13(21.1)

Without adjustment	Land	Building	Total
Proceeds per contract	$ 895,000	$ 385,000	$ 1,280,000
ACB, UCC	345,000	438,700	
Capital gain, terminal loss	550,000	(53,700)	
With subsection 13(21.1) adjustment	**Land**	**Building**	**Total**
Adjusted proceeds	$ 841,300	$ 438,700	$ 1,280,000
ACB, UCC	345,000	438,700	
Capital gain, terminal loss or recapture	$ 496,300	Nil	

There are no tax implications on the disposition of the building. Even though the deemed proceeds are less than the capital cost of the building, a capital loss can never arise on the disposition of depreciable property.

Exercise 5

Property received as an inheritance has an ACB equal to the FMV when acquired. In this case, the ACB is $60,000.

ITA: 40(1)(a), 69(1)(c)

Mary Jane has correctly calculated her capital gain. However, she only received $50,000 of the proceeds in 2013 and the balance is not due until 2015. Therefore, she can consider claiming a reserve under subparagraph 40(1)(a)(iii), calculated as follows:

$$\frac{\text{Amount not due}}{\text{Proceeds}} \times \text{capital gain}$$

$$\frac{\$150,000}{\$200,000} \times \$140,000 = \$105,000$$

OR

$\frac{4}{5}$ of gain

$\frac{4}{5} \times \$140,000 = \$112,000$

Capital gain = $140,000 − $105,000 = $35,000

Mary Jane can claim a reserve of $105,000. This reserve will then be included in income in 2014 and a reserve calculated based on proceeds not yet due. Mary Jane must file Form T2017 with her 2013 income tax return.

Chapter 9
Other Sources of Income and Deductions in Computing Income

LEARNING GOALS

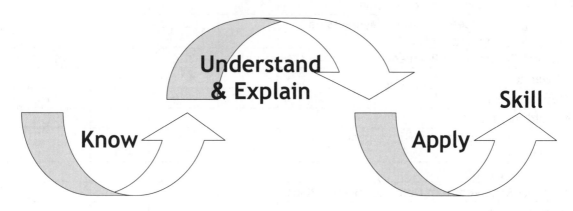

Know

By the end of this chapter you should know the basic provisions of the *Income Tax Act* that relate to other income and other deductions. Completing the Review Questions (¶9,800) and Multiple Choice Questions (¶9,825) is a good way to learn the technical provisions.

Understand and Explain

You should understand and be able to explain:

- The nature of income such as pensions, retiring allowances, support payments, and scholarships and bursaries; and
- The nature of other deductions such as RRSPs, moving expenses, child care expenses, and the disability support deduction.

Completing the Exercises (¶9,850) is a good way to deepen your understanding of the material.

Apply

You should be able to apply your knowledge and understanding of these forms of income and deductions in a way that accomplishes a client's goals. Completing the Assignment Problems (¶9,875) is an excellent way to develop your ability to apply the material in increasingly complex situations.

Chapter 9 — Learning Chart

Topic	Example Problem (✓)	Review Questions (¶9,800)	Multiple Choice (¶9,825)	Exercises (¶9,850)	Assignment Problems (¶9,875)
¶9,000 OTHER SOURCES OF INCOME					
¶9,010 Benefits in the Nature of Pensions					
¶9,015 Income splitting — Canada Pension Plan					
¶9,020 Income splitting — Pension income					
¶9,030 Retiring Allowances and Other Payments on Termination of Employment		1, 2, 17	1		5, 6, 10
¶9,040 Support Receipts and Payments		3, 4		1	
¶9,045 Overview					
¶9,050 Spousal support					
¶9,055 Child support					
¶9,060 Legal fees in connection with support payments					
¶9,070 Annuity Payments					
¶9,080 Amounts Received from Deferred Income Plans					
¶9,085 Inclusion provisions					
¶9,090 Registered education savings plan (RESP)					
¶9,095 Registered disability savings plan (RDSP)					
¶9,100 Education Assistance Payments		5			9
¶9,110 Other Inclusions		6			
¶9,120 Indirect Payments		7			
¶9,125 Overview					
¶9,130 Conditions					
¶9,135 Child Care Benefit					
¶9,140 Restrictive Covenants [Proposed]					
¶9,145 Inclusion					
¶9,150 Exceptions					
¶9,155 Schematic of the system for restrictive covenants					
¶9,200 AMOUNTS NOT INCLUDED IN COMPUTING INCOME AND EXEMPT ENTITIES					
¶9,210 Specific Examples					
¶9,220 Tax-Free Savings Account (TFSA)					1
¶9,230 Exempt Entities					
¶9,300 DEDUCTIONS IN COMPUTING INCOME					
¶9,310 Capital Element of Annuity					6
¶9,320 Registered Savings Plans				4	1, 3, 5
¶9,325 Objectives of pension reform of 1990					
¶9,330 Types of tax-assisted retirement plans		8, 9, 10			
¶9,355 Types of RRSPs					
¶9,340 Integration of limits		11, 12, 13			
¶9,345 Contribution limits for RRSPs			2	3, 6	2, 6, 10, 11
¶9,350 Definition of earned income for RRSPs			5	2	5, 6
¶9,355 Calculation of the pension adjustment (PA)					

Topic	Example Problem (✓)	Review Questions (¶9,800)	Multiple Choice (¶9,825)	Exercises (¶9,850)	Assignment Problems (¶9,875)
¶9,360 RRSP contribution room carried forward					6
¶9,365 Excess contribution		14			5
¶9,370 Contributions of property					
¶9,375 Application	✓				
¶9,380 Contributions to spousal (or common-law partner) RRSP				3	
¶9,385 Attribution on spousal (or common-law partner) RRSPs	✓			5	5
¶9,390 Withdrawals before retirement		15			
¶9,395 Home Buyers' Plan (HBP)	✓				4
¶9,400 Tax-free RRSP withdrawals for lifelong learning plan (LLP)					
¶9,405 Retirement options					
¶9,410 Registered retirement income fund (RRIFs)					
¶9,415 Treatment of RRSPs and RRIFs on death		16			
¶9,420 Transfers of Retirement Income and Sheltered Amounts					
¶9,425 Direct transfer				6	
¶9,430 Retiring allowances	✓			6	
¶9,440 Overpayments and Other Deductions					
¶9,445 Overpayments included in income					
¶9,450 Objections and appeals					
¶9,455 Legal fees to establish a right					
¶9,460 OAS clawback					
¶9,470 Moving Expenses			4, 6	7, 9	4, 7, 9, 10
¶9,475 Deductible expenditures					11
¶9,480 Flat-rate deductions by administrative practice					
¶9,485 Eligible relocation	✓				
¶9,490 Child Care Expenses			3, 5	8	4, 8, 9, 10
¶9,495 Eligibility					
¶9,500 Limitations					
¶9,505 Deduction calculation					11
¶9,510 Encouragement for parent to attend school					
¶9,515 Application	✓				
¶9,520 Disability Support Deduction	✓				
¶9,530 Expenses of Residents Absent from Canada					

Study Notes

Chapter 9 —
Discussion Notes for Review Questions

(1) The payment was made to Ms. Tang "upon or after retirement of a taxpayer from an office or employment in recognition of her long service" and as such should qualify as a retiring allowance and be included in income. An Interpretation Bulletin states that "the cessation of employment for any reason is considered as being retirement or loss of employment". Therefore, even though she quit, this amount should still qualify as a retiring allowance.

ITA: 56(1)(a)(ii), 248(1) "retiring allowance"
IT-337R4, par. 2

(2) The accumulated sick days will qualify as a "retiring allowance" and be taxed as such. However, the unused vacation days will not qualify under this definition, according to the Interpretation Bulletin, and will be taxed as employment income.

ITA: 6(3), 56(1)(a)(ii), 248(1) "retiring allowance"; IT-337R4 par. 5

(3) Since the $3,000 per month is contained in the written agreement and the $1,200 mortgage payment is part of the "allowance," the full amount should be deductible. However, the deductibility for the mortgage payment is limited to ⅕ of the original principal. In this case, ⅕ × $120,000 = $24,000. After 20 months ($24,000/$1,200), Charles will no longer be able to deduct the payments related to the mortgage and Dee will no longer have to take them into income.

ITA: 60.1(2)

(4) Under this agreement, the $500 in monthly fees paid to the financial institution will qualify as an allowance since Mark does have the discretion as to where the $500 is paid. In addition, this amount is part of the monthly spousal maintenance payment specified in the agreement.

(5) The loan would have to be included in employment income when received. Such amounts are not awards and are not subject to the rules for scholarships and research grants. As a result, neither the full exemption for scholarships nor research expenses are available as deductions. Any repayment of this repayable award is deductible provided the conditions of that paragraph are met.

ITA: 5(1), 6(3), 8(1)(n); Income Tax Folio S1-F2-C3 — Scholarships, Research Grants and Other Education Assistance
ITA: 56(1)(n), 56(1)(o)

(6) The OAS Supplement would fall into the category of "social assistance payments" since it is based on an income test. As a result, the payments are included in net income, but there is a corresponding deduction to exclude it from taxable income. The effect of these two provisions is to raise Mrs. Smith's income to a point that no one can claim her as a dependant, but at the same time not to make Mrs. Smith taxable on this amount.

ITA: 56(1)(u), 110(1)(f)

(7) The $15,000 will be taxed in Mr. Singh's hands on an indirect payment and not in Mrs. Singh's hands.

ITA: 56(2)

(8) Defined benefit pension plans are approved by and registered with the CRA. Once the CRA has agreed to the terms of the plan, the amount that the company can deduct is determined by an actuary who certifies the amount that is necessary to fund the accruing benefits of the plan.

(9) The maximum benefit that may be provided to an individual under a defined benefit plan is 2% of the individual's average best three years of remuneration times the number of years (normally a maximum of 35 years) of pensionable service, with a dollar limit of $94,383 in 2013.

(10) Under a defined benefit plan, the benefit that is to be paid is defined, usually in regard to a certain percentage of an employee's earnings in the last few years of employment, regardless of the cost to the employer or the earnings experience of the plan. The benefit that is tax-assisted is limited to an annual maximum pension of $94,383 in 2013. Under a money purchase plan, the contribution that is required by the employer and the employee is defined rather than the benefit. The retirement benefit of the employee is based on the amount accumulated in the plan at retirement and the annuity that this amount can buy at that time.

(11) The "18%" part of the limit for RRSP contributions was arrived at as follows:

(a) it is assumed that $9 of contributions buys $1 of annual pension income,

(b) pension income is limited to 2% of income per year up to an effective maximum of 35 years.

Therefore, to get $1 of pension income in the future, you will need a contribution of 18% (9 × 2%) of current income.

(12) The "$23,820" part of the RRSP limit was arrived at as follows:

(a) it is assumed that $9 of contributions buys $1 of annual pension income,

(b) pension income is limited to 2% of income per year up to an effective maximum of 35 years,

(c) the maximum pension available out of a defined benefit plan is $92,633 for 2012 (prior year),

(d) the maximum number of years that are eligible for the defined benefit calculation is normally 35 years at the 2% rate,

this amounts to $92,633/35 years = $2,647 per year. Thus, to fund the maximum pension of $92,633, a contribution of $2,647 × 9 = $23,820 is needed.

(13) The explanation is based on the fact that the two pension systems are integrated and the integration is based on how rich your pension plan is. The richness of your pension plan is determined by the Pension Adjustment calculation. For this system to work, the pension calculation has to come first. So, your maximum pension contribution is based on your current income. Then, early in the following year your pension adjustment (PA) is calculated. Finally, your RRSP limit is determined, based on your earned income and PA, both of which relate to the prior year.

(14) Using the assumptions given in the question, the calculation would be as follows:

(a) $2,000 compounded at 10% for 15 years within the RRSP minus 46% tax on withdrawal equals $4,511.

(b) $2,000 compounded at 5.4% after tax for 15 years outside the RRSP equals $4,402.

If the rate of return was only 8% the funds would have to be left in the plan for about 18.5 years:

(a) $2,000 compounded at 8% for 18.5 years within the RRSP minus 46% tax on withdrawal equals $4,488.

(b) $2,000 compounded at 4.32% after tax for 18.5 years outside the RRSP equals $4,374.

(15) The Regulations set the withholding rates based on the amount of the withdrawal — 10% of the amount if it is $5,000 or less; 20% if the amount is between $5,000 and $15,000; and 30% if the amount exceeds $15,000. The rates are one-half of these amounts in Quebec. Based on this formula, the withholdings would be 30% of $20,000 or $6,000. Instead, if she were to withdraw four payments of $5,000, then the tax withheld would amount to only 10% of $20,000 or $2,000. In both cases the $20,000 withdrawn will have to be included in her income for the year and the same amount of ultimate tax will have to be paid. The tax will have to be funded from other sources to allow for the $20,000 to be spent for the car. Alternatively, the withdrawal will have to be increased for the amount of the tax to be paid. The necessary withdrawal would be $20,000/(1 – t), where t is her marginal tax rate.   ITR: 103(4), 103(6)

(16) Since he left his RRSP to an adult child, the estate will have to pay tax on the basis that the full amount of the RRSP was included in income in the year of death. At a 50% tax rate, this will amount to $75,000 of tax which will come out of the residue or Jim's share of the estate. As a result, Kim will receive $150,000 of cash and Jim will receive the residue of the estate minus the $75,000 of tax and any other tax that may be payable. Mr. McDonald should have calculated the division of property based on the after-tax values to the estate.

(17) The following items would show up on her personal tax return:

(a) the $40,000 would be included in income as a retiring allowance;

(b) $35,000 could be deducted as a transfer of a retiring allowance in respect of pre-'96 years of service to an RRSP; and   ITA: 60(j.1)

(c) $5,000 of the $8,000 of legal fees could be deducted.   ITA: 60(o.1)

The full amount of the legal fees was deductible; however, the deduction is limited to the net of the retiring allowance less the amount transferred to the RRSP and deducted. She should have only contributed $32,000 to her RRSP from the retiring allowance.   ITA: 60(j.1)

Chapter 9 —
Solutions to Multiple Choice Questions

Question 1

(B) is the correct answer and is calculated as follows:

ITA: 60(*j*.1)

21 years employed before 1996 (1975 – 1995) × $2,000	$42,000
14 years employed before 1989 when no RPP or DPSP benefits vested (1975 – 1988) × $1,500	21,000
	$63,000

(A) incorrectly ignores the $1,500 rule for pre-89 years where RPP or DPSP benefits have not vested.

(C) incorrectly includes 1996 and 1989: 22 × $2,000 + 15 × $1,500 = $66,500.

(D) incorrectly counts 1996 to 2013 in the calculation: 39 × $2,000 + 14 × $1,500 = $99,000.

Question 2

(C) is correct. The $6,000 is calculated as follows:

The lesser of:		
the 2013 RRSP dollar limit		$23,820
18% of earned income for 2012:		
Income from employment	$44,000	
RPP contributions	1,000	
Support received	3,600	
Real estate rental income	1,400	
	$50,000 × 18%	$ 9,000
The lesser amount	$ 9,000	
minus 2012 PA	(4,000)	
add unused deduction room	1,000	
	$ 6,000	

(A) incorrectly uses $44,000 as earned income: 18% × $44,000 – $4,000 PA + $1,000 = $4,920.

(B) incorrectly excludes the unused deduction room: $9,000 – $4,000 = $5,000.

(D) incorrectly ignores the earned income calculation: $20,000 – $4,000 + $1,000 = $17,000.

Question 3

(A) is correct. The calculations are as follows:

	Meg	James	
Salary	$46,000		
Employment expenses	(2,800)		ITA: 8
Business income	—	$18,000	
Interest income	800	1,500	
Net income	$44,000	$19,500	
Earned income	$46,000	$18,000	ITA: 63

Since James has the lower net income ($19,500), he must claim the deduction, which is the least of:

(a) Eligible child care expenses: $15,000 + ($100 × 2 weeks)	$15,200
(b) Eligible children:	
$4,000 × 1 = $4,000	
$7,000 × 2 = 14,000	$18,000
(c) ⅔ × James' earned income: ⅔ × $18,000	$12,000

Since Joanne is age 17, she is not an eligible child. The deduction for the overnight camp for Susie   ITA: 63(3)
is restricted to $100 per week.

(B) is incorrect, because Meg cannot claim the deduction, since she has the higher net income.

(C) and (D) are incorrect because they are not the least amount calculated in (A) above.

Question 4

(B) is correct and is calculated as follows:

Moving van to transport household effects		$ 5,000
Travelling cost — self, spouse and two children		
Meals — flat rate ($51 × 4 persons × 5 days)	$ 1,020	
Car — flat rate (4,430 kms × $0.55)	2,437	
Hotel ($100 × 5 nights)	500	3,957
Legal fees — Vancouver house		900
Legal fees — Toronto house		1,100
Hotel costs while waiting for Vancouver house — $100 per day		
for 15 days (max.)		1,500
		$12,457

The mileage rate is determined by the province in which travel began.

(A) incorrectly excludes the legal fees on the houses and uses $3,000 as travel costs:
$12,457 − $2,000 − $3,957 + $3,000 = $9,500.

(C) incorrectly includes all the hotel costs: $12,457 + 1,500 = $13,957.

(D) incorrectly includes all the hotel costs and the house hunting trip and uses $3,000 as travel costs: $12,457 + $1,500 + $800 − $3,957 + $3,000 = $13,800.

Question 5

(D) is correct. The earned income that should be used to calculate her RRSP deduction for 2013 is   ITA: 146(1)
her 2012 earned income, which is:

	2012	
Salary	$100,000	
Taxable benefits	8,000	ITA: 6, 7
Travel expenses	(3,000)	ITA: 8
Business losses	(1,000)	
Rental income (net of expenses and CCA)	3,200	
Spousal support paid	(12,600)	
2012 Earned income	$ 94,600	ITA: 146(1)

(A) and (C) are incorrect. The earned income that should be used to calculate her child care   ITA: 63(3)
expense deduction for 2013 is $118,000:

	2013	
Salary	$110,000	
Taxable benefits	8,000	ITA: 6, 7
Earned income	$118,000	ITA: 63(3)

(A) incorrectly includes 2013 salary only ($110,000).

(C) is the 2013 net income under Division B which includes amounts for travel expenses, RPP   ITA: 63(3)
contributions, business losses, rental income and spousal support which are not part of the earned
income calculation for the child care expense deduction.

(B) is Sahar's 2013 earned income for computing her 2014 RRSP deduction: ITA: 146(1)

	2013	
Salary	$110,000	
Taxable benefits	8,000	ITA: 6, 7
Travel expenses	(2,000)	ITA: 8

Business losses	. . . .	(1,200)
Rental income (net of expenses and CCA)	. . . .	3,600
Spousal support paid	. . . .	(12,000)
Net income under Division B	. . . .	$106,400

Question 6

(D) is correct. Deductible moving costs are: ITA: 62(3)

Moving van		$2,600
Travelling costs to move Natalie and family		
Meals — flat rate ($51 × 4 persons × 3 days)	$ 612	
Car — flat rate (1,000 kms × $0.47)	470	
Hotel ($100 × 2 nights)	200	1,282
Cost of maintaining vacant former residence (maximum amount)		5,000
Cost of changing address on legal documents		100
		$8,982

(A) $25,700 incorrectly includes all expenses listed, including only $900 for travelling costs.

(B) $15,982 incorrectly includes the actual cost of maintaining the former residence (an additional $4,000) plus the $3,000 house hunting trip.

(C) $12,600 incorrectly includes all actual cost of maintaining the former residence (an additional $4,000) and uses only $900 for travel.

Chapter 9 – Solutions to Exercises

Exercise 1

The $200 monthly payments made for Ursalla's support prior to November 1st are income to Ursalla and deductions to Uriah as long as the agreement provides for their being considered as part of the agreement and the agreement makes a specific reference to subsection 56.1(3). The payments of $200 for November and December are income to Ursalla and deductions to Uriah.

ITA: 56(1)(*b*), 60(*b*)

The mortgage payments of $400 would qualify as income to Ursalla and deductions for Uriah since they are considered to be an allowance as referred to in the legislation, as long as the conditions of these provisions are met. Conceivably, if the payments are recognized in the agreement, then the conditions would be met.

ITA: 56.1(2), 56(1)(*b*), 60(*b*), 60.1(2)

The $700 monthly support payments for the children and the medical expense payments are neither income to Ursalla nor deductions for Uriah, since they are child support amounts.

ITA: 56.1(4)

Exercise 2

The definition of "earned income" is found in two places in the Act, subsections 146(1) and 63(3). The definition found in subsection 63(3) relates to child care expenses. The definition of earned income contained in subsection 146(1) is used in the calculation of the RRSP contribution limit and is quite different from the definition contained in subsection 63(3). You will note that section 146, entitled "Registered Retirement Savings Plans", appears in Division G — Deferred and Other Special Income Arrangements.

ITA: 63(3), 146(1)

The definition of "earned income" pertaining to the child care expense deduction can be seen to reflect the economic activity that the government is encouraging when taxpayers incur child care expenses. These are limited to: employment, carrying on business (in an unincorporated form), or studying where student income like a net research grant is obtained.

The definition of "earned income" pertaining to an RRSP can be seen to reflect, conceptually, a source of income that requires some amount of active involvement in the earning process, rather than a passive source, like a passive investment in stocks or bonds earning dividends or interest.

Exercise 3

The maximum amount that Don is able to deduct in respect of a spousal RRSP is his annual contribution limit, less any contributions made to his own RRSP in respect of the year.

Don's annual contribution limit for 2013 is calculated as the lesser of 18% of his 2012 earned income (i.e., $11,916 as calculated below) and the RRSP dollar limit for 2013, which is $23,820, less the PA reported by his employer in respect of 2012 of $6,084.

Don's earned income for 2012 is calculated as:

ITA: 146(1)

Employment income — Subdivision a	$68,400	
Add: RPP contribution	2,800	$71,200
Rental loss		(5,000)
Earned income		$66,200
18% thereof		$11,916

Therefore, Don is able to deduct $5,832 (i.e., $11,916 – $6,084) of RRSP contributions in 2013. Since he has already contributed $5,000 to a spousal RRSP, he can either contribute $832 to his own RRSP, or an additional $832 to the spousal RRSP for 2013.

Exercise 4

To calculate the after-tax rate of return for the first investment alternative — the bond held outside of an RRSP — you must multiply the pre-tax rate of return by $(1 - t)$. Therefore, the after-tax rate of return will be 4.4% (8% $(1 - 0.45)$), or $660. As the annual after-tax yield is reinvested at the same pre-tax 8%, the compounded yield is $8,073 (i.e., $15,000 $(1.044)^{10}$ – $150,000).

Inside the RRSP, the 8% interest compounds unhindered by tax, and in 10 years the RRSP amount grows to $17,384 (i.e., $15,000 $(1.08)^{10}$ – $15,000); however, income taxes must be paid on withdrawal from the RRSP at 45% equalling $7,823 and yielding $9,561.

The RRSP approach produces the best after-tax yield, $9,561 versus $8,073 outside the RRSP.

Exercise 5

As this was a spousal RRSP, it is subject to the three-year rule. Douglas will be required to report $6,000 as his income. Under the three-year rule, Douglas's income is the lesser of (A) and (B).

ITA: 146(1)

(A) Spousal RRSP contributions, current year $0; preceding two taxation years $6,000.

(B) RRSP withdrawn $10,000.

Donna will report the remaining $4,000 of income ($10,000 – $6,000).

While income is reported by Douglas, the income tax withholding of $2,000 remains as a credit in Donna's tax return.

Exercise 6

Mr. Reimer is able to contribute $20,900 to an RRSP for 2013 [(lesser of 18% of his earned income from 2012 (i.e., 18% of $120,000 = $20,900 and $23,820) less his 2012 PA of $700]. He may make this annual contribution to either his own or a spousal RRSP, as long as the total of the contributions does not exceed $20,900. These contributions may be made in the year or within 60 days of December 31, 2013.

He does not have to include the lump-sum transfer from his RPP in his income nor does he get an offsetting deduction, as long as it is eligible to be transferred.

ITA: 147.3(4), 147.3(9)

Mr. Reimer is able to transfer $24,000 to his RRSPs in respect of his retiring allowance. Since all of his employer's contributions have vested, he is able to contribute $2,000 for each of the 12 pre-'96 years of employment, including the part year for 1984. Since he is able to make such a transfer in the year or within 60 days of the year, he may make an additional contribution of $4,000 ($24,000 less his initial contribution of $20,000) in the first 60 days of 2014 and he will be able to deduct the full $24,000 in his 2013 return.

ITA: 60(j.1)

Exercise 7

Allowable moving expense deduction

(A) 2013

Travelling cost — air fare	$ 1,300	ITA: 62(3)(*a*)
Household effects — transporting	1,000	ITA: 62(3)(*b*)
Selling costs of Vancouver residence		ITA: 62(3)(*e*)
— legal fees	500	
— real estate commission	10,000	
Allowable purchase cost of Montreal residence		ITA: 62(3)(*f*)
— legal fees	1,000	
— Quebec transfer tax	300	
Total potential deductions	$14,100	
Less		
Amount paid by the employer not included income	$ 5,000	ITA: 62(1)(*c*)
	$ 9,100	
Deduction restricted to income from new work location — 2013	$ 7,000	ITA: 62(1)(*f*)

(B) 2014

Balance deductible from income from the new location only in 2014	2,100	ITA: 62(1)
	$ 9,100	

Exercise 8

This problem situation does not involve a single parent attending a qualifying education program or both parents attending a qualifying education program at the same time, as the legislation requires. Therefore, the limits for these situations are not applicable.   ITA: 63(2.2) ITA: 63(2.3)

Cathy's maximum deduction is the lesser of: ITA: 63

    (A) the least of:
       (i) amount paid in the year
          ($200 × 52) $10,400
       (ii) 1 × $4,000 = $ 4,000
           2 × $7,000 = $14,000 . . . . . $18,000
       (iii) $2/3$ × earned income
           ($2/3$ × ($47,000
            + $4,000)) $34,000
       least amount . . . . $ 10,400

    (B) the sum of:
       (i) $175 × 2 = $350
       (ii) $100 × 1 = 100
                 $450 × 30 weeks = $13,500
      Lesser amount $10,400

Charles' maximum deduction is the least of: ITA: 63

    (a) $200 × 52 weeks = $10,400
    (b) 1 child × $4,000 = $ 4,000
       2 children × $7,000 = $14,000 $18,000 $10,400
    (c) $2/3$ × earned income ($23,850)[1] = $15,900
  minus amount deducted by Cathy   10,400
                                   Nil

— *NOTE TO SOLUTION*

    [1] Earned income
      Gross salary $23,000
      Taxable benefits   850
      Scholarship (fully exempt)   Nil
                       $23,850

Note that earned income for child care expenses is defined differently than earned income for a registered retirement savings plan.   ITA: 63(3), 146(1)

Exercise 9

Net employment income in new location		$ 5,600

ITA: 62(3)(f)

Moving Expenses:

Transportation	$ 3,100
Travelling	3,000
Hotel and Meals ($2,500 × 15/20)	1,875
Storage fees	1,250
Lease cancellation fee	1,200
Legal fees + taxes for new residence	N/A
	$10,425

Moving allowance	4,000	(6,425)
Carryforward of moving expenses to following year		$ 825

Eligible moving expenses incurred in the year are $6,425. However, the maximum deduction is limited to net employment income of $5,600 and $825 is carried forward and available for a deduction in the following year.

Note that the legal fees incurred on the purchase of the new residence are not deductible because a former residence was not sold as a result of the move.   ITA: 62(3)(*f*)

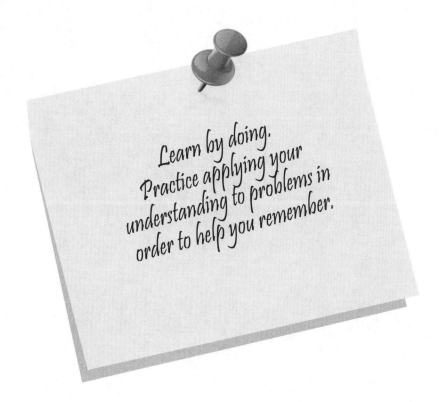

Learn by doing. Practice applying your understanding to problems in order to help you remember.

Chapter 10
Computation of Taxable Income and Taxes Payable for Individuals

LEARNING GOALS

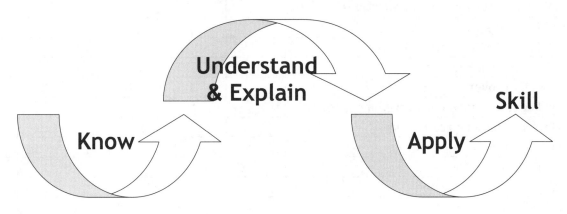

Know

By the end of this chapter you should know the basic provisions of the *Income Tax Act* that relate to the calculation of taxable income and taxes payable for individuals. Completing the Review Questions (¶10,800) and Multiple Choice Questions (¶10,825) is a good way to learn the technical provisions.

Understand and Explain

You should understand and be able to explain how taxable income is computed. With this base you should then understand and be able to explain how federal tax is calculated and how the many refundable and non-refundable tax credits are determined. Completing the Exercises (¶10,850) is a good way to deepen your understanding of the material.

Apply

You should be able to apply your knowledge and understanding of the determination of taxable income and tax liability in a way that accomplishes a client's goals. Completing the Assignment Problems (¶10,875) is an excellent way to develop your ability to apply the material in increasingly complex situations.

Chapter 10 — Learning Chart

Topic	Example Problem (✓)	Review Questions (¶10,800)	Multiple Choice (¶10,825)	Exercises (¶10,850)	Assignment Problems (¶10,875)
¶10,000 COMPUTATION OF TAXABLE INCOME FOR AN INDIVIDUAL					
¶10,005 Calculation of Taxable Income				1, 4, 16	1, 2, 6
¶10,010 Miscellaneous Division C Deductions			1, 4		
¶10,015 Employee stock options	✓				3
¶10,020 Deduction for certain receipts					
¶10,025 Home relocation loan	✓				3
¶10,030 Loss Carryovers		1		2, 3	2, 3, 4, 5
¶10,032 Legislative intent and government policy					
¶10,035 Non-capital loss carryovers					
¶10,040 Net capital loss carryovers	✓				
¶10,045 Farm loss					
¶10,060 Capital Gains Deduction					
¶10,061 Historical Overview					
¶10,065 The qualified farm property CGD					
¶10,066 The qualified fishing property CGD					
¶10,070 Ordering of Division C Deductions					
¶10,075 General ordering rules for Division C					
¶10,080 Ordering of section 111 loss carryovers	✓				
¶10,090 Taxable Income of Non-Residents					
¶10,100 COMPUTATION OF TAX FOR INDIVIDUALS					
¶10,110 Basic Computation of Tax					
¶10,115 Tax rates					
¶10,120 Annual indexing adjustment					
¶10,125 Overview of tax credit and tax calculation system					
¶10,130 Provincial and territorial tax					
¶10,135 Marginal tax rates		2, 3, 4		12, 13	
¶10,140 Section 118 Tax Credits			2, 4	5, 6, 7, 16	7, 9, 15
¶10,145 Married or common-law partnership credit					
¶10,150 Equivalent-to-married status for wholly dependent person credit					8
¶10,155 Child amount (Child tax credit)					
¶10,160 Single status — Basic personal tax credit					
¶10,165 Caregiver credit for in-home care of relative					
¶10,170 Infirm dependant credit					
¶10,173 Family caregiver tax credit					
¶10,175 Additional amount					
¶10,180 Age credit					
¶10,185 Pension income amount					
¶10,190 Canada employment credit					
¶10,195 Summary of personal tax credits	✓				

Topic	Example Problem (✓)	Review Questions (¶10,800)	Multiple Choice (¶10,825)	Exercises (¶10,850)	Assignment Problems (¶10,875)
¶10,200 Adoption Expense Tax Credit					
¶10,210 Public Transit Passes Credit					
¶10,220 Children's Fitness Credit					
¶10,222 Children's Arts Tax Credit					
¶10,225 First-Time Home Buyers' Credit and Disability Home Purchase Credit					
¶10,227 Volunteer Firefighters Tax Credit					
¶10,230 Charitable Gifts Credit					
¶10,235 Basic rules					
¶10,240 Income limit and carryforward					
¶10,245 Total charitable gifts		5			
¶10,250 Gifts of publicly traded securities					
¶10,255 Total cultural gifts					
¶10,260 Tickets to events					
¶10,265 Total Crown gifts					
¶10,270 Total ecological gifts					
¶10,275 First-time donor's super credit					
¶10,280 Medical Expense Credit					9, 10
¶10,285 Calculation of the credit					
¶10,290 Medical expenses	✓				
¶10,295 Notch provision for dependants	✓				
¶10,300 Credit for Mental or Physical Impairment (Disability Tax Credit)					9
¶10,305 Amount of and conditions for impairment credit					
¶10,310 Transfer of impairment credit					
¶10,320 Tuition, Education, and Textbook Credits			3	8	7, 12, 13, 14
¶10,325 Tuition fees					
¶10,330 Education credit					
¶10,335 Textbook credit					
¶10,340 Carryforward					
¶10,345 Transfer of tuition, education, and textbook credits to spouse and parent and grandparent	✓				
¶10,350 Credit for interest on student loans					
¶10,360 Credit for Employment Insurance Premiums and CPP Contributions		6			7
¶10,370 Transfer of Unused Credits to Spouse or Common-law Partner	✓			9	
¶10,380 Dividend Tax Credit and Subsection 82(3) Election					
¶10,385 Dividend tax credit		3	4		
¶10,390 Election to transfer dividends to spouse				10	11
¶10,400 Credits for Part-Year and Non-Residents				15	
¶10,410 Ordering of Credits					

Topic	Example Problem (✓)	Review Questions (¶10,800)	Multiple Choice (¶10,825)	Exercises (¶10,850)	Assignment Problems (¶10,875)
¶10,420 Income Not Earned in a Province					
¶10,430 Credit for Employment Outside Canada		7			
¶10,440 Refundable Goods and Services Tax/ Harmonized Sales Tax (GST/HST) Credit	✓				14
¶10,450 Refundable Medical Expense Supplement					10
¶10,460 Refundable Canada Child Tax Benefit					14
¶10,470 Working Income Tax Benefit (WITB)					
¶10,475 Overview	✓				
¶10,480 WITB supplement for persons with disabilities					
¶10,485 WITB prepayment					
¶10,490 Foreign Tax Credits				11	
¶10,500 Federal Political Contribution Tax Credit					
¶10,510 Tax on Old Age Security Benefits	✓				15
¶10,520 Tax Reduction on Retroactive Lump-Sum Payments					
¶10,530 Application of Rules for Computation of Tax and Credits	✓				
¶10,540 Minimum Tax			5	12, 14	16
¶10,545 Minimum amount					
¶10,550 Adjusted taxable income					
¶10,555 Basic exemption					
¶10,560 Basic minimum tax credit					
¶10,565 Minimum tax carryforward					
¶10,570 Impact of the minimum tax	✓				

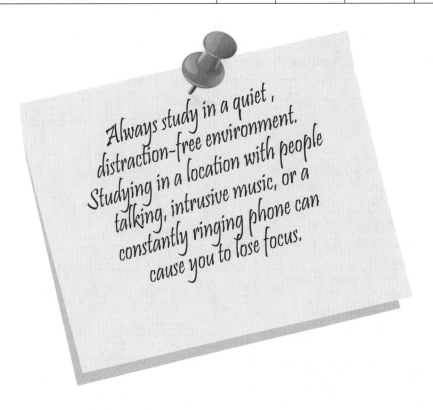

Always study in a quiet, distraction-free environment. Studying in a location with people talking, intrusive music, or a constantly ringing phone can cause you to lose focus.

Study Notes

Chapter 10 —
Discussion Notes for Review Questions

(1) There is no ordering that is required to be followed when choosing among the different kinds of losses, except that the oldest losses are always applied first. Generally, the rule of thumb is that the most restricted losses are claimed first. The factors that would have to be taken into account in making this decision are as follows:

ITA: 111(3)(b)

(a) Does she have the kind of income needed to offset the losses? She would need net taxable capital gains to offset net capital losses.

(b) Which losses are going to expire first? Net capital losses can be carried back three taxation years and forward indefinitely and non-capital losses can be carried back three taxation years and forward twenty taxation years.

(c) What is the likelihood that she will realize the type of income needed in future years to offset those losses she decides not to claim this year? If she uses up her non-capital losses this year and not her net capital losses, what is the likelihood that she will have a taxable capital gain in the future?

(2) His marginal tax rate on dividend income would be:

Cash dividend	$10,000
Gross-up 38%	3,800
Taxable dividend	$13,800
Federal tax @ 29%	$ 4,002
Dividend tax credit @ $^6/_{11}$ × $3,800	(2,073)
Basic federal tax	$ 1,929
Provincial tax @ 17% of $13,800	2,346
Provincial dividend tax credit @ $^5/_{11}$ × $3,800	(1,727)
Total tax	$ 2,548

His marginal tax rate on these dividends is $2,548/$10,000 = 25.48%.

(3) His marginal tax rate on interest income would be:

Interest earned	$10,000
Federal tax @ 29%	$ 2,900
Provincial tax @ 17% of $10,000	1,700
Total tax	$ 4,600

His marginal tax rate on this interest is $4,600/$10,000 = 46%.

(4) Her marginal tax rate on capital gains would be:

Capital gain	$10,000
Taxable capital gain (½)	$ 5,000
Federal tax @ 29%	$ 1,450
Provincial tax @ 17% of $5,000	850
Total tax	$ 2,300

Her marginal tax rate on this capital gain is $2,300/$10,000 = 23%.

(5) The Act allows an artist to designate the proceeds of the piece of art that is not established to be cultural property at anywhere between the cost and the fair market value, in this case between $200 and $8,000. Looking at the two alternatives:

ITA: 118.1(7)

(a) if she designates $200 she will report no net income since her proceeds equal her cost. However, she will receive a donation receipt for $200 which is worth a federal credit of $200 × 15% = $30;

(b) if she designated $8,000 as the proceeds, she would report an additional $7,800 in income and pay an additional federal tax of $7,800 × 15% = $1,170. However, she will also receive a donation receipt for $8,000 which will generate a federal credit of $200 × 15% + $7,800 × 29% = $2,292.

On a net basis she would have a net federal credit from this alternative of $2,292 – $1,170 = $1,122.

On a net basis, she would be further ahead to designate the full $8,000 as the proceeds. She would receive an incremental benefit of $1,092 (i.e., $1,122 – $30) plus the provincial tax effect.

If the work of art is a cultural gift, the Act deems the artist to have received proceeds of disposition equal to the cost. However, the legislation would entitle the artist to a credit based on the certified fair market value of the work. As a result, no income needs to be reported on the disposition and a credit based on the full value is available.

ITA: 118.1(7.1)
ITA: 118.1(1)

(6) Patricia will receive a personal credit of 15% times the maximum CPP contribution for the year of $2,356. The excess $2,356 will be refunded to her since it will be an overcontribution.

ITA: 118.7

(7) Given the short-term nature of the move, the fact that his family does not move with him, and the fact that he will be moving back to Canada within 15 months indicate that he will continue to be a resident of Canada for income tax purposes and he will be taxable in Canada on his worldwide income. However, since he is a Canadian resident, was employed by a Canadian resident corporation and was working outside Canada on a construction contract for more than six months, Mr. Jones will be entitled to a tax credit. The credit for 2013 will be equal to:

ITA: 122.3

the lesser of:
(a) $80,000 × 365/365 = $80,000
(b) 60% × $120,000 = $72,000   } $72,000
divided by $120,000
times the tax otherwise payable.

As a result, he will receive a credit for $72,000/$120,000 or 60% of his tax otherwise payable on his personal tax return for 2013. In 2014, the same calculation would be made prorating the $80,000 for the 90-day period abroad and reducing the percentage applied from 60% to 40%.

ITA: 122.3(1.02)

CHAPTER 10

Chapter 10 —
Solutions to Multiple Choice Questions

Question 1

    (C) is correct. Since BL is a CCPC and is at arm's length with Brad, the stock option benefit will be included in Brad's income in the year of sale (along with Brad's taxable capital gain). The stock option benefit is $3,000 (($5 – $2) × 1,000). Brad's taxable capital gain is $1,000 (½ × ($7 – $5) × 1,000). Since Brad held the shares for at least two years, he can claim a Division C deduction of $1,500 (½ × his $3,000 option benefit).

ITA: 7(1.1)

ITA: 110(1)(*d*.1)

    (A) incorrectly includes the section 7 benefit in 2011 and ignores the deduction.

    (B) incorrectly includes the employment benefit and the incorrectly calculated Division C deduction (at ¼ of the $3,000 benefit) in 2011.

ITA: 7, 110(1)(*d*.1)

    (D) incorrectly ignores the Division C deduction.

ITA: 110(1)(*d*.1)

Question 2

    (C) is correct and is calculated as follows:

Basic	$11,038		
Age: $6,854 – 15% × ($47,760 – $34,562)	4,874		
Pension	2,000		
Employment	1,117		
	$19,029 × 15% =	$2,854	
Dividend tax credit: 6/11 × $760		415	
		$3,269	

ITA: 118(1)(*c*)
ITA: 118(2)
ITA: 118(3)
ITA: 8(10)

ITA: 121

    (A) incorrectly ignores the dividend tax credit: ($11,038 + $4,874 + $2,000 + $1,117) × 15% = $2,854.

ITA: 121

    (B) incorrectly ignores the pension credit and the employment credit: ($11,038 + $4,874) × 15% + $415 = $2,802.

ITA: 118(3), 118(10)

    (D) incorrectly ignores the income restriction on the age credit: ($11,038 + $6,854 + $2,000 + $1,117) × 15% + $415 = $3,566.

ITA: 118(2)

Question 3

    (C) is correct. Shabir's net income and taxable income is calculated as follows:

Scholarship income (exempt)	$	Nil
Employment income		11,000
Moving expenses:		
to McGill University (limited to scholarship income)		Nil
to Toronto		(200)
		$10,800

    Since Shabir's income is less than $11,038, his entire tuition fee, education, and textbook credits can be transferred to his parent (up to a maximum of $5,000).

ITA: 118.9

Tuition fee	$3,900	
Education credit: 8 × $400	3,200	
Textbook credit: 8 × $65	520	
	$7,620; max. $5,000 × 15% =	$750

    (A) incorrectly computes the credit base on tuition only ($3,900 × 15% = $585).

    (B) incorrectly includes the scholarship in income and claims the full moving costs to McGill: $1,500 + $11,000 – $500 – $200 = $11,800. Since this income exceeds $11,038 ($11,800 – $11,038 = $762), then $4,238 ($5,000 – $762) can be transferred resulting in a credit of $636 to a parent.

    (D) incorrectly ignores the $5,000 limit: $7,620 × .15 = $1,143.

Question 4

(A) is correct.

Salary	$ 60,000
Canadian dividends	20,000
Gross-up 38%	7,600
Stock option benefit	200,000
Taxable capital gain (½ × $200K)	100,000
Net income	$387,600
Stock option deduction (½ × $200K)	(100,000)
Taxable income	$287,600

Tax:	
first $135,054	$ 28,580
balance @ 29% of $152,546	44,238
Basic personal amount ($11,038 × 15%)	(1,656)
Transfer of tuition, education, and textbook credits (15% × $5,000 × 3)	(2,250)
Employment (15% of $1,117)	(168)
Dividend tax credit (⁶/₁₁ × $7,600)	(4,145)
Federal tax	$ 64,599

(B) incorrectly omits the gross-up on the dividend and the dividend tax credit:
$64,599 – (29% × $7,600) + $4,145 = $66,540

(C) incorrectly omits the dividend tax credit: $64,599 + $4,145 = $68,744

(D) incorrectly omits the stock option deduction: $64,599 + 29% × $100,000 = $93,599

Question 5

(A) is correct.

Taxable income	$287,600
Add:	
30% of capital gain	60,000
⅗ of the stock option deduction	60,000
Deduct:	
Gross-up on dividends	(7,600)
Adjusted taxable income	$400,000
Less: Basic Exemption	(40,000)
Net	$360,000
Minimum tax before minimum tax credit ($360,000 × 15%)	$ 54,000
Basic personal amount ($11,038 × 15%)	(1,656)
Employment ($1,117 × 15%)	(168)
	$ 52,176

(B) incorrectly deducts the $2,250 transfer of tuition and education credits:
$52,176 – $2,250 = $49,926.

(C) incorrectly omits the adjustment to add back the stock option deduction:
$52,176 – 15% × $60,000 = $43,176.

(D) incorrectly omits the adjustment to add back the tax-free portion of the capital gain and the stock option deduction: $52,176 – 15% × $120,000 = $34,176.

CHAPTER 10

Chapter 10 — Solutions to Exercises

Exercise 1

(a) Property income

(b) Business income

(c) Employment income

(d) Employment income

(e) Business income

(f) Property income

(g) Employment income

(h) Business income

(i) Business income

(j) Other income

(k) Property income

(l) Employment income

ITA: 3

Exercise 2

(A)	2011	2012	2013	
Income from non-capital sources (≥0):				ITA: 3(a)
Property income	$ 1,000	Nil	$ 2,000	
Net taxable capital gains (≥0).				ITA: 3(b)
Taxable capital gains				
(see Schedule 1, Part (A), below)	$18,750	$25,000	$ 5,625	
Allowable capital losses	(7,500)	Nil	(11,250)	
	$11,250	$25,000	Nil	
Total income	$12,250	$25,000	$ 2,000	ITA: 3(b)
Losses from non-capital source and ABIL:				ITA: 3(d)
Property loss	Nil	$(7,000)	Nil	
ABIL	Nil	(15,000)	Nil	
Division B income	$12,250	$ 3,000	$ 2,000	ITA: 3(e)
(B) Deduct: Net capital losses (see Schedule 1, Part (B) below for maximum)	(1,212)	Nil	Nil	
Non-capital losses	Nil	Nil	Nil	
Taxable income (max. equal to personal tax credit base)	$11,038	$ 3,000	$ 2,000	

SCHEDULE 1

	2011	2012	2013
(A) Net taxable capital gains			
Taxable capital gains (TCG)	$18,750	$ 25,000	$ 5,625
Allowable capital losses (ACL)	(7,500)	—	(11,250)
	$11,250	$ 25,000	$ (5,625)

ITA: 111(1)(b),
111(1.1)(a),
111(8)(a)

(B) Net capital losses

	2011	2012	2013
Lesser of:			
(i) Net TCGs for the year	$11,250	$25,000	Nil

(ii) Total of adjusted
      net CLs .... $ 7,500 $ 5,632 $5,632

      Lesser amount ..... $7,500 $5,632   Nil

(C) Loss continuity schedule

	2009	2013	Total
Net CL	$ 7,500	$5,625	$13,125
Utilized in 2011	(1,212)	N/A	(1,212)
Available in 2014............	$ 6,288	$5,625	$11,913

Note: Only $1,212 of the Net CL was claimed in 2011 to bring taxable income down to equal the personal credit of $11,038. No Net CL was claimed in 2012 or 2013 as income was below the personal credit level.

Exercise 3

Taxpayer computation of net income for tax purposes	**A**	**B**	ITA: 3, 111
Paragraph 3(*a*)			
Section 5 Employment income	$45,000	$15,000	
Section 12 Interest income	2,000		
Section 9 Net income from a business	5,000		
Paragraph (*d*) Current-year business loss		(15,000)	
Net income for tax purposes	$52,000	0	
Non-capital loss carryforward			
Current business loss ($18,000) – loss utilized ($15,000) =		$(3,000)	

Charitable donations are a non-refundable tax credit and reduce taxes payable.

Exercise 4

DIVISION B

Par. 3(*a*)	*Subdivision a*			
	Sec. 5	Salary	$ 60,000	
	Par. 6(1)(*a*)	Taxable benefits	3,000	
	Par. 6(1)(*c*)	Director's fees	5,000	$ 68,000
	Less:			
	Par. 8(1)(*i*)	Professional engineering fees	$ 300	
	Par. 8(1)(*m*)	Registered pension plan contributions	4,000	4,300
				$ 63,700
	Subdivision b			
	Sec. 9	Business income — share of partnership tax profits	$ 10,000	
	Par. 12(1)(*c*)	Canadian bank interest	3,000	13,000
	Subdivision d			
	Par. 56(1)(*a*)	Retiring allowance........................		20,000
		Total par. 3(*a*) income		$ 96,700
Par. 3(*b*)	*Subdivision c*			
	Par. 38(*a*)	Taxable capital gain.................	$ 20,000	
	Par. 38(*b*)	Allowable capital loss	(2,000)	18,000
				$114,700
Par. 3(*d*)	*Subdivision b*			
	Ssec. 9(2):	Rental loss		
		Rental revenue	$ 25,000	
		Less: Expenses		

Par. 20(1)(*c*)	Mortgage interest	(23,000)	
Par. 18(1)(*a*)	Taxes and insurance	(4,500)	
Par. 18(1)(*a*)	Maintenance	(1,500)	(4,000)

Division B income		$110,700
Par. 111(1)(*a*)　Non-capital loss	$ 4,000	
Par. 111(1)(*b*)　Net capital loss	5,000	(9,000)
Taxable income		$101,700

Federal tax after credits
　Tax before credits . . . . 　$ 19,906

Sec. 118(1)	Personal credits	(3,312)
Sec. 118(10)	Canada employment credit	(168)
Sec. 118.7	CPP contributions credit	(353)
Sec. 118.7	EI premium credit	(134)
Sec. 118.5	Tuition credit	(68)
Sec. 118.6	Education and textbook credit transfer	(80)
Sec. 118.1	Charitable donation credit	(550)

　　　Basic federal tax . . . . 　$ 15,241

Exercise 5

(A)　Personal tax credits　　　　　　　　　　　　　　　　　　　　　　　　　　　　　ITA: 118

Basic personal tax credit base	$11,038	ITA: 118(1)(*a*)
Dolly's tax credit base: $11,038 – $3,000	8,038	ITA: 118(1)(*a*)
Child amount ($2,234 × 2)	4,468	ITA: 118(1)(*b*.1)
Don:[1] over 18 years old and not infirm	Nil	ITA: 118(1)(*d*)
Dave: caregiver credit base:[2] $6,530 – ($3,200 – $15,334)	6,530	ITA: 118(1)(*d*)
Mother's tax credit base:[3] $6,530 – ($7,000 – $6,548): claim	Nil	ITA: 118(1)(*d*)
Mother: caregiver credit base (with family caregiver amount)[3]	6,530	ITA: 118(1)(*c*.1)
Total tax credit base[4]	$36,604	
Total personal tax credits @ 15%	$ 5,491	

— *NOTES TO SOLUTION*

　[1]　Don's father may claim the transferred tuition fee, education, and textbook tax credits, since　ITA: 118.9(1)
Don's income tax will be completely offset by his basic personal tax credit.

　[2]　The infirm dependant tax credit would have the same base of $6,530 (with the family caregiver
amount), but a lower threshold of $6,548.

　[3]　The infirm dependant tax credit (with the family caregiver amount) would have a lower base of
$6,078 (i.e., $6,530 – ($7,000 – $6,548)).

　[4]　An impairment tax credit of $1,155 ($7,697 × 15%) is also available in respect of the mother　ITA: 118.3(1)
and son Dave, if their impairment is certified by a medical doctor.

Exercise 6

(A) Optimum personal tax credit:

Jack's tax credit base:

— Jack	$11,038	ITA: 118(1)(*a*)
— Jill: $11,038 – $10,600	438[(1)]	
— ETM	Nil[(2)]	ITA: 118(1)(*b*)
	$11,476	
Jack's tax credit @ 15%	$ 1,721	

Jill's tax credit base:

— Jill	$11,038	ITA: 118(1)(*b*)(i)
— one of Jill's children[(3)]	11,038	ITA: 118(1)(*b*)(ii)
— child amount[(4)]	4,468	ITA: 118(1)(*b*.1)
	$26,544	
Jill's tax credits @ 15%	$ 3,982	

(B) In 2014, Jack and Jill could each claim a basic personal tax credit. Neither is eligible for the equivalent-to-married tax credit.

— *NOTES TO SOLUTION*

[(1)] All income of a spouse during the year of marriage is used in determining a spousal tax credit.   ITA: 118(1)(*a*)(ii)

[(2)] Jack does not have the option of claiming either of the children as ETM since they were not related to nor living with him at the time during the year that he was single.   ITA: 118(1)(*b*)

[(3)] Jill has the option of claiming either Jack (however, his income is too high in this fact situation) or one of her children as ETM since she falls into both paragraphs. It would appear that Jack and Jill cannot both claim each other at the same time according to a court decision which determined that spouses cannot simultaneously support each other. (See *The Queen v. Robichaud.*)   ITA: 118(1)(*a*)   ITA: 118(1)(*b*); IT-513R, par. 27   83 DTC 5265 (F.C.T.D.)

[(4)] It appears from the legislation that Jill can claim both children for the child amount even though she is claiming one as equivalent-to-married.

Exercise 7

$300 contribution is an employment deduction.   ITA: 8(1)(*m*)

$800 is pension income.   ITA: 56(1)(*a*)

A pension credit is not available since the amount is not from a life annuity, as required in the definition of "qualified pension income".   ITA: 118(3), 118(7)

Exercise 8

(A) Division B and taxable income	$5,000
Federal tax @ 15% of $5,000	$ 750
Less: basic personal tax credit	(1,656)
Federal tax payable	Nil
Credits available for transfer:	
Tuition fee tax credit (15% of $1,800)	$ 270
Education tax credit (15% of $400 × 8)	480
Textbook tax credit (15% of $65 × 8)	78
Total	$ 828

CHAPTER 10

Amount deductible by qualified transferee:

Lesser of:

(a) $750

(b) student's tuition fee, education, and textbook tax credits — $828   } $ 750

Less: amount of tax credit required to reduce student's tax paya-
ble to nil . . . .   Nil

Net amount deductible by transferee . . . . $ 750

Note that the Employment Insurance premium and CPP contribution tax credits cannot be transferred.

(B) If Sammy was married, his wife could deduct the $750 in tuition fee, education, and textbook tax credits, since Sammy's federal tax, after his personal tax credit, is nil. Sammy's parent or grandparent can deduct all or some part of the $750 as a tax credit, if Sammy so designates.   ITA: 118.7

Exercise 9

Tax payable by Tina:

Division B income and taxable income		$ 9,755
Federal tax 15% of $9,755		$ 1,463
Less: basic personal tax credit	$1,656	
other tax credits (age ($1,028), pension (15% of $350))	1,081	(2,737)
Federal tax payable		Nil
Transferable tax credits available:		
Age credit (15% of $6,854)		$1,028
Pension credit (15% of $350)		53
Total credits available to Tina's husband		$1,081
Less: federal tax payable net of basic personal tax credit ($1,456 – $1,656)		—
		$1,081

Exercise 10

Income increased by grossed-up dividend ($900 × 1.38)			$1,242
Increase in federal tax @ 29% of $1,242			$ 360
Less increase in tax credits:			
Married credit with election [15% of ($11,038 – nil)]	$ 1,656		
Married credit without election [15% of ($11,038 – $1,242)]	(1,469)	$ 187	
Dividend tax credit ($^6/_{11}$ × $342)		187	374
Net federal tax reduction			$ 14

ITA: 82(3)

Therefore, the election should be made in this case, although it is marginal.   ITA: 82(3)

Exercise 11

Federal foreign tax credit

lesser of:

(i) $\underline{\$225}$

(ii) $\dfrac{\$1{,}500}{\$156{,}800 - \$6{,}000} \times (\$33{,}146 + \$62^*) = \underline{\$330}$ $\Big\}$ $\underline{\$225}$

* The dividend tax credit is equal to 6/11 of the gross-up of $114 (i.e., 0.38 × $300).

Exercise 12

	Regular Part I Tax			*Minimum Tax*	
(A) $100 interest	($100 × .29)		$\underline{\$29}$	($100 × .15)	$\underline{\$15}$
(B) $100 cash dividend					
($138 grossed up)	$138 × .29	$40		($100 × .15)	$\underline{\$15}$
	DTC	(21)	$\underline{\$19}$		
(C) $100 capital gains					
($50 taxable capital					
gains)	($50 × .29)		$\underline{\$15}$	($50 + $30) × .15	$\underline{\$12}$

Exercise 13

Jacob's marginal tax rate is 41% (26% + 15%) where the provincial marginal tax rate is assumed to be 15%.

ITA: 117(2), 120

Exercise 14

Taxable income		$ 98,200
Add: CCA loss on resource property shelter		103,200
		$201,400
Less: gross-up of dividends		(11,400)
Adjusted taxable income		$190,000
Less: basic exemption		(40,000)
		$150,000
Minimum tax before minimum tax credit (15% of $150,000)		$ 22,500
Less basic minimum tax credits:		
Basic personal (15% × $11,038)	$1,656	
Employment Insurance premiums	134	
CPP contributions	353	
Employment	168	2,311
Minimum amount		$ 20,189

Betty's Part I tax will be her minimum amount of $20,189 with $9,720 ($20,189 – $10,469) carried forward and applied to reduce tax payable in a subsequent year.

Exercise 15

Since Mr. and Mrs. Ataila were resident in Canada for 245 days, their non-refundable tax credits will be prorated by 245/365. For Mr. Ataila this includes the basic personal tax amount of $11,038 and the spousal amount of $11,038, the Canada Employment credit of $1,117 and the child tax credit of $6,702 ($2,234 × 3 children). Mr. and Mrs. Ataila are considered residents of Canada only for the time since May 1, and will be taxed on their worldwide income. Any income earned during the four months prior to May 1 that they were non-resident will not be subject to tax in Canada.

ITA: 118, 63

CHAPTER 10

The child care expenses are only deductible if Mrs. Ataila has earned income, is in attendance of full-time studies at an educational institution, or is mentally or physically unable to care for the children. If Mrs. Ataila attended full-time studies in order to obtain a job in the workforce, then her husband may claim the child care expenses.

Exercise 16

Pierino's taxable income is: ITA: 118, 63

Salary from Saskatoon Transit	$ 65,000	
Restricted farm loss	(5,250)	($2,500 + .50 ($8,000 – $2,500) in 2013)
Taxable capital gain	2,000	(50% ($10,000 – $6,000))
Total income	$ 61,750	
RRSP contribution	(10,000)	
Net income	$ 51,750	
Net capital losses forward	(2,000)	(maximum of taxable capital gains)
Taxable income	$ 49,750	
Personal tax credit base amounts		
Basic personal tax credit base	$ 11,038	
Canada employment credit	1,117	
Eligible dependant (ETM)	11,038	
Child	2,234	
	$ 25,427	

Chapter 11
Computation of Taxable Income and Tax After General Reductions for Corporations

LEARNING GOALS

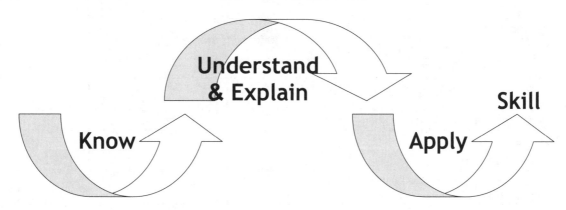

Understand & Explain

Skill

Know

Apply

Know

By the end of this chapter you should know the key provisions used in the calculation of the taxable income and the basic tax, net of some general tax credits, for a corporation. Completing the Review Questions (¶11,800) and Multiple Choice Questions (¶11,825) is a good way to learn the technical provisions.

Understand and Explain

You should understand and be able to explain:

- how to compute taxable income for a corporation;
- why most Canadian-source inter-corporate dividends are deducted in the calculation of taxable income, after having been included in Division B income for tax purposes;
- how loss carryovers are restricted — particularly, after an acquisition of control;
- how federal corporate taxes are computed with an abatement for provincial taxes; and
- how and why certain tax credits are provided to corporations to reduce basic federal tax.

Completing the Exercises (¶11,850) is a good way to deepen your understanding of the material.

Apply

You should be able to apply your knowledge and understanding of the key provisions pertaining to the calculation of:

- taxable income for a corporation to evaluate the consequences of an acquisition of control and to decide on the best strategy for dealing with losses in that situation, and
- tax for a corporation to do a basic calculation of corporate tax.

Completing the Assignment Problems (¶11,875) is an excellent way to develop your ability to apply the material in increasingly complex situations.

Chapter 11 — Learning Chart

Topic	Example Problem (✓)	Review Questions (¶11,800)	Multiple Choice (¶11,825)	Exercises (¶11,850)	Assignment Problems (¶11,875)
¶11,000 COMPUTATION OF TAXABLE INCOME FOR A CORPORATION					
¶11,010 Overview					
¶11,020 Deduction of Taxable Dividends					1
¶11,025 Purpose					
¶11,030 Dividends paid from untaxed income					
¶11,035 "After-tax financing"					
¶11,040 Dividends paid on shares subsequently sold for a loss					
¶11,050 Charitable Donations		1		1, 2	1
¶11,060 Loss Carryovers					
¶11,065 Non-capital loss	✓	2		1, 2	1
¶11,070 Treatment of allowable business investment loss	✓			4	
¶11,075 Net capital losses					1
¶11,080 Restrictions and ordering of deductions				5	
¶11,085 Choice to deduct net capital losses to preserve non-capital losses	✓			3	
¶11,090 Acquisition of Control of a Corporation and Its Effect on Losses					
¶11,095 Conceptual overview					
¶11,100 Deemed year-end		5	1		
¶11,105 Accrued or unrealized losses on inventory					
¶11,110 Accrued or unrealized losses on accounts receivable					
¶11,115 Accrued or unrealized losses on depreciable capital property			3		
¶11,120 Accrued or unrealized losses on eligible capital property					
¶11,125 Accrued or unrealized losses on non-depreciable capital property			2		
¶11,130 Elective capital gains and recapture		3			
¶11,135 Allowable business investment losses and losses from property					
¶11,140 Unused charitable contributions					
¶11,145 Deductibility of non-capital losses after an acquisition of control		4	4		
¶11,150 Loss carryback rules					
¶11,155 Summary and application	✓			6	2, 3
¶11,160 Taxable Income of a Corporation in General	✓		5	7, 8	4
¶11,200 BASIC COMPUTATION OF TAX FOR ALL CORPORATIONS					
¶11,210 Objectives of Provisions Affecting Taxation of Corporations		6			
¶11,212 Types of Corporations					
¶11,213 Private corporation					

Topic	Example Problem (✓)	Review Questions (¶11,800)	Multiple Choice (¶11,825)	Exercises (¶11,850)	Assignment Problems (¶11,875)
¶11,214 Canadian-controlled private corporation (CCPC)					
¶11,215 Public corporations					
¶11,216 Diagrammatic summary of types of corporations					
¶11,220 General Rates for Corporations					
¶11,225 Overview of rates and credits					
¶11,235 Effect of provincial corporate tax rates					
¶11,240 Effect of corporation type					
¶11,245 General rate reduction			6		8
¶11,250 Abatement from Federal Tax for Income Earned in a Province					
¶11,255 Purpose of the provision					
¶11,260 Applicable income tax regulations		7			
¶11,265 Cases on the meaning of permanent establishment	✓				5
¶11,270 Taxable income earned in a province or territory	✓				6, 9
¶11,300 TAX DEDUCTIONS/CREDITS					
¶11,310 Manufacturing and Processing Profits Deduction				10	8, 9
¶11,320 Foreign Tax Deduction					
¶11,325 Purpose and approach		8			
¶11,330 Non-business income tax deduction		9, 10		10	6, 8, 9
¶11,335 Business income tax deduction	✓			9, 10	6, 9
¶11,337 Federal Political Tax Credit				10	
¶11,340 Investment Tax Credit					
¶11,345 Overview					
¶11,350 Qualified property	✓			11, 12	8, 9
¶11,355 Qualified scientific research expenditure	✓				7
¶11,360 ITC for Apprenticeship Expenditures					
¶11,370 ITC for Child Care Spaces					
¶11,900 SUPPLEMENTAL NOTES					
¶11,910 Manufacturing and Processing Profits Deduction					
¶11,920 Eligibility					
¶11,925 Elements of the formula for determining manufacturing and processing profits					
¶11,930 Application of the rules	✓				
¶11,940 Effects on foreign tax credits	✓				

Study Notes

CHAPTER 11

Chapter 11 —
Discussion Notes for Review Questions

(1) Charitable donations are tax credits only on personal tax returns. On corporate tax returns they are deductions under Division C. Donations up to 75% of net income plus 25% of the amount of a taxable capital gain and 25% of recapture in respect of gifts of capital property with appreciated value can be deducted in the year. If the charitable donations are in excess of this amount then the excess can be carried forward for 5 years.

ITA: 110.1

(2) Income can be increased in the current year by not claiming some of the optional deductions for tax purposes. For example, the deductions for the allowance for bad debts, CCA, CECA or scientific research and experimental development expenditures can be foregone in order to increase income. These deductions will be available in future years and will not be lost. Also, the CRA will allow the revision of some permissive deductions for prior years. In addition, the company could consider the sale of any redundant assets to generate income through recapture and/or capital gain.

IC 84-1

(3) Where there has been an acquisition of control, the corporation cannot carry over its net capital losses. To the extent that the corporation has *net* taxable capital gains in the year, it may take an optional deduction of net capital losses which may in turn increase the amount of non-capital losses. Accrued capital losses are deemed to be realized in the deemed year-end immediately preceding the acquisition of control. However, there may be some relief because the corporation is allowed to trigger, on an elective basis, enough unrealized accrued capital gains to use up the net losses that are going to expire.

ITA: 111(4), 111(8)

ITA: 111(4)
ITA: 111(8)

(4) The first restriction is on the type of income against which the loss carryover can be deducted, and the second restriction is on the number of years a loss can be carried over.

Net Capital Losses: Applied against taxable capital gains only; carried back 3 years and forward indefinitely.

Non-capital Losses: Applied against all sources of income; carried back 3 years and forward 20 taxation years.

Restricted Farm Losses: Applied only against farm income; carried back 3 years and forward 20 taxation years.

Farm Losses: Applied against all sources of income; carried back 3 years and forward 20 taxation years.

(5) The deemed year-end applies whenever there is an acquisition of control even if the company acquired is not a loss company. Mr. Magee will not be able to claim a full year of CCA since CCA is prorated for a short fiscal year.

ITR: 1100(3)

(6) The three main objectives are:

 (a) alleviate double taxation;

 (b) prevent the avoidance of tax through the use of a corporation; and

 (c) provide tax incentives to corporations.

See the text in ¶11,210 of Chapter 11 for details.

(7) The gross revenue from that sale will be attributed to Alberta since, even though the sale was handled from Ontario, the order was delivered to a province in which the company had a permanent establishment.

ITR: 402(4)(a)

(8) The theory is that the country where the income is earned has the first right to tax the income. Then, in order to prevent double taxation when Canada also taxes this income, a credit is given in Canada for the foreign taxes paid.

(9) Investment income may be taxed in the foreign country even though there is no permanent establishment in that country. Canada assumes that this investment income, other than from real property, is earned through its permanent establishment in Canada and, therefore, considers this income to be earned in a province for purposes of section 124. Foreign business income, on the other hand, is assumed to be earned in a permanent establishment in the foreign country and, therefore, is not eligible for the federal abatement.

(10) Since Lossco does not have any net income or Canadian income tax, it cannot claim a foreign tax credit. No carryover is allowed for non-business income tax. However, the corporation can deduct the foreign taxes which will increase its loss for the year. This deduction will at least provide the benefit of the foreign taxes being carried forward as part of the non-capital losses.

ITA: 126(1)
ITA: 20(12)

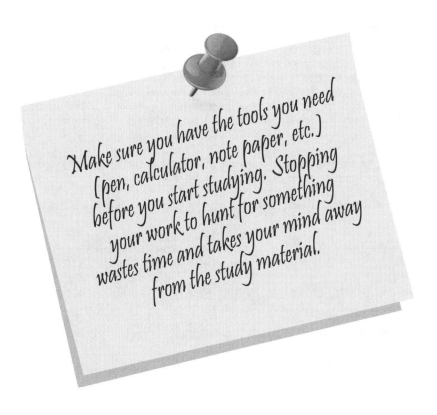

Make sure you have the tools you need (pen, calculator, note paper, etc.) before you start studying. Stopping your work to hunt for something wastes time and takes your mind away from the study material.

Chapter 11 –
Solutions to Multiple Choice Questions

Question 1

(B) is correct. Loss Co may select any date, within the 53-week period commencing February 1, 2013, as its new year end.   ITA: 249(4)(*b*), 249(4)(*d*)

(A) is incorrect, as the taxation year is deemed to have ended immediately before control was acquired. Since control was acquired on February 1, 2013, the year is usually deemed to have ended January 31, 2013. (Technically, it is possible to have an acquisition of control occur at a specific time, say, 10 a.m. on February 1, in which case, the taxation year can be deemed to have ended on February 1 at 9:59 a.m. Usually, a time is not specified, in which case, the taxation year is deemed to end the day before.)   ITA: 249(4)(*a*)

(C) is incorrect because the corporation is deemed not to have established a fiscal period yet. This being the case, the corporation is free to select any year end, within the 53-week limitation.   ITA: 249(4)(*d*)

(D) is incorrect for the same reason as (C).

Question 2

(C) is correct. The ACB of the land is reduced from $200,000 to $140,000, its FMV. The $60,000 reduction is deemed to be a capital loss for the taxation year ended May 14, 2013.   ITA: 111(4)(*c*), 111(4)(*d*)

(A) is incorrect as it includes the $25,000 accrued loss on the building which is depreciable property. Depreciable property is specifically excluded.   ITA: 111(4)(*c*)

(B) is incorrect as it includes the $20,000 accrued loss on the inventory which is not a capital property.

(D) is incorrect, because the $60,000 accrued loss on the land was reduced by the $10,000 accrued gain on the marketable securities. The recognition of the accrued gain on the marketable securities is not required. An election is available to recognize the accrued gain, if it is desirable.   ITA: 111(4)(*e*)

Question 3

(C) is correct. The UCC of the Class 45 computer equipment is reduced by $5,000, from $38,000 to $33,000. The UCC of the Class 8 office furniture and equipment is reduced by $10,000, from $58,000 to $48,000. The total of the two reductions, $15,000, is deemed to have been claimed as CCA in the year ended March 31, 2013.   ITA: 111(5.1)

(A) is incorrect as this amount adjusts the UCC of all the classes to the FMV of the classes. This amount includes an adjustment of $8,000 to increase the UCC of the Class 10 automobiles and the Class 12 assets to the FMV of the respective classes. The $8,000 is then subtracted from the $15,000 reduction calculated in (C). This is incorrect. The adjustment applies only to the classes where the UCC is higher than the FMV.   ITA: 111(5.1)

(B) is incorrect as it includes only 72% of the adjustment calculated in (C).

(D) is incorrect for the same reason as (A). The difference between (A) and (D) is that in (D) the positive and negative adjustments have been totalled, whereas in (A) they have been netted.

Question 4

(D) is correct. For its year ending December 31, 2013, Lakehead Co. will be able to deduct non-capital losses of $15,000 (maximum), provided the widget retailing business is carried on throughout the taxation year ended December 31, 2013 with a reasonable expectation of profit.   ITA: 111(5)(*a*)

(A) is incorrect as net capital losses incurred prior to the acquisition of control expire on the date control is acquired.   ITA: 111(4)(*a*)

(B) is incorrect. Non-capital losses realized prior to an acquisition of control cannot be deducted against taxable capital gains incurred after the acquisition of control. Non-capital losses are only deductible against income from the business in which the losses were incurred and income from a similar products or services.   ITA: 111(5)(*a*)

(C) is incorrect. The non-capital loss deduction has been limited to the income from a similar products or services net of the loss from the widget business. The netting of the widget business loss is not required.

ITA: 111(5)(*a*)

Question 5

(D) is correct.

Net income for tax purposes . . . . $ 600,000
Canadian dividends . . . . (100,000)
Charitable donations . . . . (200,000) – not exceeding $450,000 (75% of net income)
    $ 300,000

ITA: 112
ITA: 110.1

(A) incorrectly makes no adjustments: $600,000.

(B) incorrectly omits the deduction for charitable donations: $600,000 – $100,000 = $500,000.

(C) incorrectly omits the section 112 deduction for Canadian dividends: $600,000 – $200,000 = $400,000.

Question 6

(B) is correct.

Taxable income as per the answer to Question 5 . . . . $300,000

Part I tax on taxable income
Tax @ 38% on $300,000 . . . . $114,000
Deduct: Federal tax abatement (10% × 90% × $300,000) . . . . (27,000)
    $ 87,000
Deduct: 13% rate reduction (13% of $300,000) . . . . (39,000)
Total federal tax . . . . $ 48,000

(A) incorrectly applies the rate reduction to $500,000 of business income: $87,000 – 13% of $500,000 = $22,000.

(C) incorrectly omits the 13% rate reduction.

(D) incorrectly calculates the rate reduction as 11.5% × $300,000 rather than 13% × 300,000: $87,000 – 11.5% of $300,000 = $52,500.

Chapter 11 — Solutions to Exercises

Exercise 1

	2011	*2012*		*2013*	
Income under Division B	$(7,350)	$22,050		$14,700	
Deduct: charitable donations limited by 75% of income above					
— carried forward	Nil	$ 2,625		Nil	
— current	Nil	Nil	4,700	(7,325)	$11,025[1](11,025)
unlimited charitable donation					
— carried forward	Nil	—		$ 3,675	
— current	Nil	Nil	$14,725[2](14,725)	—	(3,675)[3]
non-capital loss from 2011[4]		Nil		Nil	Nil
Taxable income		Nil		Nil	Nil

— *NOTES TO SOLUTION*

[1] Limited to 75% of $14,700 = $11,025; $975 is available to carry forward five years to 2018.

[2] If the donation of the land gave rise to a capital gain, the taxable portion would be included in the amount of income under Division B.

[3] $1,300 ($19,700 − $14,725 − $3,675) is available to carry forward four more years to 2017.

[4] $7,350 is available to carry forward 20 taxation years to 2031.

Exercise 2

	2011	*2012*	*2013*
Option A: Claiming maximum charitable donations			
Income before CCA	$ 100,000	$115,000	$132,250
CCA	(200,000)	(101,667)[1]	(116,917)
Income (loss) under Division B	$(100,000)	$ 13,333	$ 15,333
Charitable donations:			
— Carried forward	Nil	(10,000)[1]	(11,500)[1]
— Current	Nil	Nil	Nil
Non-capital loss carried forward from 2011	N/A	(3,333)	(3,833)[2]
Taxable income	Nil	Nil	Nil
Option B: Non-capital loss utilization			
Income before CCA	$100,000	$115,000	$132,250
CCA	(107,167)[3]	(86,333)	(132,250)
Income (loss) under Division B	$ (7,167)	$ 28,667	Nil
Charitable donations:			
— carried forward	Nil	(21,500)	Nil
— current	Nil	Nil	Nil
Non-capital loss carried forward from 2011	N/A	(7,167)[3]	Nil
Taxable income	Nil	Nil	Nil
Option C: Maximum donation and non-capital loss utilization			
Income before CCA	$100,000	$115,000	$132,250
CCA	(107,166)	(101,667)	(116,917)

	2011	2012	2013
Income (loss) under Division B	$ (7,166)	$ 13,333	$ 15,333
Charitable donations:			
— Carried forward	Nil	(10,000)[4]	(11,500)[4]
— Current	Nil	Nil	Nil
Non-capital loss carried forward from 2011	N/A	(3,333)	(3,833)
Taxable income	Nil	Nil	Nil

- *Summary*

	Options		
	A	B	C
Total donations claimed	$ 21,500	$ 21,500	$ 21,500
Total CCA claimed	418,584	325,750	325,750
Unclaimed non-capital loss	92,834	Nil	Nil

— *NOTES TO SOLUTION*

[1] CCA amount selected to provide sufficient Division B income for a deduction of charitable donations (maximum of 75% of Division B income). The 2007 charitable donations would, otherwise, expire after 2012.

[2] $92,834 of non-capital loss from 2011 remains.

[3] Determined by looking forward to 2012 and creating the maximum non-capital loss in 2011 that can be fully utilized in 2012.

[4] Uses the five-year carryforward of charitable donations to the maximum — i.e., the $11,500 donations of 2008 may be carried forward to 2013, as in Option A.

Exercise 3

Sum of: loss from business		$129,000
allowable business investment loss		8,000
dividends deductible under sec. 112............................		10,750
net capital loss deducted [$27,000 – $17,200 = $9,800 remaining]......		17,200[1]
		$164,950
Less: income from property	$32,250	
net taxable capital gains [½ × ($46,400 – $12,000)]..........	17,200[1]	(49,450)
Non-capital loss for the year		$115,500

— *NOTE TO SOLUTION*

[1] The corporation may deduct the net capital loss from income even though it has no impact on the taxable income. However, the deduction is restricted to the net taxable capital gain for the year. Once deducted, the net capital loss can be included in the non-capital loss computation.

Exercise 4

Allowable capital loss (excluding ABIL)	$ 51,750
Less: taxable capital gain	(4,700)
Net	$ 47,050
Add: unutilized allowable business investment loss in respect of which the carryover period expires in the year (i.e., the 20th carryforward year)	Nil
Net capital loss for the year	$ 47,050

Exercise 5

	Option A[1]	Option B[1]
Income from business	$55,500	$55,500
Taxable capital gains	37,000	37,000

Income under Division B	$92,500	$92,500
Less: net capital losses	(37,000)[(2)]	(10,000)[(2)]
non-capital losses	(55,500)	(82,500)
Taxable income	Nil	Nil

Summary:

Unutilized non-capital losses	$27,000	Nil
Unutilized net capital losses	3,000[(2)]	$30,000[(2)]

— *NOTES TO SOLUTION*

[(1)] In Option A, maximum net capital losses are claimed before non-capital losses. In Option B, maximum non-capital losses are claimed before net capital losses.

[(2)]	*Option A*	*Option B*
1999 Net capital losses available	$60,000	$60,000
Adjusted to 2013 ($60,000 × ½ / ¾)	40,000	40,000
Utilized in 2013 (limited to TCG)	(37,000)	(10,000)
Available to carryforward	$ 3,000	$30,000

Exercise 6

Part (a)

Because of the acquisition of control by Holdco Ltd., Lofty Ltd. is deemed to have a taxation year-end on March 9, 2013. This taxation year will be only 69 days long, having commenced on January 1, 2013. The exception does not apply, since the date of the acquisition of control is more than seven days after the last year end.

ITA: 249(4), 256(9)

ITA: 249(4)(c)

Lofty Ltd. will be required to make certain adjustments as of March 9, 2013. The adjustments will increase the company's business losses of $3,000 to $48,000, as follows:

Business losses	$ 3,000
Excess of UCC ($70,000) over fair market value ($40,000) of assets in Class 8	30,000
Accrued inventory losses	Nil
Doubtful accounts receivable deemed to be actual bad debts	15,000
Losses from non-capital sources (all from business)	$48,000

ITA: 111(5.1)

ITA: 111(5.3)

The balance in the CEC account is not affected by the acquisition of control, because there was no unrealized loss at the time of the acquisition of control (i.e., ¾ of the fair market value of $68,000 = $51,000 which is greater than the $50,000 CEC account balance).

Division B income for the deemed taxation year ended March 9, 2013 would be computed as follows:

Par. 3(a):	Income from non-capital sources		Nil
Par. 3(b):	Net taxable capital gains:		
	Election under par. 111(4)(e) on land (½ × $56,000)	$28,000	
	Allowable capital losses	Nil	$28,000
Par. 3(c):	Par. 3(a) + par. 3(b)		$28,000
Par. 3(d):	Losses from non-capital sources (above)		(48,000)
Division B income and taxable income			Nil

Since the net capital losses of $30,000 will expire on March 10, 2013, if nothing is done, the corporation should deduct the net capital losses of $30,000. Although the taxable income will be unaffected, the non-capital losses can be increased by this amount.

The non-capital loss for the deemed year ending March 10, 2013, would be:

Losses from business sources	$48,000
Add: net capital losses deducted at ½ inclusion rate ($30,000 × ⁴⁄₃ × ½)	20,000
	$68,000
Less: par. 3(*c*) income determined above	28,000
Non-capital loss for deemed year	$40,000

The adjusted cost base of the land will be increased by the amount of the gain elected to $256,000 (i.e., $200,000 + $56,000) on March 10, 2013.   ITA: 111(4)(*e*)

The undepreciated capital cost in Lofty's Class 8 will be reduced from $70,000 to $40,000 as at March 10, 2013. Lofty Ltd. will be deemed to have deducted the $30,000 as capital cost allowance for taxation years ending before March 10, 2013; thereby, making Lofty Ltd. liable for recapture on that amount if the assets are subsequently sold.   ITA: 111(5.1)

Similarly, the corporation will be deemed to have made a claim for bad debts totalling $15,000. Accordingly, Lofty Ltd.'s accounts receivable will be $225,000 as at March 10, 2013, the start of its next taxation year.   ITA: 20(1)(*p*), 111(5.3)

Lofty Ltd. will be allowed the deduction of the 2012 $600,000 non-capital losses in any year up to 2032 including the short deemed taxation year (if the corporation reverts to a December 31 year end) after which they will expire. However, in order to be deducted, the widget manufacturing business must be carried on by Lofty Ltd. for profit or with a reasonable expectation of profit throughout each of those taxation years. Similarly, the $40,000 non-capital losses of the March 9, 2013 taxation year will be eligible for carryforward 20 years, under the same conditions, to December 31, 2032 if the company reverts to a December 31 year end. It appears that this condition will be met, since Holdco Ltd. will provide capital and management to turn Lofty's business around. The non-capital losses may be deducted in a carryforward year from the incomes of the widget manufacturing business and a business with similar products in that year.   ITA: 111(5)

Part (b)

Lofty Ltd. would still have business losses of $3,000 plus the deemed business loss on the Class 8 assets of $30,000 and the loss on the accounts receivable of $15,000, which gives a total of $48,000 of losses from business sources. In addition, Lofty Ltd. has a property loss of $10,000.

The 1999 net capital loss of $30,000 is $20,000 when converted from a ¾ to a ½ inclusion rate.

The minimum designated proceeds or deemed proceeds would be as follows: ITA: 111(4)(*e*)

Deemed proceeds = 2 × ($20,000 net capital losses plus $10,000 property losses)
                plus ACB of the land of $200,000
        = $260,000

Now, the Division B and taxable income for the deemed taxation year ended March 9, 2013 would be:

Par. 3(*a*)	Income from non-capital sources		Nil
Par. 3(*b*)	Net taxable capital gains:		
	Election under par. 111(4)(*e*) —		
	($260,000 – $200,000) × ½	$30,000	
	Less allowable capital losses	Nil	$30,000
Par. 3(*c*)			$30,000
Par. 3(*d*)	Losses from non-capital sources:		
	Business losses	$48,000	
	Property losses	10,000	(58,000)
Division B income			Nil
Division C deductions:			
	Net capital losses		$20,000
Taxable income			Nil

Note how just enough paragraph 3(*c*) income was created (i.e., $30,000) to offset the property loss of $10,000 plus the net capital loss of $20,000, both of which are about to expire.

The non-capital loss balance for the deemed year ended March 9, 2013 would be:

Par. 3(*d*) losses	$58,000
Add: net capital losses deducted	20,000
	$78,000
Less: par. 3(*c*) income	(30,000)
Total non-capital loss for the year ended March 9, 2013	$48,000

The non-capital loss of $48,000 for the year ended March 9, 2013 would be added to the 2012 non-capital loss balance to give a total of $648,000 to be deducted in the future. If Lofty Ltd. reverts to a December 31 year end, these could be deducted in any year that the loss business is carried on against income of the business that generated the loss or against business income from the sale of similar products up to:

2012 non-capital loss	2031
March 2013 non-capital loss	2032

The adjusted cost base of the land will now be increased to $260,000.

Exercise 7

	2012		2013	
Net income (loss) per financial accounting statements		$(53,000)		$126,000
Add total of items not deductible for tax purposes		127,700		240,700
		$ 74,700		$366,700
Less CCA ($3,378 less in 2012)		51,700		51,316
Income for tax purposes		$ 23,000		$315,384
Inter-company dividends	$23,000		$23,000	
Charitable donations (max. 75% of income):				
Carried over	—		15,000	
Current	Nil		15,000	
Non-capital loss carryover	—	23,000	18,000	71,000
Taxable income		Nil		$244,384
Taxable income originally computed		Nil		$245,060

Conclusion:

This calculation produces better results. All of the inter-company dividends are fully deductible in 2012 with the reduction of the capital cost allowance by $3,378. Both options allowed, in total, an equal amount of non-capital losses and donations to be claimed over the two-year period. Although the original calculation enabled $2,702 (i.e., $55,078 + $50,640 – $51,700 – $51,316) more capital cost allowance to be claimed in total over the two years, the original calculation could not utilize $3,378 of the potential dividend deduction. This alternative increases the future CCA write-offs by $2,702 as shown below.

Capital cost allowances were computed as follows:	Building Class 1: 6%	Equipment Class 8: 20%
2013: UCC, January 1, 2013	$ 246,667	$ 182,578*
CCA (total deduction: $51,316)	(14,800)	(36,516)
2014: UCC, January 1, 2014	$ 231,867	$ 146,062
UCC originally computed	$ 231,867	$ 143,360

* $179,200 + $3,378.

Exercise 8

Division B income		$116,850
Less: charitable donations limited to 75% of $116,850		
or $87,638		
— carried forward..................................	$10,250	
— current	77,388[1]	(87,638)
dividends from taxable Canadian corporations.....................		(12,300)
subtotal		$ 16,912
non-capital losses[2]		(16,912)
net capital losses[2] (not to exceed the taxable capital gains for the year)		(Nil)
Taxable income		Nil

— NOTES TO SOLUTION

[1] The balance of $2,612 in current charitable donations may be carried forward to the next five years.

[2] These carried-over losses may be claimed in a different sequence and in different amounts from that shown. For example, if there is little prospect of future capital gains, the corporation might make the following deductions:

subtotal...	$16,912
net capital losses ($41,000 × ½ / ¾)	(27,333)
non-capital losses	Nil
taxable income	Nil

The balance of the net capital losses may be carried forward indefinitely.

Net capital losses claimed are added to the non-capital loss balance carried forward.

Exercise 9

Income from Japan in Canadian dollars (75,593,884 yen × .0108)		$ 816,414
Total income under Division B ($2,500,000 + $816,414)		$3,316,414
Less: Dividends deductible under sec. 112	$100,000	
Net capital losses carried forward (adjusted to current year inclusion rate)	25,000	125,000
Taxable income		$3,191,414
Tax @ 38%...		$1,212,737
Less: Federal tax abatement (10% of 75% of $3,191,414)		(239,356)
General tax reduction @ 13% of 3,191,414		(414,884)
Net tax		$ 558,497

Foreign Business Tax Deduction

Least of: (a) amount paid (30,237,521 yen × .0108)	$ 326,565

$$(b) \quad \frac{\text{income from Japan}}{\substack{\text{Div. B income minus s. 112 ded.} \\ \text{and net capital loss ded.}}} \times \substack{\text{tax otherwise} \\ \text{payable before} \\ \text{abatement}}$$

$$= \frac{\$816,414}{\$3,316,414 - (\$100,000 + 25,000)} \times (\$1,212,737 - 414,884) \qquad \$ 204,103$$

(c) Part I tax otherwise payable minus foreign non-business tax credit ($558,497 – nil)	$ 558,497

Therefore, the foreign tax deduction is $204,103.

Exercise 10

Income under Division B		$2,645,000
Less: Charitable donations	$ 69,000	
Taxable dividends deductible under sec. 112	517,500	
Non-capital losses	127,600	714,100
Taxable income		$1,930,900
Tax @ 38%		$ 733,742
Less: Federal tax abatement (10% of 86% of $1,930,900)		166,057
		$ 567,685
Less: Non-business foreign tax credit (see Schedule 1)	$ 25,676	
Business foreign tax credit (see Schedule 2)	26,093	
Tax reduction (13% of $1,930,900)	251,017	
Federal political contributions tax credit (max.)	650	303,436
Part I tax payable		$ 264,249

Schedule 1: Non-business foreign tax credit

Lesser of: (a) amount paid .... $ 25,875

$$(b) \quad \frac{\text{foreign non-business income}}{\substack{\text{Div. B income minus s. 112 ded.}\\ \text{and net capital loss ded.}}} \times \substack{\text{tax otherwise payable}\\ \text{after abatement minus}\\ \text{general tax reduction}}$$

$$= \frac{\$172,500}{\$2,645,000 - (\$517,500 + 0)} \times \$316,668^{(1)} \quad .... \quad \$ \ 25,676$$

Schedule 2: Business foreign tax credit

Least of: (a) amount paid .... $ 36,800

$$(b) \quad \frac{\text{foreign business income}}{\substack{\text{Div. B income minus s. 112 ded.}\\ \text{and net capital loss ded.}}} \times \substack{\text{tax otherwise payable}\\ \text{before deductions}\\ \text{minus general tax}\\ \text{reduction}}$$

$$= \frac{\$115,000}{\$2,645,000 - (\$517,500 + 0)} \times (\$733,742 - 251,017) \quad \$ \ 26,093$$

(c) $733,742 – $251,017 – $25,676 .... $457,049

—*NOTE TO SOLUTION*

  [1] $733,742 – $166,057 – $251,017

Exercise 11

The total investment tax credit is 10% of $900,000 = $90,000.

Taxable income before CCA on eligible property		$300,000
Less: CCA on qualified property (½ × 6% of $900,000)		27,000
Taxable income		$273,000
Net federal tax: @ 15% of $273,000		$ 40,950
Less: fed. pol. contributions tax credit	$ 500	
investment tax credit (limited to ($40,950 – $500))	40,450	$(40,950)
Part I tax payable		Nil

Note that the $40,450 of investment tax credit will reduce the balance of UCC in Class 1 in the following year. The remainder of $49,550 (i.e., $90,000 – $40,450) of ITC may be carried back three taxation years and forward 20 taxation years. Any amount used to reduce tax in a particular carryover year will reduce the UCC in the year following the year of use or the year following the purchase, whichever is later.

Exercise 12

Earned investment tax credit of 10% of $3,500,000 = $350,000

Income under Division B before CCA on eligible property		$2,645,000
Less: CCA on eligible property (½ × .30 × $3,500,000)		525,000
Income under Division B.		$2,120,000
Less: charitable donations	$ 69,000	
taxable dividends deductible under sec. 112	517,500	
non-capital losses	127,600	714,100
Taxable income		$1,405,900
Tax @ 38%		$ 534,242
Less: federal tax abatement (10% of 86% of $1,405,900)		120,907
		$ 413,335
Less: non-business foreign tax credit (see Schedule 1)	$ 24,819	
business foreign tax credit (see Schedule 2)	25,223	
tax reduction (13% of 1,405,900)	182,767	
federal political contribution tax credit	500	233,309
Part I tax payable before investment tax credit		$ 180,026
Investment tax credit		(180,026)
Part I tax payable		Nil

The remaining investment tax credit of $169,974 (i.e., $350,000 – $180,026) can be carried forward 20 years.

The UCC balance in Class 10 will be reduced by $180,026 in the following year and by the amount of the $169,974 remainder in subsequent years, if that amount is deducted.

Schedule 1: Non-business foreign tax credit

Lesser of:

(a) amount paid $25,875

(b) $\dfrac{\$172,500}{\$2,120,000 - \$517,500} \times \$230,568^{(1)}$ $24,819

Schedule 2: Business foreign tax credit

Least of:

(a) amount paid . . . . $ 36,800

(b) $\dfrac{\$115,000}{\$2,120,000 - \$517,500} \times (\$534,242 - \$182,767)$ $25,223

(c) $534,242 – $182,767 – $24,819 . . . . $326,656

— *NOTE TO SOLUTION*

(1) $534,242 – $120,907 – $182,767.

Chapter 12
Integration for Business and Investment Income of the Private Corporation

LEARNING GOALS

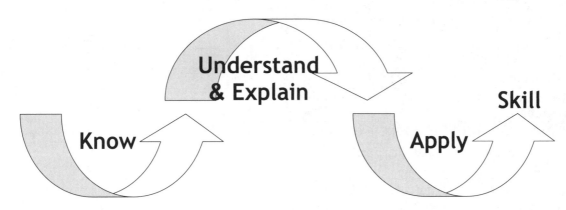

Understand & Explain

Know

Skill

Apply

Know

By the end of this chapter you should know how the income tax system works to integrate the tax on individual shareholders with the tax on private corporations for business and investment income. Completing the Review Questions (¶12,800) and Multiple Choice Questions (¶12,825) is a good way to learn the technical provisions.

Understand and Explain

You should understand and be able to explain:
- the concept of integration;
- how the small business deduction from tax is computed and how it helps to achieve integration of business income;
- the rules for the association of corporations and why they exist;
- the base on which the additional investment tax credit for a Canadian-controlled private corporation is computed and how it is limited for scientific research and experimental development expenditures;
- what investment income of a private corporation is and how it is taxed to achieve integration; and
- the advantages and disadvantages of incorporating sources of business income and sources of investment income.

Completing the Exercises (¶12,850) is a good way to deepen your understanding of the material.

Apply

You should be able to apply your knowledge and understanding of the key provisions pertaining to:
- associated corporations, where that term is used in the legislation;
- the calculation of:
  - the small business deduction,
  - the additional investment tax credit for scientific research and experimental development expenditures,
  - the income taxes on investment income of a private corporation, including refundable tax,
- the complete calculation of taxes payable by a private corporation with income from business and investment sources, and
- the decision to incorporate a source of income.

Completing the Assignment Problems (¶12,875) is an excellent way to develop your ability to apply the material in increasingly complex situations.

Chapter 12 — Learning Chart

Topic	Example Problem (✓)	Review Questions (¶12,800)	Multiple Choice (¶12,825)	Exercises (¶12,850)	Assignment Problems (¶12,875)
¶12,000 THE CONCEPT OF INTEGRATION					
¶12,010 Issues Addressed by Integration					
¶12,020 Objectives of Integration		1. 2			
¶12,030 The Major Tool for Integration in the Income Tax Act					
¶12,035 The concept		13, 14			
¶12,040 Application of the concept in theory					
¶12,045 Basis for the calculation of the dividend tax credit		3, 12			
¶12,100 INCOME FROM AN ACTIVE BUSINESS OF A CCPC					
¶12,110 Introduction to the Small Business Deduction		4, 5			
¶12,120 Mechanics of Calculation of Small Business Deduction					
¶12,125 The basic limits		6, 7	1	6	7, 9, 10, 11
¶12,130 Elimination of small business deduction for large CCPCs	✓				5
¶12,140 Definition of "Active Business"					
¶12,145 The "default" definition			2	1	1, 12, 13
¶12,150 Specified investment business	✓		2	1	1, 12, 13
¶12,155 Personal services business			2		12, 13
¶12,160 Income incidental to an active business					
¶12,170 Associated Companies					
¶12,175 Overview					
¶12,180 Related persons	✓			2	
¶12,185 Basic association rules	✓		5, 6	3, 4, 10, 13	2, 3, 12, 13
¶12,190 Concept of control					4
¶12,195 Extended meaning of control			6		4
¶12,200 Ownership of shares					3
¶12,205 Association with third corporation	✓		5		2, 3, 12
¶12,210 Deemed association				4, 5	3, 4
¶12,220 Corporate Partnerships					
¶12,230 Manufacturing and Processing Profits and the Small Business Deduction	✓	10	3	6	7, 9
¶12,235 General Rate Reduction Revisited				6, 8, 9	5, 7, 9, 10, 11
¶12,240 Investment Tax Credit Revisited					
¶12,245 Overview					
¶12,250 The ITC rate for CCPCs					6, 9
¶12,255 Refundable investment tax credit	✓				6
¶12,260 Prescribed proxy amount					6

Topic	Example Problem (✓)	Review Questions (¶12,800)	Multiple Choice (¶12,825)	Exercises (¶12,850)	Assignment Problems (¶12,875)
¶12,265 Capital expenditures	✓				6
¶12,270 Incorporated Business Income and Integration					15
¶12,275 Corporate tax rate incentives to incorporate in general					
¶12,280 Specific tax savings (cost) and deferral (prepayment) possibilities					
¶12,285 Summary of advantages and disadvantages of incorporating active business income		8, 9			
¶12,300 INCOME FROM INVESTMENTS OF A CCPC					
¶12,310 Overview of Integration for Income from Investments of a CCPC					
¶12,315 Purpose					
¶12,320 Conceptual illustration of integration		15			
¶12,330 Special Refundable Taxes in Respect of Income from Investments of a CCPC					
¶12,335 Aggregate investment income					9
¶12,340 Additional refundable tax (ART)					5, 7, 9, 11, 13
¶12,345 "Refundable dividend tax on hand" (RDTOH)		12		13	8, 11, 13
¶12,350 "Deeming rules"		16		11, 13	12, 13
¶12,355 Part IV tax on portfolio and other dividends	✓	11, 12, 17, 18	4	7, 10	8, 9, 11, 12
¶12,360 Dividend refund		12			8, 9, 11
¶12,365 Anti-avoidance rule					8, 9
¶12,370 Summary of conditions for Part IV tax					
¶12,375 Application of non-capital losses					
¶12,380 Actual Application of the Scheme	✓			12	14
¶12,390 Summary of advantages and disadvantages of incorporating investment income eligible for refundable tax					
¶12,400 Imperfections and Policy Choices in the Integration System for Income of a CCPC					
¶12,405 Imperfections					
¶12,410 A deferral of tax as a government policy choice					
¶12,415 ANALYZING TAX DECISION TO INCORPORATE					15
¶12,500 COMPREHENSIVE SUMMARY OF TYPES OF CORPORATE INCOME AND FEDERAL CORPORATE INCOME TAX RATES	✓			8, 9	9, 10, 11, 15
¶12,900 SUPPLEMENTAL NOTES					
¶12,910 Common Law Background to Current Legislation on Definition of "Active Business"					

Study Notes

Chapter 12 –
Discussion Notes for Review Questions

(1) The purpose of integration is to avoid the double taxation of income earned through a corporation. Integration should cause the total tax paid by a corporation and its shareholders to be equal to the total tax paid by an individual who carries on the same economic activity directly and not through a corporation. The system should be neutral as to the form of organization used.

(2) Ideal integration depends on:

(a) When the corporation itself pays tax, the shareholder must include in income and pay tax on the full pre-tax income earned by the corporation and then get a full credit for all the income tax paid by the corporation.

(b) All after-tax income would have to be either paid out as dividends in the year earned or taxed in some manner at the shareholder level in that year to avoid the indefinite deferral of tax that might otherwise be available if the corporate rates were lower than individual tax rates. This would equate the position of the shareholder with the position of the proprietor, partner or owner of investments who must pay tax on income from his or her economic activity whether or not it is distributed.

(3) The gross-up is intended to add to the dividend received by the individual shareholder an amount equal to the total income tax paid by the corporation on the income that gave rise to the dividend. Thus, the grossed-up dividend is intended to represent the corporation's pre-tax income. The shareholder will pay tax on the grossed-up dividend at his or her personal rate. The tax credit is intended to give the shareholder credit for the total tax paid by the corporation on the shareholder's behalf. This procedure is intended to equalize the tax paid on the income that is flowed through the corporation to its shareholders with the tax paid on the same income that is earned directly. When the gross-up is 25% [18% for dividends paid after 2013] and the total (i.e., federal and provincial) corporate tax rate is 20% [15.3% for the 18% gross-up], integration is theoretically perfect. When the gross-up is 38% and the total (i.e., federal and provincial) corporate tax rate is 27.5%, integration is, also, theoretically perfect.

(4) Its purpose is to help small CCPCs retain capital in order to expand their businesses. This is accomplished by using a relatively low corporate tax rate after the small business deduction to defer tax until the income is paid out as a dividend.

(5) There is a deemed year end on July 14 as a result of the acquisition of control and he is deemed to acquire control at the commencement of that day. Mr. Smith can now choose any year-end he wants and the company should qualify as a CCPC throughout the year.   ITA: 249(4), 256(9)

(6) Paragraph 125(1)(*a*) deals with Division B income (net of expenses) while paragraph 125(1)(*b*) starts off with taxable income. Therefore, if there are Division C deductions such as donations or loss carryforwards then paragraph 125(1)(*b*) could be lower.

(7) The concept is that foreign income which is not taxed in Canada because of a foreign tax credit should be removed from the base amount on which the small business deduction is calculated.

A $^{100}/_{28} \times$ factor is applied to the non-business foreign tax credit in order to estimate the foreign non-business income. This is based on the theory that the corporate rate is 28%.

A $4 \times$ factor is applied to the business foreign tax credit in order to estimate the foreign business income. This is based on the theory that the corporate rate is 38% less the general tax reduction of 13% on foreign business income. The abatement is not applied since it is assumed that the income is attributable to a permanent establishment outside of Canada.

(8) Some advantages of incorporation are:

- limited liability except for personal guarantees;

- tax savings if the combined corporate tax rate is under 20% [15.3% after 2013];

- tax deferral;

- income splitting with family members as employees or shareholders (beware of the attribution rules and the tax on split income);

- estate freezing;

- availability of registered pension plans to the owner;

- separation of business and personal activities;

- greater flexibility as to the timing of income received personally;

- continuity of separate legal entity;

- deferral of accrued capital gains on transfer of shares to a spouse;

- access to financing;

- availability of capital gains exemption on QSBCS; and

- availability of deferral of capital gains on shares of an SBC.

(9) Some disadvantages of incorporation are:

- tax cost if combined corporate tax rate is over 20% [15.3% after 2013] for income eligible for the small business deduction and 27.5% for other business income;

- a prepayment of tax at lower levels of personal income on business income not eligible for the small business deduction;

- additional legal and accounting costs; and

- inability to deduct losses against personal income. This disadvantage may be offset somewhat by the availability of the ABIL.

(10) He will not be able to get the M&P profits deduction on income eligible for the small business deduction. In addition, the question does not indicate whether this venture is incorporated. If it is not, then these deductions are not available since they are only available to incorporated businesses.   ITA: 125.1(1)(*a*)

(11) Part IV tax of 33⅓% on portfolio dividends prevents a significant deferral of tax.

(12) (a) Refundable Part I tax;

   (b) Part IV tax;

   (c) Dividend gross-up and tax credit;

   (d) Refundable dividend tax on hand; and

   (e) Dividend refund.

(13) The gross-up is intended to place the shareholder in an income position equivalent to that of the corporation before it paid corporate taxes. At an assumed corporate tax rate of 20% [15.3% after 2013] or 27.5%, the 25% [18% after 2013] or 38% gross-up, respectively, represents the underlying corporate tax. This is added to the after-tax dividend to tax, theoretically, the pre-tax corporate profits in the hands of the individual shareholder.

(14) The dividend tax credit is intended to give the shareholder credit against his or her taxes for the taxes paid by the corporation on the income from which the dividend was paid. Since the gross-up theoretically takes the dividend up to the pre-tax corporate income level, the dividend tax credit is needed to reduce the individual tax by the theoretical amount of corporate tax already paid on that income. At a corporate tax rate of 20% [15.3% after 2013], for example, tax of $20 [$15.30 after 2013] would be paid on corporate income of $100. The gross-up of 25% [18% after 2013] would take the individual's income on that dividend of $80 [$84.70 after 2013] back up to the $100 of corporate pre-tax income level. Assuming a provincial dividend tax credit of ⅓ of the gross-up [⁵⁄₁₈ after 2013] the total dividend tax credit would be 20% [15.3% after 2013] of the grossed-up dividend or $20 [$15.30 after 2013]. Thus the dividend tax credit represents the underlying corporate tax paid on the dividend.

(15) Of the $1,000 capital gain, $500 is not taxable and is allocated to the capital dividend account to be passed out to the shareholders tax-free as a capital dividend. This provides for the tax-free receipt of this $500 whether the capital gain is realized in the corporation or by the individual directly.   ITA: 82(3)

The remaining $500 is theoretically taxed at an approximate initial rate of Part I tax of 40%. An additional refundable tax of 6⅔% is also levied and added to this account. Then, 26⅔% of the income is classified as refundable Part I tax and added to the refundable dividend tax on hand account. Dividend payments result in a return to the corporation of $1 for every $3 of dividends that are paid. This would leave an effective tax rate in the corporation on taxable capital gains of 20% which is higher than the 15.3% [after 2013] level at which integration works.

(16) Ordinarily the interest would be taxed at the full rate of 38% plus the 6⅔% additional refundable tax under Part I with part of this being classified as refundable Part I tax and added to the refundable dividend tax on hand account. However, since the two companies are associated and the interest is being deducted against the active business income of Opco, the deeming rules will deem the interest income to be active business income and not eligible for the refundable tax treatment.

ITA: 129(6)

(17) While A Ltd. does not have more than 10% of the votes and value of B Ltd., A Ltd. does have control, since A Ltd. and the son of the only shareholder are related and do not deal at arm's length. Thus, over 50% of the voting shares belong to a person with whom A Ltd. does not deal at arm's length.

ITA: 186(2)

(18) The factors to be considered are:

- the same non-capital losses cannot be deducted under both provisions;
- the normal corporate tax rates under Part I are usually higher than the 33⅓% Part IV tax;
- the Part IV tax is a refundable tax and not a permanent tax like Part I tax;
- the non-capital losses would otherwise expire without any value; and
- the corporation is not expected to pay a dividend to claim the refund until years in the future.

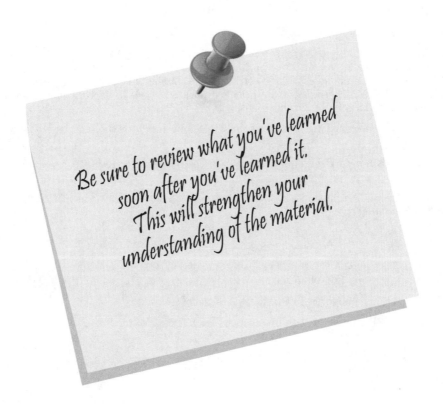

Be sure to review what you've learned soon after you've learned it. This will strengthen your understanding of the material.

Chapter 12 —
Solutions to Multiple Choice Questions

Question 1

(B) $19,550 is correct. It is calculated as follows:

Least of:	(a)	income from an active business carried on in Canada	$120,000
		net of loss from an active business carried on in Canada	(0)
			$120,000
	(b)	taxable income	$132,000
	(c)	business limit: $500,000 – $385,000	$115,000

The least is (c): $115,000 × 17% = $19,550

(A) $17,000 is incorrect. The foreign business loss of $20,000 has been netted against the $120,000 of Canadian business income.

(C) $20,400 is incorrect. This amount is 17% of the Canadian active business income.

(D) $22,440 is incorrect. This amount is 17% of the taxable income.

Question 2

(D) is correct. M Ltd. is carrying on an active business. The business is not a personal services   ITA: 125(7)
business as the services are provided to an associated corporation. M Ltd. and ACC Ltd. are associated.   ITA: 256(1)(*d*)
M Ltd. is not a specified investment business as the principal purpose is not to derive income from
property. Thus, by default, it is carrying on an active business.

(A) is incorrect. M Ltd. is not carrying on a personal services business for the reasons outlined above.

(B) is incorrect. M Ltd. is not carrying on a personal services business for the reasons outlined above.

(C) is incorrect. M Ltd. is not carrying on a specified investment business as the principal purpose is not to derive income from property.

Question 3

(B) $3,250 is correct. This amount is 13% of taxable income of $520,000 in excess of ABI eligible for the SBD, which is $495,000 (i.e., 13% of $520,000 – $495,000).

(A) $2,600 is incorrect. This amount is 13% of taxable income in excess of $500,000.

(C) $53,411 is incorrect. This amount is 13% of Canadian ABI in excess of the SBD of $84,150 (i.e., 17% of $495,000).

(D) $67,600 is incorrect. This amount is 13% × taxable income.

Question 4

(C) $68,000 is correct.   ITA: 186(1), 186(4)

Dividend received from non-connected corporation, C Ltd.:	
$120,000 × ⅓	$40,000
70% of $40,000 dividend refund received by connected	
corporation, B Ltd.	28,000
	$68,000

B Ltd is connected to A Ltd., because of *de jure* control and because A Ltd. holds more than 10% of   ITA: 186(2), 186(4)
the issued share capital in both votes and value.

(A) $60,000 is incorrect. This amount is 70% and 8% of the dividend refunds received by B Ltd. and C Ltd., respectively.

(B) $64,000 is incorrect. This amount applies the Part I tax rate on investment income, 26⅔%, to the total dividends received.

(D) $80,000 is incorrect. This amount is ⅓ × the dividends received and ignores the special rules for connected corporations.

Question 5

(D) is correct. Neither J Co. nor D Co. is associated with R Co., since neither Joanne nor David own at least 25% of the shares of R Co. through J Co. and D Co. Their ownership is only 22% (i.e., 55% of 40%). Hence, J Co. and D Co. cannot be associated through R Co.

ITA: 256(2)

(A) and (B) are incorrect because Joanne controls J Co. and her spouse controls D Co. Two corporations are associated under paragraph 256(1)(*c*), if related persons control each corporation and either person owns at least 25% of the shares of the related persons' corporation. Spouses are related by marriage.

ITA: 251(6)(*b*)

(C) is incorrect because if a trust for their twin daughters controls a third company, T Co., those shares are deemed to be owned by the beneficiaries. In addition, because those beneficiaries are minors, their shares are deemed to be owned by each of Joanne and Doug. Therefore, J Co. and T Co. are associated because they are deemed to be controlled by the same person (Joanne). The same is true for D Co. and T Co. (each deemed to be controlled by Doug). The two corporations are associated with each other unless an election is made to deem the third corporation (T Co.) to have a business limit of nil.

ITA: 256(1.2)(*f*)(ii), 256(1.3)
ITA: 256(1)(*a*)

ITA: 256(2)

Question 6

(C) is correct. X Ltd. and Y Ltd. are not associated because although X Ltd. is controlled by a person who is related to each member of the various groups of persons (i.e., an pair of the two daughters and one son or all three) who controls Y Ltd., there is no cross-ownership of at least 25%. Thus, X Ltd. and Y Ltd. are not associated.

ITA: 256(1)(*d*)

(A) is not correct. X and Y are associated. The same group (Rod and Patrick) controls both corporations. This group controls X Ltd., despite the fact that Patrick himself controls X Ltd. It does not matter that the individuals are not related.

ITA: 256(1)(*b*)
ITA: 256(1.2)(*b*)(i)

(B) is not correct because X Ltd. and Y Ltd. are associated because they are controlled by related persons (a parent and son are related by blood) and one of the persons owns not less than 25% of the shares of both companies.

ITA: 256(1)(*c*)
ITA: 251(6)(*a*)

(D) is not correct. Sibco and Parentco are associated. Sibco is controlled by a related group of two, three, or four of its shareholders. Parentco is controlled by the related group of the mother and father. Each member of any related group that controls Sibco is related to each member of the related group that controls Parentco. The mother and father, together, own at least 25% of the shares of both corporations.

ITA: 256(1)(*e*)

Chapter 12 — Solutions to Exercises

Exercise 1

[Note: The facts of this case are those of *The Queen v. Rochmore Investments Ltd.* However, the legislation under which the case was decided did not contain a definition of "active business" or "specified investment business".]

76 DTC 6156 (F.C.A.)

Under the current legislation, "active business" is defined to exclude "a specified investment business" in such a way that if a business is not a specified investment business (and is not a personal service business), it is an active business. Note that the definition includes an adventure in the nature of trade and is only applicable in respect of the small business deduction.

ITA: 125(7), 248(1)

In this particular case, the facts indicate that it is carrying on a specified investment business. It would appear that the principal purpose of the corporation's business is to derive income from interest on mortgage loans. It does not appear to be carrying on the business of a credit union and it is not in the business of leasing movable property. If it did, the corporation would be considered to be carrying on an active business. Since the corporation had no full-time employees, it cannot escape the definition of a specified investment business, to be treated as an active business, through paragraph (*a*) of the definition, which requires more than five full-time employees.

ITA: 125(7)

The only possibility for escape is in paragraph (*b*) of the definition of "specified investment business". If the taxpayer company did not have more than five full-time employees because another corporation associated with it provided the services to the taxpayer corporation that would otherwise be performed by its own full-time employees, then the taxpayer corporation could be considered as carrying on an active business. In this case, the two principal operators of the taxpayer corporation own and manage a number of other companies. Further facts are required to determine if any of these other corporations are associated with the taxpayer corporation and if such an associated corporation provides services that would otherwise be provided by more than five full-time employees of the taxpayer corporation. This seems unlikely given the facts outlined in the case.

ITA: 125(7)

The taxpayer corporation, therefore, is likely carrying on a specified investment business. It is not carrying on a personal services business because it is not likely that the principals of the taxpayer corporation would reasonably be regarded as employees of the persons to whom the mortgage loans were made.

Exercise 2

(A) (i)   Mr. Beta is at arm's length with the corporation because his 25% ownership does not give him control. However, paragraph 251(1)(*b*) could always apply if the facts indicate that the non-related persons are not dealing at arm's length at a particular moment in time.

ITA: 251(2)(*b*)

(ii)   Mr. Beta and his brother are not at arm's length with the corporation. Mr. Beta and his brother form a related group; since they are siblings, each is related by blood.

ITA: 251(2)(*b*)(ii), 251(6)(*a*)

(iii)   Mr. Delta is not at arm's length with the corporation because of the share purchase option. This provision deems Mr. Delta to control Alpha Corp. unless the exceptions in this subparagraph are met.

ITA: 251(5)(*b*)(i)

(iv)   Mr. Epsilon is at arm's length with the corporation because of the exception, which is contingent on the death of Mr. Beta, unless paragraph 251(1)(*b*) applies, as described in (i), above.

ITA: 251(5)(*b*)(i)

(B) (i)   The corporations are not at arm's length. This subparagraph applies where Lambda Corp. is controlled by a person (i.e., A) and Tau Corp. is controlled by a related group (i.e., A and B). A is related to himself for purposes of share ownership and to his brother.

ITA: 251(2)(*c*)(iii), 251(5)(*c*), 251(6)(*a*)

(ii)   The corporations are at arm's length because subparagraph 251(2)(*c*)(iv) does not apply where there is an unrelated group of persons controlling one corporation, unless the person controlling the other corporation is related to each member of the unrelated group. For example, if two first cousins control one corporation and their grandfather controls the other, the two corporations would be related. Of course, factual non-arm's length can always apply as described in (A)(i), above.

(iii)   The corporations are related and, hence, they are not at arm's length. This provision deems two corporations to be related where each corporation is related to another common corporation.

ITA: 251(3)

Exercise 3

(A) Jay-one Ltd. and Jay-two Ltd. are associated, both being controlled by the same person. Jay-one Ltd. and Jay-three Ltd., are associated. Since Ava has voting control of Jay-one Ltd. and Jay-one Ltd. in turn has voting control of Jay-three Ltd., then Ava controls Jay-three Ltd. Therefore, all three corporations are controlled by the same person. As a result of this application of the association rule in paragraph 256(1)(*b*), the election under subsection 256(2) is not available to Jay-one Ltd., because Jay-three Ltd. and Jay-two Ltd. are associated without subsection 256(2).

ITA: 251(1)(b), 256(1)(a), 256(1)(b)

(B) Benco Ltd. and Rayco Ltd. are associated. Benco Ltd. is controlled by Abigail's mother and Rayco Ltd. is controlled by Abigail. Abigail and her mother are related. Abigail owns at least 25% of the shares, which are not of a specified class, of both corporations.

ITA: 256(1)(a), 256(1)(c)

(C) Adamco Ltd. and Kidco Ltd. are associated. Adamco Ltd. is controlled by Adam. Kidco Ltd. is controlled by the group consisting of Adam, his daughter and his son-in-law. Adam is related to himself, to his daughter and to his son-in-law. Adam owns at least 25% of the shares which are not of a specified class of Kidco Ltd.

ITA: 252(1)(e), 256(1)(d), 256(1.5), 251(6)(a), 251(6)(b)

(D) Since both corporations are controlled by a group, paragraph 256(1)(*e*) is the only possibility for association. However, while Sisco Ltd. is controlled by a related group of sisters, Cousco Ltd. is not controlled by a related group. The two sisters as a group do not control Cousco Ltd. One sister and her daughter do not control the company. Finally, cousins and aunts and nieces are not related by the rules. Therefore, the condition in paragraph 256(1)(*e*) fails and the two corporations are not associated unless subsection 256(5.1) can be used with the argument that control in fact is exercised by Sister One and Sister Two through direct or indirect influence on their daughters or unless subsection 256(2.1) is invoked on the basis that one of the main reasons for the separate existence of the two corporations is to reduce taxes.

ITA: 251(6)(a)

ITA: 251, 252

Exercise 4

Taxit and Sibling are associated:

ITA: 256(1)(c)

— each corporation is controlled by one person;

— the person who controlled one was related to the person who controlled the other;

— one of these persons owned not less than 25% of the shares which are not of a specified class of each corporation.

Since the two corporations are associated, they must share the small business deduction on a maximum of $500,000 of active business income. The Act requires that the corporations file an agreement, in prescribed form, allocating the $500,000 business limit. If an agreement is not filed within the time period indicated in subsection 125(4), that subsection empowers the Minister to make an allocation.

ITA: 125(3)

They could each gain their eligibility for the small business deduction on a full $500,000 by having Beta reduce her holdings in Taxit to below 25% or by having Beta convert her holdings in Taxit to shares of a specified class (i.e., in essence, non-voting preferred shares). However, this strategy would work only as long as there are no factors present of the kind that would enable the deeming provisions to apply.

ITA: 256(2.1)

Exercise 5

Since neither corporation is controlled by one person, and both corporations are not controlled by the same group of persons, the only provision in subsection 256(1) that can potentially apply is paragraph 256(1)(*e*). That paragraph sets out three conditions, each of which must be met by the facts of the case for association.

(1) Each corporation must be controlled by a related group. — The group of brothers controlling Chutzpah Enterprises Limited is related. The group consisting of Bett and Dalled Chutzpah controlling Schlock Sales Limited are related as brother-in-law and sister-in-law or by paragraph 251(6)(*a*) and paragraphs 252(2)(*b*) and (*c*). Therefore, the condition is met.

ITA: 251(2)(a), 251(6)(a)
ITA: 251(6)(b)

(2) Each of the members of one of the related groups was related to all of the members of the other related group. — Consider the group consisting of Aleph and Bett Chutzpah which is a related group controlling Chutzpah Enterprises Limited and the group Bett and Dalled Chutzpah which is a related group controlling Schlock Sales Limited. Aleph is related to his brother Bett, as discussed above, and to Dalled. Bett is related to himself and his sister-in-law, Dalled, as discussed above. Therefore, the condition is met.

ITA: 251(2)(a), 251(6)(a), 256(1.5)

(3) One or more members of both related groups must own, either alone or together, not less than 25% of the issued shares of any class, other than a specified class, of shares of the capital stock of the other corporation. — Bett, who is a member of both related groups, owns alone the minimum 25% of the shares necessary to meet this condition. Common shares are not shares of a specified class.   ITA: 256(1.1)

Exercise 6

Part I tax payable

Part I Tax on Taxable Income

Taxable income	$ 79,700
Tax @ 38% on $79,700	$ 30,286
Deduct: Federal tax abatement (10% of $79,700)	7,970
Net	$ 22,316

Additional refundable tax (ART) — $6\frac{2}{3}$% × lesser of:

(a) AII	$ 7,000	
(b) TI – SBD income amount (Schedule 1)	$ 3,750	
$6\frac{2}{3}$% of $3,750 (i.e., $79,700 – $75,950)		250
Total		$ 22,566

Deduct: Non-business foreign tax credit (assumed)	$ 1,050	
Small business deduction (see Schedule 1)	12,912	
General reduction (see Schedule 2)	Nil	13,962
Part I federal tax payable		$ 8,604
Provincial tax @ 5% of $79,700		3,985
Total tax payable		$ 12,589

Schedule 1: *Small Business Deduction*

17% of the least of:

Income from an active business		$110,000(I)
Taxable income	$79,700	
Less: $^{100}/_{28}$ × foreign non-business tax credit (see above) ($^{100}/_{28}$ × $1,050)	3,750	$ 75,950(II)
Business limit		$500,000(III)

Small business deduction — 17% of $75,950 = $12,912

Schedule 2: *General Reduction*

taxable income		$ 79,700
less: income eligible for the small business deduction	$75,950	
AII	7,000	(82,950)
net		Nil
13% of Nil		Nil
Total		$ Nil

Exercise 7

Paragraph 186(1)(*b*) requires that Part IV tax be calculated as follows:

$$\frac{\$90,000}{\$120,000} \times \$18,000 = \$13,500$$

Exercise 8

(A) *Computation of Taxable Income*

Net income for income tax purposes		$186,250
Deduct: taxable dividends	$18,750	
non-capital losses	37,500	
net capital losses ($68,750 × ½ / ¾; limited to TCG)	37,500	93,750
Taxable income.		$ 92,500

Part I Tax on Taxable Income

Tax @ 38% of $92,500.		$ 35,150
Deduct: federal tax abatement (10% of $92,500)		9,250
Net		$ 25,900
Additional refundable tax (ART) — 6⅔% of lesser of:		
(a) AII ($37,500 + $45,000 + $18,750 − $37,500 − $18,750) = $45,000		
(b) TI − SBD income amount ($92,500 − $85,000) = $7,500		500
		$ 26,400
Deduct: small business deduction (see Schedule 1)	$14,450	
general reduction	Nil	$ 14,450
Part I tax payable (federal)		$ 11,950
Provincial tax @ 8% of $92,500		7,400
Total tax payable		$ 19,350

Schedule 1: Small Business Deduction

Income from active business	$ 85,000(I)
Taxable income (no foreign tax credits)	$ 92,500(II)
Business limit	$500,000(III)
17% of the least of amounts (I), (II), and (III)	$ 14,450

(B) *Refundable Portion of Part I Tax*

Least of:

(a) 26⅔% × aggregate investment income (26⅔% × ($45,000 + $37,500 + $18,750 − $37,500 − $18,750))		$ 12,000
(b) Taxable income	$ 92,500	
Less: Amount eligible for the SBD	(85,000)	
26⅔% × $7,500 =		$ 2,000
(c) Part I tax		$ 11,950
Refundable portion of Part I tax — the least amount		$ 2,000

Part IV Tax on Taxable Dividends Received

Taxable dividends subject to Part IV tax × ⅓ ($18,750 × ⅓)	$ 6,250
Deduct: non-capital loss claimed for Part IV × ⅓ (all claimed under Part I)	Nil
Tax	$ 6,250

Refundable Dividend Tax on Hand

Refundable dividend tax on hand at end of last year	Nil	
Deduct: dividend refund for last year	Nil	
	Nil	
Add: refundable portion of Part I tax	$ 2,000	
Part IV tax	6,250	$ 8,250

Dividend Refund

Taxable dividends paid in the taxation year ($112,500 × ⅓)	$ 37,500(VI)
Refundable dividend tax on hand	$ 8,250(VII)
Dividend refund — lesser of (VI) and (VII)	$ 8,250

Exercise 9

(A) *Part I Tax on Taxable Income*

Tax @ 38% of $130,000		$ 49,400
Deduct: federal tax abatement (10% of 95% of $130,000)		12,350
Net		$ 37,050
Additional refundable tax (ART) — $6\frac{2}{3}$% of lesser of:		
(a) AII ($50K + $30K + $20K + $50K – $20K – $50K) = $80,000		
(b) TI – SBD income amount ($130K – $90K) = $40,000		2,667
Total		$ 39,717
Deduct: non-business foreign tax credit (given)	$ 4,000	
business foreign tax credit (given)	1,000	
small business deduction (see Schedule 1)	15,300	
general reduction	Nil	20,300
Part I tax payable (federal)		$ 19,417
Provincial tax @ 7% of 95% of $130,000		8,645
Total tax		$ 28,062

Schedule 1: *Small Business Deduction*

17% of least of:

Income from active business			$ 90,000(I)
Taxable income		$130,000	
Deduct: non-business foreign tax credit × $\frac{100}{28}$	$14,286		
business foreign tax credit × 4	4,000	18,286	$111,714(II)
Business limit			$500,000(III)
Small business deduction — 17% of $90,000			$ 15,300

(B) *Refundable Portion of Part I Tax*

Least of:

(a) $26\frac{2}{3}$% × aggregate investment income ($26\frac{2}{3}$% × $80,000)			$ 21,333
Less: non-business foreign tax credit	$4,000		
minus: $9\frac{1}{3}$% × foreign investment income ($9\frac{1}{3}$% × $30,000)	(2,800)	(1,200)	$ 20,133
(b) Taxable income		$130,000	
Less: amount eligible for SBD		(90,000)	
$\frac{100}{35}$ × non-business FTC ($4,000)		(11,429)	
4 × business FTC ($1,000)		(4,000)	
	$26\frac{2}{3}$% × $24,571 =		$ 6,552
(c) Part I tax			$ 19,417
Refundable portion of Part I tax — The least			$ 6,552

Part IV Tax on Taxable Dividends Received

Taxable dividends subject to Part IV tax:

Non-connected corporations × $\frac{1}{3}$ ($30,000 × $\frac{1}{3}$)	$ 10,000
Connected corporations to the extent of share of dividend refund to payer	4,000
Total Part IV tax payable	$ 14,000

Refundable Dividend Tax on Hand

RDTOH at end of last year	Nil	
Deduct: Dividend refund for last year	Nil	Nil

Add: Refundable portion of Part I tax	$ 6,552
Part IV tax	14,000
RDTOH at end of year	$ 20,552

Dividend Refund

Taxable dividends paid in year ($70,000 × ⅓)	$ 23,333(VI)
RDTOH at end of year	$ 20,552(VII)
Dividend refund — lesser of (VI) and (VII)	$ 20,552

Exercise 10

(A) Sunlight Limited and H Ltd. are associated. H Ltd. is controlled by one person, Mr. Bennett. He is related to each member of the group, H Ltd. and W Ltd. that controls Sunlight Limited, because he is related to H Ltd. which he controls and he is related to W Ltd., which is controlled by his wife. Also, he owns not less than 25% of the shares of Sunlight Limited through his ownership of shares in H Ltd. These shares are not specified shares. By a similar analysis, Sunlight Limited and W Ltd. are associated.

ITA: 256(1)(*d*)
ITA: 251(2)(*b*)(i), 251(2)(*b*)(iii)
ITA: 256(1.2)(*d*)

Since the rental income would be deductible as an expense from the income of an active business of an associated payer, it will not be income from property of the recipient. It will be deemed to be income from an active business of the recipient, H Ltd. Since H Ltd. has only dividend income it will be eligible for the small business deduction in respect of the rental income as long as it is allocated a part of the business limit of the associated corporations.

ITA: 129(6)(*a*)(i)
ITA: 129(6)(*b*)(i)
ITA: 125(1)

(B) Since Sunlight is connected with both holding companies there will be no Part IV tax liability unless Sunlight gets a dividend refund as a result of the dividends it pays. However, Sunlight earns only active business income which is not subject to refundable taxes and dividend refunds.

Exercise 11

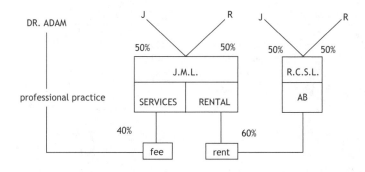

(A) Rent from RCSL:

   (i) RCSL is associated with JML;

ITA: 256(1)(*b*)

   (ii) RCSL deducts the rent from its active business.

Therefore, the rent is deemed to be income of JML from an active business, eligible for the small business deduction.

ITA: 125(1), 129(6)(*b*)(i)

(B) Services fee from Dr. Adam:

   (i) JML's income from providing services would be considered income from an active business unless further facts indicate that it is carrying on a personal services business;

   (ii) the business of providing services would be a personal services business if one or both of the shareholders of JML, who are specified shareholders (because they own at least 10% of the shares of JML), performed the services and would be regarded as an employee of the professional practice of Dr. Adam.

Therefore, if the services fee is considered income from an active business, it would qualify for the small business deduction.

CHAPTER 12

Exercise 12

Interest income		$ 7,000
Dividends grossed up (1.18 × $15,000)		17,700
Taxable capital gains (½ × $6,000)		3,000
Incremental taxable income		$27,700

Federal tax on total taxable income of $47,700
(i.e., $27,700 incremental + $20,000 other income):

Tax on first $43,561	$ 6,534	
Tax on next $4,139 @ 22%	911	$ 7,445
Less: dividend tax credit (¹³/₁₈ × 18% of $15,000)	$ 1,950	
other personal tax credits	1,800	(3,750)
Basic federal tax		$ 3,695
Provincial tax		
Tax on first $43,561	$ 4,356	
Tax on next $4,139 @ 12%	497	4,853
Less: dividend tax credit (⁵/₁₈ × 18% of $15,000)	$ 750	
other personal tax credits	1,200	(1,950)
Total tax on taxable income of $48,750		$ 6,598

Taxation of Income from Investment Portfolio through a Corporation

Corporation		*Available cash*
Interest income	$ 7,000	
Dividends	15,000	
Taxable capital gains	3,000	
Income	$25,000	$25,000[1]
Less: dividends [sec. 112]	15,000	
Taxable income	$10,000	
Tax under Part I @ 43.5% (38% − 10% + 15.5%)	$ 4,350	
Additional refundable tax at 6⅔% of $10,000 ($7K + $15K + $3K − $15K)	667	
Tax under Part IV @ 33⅓% of $15,000	5,000	10,017
Retained in corporation[1]		$14,983
Refundable tax:		
Part I (26⅔% of ($7K + $15K + $3K − $15K))	$ 2,667	
Part IV (33⅓% × $15,000)	5,000	7,667
Available for distribution to shareholders as taxable dividend		$22,650[2]

Shareholder		
Taxable dividend (per requirements)		$15,000
Gross-up (18% of $15,000)		2,700
Incremental taxable income		$17,700

Federal tax on total taxable income of $37,700
(i.e., $17,700 incremental + $20,000 other income):

Tax @ 15%		$ 5,655
Less: dividend tax credit (¹³/₁₈ × 18% of $15,000)	$1,950	
other personal tax credits	1,800	(3,750)
Basic federal tax		$ 1,905
Provincial tax		
Tax @ 10%		$ 3,770
Less: dividend tax credit (⁵/₁₈ × 18% of $15,000)	$ 750	
other personal tax credits	1,200	(1,950)
Total tax on taxable income of $38,750		$ 3,725

Total Taxes Paid

Through corporation:

Corporation after refund on $15,000 of dividends paid ($10,017 – ⅓ × $15,000)	$ 5,017
Shareholder	3,725
Total[3]	$ 8,742
Received directly	$ 6,598

— NOTES TO SOLUTION

[1] Ignores the non-taxable portion of capital gain which can be distributed tax free.

[2] Note that a dividend of $22,650 will result in a dividend refund of only $7,550 (i.e., $22,650 × ⅓), not the $7,667 that was added to the RDTOH for the year. This deficiency results from imperfections in the tax rates. A larger dividend of $23,000 (i.e., 3 × $7,667) would have to be paid, using other sources of funds, to clear the RDTOH. Alternatively, the maximum dividend that can be paid in this case is $22,475, determined algebraically, as follows:

$$R = ⅓\,D$$
$$D = N - T + R$$
where:
R = dividend refund
$$= N - T + ⅓\,D$$
D = dividend
$$= (N - T) × ³⁄₂$$
N = Division B net income
$$= (\$25,000 - \$10,017) × ³⁄₂$$
T = total tax
$$= \$22,475$$
$$R = \$7,492$$

This is not an immediate issue, since only $15,000 of dividends are required to be paid in the year.

Note that if the provincial corporate tax rate had been only 7.3%, before the additional refundable tax and the dividend refund, the amount available for dividends would be sufficient to clear the RDTOH.

[3] This amount is higher because not all of the corporate tax has been refunded as yet, and because the provincial corporate tax is 8.2% higher than the theoretical rate of 7.3%.

Exercise 13

The two corporations are considered associated for Canadian tax purposes. Generally, interest income received from an associated corporation that is deductible in computing that corporation's active business income would be considered active business income. However, as the interest is U.S.-sourced, and not from a "source in Canada", and is not deductible in computing active business income in Canada, it will be considered investment income to the Canadian corporation and not income from an active business. Hence, the small business deduction will not apply.

ITA: 256
ITA: 129(6)

The interest will be subject to the full corporate tax rate, including the 6⅔% additional refundable tax on investment income. The addition to RDTOH (26⅔%) will also apply.

ITA: 123.3, 129(1)

Chapter 13
Planning the Use of a Corporation and Shareholder-Manager Remuneration

LEARNING GOALS

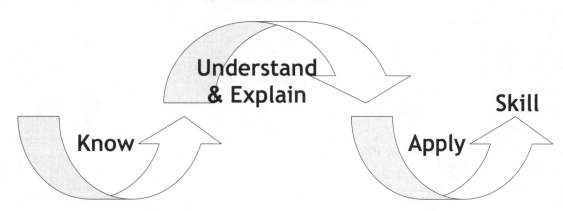

Know

By the end of this chapter, you should know the basic provisions of the *Income Tax Act* that relate to the compensation of a corporation's owner-manager and that relate to the general anti-avoidance rule. Completing the Review Questions (¶13,800) and Multiple Choice Questions (¶13,825) is a good way to learn the technical provisions.

Understand and Explain

You should understand and be able to explain:

- the more common elements in the remuneration of a shareholder-manager, including salary, bonus, dividend, and loan and the considerations needed to make a choice;
- the salary versus dividend trade-off, including the amount of dividends that can be distributed tax free;
- the reasons for the use of a holding corporation, the benefits of the capital gains deduction, and rules that inhibit family income splitting through a corporation; and
- why the general anti-avoidance rule exists and how it has been interpreted and used.

Completing the Exercises (¶13,850) is a good way to deepen your understanding of the material.

Apply

You should be able to apply your knowledge and understanding of the key elements of compensation to:

- choose the optimal compensation components to minimize remuneration costs in a particular owner-manager situation;
- maintain the eligibility of shares for the capital gains exemption;
- avoid the adverse income tax effects of using a corporation to split family income; and
- generally determine whether the general anti-avoidance rule might apply in a particular planning situation.

Completing the Assignment Problems (¶13,875) is an excellent way to develop your ability to apply the material in increasingly complex situations.

Chapter 13 — Learning Chart

Topic	Example Problem (✓)	Review Questions (¶13,800)	Multiple Choice (¶13,825)	Exercises (¶13,850)	Assignment Problems (¶13,875)
¶13,000 EMPLOYMENT REMUNERATION					
¶13,010 Considerations in Choosing Elements of Shareholder-Manager Remuneration					
¶13,015 Cash needs					
¶13,020 Individual's tax bracket					
¶13,025 25% dividend gross-up and credit					
¶13,030 45% dividend gross-up and credit					
¶13,035 Availability of tax deferral					
¶13,040 Avoid exceeding the business limit for the small business deduction					
¶13,050 Salaries, Bonuses, and Other Payments to the Shareholder-Manager					
¶13,055 General guidelines		7			
¶13,060 Salaries and bonuses		2			
¶13,065 Accrued bonuses and other amounts		1, 3, 4	3	1	3
¶13,070 Shareholder Benefits and Loans					
¶13,075 Shareholder benefits	✓				1
¶13,080 Shareholder loans	✓	5, 6	1, 2	2, 3, 4	2, 3, 4
¶13,090 Other Planning Considerations for Shareholder-Manager Remuneration					
¶13,095 Income splitting					
¶13,100 Fringe benefits				5	
¶13,200 SALARY VERSUS DIVIDENDS					
¶13,210 The Basic Trade-Off					
¶13,220 Approximate Amounts of Taxable Dividends That Can Be Distributed Tax-Free					
¶13,230 Distribution Out of Income Taxed at Small Business Rate	✓	8		6, 7	5, 6, 7
¶13,240 Distributions Out of Income Not Eligible for the Small Business Deduction					
¶13,250 Summary of the Salary Versus Dividends Issue					
¶13,300 OTHER PLANNING ASPECTS OF USING CORPORATIONS					
¶13,310 Use of Holding Companies					
¶13,315 An extension of integration					
¶13,320 Compensation					
¶13,325 Deferral of tax on dividends					
¶13,330 Implementing an estate freeze					
¶13,340 Qualified Small Business Corporation Share (QSBCS)					
¶13,345 Small business corporation (SBC)	✓	10, 11	7	8	
¶13,350 Basic QSBCS rules applied to a single corporation	✓				8

Topic	Example Problem (✓)	Review Questions (¶13,800)	Multiple Choice (¶13,825)	Exercises (¶13,850)	Assignment Problems (¶13,875)
¶13,355 Modification of the asset test (stacking rule)	✓				9
¶13,360 Capital Gains Deduction					
¶13,365 Overview					
¶13,370 Computation of deduction				9	10
¶13,375 Allowable business investment losses		9			
¶13,380 Cumulative net investment loss (CNIL)					
¶13,385 Other related provisions	✓				
¶13,390 Attribution Through a Corporation		12	6	10	11
¶13,395 Imputed interest	✓				
¶13,400 Income-Splitting Tax ("Kiddie Tax")					
¶13,500 GENERAL ANTI-AVOIDANCE RULE UNDER THE INCOME TAX ACT					
¶13,510 The Statutory Provision			4	11, 12	
¶13,515 Purpose					
¶13,520 Defined terms					
¶13,525 Limitation					
¶13,530 Examples in the technical notes					
¶13,535 Administration and application			5		12, 13
¶13,540 Federal Court of Appeal — OSFC Holdings Ltd.					
¶13,545 The findings					
¶13,550 Application of OSFC case analytical framework					
¶13,560 Supreme Court of Canada — *Canada Trustco* and *Mathew et al.*					
¶13,565 The transactions					
¶13,570 Application of the OSFC tests and interpretations					
¶13,580 The Saga Continues — Decisions Since *Canada Trustco*					
¶13,585 *Earl Lipson and Jordan B. Lipson* 2006 DTC 2687 (T.C.C.)/2007 DTC 5172 (F.C.A.)/2009 DTC 5015 (S.C.C.))					
¶13,586 *Copthorne Holdings Ltd. v. The Queen*, 2012 DTC 5007 (S.C.C.)					
¶13,600 Proposals To Require Information Reporting of Tax Avoidance Transactions					
¶13,900 SUPPLEMENTAL NOTES					
¶13,910 General Anti-Avoidance Rule Under the *Excise Tax Act*					

Study Notes

Chapter 13 —
Discussion Notes for Review Questions

(1) Mr. Smith can pay the bonus within the 179-day limit and loan the net after-tax amount back to the company. If he actually does this, he should consider charging interest to the company in order to reduce payroll taxes by converting his salary into interest income. This will also protect his ability to claim a capital loss or an ABIL in the event the company was unable to repay the loan. He should also consider securing the loan.

ITA: 78(4)

(2) (a) If he leaves the money in the company, the income over $500,000 will not be eligible for the small business deduction, but it will be eligible for the general rate reduction. The marginal tax rate will be 28% (i.e., 38% − 10% − 13% + 13%).

(b) If he declares and pays the bonus the personal marginal tax rate will be 46% (i.e., 29% + 17%).

(c) He can defer approximately 18.3% (see calculation below) of tax by leaving the income in the company to be taxed.

(d) If he leaves the income in the company to be taxed, he will have to pay tax on the dividend when he eventually pays it out. The combined tax rate at that point, assuming the 38% dividend tax credit, will be approximately 46.3% which is slightly above the 46% personal tax cost of paying out the bonus now. That small tax cost is offset by the deferral of tax until the dividend is paid.

(e) Calculation:

Corporate income	$1,000
Corporate tax @ 28	(280)
After-tax income	$ 720
Dividend paid	$ 720
Gross-up (38%)	274
Taxable dividend	$ 994
Tax @ 46%	$ 457
Dividend tax credit	(274)
Net personal tax	$ 183
Net cash after tax	$ 537
Total tax ($280 + $183)	$ 463

(3) If he or she chooses a fiscal year-end on or after July 6, but no later than December 31, then the bonus can be paid within the 179 days in either this calendar year or on January 1 of the next calendar year.

ITA: 78(4)

(4) The following are the five criteria for the deductibility of bonus accruals as decided in the *Totem Disposal* case:

- reasonableness of the bonus in relation to profit and services rendered;

- payment for real and identifiable service;

- some justification for expecting a bonus over regular salary (e.g., a company policy);

- reasonableness of the time between determining profit and establishing the bonus; and

- a legal obligation to pay the accrued bonus.

(5) Mr. Chow is related to his brother-in-law. Therefore, they are deemed not to deal with each other at arm's length and the brother-in-law is connected with Mr. Chow. As a result, the conditions in the shareholder loan rule are met and none of the exceptions are met. Therefore, the brother-in-law will be required to take the full amount of the loan into income in 2013 since none of it was repaid by December 31, 2014. In 2015 and 2016, the brother-in-law will be able to deduct the principal repayments. The imputed interest benefit included in his 2013 tax return can be removed through an amended return to eliminate the benefit.

ITA: 15(2.1), 251(2)
ITA: 15(2), 15(2.4)
ITA: 20(1)(*j*)

ITA: 80.4(3)(*b*)

(6) Since Ms. Jones is a shareholder and received a loan, the shareholder loan rules apply. Although Ms. Jones is an employee, the boat does not fit into one of the exceptions. Therefore, Ms. Jones will have to take the $25,000 into income unless she repays it within one year from the end of the taxation year in which she received the loan. If she has to include the principal in income then the imputed interest rules will not apply.

ITA: 15(2)
ITA: 15(2.4)(*b*)–(*d*), 15(2.6)
ITA: 80.4, 80.4(3)(*b*)

(7) This provincial tax holiday would bring the combined corporate tax rate on income eligible for the small business deduction down below 15.3% [after 2013] and would provide a tax incentive to flowing active business income through a corporation, paying corporate tax and then paying dividends. Thus, there would then be an advantage to paying dividends instead of salary to the owner due to the fact that the dividend tax credit is greater than the underlying corporate tax.

(8) With the 18% dividend gross-up [for dividends paid after 2013] his taxable income would be $35,400. The federal tax would be $5,310 less the dividend tax credit of $3,900 and the personal credit of $1,656 (in 2013) leaving basic federal tax of nil. Provincial tax on $35,400 would be $3,540, less the provincial dividend tax credit of $1,500 (i.e., $5/18 \times \$5,400$) and the provincial personal tax credit of $1,104 (i.e., $11,038 \times .10$), leaving provincial tax of $936.

(9) It is true that in order to claim an ABIL the shares need to be shares in a small business corporation. However, the definition of small business corporation allows the status as a small business corporation to continue for 12 months for purposes of the ABIL provisions. Since she sold the shares within six months she should be able to claim the loss as an ABIL.

ITA: 248(1)
ITA: 39(1)(*c*)

(10) In several Interpretation Bulletins, the CRA states that the phrase means at least 90%. It should be noted that this phrase has not been specifically determined by the courts and it is unclear whether the courts would allow 85% or require 95% as the percentage necessary to meet this test. Practitioners generally use 90%.

IT-151R5, par. 31 (for example)

(11) This corporation is neither, since in order to meet the definition of "small business corporation" it has to meet the 90% test at the determination time. Since the corporation does not meet this test it is neither an SBC nor a QSBC.

(12) The preamble to the corporate attribution rule refers only to situations where "individuals have transferred or loaned property." In this case his corporation has loaned the funds to her corporation. It could not even be said that he did it indirectly since he has not loaned or transferred any money to his own corporation. Therefore, even though her corporation is not an SBC, the corporate attribution rules should not apply. However, GAAR should be considered.

ITA: 74.4(2)

Chapter 13 –
Solutions to Multiple Choice Questions

Question 1

(B) is correct under administrative practice outlined in the text. If $40,000 of the loan is repaid within one year of the end of the year of S Ltd. in which the loan was made, then $160,000 must be included in the year of the loan. Subsequent repayments are deductible in the year of the repayment.

ITA: 15(2)
ITA: 15(2.6)
ITA: 15(2.4)

(A) is incorrect under administrative practice. Only the part of the loan ($160,000) that was not paid before the one-year limit will be included in Stan's income in 2013, the year he received the loan. The limit is one year after the end of the taxation year of the lender in which the loan was made. He does not meet the other criteria for exclusion. Since such a loan is not available to other employees, it is not reasonable to conclude that he received the loan because of his employment.

(C) is incorrect. There is no imputed interest benefit when the loan is included in income. If there was an imputed interest benefit the prescribed rate protection rule would not apply as the loan was not received because of his employment.

ITA: 80.4(1), 80.4(3)(*b*), 80.4(4)

(D) is incorrect. One year after the end of the calendar year in which the loan is received has no significance. The shareholder loan rule includes the loan in income in the year it is *received* unless it is repaid by one year after the end of the taxation year of the *lender* in which the loan was made, or the loan meets one of the specific exclusions.

ITA: 15(2)

Question 2

(C) is the correct answer. The shareholder loan rule would include the principal amount of the loan in Mrs. C's income in 2013 because none of the exception tests are met.

ITA: 15(2.2), 15(2.3), 15(2.4), 15(2.6)

(1) The exception test in subsection 15(2.2) does not apply because Mrs. C is resident in Canada.

(2) The exception in subsection 15(2.3) does not apply since the money is not lent in the ordinary course of money lending business.

(3) None of the exceptions for employees in subsection 15(2.4) are met, because it is not reasonable to conclude that the loan is received because of employment since no other employees have received similar loans.

(4) The exception in subsection 15(2.6) does not apply since the debt was repaid on April 1, 2015, which is more than one year from the end of S Ltd.'s December 31, 2013 fiscal year.

The loan in (A) would not be included in Mrs. A's income because the one-year repayment exception test applies: the debt is repaid on April 1, 2014, which is within one year from the end of S Ltd.'s December 31, 2013 fiscal year. Note, however, that the imputed interest benefit rule would apply to compute a deemed interest benefit on the loan.

ITA: 15(2.6)

ITA: 80.4(2)

The loan in (B) would not be included in B Ltd's income because the shareholder loan rule does not apply to corporate shareholders resident in Canada.

ITA: 15(2)

The loan in (D) would not be included in Mr. D's income because one of the exceptions for employees is met: Mr. D is not a specified employee and it is reasonable to conclude that the loan is received because of employment, since the computer is for employment use and other employees currently working at home have received similar loans. Since Mr. D is not a specified employee, the loan does not have to be for any specified purpose. A specified employee is an employee who is either a specified shareholder (i.e., generally, a person who owns at least 10% of the shares of any class of the corporation) or a person who does not deal at arm's length with the corporation. Since Mr. D owns only 5% of the shares of S Ltd. and deals at arm's length with the corporation, he is not a specified employee.

ITA: 15(2.4), 248(1)

Question 3

(D) is correct. Since the $300,000 bonus is unpaid on the 180th day after the end of the taxation year of Fortelli Inc. in which the expense was incurred, it is not deductible until 2014, the taxation year in which it is actually paid.

ITA: 78(4)

(A) is incorrect. This amount refers to the rules in subsection 78(1) for unpaid amounts due to related persons, other than pension benefits, retiring allowances, salary, wages, or other remuneration.

(B) is incorrect. Subsection 78(4) does not distinguish between amounts owed to related and unrelated persons.

(C) is incorrect for the same reason as (A).

Question 4

The correct answer is (B). There is no penalty. The tax benefit that would otherwise have been enjoyed is denied.   ITA: 245(2)

(A) is incorrect as it is true in accordance with subsection 245(2).

(C) is incorrect as it is true in accordance with subsection 245(3).

(D) is incorrect as it is true in accordance with subsection 245(4).

Question 5

(C) is correct. The purpose of the transaction seems to be the reduction or avoidance of tax on the income earned on the $10,000 gift. This transaction goes against the spirit of the Act, read as a whole, and falls within the definition of an avoidance transaction. Note that an attribution rule would apply if it was a loan instead of a gift.   ITA: 245(3)
ITA: 56(4.1)

(A) is incorrect. The transaction is an estate freeze which can reasonably be considered to have been undertaken for *bona fide* purposes other than to obtain the tax benefit. This transaction does not result in a misuse or abuse of the Act, read as a whole.   IC 88-2, par. 10

(B) is incorrect. The incorporation of a business and the claiming of a small business deduction by a CCPC is specifically provided for in the Act. This transaction does not result in a misuse or abuse of the Act, read as a whole.   IC 88-2, par. 11

(D) is incorrect. The Act will deny the deduction of the bonus to the extent it is in excess of a reasonable amount. To the extent the transaction is reasonable, it does not result in a benefit. Corporate tax will be reduced by the accrual, but Mary will pay tax on the income personally.   ITA: 67; IC 88-2, par. 18

Question 6

(D) is correct. All the conditions for corporate attribution are met. As a result, Mr. Boehmer is deemed to have income of 3% $\times$ $1,000,000 = $30,000.   ITA: 74.4

(A) incorrectly attributes the cash dividend received by Mrs. Boehmer to Mr. Boehmer: $10,000.

(B) incorrectly attributes the grossed up dividend received by Mrs. Boehmer to Mr. Boehmer: $11,800 [using the 18% gross-up for dividends paid after 2013].

(C) incorrectly computes the attributed amount to Mr. Boehmer based on $500,000:   ITA: 74.4
3% $\times$ $500,000 = $15,000.

Question 7

(C) is correct. In order to be a small business corporation, the percentage of assets used in an active business by the corporation and the corporation controlled by Ms. Prentice's brother must be at least 90%. It is now 80% (60% + 20%) or $3,200,000.   ITA: 248(1) "small business corporation"

Therefore total assets must be $3,200,000/90% or $3,555,555.

Therefore $444,445 ($4,000,000 – $3,555,555) of the non-active business assets must be sold.

(A) is incorrect because the corporation does not currently meet the 90% test.

(B) incorrectly assumes that 10% of the assets must be sold: 10% $\times$ 4,000,000 = $400,000.

(D) incorrectly ignores the assets used by the related corporation and calculates that since active business assets are $2,400,000 (60% $\times$ $4,000,000), total assets must be $2,400,000/90% or $2,666,666 to meet the 90% test. As a result, $1,333,333 ($4,000,000 – $2,666,666) of the non-active business assets must be sold.

Chapter 13 — Solutions to Exercises

Exercise 1

(A) The bonus must be paid on or before 179 days from the end of the year in which it was deducted. In this case, it must be paid on or before March 28, 2014. (Administrative practice would allow payment on the 180th day.)

IT-109R2, par. 10

(B) If the bonus is not paid on or before March 28, 2014, the corporation may not deduct the bonus in its 2013 taxation year. The bonus may only be deducted when it is paid.

(C) (i) The rent must be paid within two years from the end of the year in which it was deducted. In this case, it must be paid by September 30, 2015.

(ii) If the rent is not paid by September 30, 2015, the corporation must add the $10,000 to its income for its 2016 taxation year beginning October 1, 2015. This does not cancel the payable, such that if the rent is ever paid, the shareholder will declare the rental income, but there will be no deduction for the corporation.

(iii) An election can be filed before the date on which the corporation must file its tax return for 2016. In this case, that date is March 31, 2017. If such an election is filed, Mr. Schneider will be deemed to have income of $10,000 and to have loaned that amount back to the corporation on October 1, 2015. When the loan is repaid to Mr. Schneider, there are no tax consequences since the amount of the loan has already been taxed. The election can be filed late. However, $2,500 (effectively, a late-filing penalty) will be added back to the income of the corporation for its 2016 fiscal year. Mr. Schneider's tax position is not affected by this late-filed election.

ITA: 78(1)(b)

ITA: 78(3)

Exercise 2

(A) *Employee*

Principal-Amount

— Note that the shareholder loan rule applies in this case because he is a shareholder.

ITA: 15(2)

(a) House Loan

The Act would exempt the principal amount of this loan from income since Mr. Nesbitt received the loan in his capacity as an employee (i.e., by virtue of his employment), the purpose of the loan was to purchase a house and *bona fide* arrangements were made for repayment of the loan within a reasonable time;

ITA: 15(2.4)(b)

— however, an interest benefit on a "home purchase loan" would be included in income as shown in the calculation below.

ITA: 80.4

(b) Furniture Loan

There is no exemption from income for this loan because it was not repaid within one year of the 2013 taxation year of the corporation;

ITA: 15(2.3), 15(2.4), 15(2.6)

— since the loan is included in income in 2013, it is an exception for the purposes of the imputed interest benefit and, hence, there is no interest benefit.

ITA: 15(2), 80.4(3)(b)

(c) Share Purchase Loan

This loan is exempt from income because Mr. Nesbitt received the loan in his capacity as an employee and *bona fide* arrangements were made to repay the loan within a reasonable time;

ITA: 15(2.4)(c)

— since this type of loan is not an exception to the imputed interest rules, there is an interest benefit as shown in the calculation below.

ITA: 80.4

Interest Benefit

(a) interest on "home purchase loan" made to an officer or employee computed, at lesser of: (i) the prescribed rate in effect during the period in the year that the loan was outstanding, and (ii) the prescribed rate in effect at the time the loan was made. This "lesser of" choice can be made on a quarter-by-quarter comparison of tax rates. In this case, the 3% prescribed rate in June 2013, when the loan was received, is less than the rate for the other two quarters of 2013 in which the loan was outstanding. Therefore, the benefit would be based on the following calculation:

ITA: 80.4(1)(a), 80.4(4)

June–Dec. 2013: 3% of $75,000 $\times$ $^{214}/_{365}$ $1,319

(b) interest on share purchase loan computed at prescribed rates in effect
during the period in the year that the loan was outstanding

ITA: 80.4(1)(a)

June 2013: 3% of $10,000 × 30/365 = $ 25

July–Sept. 2013: 4% of $10,000 × 92/365 = 101

Oct.–Dec. 2013: 4% of $10,000 × 92/365 = 101   227

Subtotal $1,546

(c) Less: interest paid on above loans (2% of $75,000 × 214/365) 879

Benefit calculated under ssec. 80.4(1) and included in employment income $ 667

ITA: 61(1)(a), 6(9)

Less: deduction for imputed interest on loan to buy shares 227

ITA: 20(1)(c), 80.5

Net benefit under Division B .... $ 440

Since the loan to purchase the house is a "home relocation loan", the Act provides for a deduction from taxable income in Division C, calculated as the least of:

ITA: 248(1). 110(1)(j)

(a) the net imputed interest on the home purchase loan computed
under paragraph 80.4(1)(a) as the lesser amount above $1,319
less: interest paid in respect of the year, ... 879 $ 440

(b) interest on $25,000 computed under paragraph 80.4(1)(a) as
the lesser amount above ($25,000/$75,000 × $1,319) .... $ 440

(c) benefit deemed received under section 80.4 for the year ...... $ 667

Therefore, the deduction would be $440.

ITA: 110(1)(j)

(B) *Shareholder*

If Mr. Nesbitt received the loans by virtue of being a shareholder, then all the loans would be included in income in the year that the loans were received, unless the loans were repaid by the end of the fiscal year in which the loans were made. Where a loan is outstanding in the year in which the loan was made, there would be an imputed interest inclusion. However, the inclusion would be reversed on the filing of the amended return for the loan inclusion.

ITA: 80.4(2)
ITA: 15(2)

For imputed interest, the main difference is that the benefit on the loan to purchase the house would be based only on the prescribed rate in effect during the period in the year that the loan was outstanding and reduced by the amount of interest paid on the loan by the shareholder in the period not later than 30 days after the corporation's year-end. This is because the calculation of the imputed interest benefit by virtue of shareholdings does not take into account the special rules for a "home purchase loan" or a "home relocation loan". Therefore, there would also not be a deduction available.

ITA: 80.4(2), 80.4(7), 248(1)
ITA: 110(1)(j)

Exercise 3

(A) The CRA indicates that it examines the balance in the account at the end of each year of the lender considering a net increase as a loan to be included in the income of the borrower and a net decrease as a repayment to be deducted from the income of the borrower. This approach would result in the following:

IT-119R4, par. 34-35

Lender's year end	Change from previous year	Income [ssec. 15(2.6)] or repayment [par. 20(1)(j)]
Year 2	$45,000	income
Year 3	(32,000)	repayment
Year 4	(2,000)	repayment
Year 5	12,000	income
Year 6	(14,000)	repayment

(B) If there is no series of loans and repayments, then repayments are considered to apply first to the oldest loan outstanding unless the facts clearly indicate otherwise. Applying this approach would result in the following:

IT-119R4, par. 27

Lender's year end	Net inclusion (or deduction)	Explanation
Year 2	$25,000	— only the $20,000 borrowed in year 2 is repaid within one year of year 2; the $25,000 loan was not fully repaid within one year, so it must be taken into income in year 2
Year 3	(12,000)	— repayment of $12,000 of the $25,000 year 2 loan previously included
Year 4	(12,000)	— repayment of part of balance of year 2 loan
	Nil	— Nov. 30/year 4 loan repaid within one year of year 4
Year 5	(1,000)	— repayment of remainder of April 30/ year 2 loan
	23,000	— full amount of Nov. 30/year 5 loan, since not fully repaid within one year of year 5
Year 6	(14,000)	— repayment of $14,000 of year 5 loan

Note that these methods of calculation are based on administrative practice and are not stipulated by the Act. Note that based on these methods, while total inclusions net of deductions over the period amount to $9,000 under each alternative, the time pattern of net inclusion is more favourable in this case if there is no series of loans and repayments considered.

If the loans are all part of a single running loan account, they are likely a series of loans and repayments. However, if the loans are for separate purposes, with differing repayment or other terms, and the repayments relate to specific loans, the facts might suggest there was no series of loans and repayments.

Exercise 4

Since he is a shareholder of the corporation, the shareholder loan rule applies and the loan that was received by the taxpayer should be included in income. However, the Act provides an exclusion for the $35,000 principal amount of the loan because:

ITA: 15(2)
ITA: 15(2.4)(d)

— the taxpayer is an employee of the lender;

— the loan is to enable him to acquire a motor vehicle to be used by him in the performance of his employment duties;

— the taxpayer received the loan because of his employment, not because of his shareholdings, since other employees were eligible for a loan; and

— *bona fide* arrangements were made, at the time the loan was made, for repayment within a reasonable time.

Since the loan is a low-interest loan, the imputed interest benefit rule applies to impute an interest benefit calculated as follows:

ITA: 80.4(1)

April 1 to June 30: $91/365 \times 4\%$ of $35,000 = ...		$ 349
July 1 to Sept. 30: $92/365 \times 5\%$ of $35,000 = ...		441
Oct. 1 to Dec. 31: $92/365 \times 6\%$ of $35,000 = ...		529
Total		$1,319
Less: interest *paid* (not payable) ($214/365 \times 3\%$ of $35,000)		616
Net interest benefit		$ 703

The Act deems the imputed interest benefit of $703 to have been paid in the year. As a result, a part of the interest will qualify as a deduction of interest *paid* limited as follows:

ITA: 80.5
ITA: 8(1)(j), 67.2

Lesser of:

(a) interest deemed paid	$703	
interest *paid* ($214/365 \times 3\%$ of $35,000)	616	$1,319

CHAPTER 13

(b) $\dfrac{\$300}{30}$ × 214 days of interest paid $2,140

Lesser amount × 60% business usage (60% of $1,319) . . . . $ 791

Exercise 5

Shareholder-Manager Pays Tax on Benefit

Benefit from use of car:

standby charge[1] (10,000 km/20,004 km ×²/₃ × $6,000)   2,000

value of operating costs of personal use[2]   1,000   ITA: 6(1)(*e*)

Incremental taxable income . . . . $ 3,000

Tax @ 46% on $3,000 of incremental taxable income . . . . $ 1,380

Shareholder-Manager Leases Car Personally

Incremental taxable income ($2,880 + $6,000) . . . . $ 8,880

Less: deduction for business use of car [66²/₃% of ($6,000 + $2,880)] . . . .   (5,920)

Add: HST rebate (13/113 × $5,920)[3]   681

Incremental taxable income . . . . $ 3,641

Tax @ 46% on $3,641 of incremental taxable income . . . . $ 1,675

Tax net of HST rebate ($1,675 – $681) . . . . $ 994

Notice that the second alternative is the better by $386.

— NOTES TO SOLUTION

[1] This calculation assumes that business usage of 66²/₃% meets the test that the primary distance   ITA: 6(2)
travelled was for business. Generally, the term "primarily" has been interpreted by the CRA to mean
more than 50%.

[2] The election includes a benefit of 50% of the standby charge of $2,000 (i.e., $1,000) which is less   ITA: 6(1)(*k*)
than 27¢ × 10,000 km or $2,700.

[3] In reality, the HST rebate would have to be taken into income in the following year. Note that
the present value considerations on the rebate have been ignored. Also, ignored is the effect of the input
tax credit (ITC) received by the corporation if it incurs the annual lease and operating costs. If the
corporation pays additional salary equal to its net costs for these items after ITC and, hence, if the
shareholder manager must pay the HST from other sources, it can be shown that the shareholder-
manager's after-tax retention is reduced by the after-tax equivalent of the HST costs. This would reduce
the advantage of the second alternative.

Exercise 6

	Remuneration alternatives		
Corporation	*Salary*	*Dividends*	*Combination*
Income before salary and taxes	$ 20,000	$20,000	$ 20,000
Salary	(20,000)	—	(10,000)
Taxable income	Nil	$20,000	$ 10,000
Tax @ 15% (i.e., 38% – 10% – 17% + 4%)	—	(3,000)	(1,500)
Available for dividends	Nil	$17,000	$ 8,500
Shareholder			
Employment income (ssec. 8(1) deductions not considered)	$ 20,000	—	$ 10,000
Grossed-up dividends (1.18 × dividend)	—	$20,060	10,030
Taxable income	$ 20,000	$20,060	$ 20,030
Federal tax before dividend tax credit . . .	$ 3,000	$ 3,009	$ 3,005
Dividend tax credit (¹³/₁₈ of gross-up)	—	(2,210)	(1,105)
Personal tax credits	(2,000)	(2,000)	(2,000)
Basic federal tax*	$ 1,000	$ Nil	$ Nil

	Remuneration alternatives		
	Salary	*Dividends*	*Combination*
Provincial tax...................	2,000	2,006	2,003
Provincial dividend tax credit ($^5/_{18}$ of gross-up)	—	(850)	(425)
Provincial personal tax credits	(1,290)	(1,290)	(1,290)
Total tax*	$ 1,710	Nil	$ 288

Summary

Income before salary and taxes	$ 20,000	$20,000	$ 20,000
Less: tax paid by corporation	Nil	(3,000)	(1,500)
tax paid by shareholder	(1,710)	Nil	(288)
Net cash to shareholder	$ 18,290	$17,000	$ 18,212

Excess federal dividend and personal tax credits ($3,009 – $2,210 – $2,000)		$ 1,201	

* Cannot be negative.

Effect of additional $100 of salary on all-dividend alternative at the corporate level when all of the income is distributed:

Increase in salary expense	$ 100.00
Decrease in corporate tax @ 15%	(15.00)
Decrease in amount available for dividend	$ 85.00

Effect of additional $100 in salary on all-dividend alternative at shareholder level:

Increase in salary	$ 100.00
Decrease in dividend	(85.00)
Decrease in gross-up	(15.30)
Decrease in taxable income	$ (0.30)
Decrease in federal tax @ 15% of $0.30	$ (.05)
Decrease in federal dividend tax credit ($^{13}/_{18} \times$ .18 $\times$ $85.00)	11.05
Increase in tax	$ 11.00
Additional salary to eliminate $1,201 in excess tax credit ($1,201/.11)	$ 10,918

Corporation:

Income before salary	$ 20,000
Salary	(10,918)
Taxable income	$ 9,082
Corporate tax @ 15%	(1,362)
Available for dividend	$ 7,720

Shareholder:

Income from salary	$ 10,918
Income from dividend	7,720
Gross-up @ 18%	1,390
Taxable income	$ 20,028
Federal tax	$ 3,004
Dividend tax credit ($^{13}/_{18} \times$ $1,390)	(1,004)
Personal tax credits	(2,000)
Net federal tax (cannot be negative)	Nil
Provincial tax	2,003
Provincial dividend tax credit ($^5/_{18} \times$ $1,390)	(386)
Provincial personal tax credits	(1,290)
Total tax	$ 327
Net cash to shareholder ($20,000 – $1,362 – $327)	$ 18,311
Improvement ($18,311 – $18,290)	$ 21

CHAPTER 13

Exercise 7

(A)   *Taxation of Income from Sole Proprietorship*

Income from business and taxable income		$80,000
Federal tax		
Tax on first $43,561	$ 6,534	
Tax on next $36,439 @ 22%	8,017	$14,551
Personal tax credits		(2,100)
Basic federal tax		$12,451
Provincial tax (12% of ($80,000 − $43,561) + $4,356)...............		8,729
Provincial personal tax credits		(1,400)
Total tax paid		$19,780

(B)   *Taxation of Income through a Corporation*

	Remuneration alternatives		
	All salary	*All dividends*	*Combination*
Corporation			
Income before salary and taxes	$ 80,000	$ 80,000	$ 80,000
Salary	(25,000)	—	(4,630)[3]
Taxable income	$ 55,000	$ 80,000	$ 75,370
Tax @ 15% (i.e., 38% − 10% − 17% + 4%)	(8,250)	(12,000)	(11,306)
Available for dividend	$ 46,750	$ 68,000	$ 64,064
Shareholder			
Salary[1] .... (A)	$ 25,000	—	$ 4,630
Dividend .... (B)	—	$ 25,000	20,370
Gross-up @ 18% of dividend	—	4,500	3,667
Income	$ 25,000	$ 29,500	$ 28,667
Federal tax	$ 3,750	$ 4,425	$ 4,300
Dividend tax credit ($^{13}/_{18}$ × gross-up) ...	—	(3,250)	(2,648)
Personal tax credits	(2,100)	(2,100)	(2,100)
Basic federal tax	$ 1,650	Nil	(448)[4]
Provincial tax	2,500	2,950	2,867
Provincial dividend tax credit ($^{5}/_{13}$ × gross-up)	Nil	(1,250)	(1,019)
Provincial personal tax credits	(1,400)	(1,400)	(1,400)
Total tax .... (C)	$ 2,750	$ 300	Nil
Disposable income (A + B − C)	$ 22,250	$ 25,000	$ 25,000
Total Taxes paid			
Through corporation:			
Corporation	$ 8,250	$ 12,000	$ 11,306
Shareholder	2,750	300	Nil
Total	$ 11,000	$ 12,300	$ 11,306
Paid directly by proprietor	$ 19,780	$ 19,780	$ 19,780
Tax Saving (maximum[2])	$ 8,780	$ 7,480	$ 8,474

At these rates, all salary results in the biggest tax savings, assuming that dividends will be distributed when the owner-manager's income will be such that there will be no tax on the dividends.

— NOTES TO SOLUTION

[1] Assumes no deductions available to employee.

[2] Assumes amount retained in the corporation can be distributed as taxable dividends in amounts that will not attract tax after personal tax credits.

[3] Note that the marginal analysis used in Example Problem 13-5 in ¶13,230 of the book can be used to derive this amount. The excess tax credits in the all-dividend alternative amount to $625 (i.e., $4,425 − $3,250 − $2,100 + $2,950 − $1,250 − $1,400), assuming that all excess federal credits can be used on other income, as required in this problem. Since only part of the corporate income is being distributed, the focus is on the shareholder-manager. If salary is increased by $100, the following would occur:

Increase in salary	$ 100.00
Decrease in dividend	(100.00)
Decrease in gross-up	(18.00)
Decrease in taxable income	$ (18.00)
Decrease in tax @ 25% (i.e., 15% federal and 10% provincial) of $18.00	$ (4.50)
Decrease in dividend tax credit ($^{18}/_{18}$ × .18 × $100.00)	18.00
Increase in tax	$ 13.50
Increase in salary to eliminate $625 of excess tax credits ($625/.135)	$4,630.00

[4] Negative allowed only due to assumption in the required.

Exercise 8

In each of the cases, the test to be applied to the facts is whether all or substantially all (i.e., at least 90%) of the fair market value of the assets are:

(a) used principally in an active business carried on primarily in Canada by the corporation (or a related corporation);

(b) shares or debt of a connected SBC; or

(c) a combination of (a) and (b).

(A) This situation depends on whether the marketable securities are used in the active business or are passive investments not necessary to the active business. If the marketable securities are used in the active business, then the 90% test is met. This would be the case, for example, if the marketable securities represented a short-term investment of cash surpluses, awaiting the purchase of inventory for the next season.

(B) In this situation, the 90% test is met with a combination of active business assets and shares in a connected SBC.

(C) In this case, the marketable securities cannot be considered to be used in an active business, because the corporation has no other active business assets to carry on such a business. Since the shares of a connected SBC represent only 80% of the total fair market value of the corporation's assets, the 90% test is not met.

(D) Again, this case fits the definition of an SBC if the marketable securities are considered to be used in an active business. If the facts of this case so indicate, then the 90% test is met by a combination of active business assets (including the marketable securities) and the shares of a connected SBC.

Exercise 9

(A) Unused lifetime deduction in 2014:

Lifetime cumulative deduction limit [as proposed for 2014]	$ 400,000
Less: prior years' deductions:	
Capital gains deduction claimed in 2012	75,000
Capital gains deduction available for 2014	$ 325,000

(B) Annual gains limit for 2014:

Net taxable capital gains for 2014[1]	$ 225,000
Minus:	

Net capital losses deducted in 2014		Nil	
ABILs realized in 2014[1]		5,000	5,000
Annual gains limit for 2014			$ 220,000

(C) Cumulative gains limit for 2014:

Cumulative net taxable capital gains ($75,000 + $225,000)			$ 300,000
Minus:			
Cumulative net capital losses deducted		Nil	
Cumulative ABILs realized	$	5,000	
Cumulative capital gains deductions		75,000	
Cumulative net investment loss:			
Investment expenses —			
Cumulative carrying charges	$ 1,075		
Cumulative net rental losses			
($1,100 + $220)	1,320		
	$ 2,395		
Investment income —			
Cumulative interest income			
($600 + $1,200)	(1,800)		
Cumulative grossed-up dividends	(140)	455	80,455
Cumulative gains limit for 2013			$ 219,545

(D) Least of (A), (B), (C) . . . . $ 219,545

— *NOTE TO SOLUTION*

[1] Allowable business investment loss (ABIL):

BIL before ssec. 39(9) reduction			$ 160,000
Disallowed portion — Lesser of:			
(a) BIL		$ 160,000	
(b) Adjustment factor × cumulative			
CG deductions of previous			
years (2 × $75,000)	$150,000		
Minus: Cumulative disallowed			
BIL of prior years	Nil	$ 150,000	
Lesser of (a) and (b)			(150,000)
BIL after adjustment			$ 10,000
ABIL (½ × $10,000)			$ 5,000
Allowable capital loss (ACL):			
Disallowed portion of BIL			$ 150,000
ACL (½ × $150,000)			$ 75,000
Net TCG for 2014:			
TCG			$ 300,000
Less: ACL			75,000
Net TCG			$ 225,000

Exercise 10

The disposition of the real estate is a transfer for tax purposes in 2013. The facts do not provide enough details on the cost base to determine the tax effect of the disposition.

In this case it can likely be established that one of the main purposes of the transfer of the building may reasonably be considered to be to reduce the income of Mr. Albert and to benefit Mrs. Albert who is a designated person and a specified shareholder. Had Mr. Albert kept the building himself he would have earned $20,000 of rental income on which he would have been taxable. Instead, he will receive $1,000 of interest and $2,000 of dividends. Mrs. Albert benefited from the rental income since this will accrue to the common shares of the corporation. Therefore, it may be argued that the purpose test will have been met.

Furthermore, the corporation will no longer be a "small business corporation", since the fair market value of the assets of the corporation will be as follows:

ITA: 248(1)

Retail assets, 75%	$600,000
Building, 25%	200,000
Total	$800,000

Even if 20% of the building (FMV $40,000) is classified as an active business asset, the corporation will still not be a small business corporation since all or substantially all of the fair market value of the assets are not used principally in an active business carried on primarily in Canada.

Mr. Albert's attributed amount	
FMV of the building transferred	$200,000
Less: cash received	(60,000)
Outstanding amount	$140,000
Interest imputed at 4%	$5,600
Less: interest received (5% of $20,000)	(1,000)
1.18 × dividends received	(2,360)
Attributed amount	$2,240
Mr. Albert would also have	
Interest income	1,000
Taxable dividends ($2,000 × 1.18)	2,360
Total income	$5,600

Exercise 11

The following comments are based on the application of the logic presented in Exhibit 13-11 to the facts of this situation.

(1) Does any other provision of the Act or other rule of law apply to stop the taxpayer from achieving the intended advantage? No, the amount paid is considered to be reasonable and, hence, is not prohibited. Remuneration is considered to be an expense incurred to produce income from business and, thus, is not prohibited.

ITA: 67

ITA: 18(1)(*a*)

(2) Does the transaction result, directly or indirectly, in a tax benefit, i.e., a reduction, avoidance or deferral of tax or an increase in a refund? On the one hand, corporate tax is reduced, but on the other hand the individual receives income subject to tax at a higher rate. However, the reduction of income to the corporation reduces the potential for double taxation on income taxed at more than a 27.5% rate in the corporation which may be considered to be a tax benefit. If it is concluded that there is no tax benefit, GAAR should not apply.

ITA: 245(1)

(3) Is the transaction part of a series of transactions, which would result, directly or indirectly, in a tax benefit? If the answer to question 2 is yes, then proceed directly to question 4.

(4) Can the transaction reasonably be considered to have been undertaken or arranged primarily for *bona fide* purposes other than to obtain the tax benefit? No, a tax reduction for the corporation was probably the primary purpose. On the other hand, it might be argued that, since the amount paid was reasonable, it is necessary remuneration.

(5) Can it reasonably be considered that the transaction would result directly or indirectly in a misuse of the provisions of the Act or an abuse having regard to the provisions of the Act read as a whole? No, "the Act recognizes the deductibility of reasonable business expenses".

IC 88-2, par. 18

Exercise 12

The general anti-avoidance rule allows for transactions or a series of transactions to be disregarded if they are without a *bona fide* purpose. If your client's spouse and children are not providing any services to her business, it is obvious that the transactions were arranged primarily to obtain a tax benefit with no *bona fide* purpose, and they will be disregarded by the CRA. Any tax benefit derived from the transactions will be eliminated. If there is some service being provided to justify a salary, the amount of salary must be reasonable in the circumstance or the deduction by your client can be disallowed without the need to apply the GAAR. In fact, if the unreasonable salaries are still taxed in the hands of the spouse and children, after the expense is disallowed, the result is worse than the application of the GAAR that disregards the payment.

Make sure your study notes are neatly written and structured. The more organized your notes, the more likely your brain will retain the information.

Chapter 14
Rights and Obligations Under the Income Tax Act

LEARNING GOALS

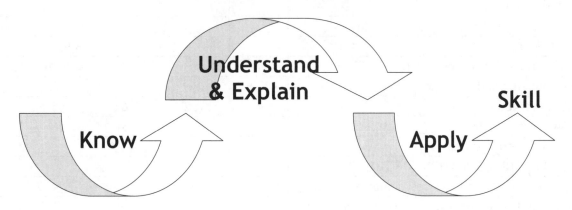

Know

By the end of this chapter you should know the basic provisions of the *Income Tax Act* and the *Excise Tax Act* that relate to the taxpayer compliance rules, the powers of the Canada Revenue Agency (CRA), and a taxpayer's rights and requirements on appeals. Completing the Review Questions (¶14,800) and Multiple Choice Questions (¶14,825) is a good way to learn the technical provisions.

Understand and Explain

You should understand and be able to explain:

- The requirements for taxpayers of income tax and registrants for GST/HST to make payments, file returns, and, possibly, incur penalties and interest, if the taxpayer does not comply with the legislation on an accurate and timely basis;
- The powers and obligations of the CRA to assess and reassess a taxpayer's or registrant's filings;
- The rights of taxpayers and registrants to appeal within deadlines; and
- The compliance rules applicable to employers, other payers of tax, and representatives of deceased taxpayers.

Completing the Exercises (¶14,850) is a good way to deepen your understanding of the material.

Apply

You should be able to apply your knowledge and understanding of the key elements of compliance pertaining to payment of tax and filing returns and appeals to achieve a client's goals of minimizing interest and penalties in the early stages of the process. Completing the Assignment Problems (¶14,875) is an excellent way to develop your ability to apply the material in increasingly complex situations.

Chapter 14 — Learning Chart

Topic	Example Problem (✓)	Review Questions (¶14,800)	Multiple Choice (¶14,825)	Exercises (¶14,850)	Assignment Problems (¶14,875)
¶14,000 OBLIGATIONS OF THE TAXPAYER UNDER THE INCOME TAX ACT					
¶14,010 Returns, Penalties, and Criminal Offences		1		1	
¶14,015 Returns					
¶14,018 Functional currency tax reporting					
¶14,020 Penalties			1	8,9,10,12	3, 4
¶14,025 Criminal offences				8, 10	
¶14,030 Payments and Interest				11	
¶14,035 Individuals	✓	1, 2	6	5	1
¶14,040 Corporations	✓		5	6	2, 3
¶14,050 Books and Records					
¶14,100 POWERS AND OBLIGATIONS OF THE CRA					
¶14,110 Assessments and Reassessments	✓	5	2, 3	2, 4, 7	
¶14,120 Refunds and Interest		3		11, 15	
¶14,200 RIGHTS OF THE TAXPAYER					
¶14,210 Objections and Appeals		4		13	
¶14,220 Amended Returns					
¶14,300 OBLIGATIONS OF PAYERS AND OTHER PERSONS					
¶14,310 Employers	✓			3	
¶14,320 Obligations of Other Payers, Trustees, etc.					
¶14,322 Liability of directors					
¶14,324 Taxpayer's legal representative					
¶14,325 Payments to residents of Canada				3	
¶14,330 Payments to non-residents				14	5, 6, 7
¶14,335 Foreign reporting requirements	✓				7
¶14,340 Deceased Taxpayers		6			
¶14,345 Tax returns			4	17	8
¶14,350 Rights or things				16, 17	8
¶14,355 Other return				16	
¶14,360 Personal tax credits				10	
¶14,365 Summary of filing deadlines					
¶14,400 OBLIGATIONS OF THE REGISTRANT UNDER THE EXCISE TAX ACT					
¶14,410 Collection and Remittance of Tax					9
¶14,420 Disclosure of Tax					
¶14,430 Returns and Reporting Periods					9
¶14,440 Remittance of Tax					
¶14,450 Books and Records					9
¶14,500 POWERS AND OBLIGATIONS OF THE CRA IN RESPECT OF THE EXCISE TAX ACT					
¶14,510 Assessments and Reassessments					
¶14,520 Refunds and Interest					

Topic	Example Problem (✓)	Review Questions (¶14,800)	Multiple Choice (¶14,825)	Exercises (¶14,850)	Assignment Problems (¶14,875)
¶14,600 RIGHTS OF THE REGISTRANT					
¶14,610 Objections and Appeals					
¶14,620 Amended Returns and GST/HST Adjustments					
¶14,700 SIMPLIFIED METHOD AND QUICK METHOD					
¶14,900 SUPPLEMENTAL NOTES					
¶14,910 Penalties	✓				
¶14,920 Objections and Appeals	✓				
¶14,930 Late-Filed or Amended Elections					
¶14,940 Enforcement and Collections					

CHAPTER 14

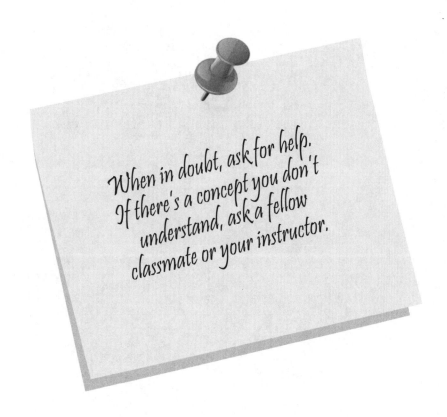

When in doubt, ask for help. If there's a concept you don't understand, ask a fellow classmate or your instructor.

Study Notes

Chapter 14 —
Discussion Notes for Review Questions

(1) (a) False. All corporations resident in Canada have to file tax returns within six months of the end of the year.

ITA: 150(1)(*a*)

(b) True. An individual is required to file a tax return if he or she "has disposed of a capital property". Even if there is no taxable income or tax liability a return must be filed. In addition, Mr. Austen may lose his capital gains deduction in respect of this transaction, if he does not file the return.

ITA: 110.6(6), 150(1)

(c) False. Instalments must be paid on the 15th of each of those months.

ITA: 156(1)

(2) An instalment interest offset is available on prepaid or overpaid instalments. However, this credit offset can only be applied against instalment interest owing; it is not refundable and may not be applied against any other debt. To benefit, he would have to pay the December 15 instalment on September 15 which would offset the fact that the June 15 instalment was three months late. In addition, the prescribed interest rate for the last quarter would have to be equal to or greater than the prescribed interest rate for the second quarter.

ITA: 161(2.2)

(3) They will not be able to collect interest for the last three years. Interest will not be paid for the period prior to the filing of the tax return for the year in which the request is made to carry the loss back.

ITA: 164(5)

(4) Since the accountant sent a letter to the CRA, it may take some time before a reply is received. If the reply is received late and there is disagreement, it may be too late to file a Notice of Objection. Therefore, it may be prudent to file the Notice of Objection in the first place unless the matter is a minor one.

ITA: 165(1)

(5) In order to amend the tax returns for the third preceding year the company would have had to file form T2A by the time the corporate tax returns are due for the loss year which is six months after the fiscal year-end. However, Murray Corp. did not meet this deadline since it did not file until seven months after the year-end. Therefore, the CRA will not have to let the corporation carry the loss back at all. However, the loss will still be available to be carried forward.

ITA: 152(6)

(6) The following are the three returns that can be filed:

(a) Terminal return — This return reports the income for the period in the year before the date of death and includes any gain or loss on the deemed disposition on death. Full personal credits may be claimed.

ITA: 70(1)

(b) Rights or things — "Rights or things" can be reported on a separate return to take advantage of the lower marginal tax brackets. Also, the full personal tax credits allowed can be claimed again.

ITA: 70(2), 118(1), 118(2)

(c) Trust return — Similar rules to those in (c) above apply to those situations that have more than one trust year-end in the same calendar year. This would only apply in the case of a testamentary trust since they are the only ones that can have an off-calendar year-end. Again, the lower marginal tax rates and the personal tax credits are available.

ITA: 104(23)(*d*)

Chapter 14 —
Solutions to Multiple Choice Questions

Question 1

(B) is correct. The penalty is $900. The initial penalty rate of 5% is increased by 1% for each *complete* month after April 30, 2013 that the return was not filed to a maximum penalty of 5% + 4% = 9%.   ITA: 162(1)

(A) is incorrect as it includes only the initial penalty of 5% of the unpaid tax.

(C) is incorrect as it includes ½% for the half month of September. Only complete months should be counted for purposes of the penalty.

(D) is incorrect as it includes 1% for the month of September. Only complete months should be counted for purposes of the penalty.

Question 2

(B) August 15, 2016 is correct. The normal reassessment period for a CCPC ends three years after the day of mailing of a notice of assessment for the year.   ITA: 152(3.1)

(A) December 31, 2015, three years after the end of the taxation year, is incorrect. The three-year period commences with the date of mailing of the notice of assessment, not the last day of the fiscal year.

(C) December 31, 2016, four years after the end of the taxation year, is incorrect.

(D) August 15, 2017, four years after the day of mailing of a notice of assessment for the year, is incorrect. It would be correct if the taxpayer were a corporation other than a CCPC.   ITA: 152(3.1)

Question 3

(D) June 15, 2014 is correct. The notice of objection filing due date is one year after Darol's filing-due date for 2012.   ITA: 165(1)

(A) December 31, 2013, being one year after the end of the taxation year, is incorrect.

(B) January 14, 2014, being 90 days after the date of mailing of the notice of assessment, is incorrect in this case. For an individual and a testamentary trust, the due date is the later of this date and one year after the filing-due date for the tax return.

(C) April 30, 2014, being one year after the filing-due date for 2012 for an individual *not* carrying on a business, is incorrect. Darol's filing-due date for 2012 was June 15, 2013, as he carried on business in 2012.

Question 4

The correct answer is (D) September 30, 2013, being six months after the date of death.   ITA: 150(1)(*b*)

(A) is incorrect. It is the most common due date for 2012 personal tax returns. This date is not correct for two reasons: first, he has income from carrying on business, and second, he has at least six months from the date of death.   ITA: 150(1)(*a*)(i)

(B) is incorrect. It is the date the return would have been due if he had not died.   ITA: 150(1)(*a*)(ii)

(C) is incorrect as it is six months after the end of the year for which the return is being filed.

Question 5

(A) is correct. The minimum monthly instalment is the least of:

– $1/12$ of the estimated taxes payable: $1/12 \times \$200,000 = \$16,667$

– $1/12$ of the prior year's taxes payable: $1/12$ of $\$140,000 = \$11,667$

– $1/12$ of the second prior year's taxable payable ($1/12$ of $\$180,000 = \$15,000$) for two months and 10 payments of $11,000 ($1/10 \times [\$140,000 - 2 \times \$15,000]$).

The least of these is either the prior year method or the second prior year method. Only the prior year method ($11,667 per month) is listed as a choice in this question. Because X Ltd. had taxable income in the prior year of more than the small business deduction limit, it must pay its final balance due within two months of year end (February 28, 2014).

(B) and (C) incorrectly base the instalments on estimated taxes payable. (B) has the correct final due date. (C) incorrectly uses the balance-due day that is three months after the end of the year which is applicable only for Canadian-controlled private corporations that have taxable income that is less than the small business deduction limit in the prior year.

(D) incorrectly uses the amount for the first two payments of the second prior year method for all 12 payments but has the correct final due date for the balance due. (D) would have been a correct answer had it indicated that the payments for the last 10 months would be $11,000 per month.

Question 6

(D) is correct (two payments of $3,825 and two payments of $4,375). The minimum monthly instalment is the least of:

– $\frac{1}{4}$ of the estimated taxes payable: $\frac{1}{4} \times \$25,000 = \$6,250$

– $\frac{1}{4}$ of the prior year's taxes payable: $\frac{1}{4}$ of $16,400 = \$4,100$

– $\frac{1}{4}$ of the second prior year's taxable payable ($\frac{1}{4}$ of $15,300 = \$3,825$) for two months and two payments of $4,375 ($\frac{1}{2} \times [\$16,400 - 2 \times \$3,825]$).

(A) is incorrect because four payments of $6,250 is not the minimum payment.

(B) is incorrect because two payments of $4,100 and two payments of $6,250 is not the minimum amount. Four payments of $4,100 would result in the minimum amount.

(C) is incorrect because two payments of $3,825 and two payments of $4,100 is not the minimum amount. If the first two payments are $3,825, the last two payments must be $4,375. Alternatively, four payments of $4,100 can be made.

Chapter 14 – Solutions to Exercises

Exercise 1

Subsection 150(1):

(a) corporations — within 6 months from the end of the taxation year;

(b) deceased persons — the tax return for the year in which the individual died is due on or before the later of 6 months after the day of death and the day the return would otherwise be due, i.e., by April 30 (or June 15, if the deceased individual or his or her spouse carried on a business in the year of death) following the year of death;

(c) trust — within 90 days from the end of the taxation year;

(d) individual — on or before April 30 of the next calendar year unless the individual or his or her spouse carried on a business, in which case the deadline is June 15 of the next year.

Exercise 2

Subsection 152(4):

— No limit if fraud or misrepresentation in the 2012 return can be established or on a matter for which the taxpayer has filed a waiver of the limit by May 27, 2016;

— Otherwise, the reassessment must be made within three years of May 27, 2013.

Exercise 3

Subsection 153(1):

(a) salary or wages or other remuneration, including stock option benefits, from employment;

(b) a superannuation or pension benefit;

(c) a retiring allowance;

(d) a death benefit for long service from an employer;

(e) an Employment Insurance benefit;

(f) a benefit under a supplementary unemployment benefit plan;

(g) an annuity payment;

(h) a benefit from a deferred profit sharing plan;

(i) fees, commissions and other amounts for services;

(j) a payment under a registered retirement savings plan;

(k) certain amounts resulting from an income averaging annuity;

(l) a payment from a registered retirement income fund.

Exercise 4

Inheritance, gambling winnings, lottery prize, etc.

Exercise 5

As his net tax owing in the current year and one of the two preceding years is in excess of $3,000, he is required to make instalments.

Instalments of $750 ($\frac{1}{4}$ × $3,000) must be paid by March 15 and June 15 and instalments of $1,250 (i.e., ($4,000 – 2 × $750) × $\frac{1}{2}$) must be paid by September 15 and December 15. The balance of the tax liability must be remitted by the balance-due date of April 30, 2015.

Exercise 6

As the corporation's estimated taxes payable for the current year and the taxes paid for the preceding year exceed $3,000, instalments are required.

The Act would allow the following: ITA: 157(1)(*a*)(iii)

January 31 and February 28, 2014 — $^1/_{12}$ of $158,400 or $13,200;

Last day of March to December 2014 — $^1/_{10}$ of ($237,600 – 2 × $13,200) or $21,120;

Balance on the last day of the third month after the taxation year-end, where a small business deduction was taken by virtue of section 125 in the current or preceding year and the corporation and associated corporations' aggregate taxable incomes for the preceding year did not exceed the small business deduction limit, or, in this particular case, the last day of February 2015, as applicable to any other case.

Exercise 7   ITA: 165, 169

Rachel should ensure that the required forms are filled out correctly and that they are signed by her employer. If all the forms are in order, she has the right under section 165 to object to an assessment made by the CRA by filing a notice of objection within one year of the April 30 filing due date, or within 90 days after the day of mailing of the assessment notice, whichever is later. If Rachel is not satisfied with the reassessment, she can appeal to the courts as outlined under section 169.

Exercise 8

Subsection 150(1):

Y and Z will incur no penalties; furthermore, Y is not required to file since no tax is payable, unless he disposed of capital property.

Subsection 162(1):

Failure to file when required — 5% of unpaid tax plus 1% of unpaid tax per complete month past due for a first offence:

X — 5% of $4,700 or $235 plus 1% of $4,700 × nil = $235.

Y — 5% of nil or nil.

Z — no penalty as the return is not due until June 15. Interest charges on the unpaid tax from April 30 will, however, apply.

Subsection 238(1):

Failure to file as or when required — liable on summary conviction to a fine of $1,000 to $25,000 or a fine and imprisonment for up to 12 months;

— Y could be fined if there has been a demand to file under subsection 150(2).

Exercise 9

(A) Facts to be determined:

(i) Date of mailing of 2009 original assessment in order to determine the three-year limit (i.e., the   ITA: 152(4)
normal reassessment period for an individual).

(ii) Obtain date of mailing of notice of reassessment.

(iii) Assuming Mr. DeHaan is correct as to the date of the reassessment, determine if the date of the original assessment was prior to June 15, 2010 and if so, whether Mr. DeHaan has filed a waiver of the three-year limit.

(iv) If the date of the original assessment was prior to June 15, 2010, you should determine whether Mr. DeHaan is alleged to have made any misrepresentation due to neglect, gross carelessness, wilful default, or has committed a fraud in filing his 2009 return.

(B) Steps to be taken:

(i) Procure an engagement letter or a signed consent form which gives permission to discuss   Form T1013
Mr. DeHaan's case with officials of the CRA.

(ii) Start discussions with the CRA.

(iii) File a Notice of Objection prior to the expiry of the 90-day period based upon the date of mailing determined above (i.e., September 12, 2013, if mailed on June 15, 2013).

(iv) Warn Mr. DeHaan that certain second-time offences may carry heavier penalties than the first-time offence.

(C) A penalty of 10% of unreported income could be imposed on Mr. DeHaan, if the current reassessment is his second offence within three years of the first offence. Under the CRA's voluntary disclosure program, a valid voluntary disclosure may result in a waiver of penalties.

ITA: 163(1), IC 00-1R

Exercise 10

The backdating of the document would be considered to be participating in the making of a false statement or omission in a return. As a result, a penalty is imposed equal to the greater of $100 and 50% of the difference in tax liability.

ITA: 163(1)

In addition, a fine of not less than 50% and not more than 200% of the amount of the tax that was evaded, or the fine plus imprisonment for a term not exceeding two years, would be imposed.

ITA: 238(1)

Both Mr. Turner and Ms. Blackford would be subject to the above fines and penalties.

Ms. Blackford may also be subject to disciplinary measures by her professional accounting association.

Ms. Blackford could be liable for the civil penalty imposed on third parties for a false statement.

ITA: 163.2

Exercise 11

The Act computes interest at a basic prescribed rate plus 4% on amounts owing to the CRA from the earliest date the amount was due until the date it was paid;

ITA: 161

— the interest is not tax deductible.

Interest is computed at the same basic prescribed rate plus 2% on refunds by the CRA to non-corporate taxpayers and at the basic prescribed rate to corporate taxpayers;

ITA: 164(3)

— the interest is taxable;

— if the interest relates to instalments, an interest offset is computed using the 4% addition, against interest owing on late instalments for interest earned on early instalments.

ITA: 161(2.2)

Both interest calculations are based on daily compounding.

Interest on the overpayment of taxes for individuals will start to accrue 30 days after the later of the balance due day for the return (i.e., April 30, 2014 for 2013 returns) or the date the return is filed.

An individual's refund interest accruing over a period can be offset by any arrears interest that accrues over the same period, to which the refund interest relates. Hence, only the excess refund interest is taxed to the individual.

Exercise 12

The CRA has commented on this type of situation. The conclusion is that the good faith defence is available, since the income statement reveals nothing that would lead you to question the validity of the information provided to you. As a result, the preparer penalty would not apply in your situation.

IC 01-1

Use of the flowchart presented in the chapter may be helpful in analyzing this situation and reaching this conclusion.

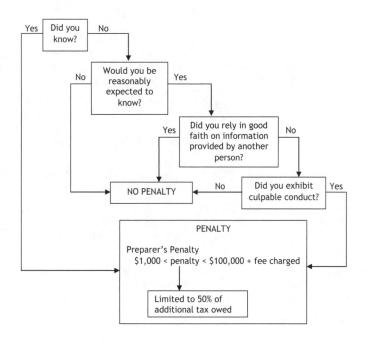

Exercise 13

(a) Notice of objection: ITA: 165(1)

— to be filed by *individual* taxpayers by the later of:

(i) one year after the filing-due date, which is normally April 30 or June 15 except for trusts and deceased persons, and ITA: 248(1)

(ii) the 90th day after the mailing date of the notice of assessment;

— to be filed within 90 days of mailing of notice of assessment for all other taxpayers;

— a prescribed form is not required.

(b) Appeal to the Tax Court of Canada: ITA: 169

— after 90 days of date of decision on notice of objection or 90 days after the mailing of the notice of objection if there has been no response to it;

— may be able to elect informal procedure under subsection 18(1) of the *Tax Court of Canada Act.*

(c) Appeal to the Federal Court of Appeal (section 17.6 of the *Tax Court of Canada Act*):

— within 30 days from date of mailing of decision of the Tax Court of Canada only if that taxpayer chose the general procedure in the Tax Court of Canada.

(d) Appeal to Supreme Court of Canada:

— on recommendation of Federal Court of Appeal;

— with permission of Supreme Court of Canada.

Exercise 14

A tax return may be filed by a non-resident within two years after the end of the year that rents were paid. In that return, rental income for the year, net of expenses, would be reported and any withholding tax paid in the year in respect of rental revenue would be considered taxes paid for the year. ITA: 216

This individual is eligible to file this return for 2011, 2012, and 2013. The 2008, 2009, and 2010 rents do not fall into the eligible filing period. However, the Minister may extend the time for filing a return. The individual may consider requesting such an extension. ITA: 216
ITA: 220(3.2)

Exercise 15

Steve will receive interest on the $9,000 only from 30 days after June 15, 2013 (i.e., July 15, 2013) to the date the cheque was mailed. When he determined he had paid excess instalments, he could consider requesting that the instalments be transferred to his employer remittance account, if he has employees from whom he withholds tax.

Exercise 16

(A) The accrued interest is a periodic payment to be reported on the terminal T1 return, due April 30, 2014.

ITA: 70(1)

(B) Since the dividend is not payable until declared, it does not have to be accrued. Because it was declared after death, it is not a right or thing. Therefore, it is income of his estate.

ITA: 70(1), 70(2)

(C) The $800 of CPP would be reported on the terminal T1 return, since no amount was unpaid at the date of death that related to a *completed* pay period. Hence, CPP earned from September 1 to the date of death on September 10 is not considered to be a right or thing, since it is not legally receivable for a completed pay period on the date of death.

(D) The donations are creditable, to the extent of 100% of net income reported, on all the year of death returns combined or in the preceding year's return. Only personal tax credits may be deducted on each of the separate returns for the year of death.

ITA: 118(1), 118(2)
ITA: 118.93

(E) Net capital losses are deductible from any source of income in the year of death and the preceding year.

ITA: 111(2)

(F) Trust income of $900 for the year ended May 31, 2013 must be reported on the terminal return. An election is permitted to report the trust income payable to Sam for the stub period, June 1, 2013 to September 10, 2013 on a separate return, also due April 30, 2014. The personal tax credits can be deducted on this return.

ITA: 104(23)(*d*)

ITA: 118(1), 118(2)

(G) Life insurance proceeds received on death are not taxable.

Exercise 17

Ms. Kaye's 2013 terminal personal tax return is required to be filed by April 30, 2014. In Ms. Kaye's 2013 return all accrued income earned on a periodic basis during the period January 1 to May 1, 2013 should be included. In addition, all capital property (such as her Flying High shares) is deemed to have been disposed of at the fair market value. A claim for the full personal tax credits can be made on the terminal return even though Ms. Kaye died on May 2, 2013. The RRSP contribution of $9,000 is deductible on her 2013 terminal return, since it is less than the maximum amount (i.e., lesser of $22,000 and 18% of $80,000).

ITA: 150(1)(*d*)
ITA: 70(1)
ITA: 70(5)

Ms. Kaye's 2013 terminal return will include the following:

Salary	$22,000
Bond interest	950
Savings account interest	150
GIC interest	140
Dividend income	250
Taxable capital gain [½ ($25 − $10) × 100]	750
RRSP accumulation	34,000
RRSP contribution	(9,000)
Taxable income	$49,240

Ms. Kaye's legal representative can report amounts which were receivable but not received at the date of death, on a separate tax return, called a "rights or things" return, instead of on the terminal return.

ITA: 70(2)

The unpaid vacation pay of $2,000, interest payable of $950 and $250 of grossed-up dividend income would qualify as income from "rights or things." Personal tax credits equal to the amounts claimed in the terminal return may be claimed again on the "rights or things" return. This return is due on the date that is the later of one year after death and 90 days after assessment of any return for the year of death.

Alternatively, the legal representative can assign the income from "rights or things" to a particular beneficiary.

ITA: 70(3)

Chapter 15

Corporate Distributions, Windings-Up, and Sales

LEARNING GOALS

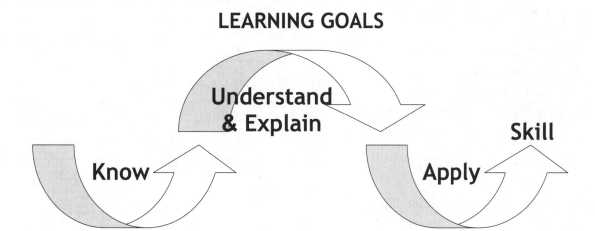

Know

By the end of this chapter you should know the basic provisions of the *Income Tax Act* pertaining to corporate surplus and its distribution in a variety of ways. Completing the Review Questions (¶15,800) and the Multiple Choice Questions (¶15,825) is a good way to learn the technical provisions.

Understand and Explain

You should understand and be able to explain:

- the tax-paid or tax-free components of corporate surplus;
- the income tax effects of distributing corporate surplus in a variety of situations; and
- the process for analyzing the tax consequences of two options for selling an incorporated business.

Completing the Exercises (¶15,850) is a good way to deepen your understanding of the material.

Apply

You should be able to apply your knowledge and understanding of the key elements of corporate surplus distributions to the analysis of the tax consequences of

- distributing a variety of types of dividends, and
- the options available on the sale of an incorporated business.

The objectives of this analysis should be to support a client's decisions and accomplish the client's goals in these areas. Completing the Assignment Problems (¶15,875) is an excellent way to develop your ability to apply the material in increasingly complex situations.

Chapter 15 — Learning Chart

Topic	Example Problem (✓)	Review Questions (¶15,800)	Multiple Choice (¶15,825)	Exercises (¶15,850)	Assignment Problems (¶15,875)
¶15,000 CORPORATE SURPLUS BALANCES					
¶15,010 Overview					
¶15,020 Paid-Up Capital of Shares					
¶15,025 The tax concept					
¶15,030 Technical tax aspects			5		
¶15,035 The effect of corporate law		1, 2, 3			
¶15,040 Effect of PUC in a redemption of shares				3	4
¶15,045 Effect of PUC in other corporate distribution		6		3, 5	3
¶15,050 Capital Dividend Account					
¶15,055 Components of the account		4	1	1, 2	1, 2
¶15,060 "The period"					
¶15,065 Example of disposition of eligible capital property	✓	5	6		1, 2
¶15,100 USE OF CORPORATE SURPLUS BALANCES					
¶15,110 Income Tax Treatment of Taxable Dividends Received or Deemed to be Received					
¶15,115 Treatment of taxable dividends					
¶15,120 Source of taxable dividends				3	
¶15,130 Cash or Stock Dividends				3, 4	3
¶15,140 Dividends in Kind					
¶15,150 Deemed Dividends					
¶15,155 Deemed dividend on increase in PUC				5	3
¶15,160 Deemed dividend on winding-up					
¶15,165 Deemed dividend on redemption, acquisition, or cancellation of shares	✓	9	2	4	4
¶15,170 Deemed dividend on reduction of PUC				5	
¶15,180 Capital Dividend	✓				
¶15,200 WINDING-UP OF A CANADIAN CORPORATION					
¶15,210 Disposition of Net Assets of the Corporation		8	3		
¶15,220 Deemed Dividend on Winding-Up					
¶15,225 Timing of winding-up					
¶15,230 Components of the winding-up distribution		7, 9	4		
¶15,240 Application of the Winding-Up Rules	✓			6, 7, 8	5, 6, 7, 8
¶15,300 SALE OF AN INCORPORATED BUSINESS					
¶15,310 Assets Versus Shares					
¶15,315 Allocation of Amounts in Consideration for Disposition of Property					
¶15,320 Analysis for the Decision	✓				9

Topic	Example Problem (✓)	Review Questions (¶15,800)	Multiple Choice (¶15,825)	Exercises (¶15,850)	Assignment Problems (¶15,875)
¶15,330 Summary of Steps for the Sale of an Incorporated Business					
¶15,400 GST/HST AND THE WINDING-UP OF A CANADIAN CORPORATION					6
¶15,900 SUPPLEMENTAL NOTES					
¶15,910 GST/HST and the Sale of an Incorporated Business					

CHAPTER 15

Study Notes

Chapter 15 —
Discussion Notes for Review Questions

(1) Dr.: Cash $30,000

    Cr.: Share capital $10,000

    Cr.: Contributed surplus $20,000

(2) In these jurisdictions, the paid-up capital is the "stated capital" as determined by the directors of the corporation under corporations law. Generally, this stated capital will be the fair market value of the consideration for which the shares were issued. However, these statutes provide that, in connection with certain non-arm's length transactions, the corporation may establish an amount which is less than the consideration for which the shares were issued as the stated capital and such amount as so determined will then be the amount of PUC for tax purposes.

(3) In no par value jurisdictions, in certain non-arm's length situations, the stated capital (PUC) can be set at less than the fair market value of the consideration received by the corporation. In these situations, the PUC may be kept low to avoid certain penalty provisions of the Act. This will result in the redemption value of the shares being high to represent the value of the assets transferred and the PUC being low to avoid tax penalties or to benefit from a deemed dividend on redemption rather than a capital gain, since the tax on dividends is lower than the tax on an equal amount of capital gain. This ignores the capital gains exemption.

(4) The five basic components of the capital dividend account are:

    (a) the non-taxable portion of net capital gains;

    (b) capital dividends received from other corporations;

    (c) the untaxed portion of the proceeds of eligible capital property;

    (d) proceeds from life insurance policies net of their adjusted cost base; and

    (e) capital dividends paid, which reduce the account.

(5)

CEC balance	$6,000
Proceeds ($\frac{3}{4} \times$ $100,000)	(75,000)
	$(69,000)
Previous CECA claims (($\frac{3}{4} \times$ $10,000) – $6,000)	1,500
	$(67,500)
Income (($\frac{2}{3} \times$ $67,500) + $1,500)	$46,500
Capital dividend account ($\frac{2}{3} \times$ $67,500)	$45,000

Conceptually, the $45,000 added to the CDA is one-half of the economic gain of $90,000 (i.e., $\frac{1}{2}$($100,000 – $10,000)).

Even though the goodwill may not relate to the customer list, the two are both included in the same calculation as long as they both relate to the same business.

(6) The $8,000 reduction in capital will not cause a deemed dividend. However, the extra $1,000 of payment will be a deemed dividend since it is considered to be a distribution out of taxable surplus.   ITA: 84(4)

(7) The three components of a distribution are: ITA: 88(2)

    (a) paid-up capital which is returned tax-free;

    (b) a capital dividend to the extent of the capital dividend account and the election of a capital dividend; and   ITA: 83(2)

    (c) a taxable dividend to the extent of the balance.

(8) On the winding-up of the corporation, subsection 13(21.2) does not apply. Therefore, the terminal loss will be allowed as a deduction to the corporation.   ITA: 69(5)(*d*)

(9) The Act provides the definition of "proceeds of disposition" for purposes of the calculation of capital gain or loss. The proceeds do not include the deemed dividend on the winding-up distribution. Therefore, the proceeds are calculated as the amount distributed less the deemed dividend.   ITA: 54 ITA: 84(2)

CHAPTER 15

Chapter 15 — Solutions to Multiple Choice Questions

Question 1

(D) is false. Only taxable dividends paid are included in the computation of dividend refunds.   ITA: 129(1)

(A) is true.   ITA: 83(2)(*b*)

(B) is true.   ITA: 83(2)

(C) is true.   ITA: 89(1) "capital dividend account" (*a*)

Question 2

(D) is correct.

Redemption amount	$ 60,000
PUC	(10,000)
Dividend	$ 50,000

ITA: 84(3)

Redemption amount	$ 60,000
Dividend	(50,000)
Proceeds of disposition	$ 10,000
ACB	(20,000)
Capital loss	$(10,000)

ITA: 54

(A) is incorrect. This amount ignores the redemption deemed dividend.   ITA: 84(3)

(B) is incorrect. This amount calculates the dividend using the cost as opposed to the PUC.

(C) is incorrect. The dividend has not been subtracted from the redemption amount to arrive at the proceeds of disposition.

Question 3

(B) is correct.

Funds available for distribution	$ 40,000
PUC	(2,000)
Deemed dividend	$ 38,000
Elected amount of capital dividend	(8,000)
Taxable dividend	$ 30,000

ITA: 84(3)

Funds available for distribution	$ 40,000
Deemed dividend	(38,000)
Proceeds of disposition	$ 2,000
ACB	(1,000)
Capital gain	$ 1,000

ITA: 54

(A) is incorrect. Only subsidiaries in which the parent company owns at least 90% of the shares can wind up on a tax-deferred basis.

(C) is incorrect. The capital dividend has not been subtracted in the calculation of the proceeds.

(D) is incorrect. The ACB has been subtracted from the funds available to arrive at a $39,000 capital gain. The general winding-up rule and the deemed dividend on winding-up have been ignored.   ITA: 84(2), 88(2)

Question 4

(C) $1,561,333 is correct.

	Deemed proceeds	Business income	Investment income	CDA	RDTOH
Opening balance		Nil	Nil	$ 10,000	$ 30,000
Cash	$ 45,000				
Land	850,000		$300,000	300,000	
Building	780,000	$200,000	200,000	200,000	
	$1,675,000		$500,000	$510,000	
Liabilities	$ (20,000)	× 16%	× 45%		
Tax	(257,000)	$ 32,000	$225,000		$133,333
RDTOH	163,333				$163,333
	$1,561,333				

(A) $485,000 is incorrect. The liabilities of $20,000 have been subtracted from the asset total of $505,000 on the balance sheet.

(B) $1,398,000 is incorrect. The RDTOH has been omitted.

(D) $1,838,333 is incorrect. The liabilities and the income tax have not been deducted in the computation of the amount available for distribution.

Question 5

(A) is correct. The total paid-up capital of the common shares is $25,000, ½ of which is attributable to Mr. C and ½ is attributable to Mr. B. The total paid-up capital of the common shares is

100 common shares issued to Mr. A $10,000
100 common shares issued to Mr. B 15,000
$25,000

(B) and (D) are incorrect. The total paid-up capital of the common shares is not $35,000. The sale by Mr. A to Mr. C for $20,000 does not affect the paid-up capital of the shares.

(C) is incorrect because the $25,000 total paid-up capital of the common shares is split equally among the shares and is not based on the issue price of the shares.

Question 6

(B) is correct. The ¾ × the proceeds would be deducted from the CEC pool which would cause it to have a negative balance of $750,000. The Act states that this negative balance should be multiplied by ⅔, which makes it $500,000. The definition of the capital dividend account requires the tax-free portion of the gain ($500,000) to be included in the capital dividend account.

ITA: 14(1)(*b*)
ITA: 89(1) "capital dividend account" (*c*.2)

(A) and (D) are incorrect because there is no taxable capital gain on the sale of goodwill. As well, the reference in (D) to the refundable dividend tax on hand account is incorrect. The account is not affected.

(C) is incorrect as it does not take into consideration the business income inclusion or paragraph (*c*.2) of the definition of "capital dividend account".

ITA: 14(1)(*b*), 89(1)

CHAPTER 15

Chapter 15 — Solutions to Exercises

Exercise 1

	A	B	C
Proceeds of disposition	$ 4,000	$ 1,000	$ 2,000
Less: adjusted cost base	(2,000)	(2,000)	(2,000)
selling expenses	(400)	(100)	(200)
Capital gain (loss)	$ 1,600	$(1,100)	$ (200)
Adjustment to CDA (½ × capital gain (loss))	$ 800	$ (550)	$ (100)

Exercise 2

(A) Net income for tax purposes	Property 1		Property 2	
Proceeds of disposition		$110,000		$ 11,000
Less: ACB	$75,000		$40,000	
selling costs	11,000	86,000	5,500	45,500
Capital gain (loss)		$ 24,000		$(34,500)
Taxable capital gain (allowable capital loss)		$ 12,000		$(17,250)
(B) Adjustment to CDA (½ × capital gain (loss))		$ 12,000		$(17,250)

Exercise 3

(A) Where Investment Limited redeems the preferred shares, Mr. Duong will have a deemed dividend equal to: ITA: 84(3)

Redemption amount	$60,000
Less: PUC (800 × $15)	12,000
Deemed dividend	$48,000

ITA: 84(3)

Mr. Duong will not have a capital gain on the transactions because the adjusted proceeds of disposition equals the ACB of shares as demonstrated below:

Proceeds of disposition	$60,000
Deemed dividend	48,000
Adjusted proceeds of disposition	$12,000
Less: ACB (800 shares × $15)	12,000
Capital gain	Nil

ITA: 84(3)

ITA: 54 "proceeds of disposition" (*j*)

(B) The dividend payment of $60,000 will be a taxable dividend unless Investment Limited makes an election to treat the cash dividend as a distribution from the capital dividend account. Where this election is made, the dividend will be tax-free to Mr. Duong.   ITA: 83(2)

(C) A non-dividend distribution to Mr. Duong in excess of the PUC of the preferred shares will result in a deemed dividend of $45,000 (i.e., $60,000 – $15,000). The ACB of the shares will be reduced by the non-taxed portion of the payment of $15,000. The PUC of the shares must be reduced by the $15,000 in this case to reflect the tax-free distribution of PUC If PUC is not reduced by $15,000 in this transaction, an additional $15,000 will be treated as a deemed dividend.   ITA: 84(4) / ITA: 53(2)(*a*)(ii) / ITA: 84(4)(*a*)

Exercise 4

(A) The amount of the stock dividend is $1.00 per share and must be grossed up and included in income of the shareholder. Thus, income would total $11.80 (1.18 × $1.00 × 10 shares, using the 18% gross-up for dividends paid after 2013). The dividend tax credit would be available on the $1.00 amount of the stock dividend or about $0.18 total (including provincial tax effect) per share. The adjusted cost base of the shares on the acquisition date would be $10.00 in total (i.e., $1.00 per share).

(B) The corporation will be deemed to have paid a dividend of $10.00 for determining its dividend refund and other amounts dependent on dividends paid.

(C) P of D (10 shares @ $1,000 FMV) $10,000
     ACB (see (A), above) .... (10)

     Capital gain .... $ 9,990

     Taxable capital gain (eligible for capital gains deduction) .... $ 4,995

(D) (i)   Redemption amount (10 shares @ $1,000) $10,000
         PUC (10 shares @ $1.00) .... (10)

         Deemed dividend on redemption .... $ 9,990   ITA: 84(3)

   (ii) Proceeds of disposition (above) $10,000

         Less: deemed dividend .... (9,990)   ITA: 54 "proceeds of disposition" (*j*)

         Adjusted proceeds of disposition .... $ 10
         ACB .... (10)

         Capital gain.. Nil

Exercise 5

(a) This transaction would cause an immediate deemed dividend of $50 since the daughter could immediately retract the shares and receive $150 tax free whereas the price paid for the shares was only $100.   ITA: 84(1)

Deemed dividend   ITA: 84(1)
     PUC increase $150
     PUC decrease .... (Nil)

                              $150
     Increase in net assets .... (100)
     Deemed dividend .... $ 50   ITA: 84(1)

This $50 deemed dividend would be added to the ACB of the preferred shares acquired by the daughter.

In addition, there would be a subsection 84(3) deemed dividend on the ultimate redemption of the preferred shares as calculated below:

Redemption of shares
     Redemption amount $1,000
     PUC — Special share .... (150)

     Deemed dividend on redemption .... $ 850   ITA: 84(3)

     Proceeds of disposition $1,000
     Less: deemed dividend 850   ITA: 54 "proceeds of disposition" (*j*)

     Adjusted P of D .... $ 150
     ACB
        — original cost $100
        — ssec. 84(1) deemed dividend 50   (150)   ITA: 53(1)(*b*)

     Capital gain .... Nil

Economic consequences
     Redemption amount $1,000
     Actual price paid .... (100)

Economic gain on redemption	$ 900	

Tax results:

Deemed dividend	$ 50	ITA: 84(1)
Deemed dividend	850	ITA: 84(3)
Total gain taxed ($1,000 – $100)	$ 900	

(b) As long as there is no capital gain or loss triggered on the transfer, the gift of land to the corporation should have no other immediate tax consequences. The accounting and tax records would show an increased balance in the contributed surplus account. However, the withdrawal of this contributed surplus can only be in the form of taxable dividend subject to the gross-up and tax credit mechanism. However, the Act permits the capitalization of the contributed surplus into PUC as long as the amount did not arise under one of the corporate tax-free rollover provisions, discussed in the next few chapters.

ITA: 84(1)(c.3)

(c) Y has received $2,000 more in consideration than the cancelled debt (i.e., $2,000 + $20,000 versus $20,000); therefore, Y will have an income inclusion of:

PUC increase	$2,000	
Net asset increase ($20,000 – $20,000)	Nil	
Deemed dividend	$2,000	ITA: 84(1)

The cost of the shares is nil since the $20,000 cash cancelled the debt; however, there will be an increase in ACB equal to the deemed dividend of $2,000.

ITA: 53(1)(b)

(d) (i) Since the payment of $5,000 is less than the PUC of the outstanding share(s) (i.e., $10,000), there are no immediate tax consequences because this payment is a return of the original investment in the corporation with tax-paid funds. However, the adjusted cost base of the shares is reduced to $15,000 (i.e., $20,000 – $5,000) by the amount of the return of capital which would result in a potential higher capital gain on the ultimate disposition of the shares.

ITA: 53(2)(a)(ii)

Deemed dividend

ITA: 84(1)

PUC before distribution	$10,000	
PUC after distribution	(5,000)	
PUC decrease (not an increase)	$ 5,000	

Adjusted cost base

ACB prior to distribution	$20,000	
Distribution amount	(5,000)	
New ACB	$15,000	

(ii) Since the payment of $18,000 exceeds the PUC of the outstanding share(s), there will be a deemed dividend of $8,000. However, the ACB of the share(s) will only be reduced by the non-taxed portion of the payment to $10,000.

ITA: 84(4)

Exercise 6

(A)

Funds available for distribution to shareholder	$1,000,000	
Less: paid-up capital	(625,000)	
Deemed dividend on winding-up	$ 375,000	ITA: 84(2)
Less: capital dividend elected	(150,000)	ITA: 83(2), 88(2)(b)(i)
Taxable dividend (sufficient to clear RDTOH)	$ 225,000	

(B) Taxable capital gain (allowable capital loss) to Mr. Siewert:

Proceeds on winding-up	$1,000,000	
Less: deemed dividend	(375,000)	ITA: 54 "proceeds of disposition" (j)
Proceeds of disposition	$ 625,000	
ACB	350,000	
Capital gain	$ 275,000	
Taxable capital gain (½)	$ 137,500	

Exercise 7

Funds available for distribution		$30,000
Less: paid-up capital		(2,000)
Deemed dividend or winding-up		$28,000
Less: capital dividend elected		(2,000)
Deemed taxable dividend		$26,000

ITA: 84(2)
ITA: 83(2), 88(2)(*b*)(i)

Capital gain or loss on disposition of shares:

Actual proceeds from distribution	$30,000
Less: deemed dividend	(28,000)
Proceeds of disposition	$ 2,000
Cost	(2,000)
Capital gain (loss)	Nil
Taxable capital gain	Nil

ITA: 54 "proceeds of disposition" (*j*)

Net cash retained:

Funds distributed		$30,000
Tax on incremental income from distribution:		
Deemed taxable dividend	$26,000	
Gross-up (18% × $26,000)	4,680	
Taxable capital gain	Nil	
Incremental taxable income	$30,680	
Combined federal and provincial tax @ 46%	$14,113	
Less: combined dividend tax credit in province @ (^{13}/₁₈ + ⁵/₁₈) × .18 × $26,000	(4,680)	9,433
Net cash retained		$20,567

Exercise 8

(A)

		Income			
	Proceeds	Bus.	Invest.	C.D. a/c	RDTOH
Opening balances		Nil	Nil	Nil	$ 10,000
Cash	$ 20,000	Nil	Nil		
Inventories	220,000	$ 20,000	Nil		
Land[(1)]	70,000	Nil	$ 15,000	$15,000	
Buildings[(2)]	300,000	140,000	50,000	50,000	
Equipment[(3)]	80,000	40,000	Nil		
Liabilities	(50,000)				
Income taxes[(5)]	(60,333)	$200,000[(4)]	$ 65,000		17,333
RDTOH[(6)]	27,333				$ 27,333
	$607,000			$65,000	

(B)

Funds available for distribution to shareholder		$607,000
Less: paid-up capital		2,000
Deemed dividend on winding-up		$605,000
Less: capital dividend elected		65,000
Deemed taxable dividend (clears RDTOH)		$540,000

ITA: 84(2)
ITA: 83(2)

CHAPTER 15

(C)   Taxable capital gain to Mr. Warren

Actual proceeds on winding-up	$607,000
Less: deemed dividend	605,000
Proceeds of disposition	$ 2,000
Cost	(1,000)
Capital gain	$ 1,000
Taxable capital gain (½ × $1,000)	$ 500

(D)

Where a corporation is wound up and the general winding-up rules of the Act apply, the supply of property on the wind-up is subject to HST. HST is payable on any taxable supplies of property. However, an election may be available, in which case the payment of HST is not required. In order to qualify, a registrant must have sold or transferred all or substantially all of the assets used in a commercial activity that is part of a business carried on. Since Dwight Ltd. is being wound up by Mr. Warren it would qualify for this election.   ITA: 88(2)   ETA: 167(1)

— *NOTES TO SOLUTION*

(1)
Proceeds on sale of land	$ 70,000
Cost	(40,000)
Capital gain	$ 30,000
Taxable capital gain (½ × $30K) (investment income)	$ 15,000
Capital dividend account (½ × $30K)	$ 15,000

(2)
Actual proceeds on sale of building	$300,000
UCC	(60,000)
Gain	$240,000
Recapture ($200K – $60K) (business income)	$140,000
Taxable capital gain (½ × ($300K – $200K)) (investment income)	$ 50,000
Capital dividend account (½ × ($300K – $200K))	$ 50,000

(3)
Actual proceeds on sale of equipment	$ 80,000
UCC	(40,000)
Gain	$ 40,000
Recapture ($80K – $40K) — fully accounts for gain (business income)	$ 40,000

(4) The $500,000 business limit for the small business deduction must be prorated for the number of days in the taxation year. Since the winding-up may take some time to complete, this solution assumes that the corporation maintains its eligibility for the small business deduction in the year in which the sale of assets occurs. In this case, there would be no need to bonus down to the business limit for the small business deduction, given active business income of $200,000.   IT-73R6, par. 9

(5)   Income taxes

15% × ABI ($200,000)	$30,000	
46⅔% × investment income ($65,000)	30,333	$ 60,333
RDTOH (26⅔% of $65,000)		$ 17,333

(6) Assumes a minimum $81,999 (i.e., 3 × $27,333) is to be distributed as a taxable dividend to produce a refund of the full RDTOH.

Chapter 16
Income Deferral: Rollover on Transfers to a Corporation and Pitfalls

LEARNING GOALS

Know

By the end of this chapter you should know the basic provisions of the *Income Tax Act* pertaining to the transfer of property to a corporation, by a person who will be a shareholder of the corporation, on a tax deferred or rollover basis. Completing the Review Questions (¶16,800) and Multiple Choice Questions (¶16,825) is a good way to learn the technical provisions.

Understand and Explain

You should understand and be able to explain:
- The basic tax consequences of the transfer of property to a corporation by a shareholder on a rollover basis where applicable;
- Options for the transfer of property to a corporation;
- The means that a corporation can use to pay for the assets transferred and their tax consequences; and
- Two potential traps or pitfalls on the transfer of shares to a corporation, the cause of the issues that arise and how to avoid them.

Completing the Exercises (¶16,850) is a good way to deepen your understanding of the material.

Apply

You should be able to apply your knowledge and understanding of the key elements of the rollover on the transfer of property to a corporation in a variety of tax planning situations, including the incorporation of an unincorporated business, while avoiding the pitfalls of doing so, and in a way that accomplishes a client's goals. Completing the Assignment Problems (¶16,875) is an excellent way to develop your ability to apply the material in increasingly complex situations.

Chapter 16 — Learning Chart

Topic	Example Problem (✓)	Review Questions (¶16,800)	Multiple Choice (¶16,825)	Exercises (¶16,850)	Assignment Problems (¶16,875)
¶16,000 TRANSFER OF PROPERTY TO A CORPORATION BY A SHAREHOLDER					
¶16,010 The Basic Concepts					
¶16,015 Situation one					
¶16,020 Situation two					
¶16,025 Situation three					
¶16,030 Basic Technical Rules on the Transfer					
¶16,035 Use of the rollover		1			
¶16,040 Conditions for the rollover to apply		2			
¶16,045 Elected transfer price		3	1	1, 2	1
¶16,050 Non-share consideration or boot		4, 5, 9	2	1, 2	1
¶16,060 Application of the Basic Rules	✓			5, 7	2, 3
¶16,070 The Corporation's Position			3	7	2, 3
¶16,080 The Shareholder's Position	✓	7, 11	4	3	
¶16,090 Paid-Up Capital Reduction on Shares Issued as Consideration					
¶16,095 The issue in concept					
¶16,100 The technical solution			6		
¶16,105 Illustration of application				5	
¶16,110 The effect	✓			3	
¶16,120 Other Rules Applicable in the Rollover					
¶16,125 Depreciable capital property		6			
¶16,130 Transfer of non-depreciable capital property with unrealized capital losses to affiliated persons		8			
¶16,135 Summary of stop-loss rules					
¶16,140 Benefits Conferred on Shareholders and Related Persons					
¶16,145 Conceptual example					
¶16,150 Benefit conferred on a related person — Technical rules		12		4	
¶16,155 Subsection 15(1) benefit conferred on a shareholder — Technical rules		10			
¶16,160 Summary of Rules					
¶16,170 Fair Market Value					
¶16,180 Section 22 Election			5		4, 5, 6
¶16,190 Application	✓			6	4, 5, 6
¶16,200 TRANSFER OF SHARES					
¶16,210 Non-Arm's Length Sale of Shares		13			
¶16,215 The situation: QSBC shares		14			
¶16,220 Conditions for section 84.1 to apply					
¶16,225 The basic rules formulated					

Topic	Example Problem (✓)	Review Questions (¶16,800)	Multiple Choice (¶16,825)	Exercises (¶16,850)	Assignment Problems (¶16,875)
¶16,230 Application of rules	✓			8, 9	7, 8
¶16,240 Sale of Shares by a Corporation to an Unrelated Person					
¶16,245 Situation addressed by section 55					
¶16,250 Illustration of the effect of section 55				10	9
¶16,255 Exceptions to the application of section 55					
¶16,900 SUPPLEMENTAL NOTES					
¶16,910 GST/HST and Section 85 Rollovers					

Study Notes

Chapter 16 —
Discussion Notes for Review Questions

(1) In general, a rollover allows for a partial or complete deferral of the recognition of income on the transfer of property from one person to another. The transferor, in return for the property transferred, should receive a package of consideration, the total fair market value of which should be equal to the fair market value of the property transferred. The transferor is the one who is deferring the recognition of income. The transferee usually steps into the position of the transferor in terms of the tax value of the asset received. Therefore, on the ultimate disposition of the asset by the transferee, the income will be recognized. Examples of rollovers include subsections 73(1), 85(1), 88(1) and sections 51 and 86.

(2) In order to use section 85, the corporation must be a "taxable Canadian corporation" which is defined to be a "Canadian corporation" that is not exempt from tax. A "Canadian corporation" is defined to include a company that is resident in Canada and was either incorporated in Canada or resident in Canada since before June 18, 1971. In this case, Della Inc. has been resident in Canada only since 1973 and, therefore, is not a Canadian corporation and not a taxable Canadian corporation. Although the real estate is capital property to Mr. Della and, thus, it is "eligible property", this property cannot be transferred using section 85 since the transferee is not a taxable Canadian corporation. `ITA: 85(1.1)` `ITA: 89(1)`

(3) The following are the four uses of the elected price:

(a) it is the proceeds of disposition to the transferor;

(b) it is the cost of the property to the corporation;

(c) it is used to determine the ACB of the package of consideration taken by the transferor from the corporation in return for the assets transferred to the corporation; and

(d) it is used to calculate the paid-up capital of the shares taken as consideration by the transferor from the corporation.

(4) On the transfer, the only decision variable you have is the non-share consideration or boot. If the boot is higher than the lower limit for the particular asset transferred, then the lower limit is increased. The boot cannot, however, raise the upper limit above fair market value. `ITA: 85(1)(b), 85(1)(c)`

(5) The maximum "boot" that should be taken in order to maximize the deferral is the lower limit on the election range as determined by the tax value, unless the FMV is lower. This will cause a problem if the asset being transferred is shares and section 84.1 applies. This problem could occur if the shares being transferred were QSBCS. and an amount was elected to trigger a gain equal to the available exemption. When section 84.1 applies, the maximum boot should be the greater of the PUC and the arm's length cost, not a higher elected amount.

(6) The Regulations would still apply. She may have heard about another regulation which allows the transferee to avoid the half-year rule as long as the transferor was not dealing at arm's-length with the corporation at the time of the transfer (which is true in this situation) and the property was owned continuously by the transferor (Ms. Smith) for the period from at least 364 days before the end of the taxation year of the corporation in which the asset was acquired to the date of the election. If the taxation year of the corporation occurs at least 364 days after the purchase of the equipment, then the condition is met. `ITR: 1100(2), 1100(2.2)`

(7) The elected transfer price is equal to the total cost of the consideration taken back. This elected amount is allocated among the different types of consideration in the following manner:

First: to non-share consideration (boot) up to the FMV of that property as long as that FMV does not exceed the FMV of the assets transferred to the corporation; `ITA: 85(1)(f)`

Second: to preferred shares up to the FMV of those shares after the transfer but only to the extent that there is a balance left after the boot has been deducted from the elected amount; and `ITA: 85(1)(g)`

Third: to common shares to the extent that the elected amount exceeds the FMV of the boot and the cost allocated to the preferred shares. `ITA: 85(1)(h)`

(8) Normally, the sale of shares in an SBC would allow Bar Ltd. to claim the loss as a business investment loss. However, the ABIL is denied, since it must sell to an arm's length person. Bar Ltd. and Spouse Ltd. do not deal at arm's length since they are related. Therefore, the loss would be an ordinary capital loss. `ITA: 39(1)(c)` `ITA: 251`

However, in this case, Bar Ltd. is transferring the shares to a corporation controlled by the sole shareholder's wife, an affiliated person; therefore, the superficial loss will be denied to Bar Ltd. However, Spouse Ltd. can take advantage of the ability to add the loss to the cost base of the Lite Ltd. shares now owned by Spouse Ltd. An election under section 85 is not required in order to apply. The rule applies whenever a taxpayer disposes of capital property to an affiliated person, including a corporation that was controlled, directly or indirectly in any manner whatever, by the taxpayer, by the spouse of the taxpayer or by other affiliated persons.

ITA: 53(1)(f), 54, 251.1
ITA: 40(2)(g)

ITA: 40(2)(g)

(9) The "elected amount" determines how much can be withdrawn tax-free since this is the starting point for determining the ACB and the PUC of the shares. In addition, it is the amount that is used to determine how much boot to take back on the transaction to fully defer the accrued income.

(10) The elected amount is correct since the upper limit is the FMV of $8,000. Ms. Smith will realize a capital gain of $3,000. The company will have a cost in the portfolio shares of $8,000 which is the elected amount. There will be a paid-up capital reduction to reduce the PUC to $8,000. Thus, on redemption, she will have a deemed dividend for $2,000 (i.e., $10,000 of redemption value – $8,000 of PUC).

ITA: 85(1)(b)

ITA: 85(2.1)

(11) If boot is equal to the elected amount and equal to the tax value of the property being transferred, then the ACB and PUC of the shares will be nil. However, if the transaction results in a capital loss, the stop-loss rules may deny the loss. The capital loss can then be added to the adjusted cost base of the property held by the transferee corporation. If the benefit rule applies, then the PUC will exceed the ACB by the amount of the benefit. If section 84.1 applies, then the ACB will exceed the PUC by the amount of the PUC reduction.

ITA: 40(2)(g), 54
"superficial loss"
ITA: 53(1)(f)
ITA: 85(1)(e.2)

(12) Price adjustment clauses are often used to provide for an adjustment to the consideration taken back in the event that the assessed value is different than what was originally used. The courts have determined that the price adjustment clause will only be recognized if the parties have reasonably and in good faith attempted to determine fair market value. The CRA's position on them is outlined in an Interpretation Bulletin.

IT-405

(13) The provision is designed to prevent an individual from stripping the fair market value in excess of the greater of his or her arm's length cost or the PUC out of the company without selling the shares in an arm's length transaction (i.e., a share redemption).

(14) He can reduce the PUC of the shares by $100,000. This will cause his ACB in the shares to become negative $90,000 which will give rise to an immediate capital gain. Alternatively, he can transfer his shares to a holding company under section 85 and take back a note for $100,000 and one share with a nominal value of, say, one cent. Section 84.1 will not give rise to a deemed dividend, since the boot does not exceed the greater of the arm's length cost and the PUC. In either case, he can use his capital gains exemption to shelter the gain.

ITA: 40(3), 53(2)(a)(ii),
84(4)

Chapter 16 —
Solutions to Multiple Choice Questions

Question 1

(C) is correct. Electing at $800, the UCC of the transferred asset, will defer recapture as well as the capital gain. ITA: 85(1)(*e*)

(A) is incorrect. The spousal rollover applies to transfers to a spouse or a spousal trust, but never to a corporation. ITA: 73(1)

(B) is incorrect. Electing at $2,200 will defer the capital gain, but recapture of $1,400 will be incurred.

(D) is incorrect. Since the corporation will have acquired the depreciable asset from a non-arm's length individual, $2,600 (i.e., $2,200 + ½ ($3,000 – $2,200) is the maximum amount that the capital cost could be. ITA: 13(7)(*e*)

Question 2

(D) $25,000 is correct. In order to defer the gain, Steve will elect at $40,000, the ACB of the asset. The elected amount cannot be less than the non-share consideration. Since S Ltd. assumed the mortgage of $15,000, an additional $25,000 of non-share consideration is the maximum that can be taken. ITA: 85(1)

(A) $100,000 is incorrect. This amount would result in a capital gain of $60,000 as well as a shareholder benefit of $15,000. ITA: 15(1)

(B) $85,000 is incorrect. This amount would result in a capital gain of $60,000.

(C) $40,000 is incorrect. This amount would result in a capital gain of $15,000.

Question 3

(B) $110,000 is correct. Since the corporation has acquired the depreciable property from a non-arm's length individual, the capital cost is limited to the transferor's capital cost, $100,000 plus the taxable capital gain on the transfer, $10,000. This totals $110,000. ITA: 13(7)(*e*)

(A) $120,000, the elected transfer price, is incorrect for the same reason that (B) is correct.

(C) $90,000, the transferor's UCC plus the taxable capital gain on the transfer, is incorrect. The starting point is the transferor's capital cost, not UCC. ITA: 13(7)(*e*)

(D) $75,000, the transferor's UCC, is incorrect for the same reason that (B) is correct.

Question 4

(D) $20,000 is correct.

Elected transfer price		$40,000
Allocated to non-share consideration:		
Cash	$3,000	
Debt	2,000	$ 5,000
Allocated to the preferred shares, up to their FMV		15,000
Allocated to the common shares, remainder		20,000
		$40,000

ITA: 85(1)(*g*)
ITA: 85(1)(*h*)

(A) $35,000 is incorrect. The elected amount, in excess of the non-share consideration, has all been allocated to the common shares.

(B) $23,000 is incorrect. None of the elected amount has been allocated to the cash.

(C) $23,333 is incorrect. The allocation between the preferred and common shares has been done based on proportionate values.

Question 5

(D) is correct because a section 22 election ensures that the purchaser will be able to take a doubtful debts reserve on the accounts receivable.

(A) and (B) are incorrect because a section 22 election ensures that the loss to the vendor is a business loss rather than a capital loss or superficial loss. If no section 22 election is made, the vendor will realize a loss that is a capital loss. Further, if the vendor and purchaser are affiliated persons, the loss will be denied and will be a superficial loss.

ITA: 54

(C) is incorrect because the vendor is always required to add the prior year's doubtful debts reserve. It does not matter whether or not a section 22 election is made.

ITA: 12(1)(*d*)

Question 6

(D) is correct. Because the promissory note is $60,000, the elected amount is deemed to be $60,000. The elected amount determines the proceeds of disposition to Rebecca, R Co.'s cost of the land, the cost of the consideration to Rebecca, and the paid-up capital of the shares issued as consideration after the paid-up capital reduction.

ITA: 85(2.1)

(A) is incorrect because the proceeds to Rebecca are deemed to be $60,000 not $50,000 as discussed above.

(B) is incorrect because R Co.'s cost of the land is deemed to be $60,000, not $50,000 as discussed above.

(C) is incorrect because Rebecca's cost of the preference shares is zero. It is calculated as the elected amount minus the boot ($60,000 – $60,000 demand note).

ITA: 85(1)(*g*)

Chapter 16 — Solutions to Exercises

Exercise 1

		A	B	C	D	E	F	G
(A)	Minimum elected amount or deemed proceeds	$120	$100	$ 80	$ 75	$100	$ 90	$ 50
(B)	Proceeds	$120	$100	$ 80	$ 75	$100	$ 90	$ 50
	Cost	100	75	100	75	100	75	100
	Capital gain	$ 20	$ 25	Nil*	Nil	Nil	$ 15	Nil
	Taxable capital gain (½)	$ 10	$ 13	Nil	Nil	Nil	$ 8	Nil
	Lesser of cost or proceeds	$100		$ 80		$100		$ 50
	UCC of class	200		50		150		50
	Recapture	Nil		$ 30		Nil		Nil
	Income from shareholder benefit	$ 30	$100	Nil	Nil	Nil	Nil	Nil
(C)	Maximum "boot"	$100	$ 75	$ 50	$ 75	$100	$ 75	$ 50

ITA: 15(1)

* No capital loss on depreciable property.

Exercise 2

(A) Cost of consideration received:

	A	B	C
Elected transfer price	$5,000	$5,000	$5,000
Allocated to note up to FMV	5,000	2,500	4,000
Allocated to preferred up to FMV	Nil	$2,500	Nil
Allocated to common shares	Nil	Nil	$1,000

(B)

	A	B	C
LSC before reduction	$5,000	$7,500	$6,000

Reduction in PUC   ITA: 85(2.1)

	A	B	C
(a) Increase in LSC of all shares	$5,000 (A)	$7,500 (A)	$6,000 (A)
(b) Elected amount	$5,000	$5,000	$5,000
Less: boot	5,000	2,500	4,000
Excess, if any	Nil (B)	$2,500 (B)	$1,000 (B)
Total reduction in PUC (A – B)	$5,000	$5,000	$5,000

(c) Allocation of reduction to different classes:

Preferred shares

$$\$5,000 \times \frac{\$4,500}{\$5,000} = \underline{\$4,500}$$

Common shares

$$\$5,000 \times \frac{\$500}{\$5,000} = \underline{\$\ 500}$$

Tax PUC	A	B	C
Preferred shares	Nil	$2,500	
Common shares	Nil		$1,000

Note how the PUC after reduction is equal to the amount of the $5,000 ACB of the original capital property that has not been recovered through the notes received as consideration.

CHAPTER 16

Exercise 3

(A) The elected amount becomes the proceeds of disposition of the assets transferred by Mr. Good. Since his adjusted cost base on the land and his undepreciated capital cost on the building are equal to these proceeds, there will be no capital gain on that land and no recapture on the building. The corporation is deemed to acquire these assets at a cost equal to the elected amount. On the building, the corporation is deemed to have a capital cost of $436,224 and to have taken capital cost allowance of $8,724 making it liable for future recapture and for a potential future capital gain if ultimate proceeds exceed $436,224. This places the corporation in the same position as Mr. Good was in with respect to the building prior to the transfer.

(B) (i) The cost of the debt and shares taken as consideration would be computed as follows:

Elected transfer price		$577,500
Allocated to debt:		
— mortgage assumed	$247,500	
— new debt issued	330,000	577,500
Allocated to shares		Nil

(ii) LSC before reduction . . . . $322,500   ITA: 85(2.1)

Reduction in PUC

(1) Increase in LSC of all shares		$322,500 (A)	
(2) Elected amount	$577,500		
less: boot ($247,500 + $330,000)	577,500		
Excess, if any		Nil (B)	
Total PUC reduction (A – B)			(322,500)
Tax PUC after reduction			Nil

(C) (i) If the new debt is redeemed for $330,000, given its adjusted cost base in Mr. Good's hands of $330,000, there would be no gain or loss. However, on the disposition of the shares, the following would result:

Proceeds of disposition	$425,000
Adjusted cost base	Nil
Capital gain	$425,000
Taxable capital gain	$212,500

(ii)

Redemption amount	$425,000	
Less: PUC	Nil	
Deemed dividend	$425,000	ITA: 84(3)
Redemption amount	$425,000	
Less: deemed dividend	425,000	
Proceeds of disposition	Nil	ITA: 54 "proceeds of disposition" (j)
Less: adjusted cost base	Nil	
Capital gain	Nil	

Exercise 4

The benefit rule would apply. The amount of the benefit would be equal to: ITA: 85(1)(e.2)

Fair market value of property transferred		$125,000
Less greater of:		
(a) fair market value of all consideration received	$101,000	101,000
(b) elected amount	$100,000	
Benefit		$ 24,000

CHAPTER 16

The proceeds of disposition of the securities to Mother would be increased by the amount of the benefit, $24,000, to $124,000 resulting in a capital gain of $24,000 on the transfer. The cost of the property to the corporation would also be increased by $24,000 to $124,000. However, the cost of the consideration received would be as follows:

Elected amount	$100,000
Allocated to note (up to FMV)	100,000
Allocated to preferred share	Nil

Thus, the cost of the consideration received or of the shares owned by Daughter, which would increase in value by $24,000, is not increased by the amount of the benefit resulting in potential double taxation.

The $1,000 LSC of the preferred share would not be reduced and would equal tax PUC.

Reduction in PUC   ITA: 85(2.1)

(a) Increase in LSC		$ 1,000 (A)
(b) Elected amount (as increased by benefit)	$124,000	
Less: boot	100,000	
Excess, if any		24,000 (B)
Total PUC reduction (A – B)		Nil

ITA: 257

To avoid the problem of the $24,000 benefit being potentially taxed twice, Mother should have taken more share consideration in the amount of $24,000 such that the fair market value of all consideration received was equal to the fair market value of the property transferred. The PUC of these shares will be reduced to nil by the above formula, but this will not have any immediate tax consequences.

ITA: 85(2.1)

Exercise 5

Elected amount	*Range*
Asset #1	$5,000 — $20,000
Asset #2	$8,000 — $14,000

However, the Act forces the minimum elected amount to be $18,000 because of the non-share consideration taken in that amount.

ITA: 85(1)(*b*)

Assign the elected amount as follows:

Asset #1	$ 5,000
Asset #2	13,000
	$18,000

Note that the minimum amount is assigned to the depreciable asset to avoid recapture being fully taxed.

Income

Asset #1	P of D	$ 5,000
	ACB	10,000
	CL	Nil
Asset #2	P of D	$13,000
	ACB	8,000
	CG	$ 5,000
	TCG	$ 2,500

Under corporate law[1], the paid-up capital of the one common share would be equal to the net fair market value of the assets transferred to the corporation. In this case, the PUC would be $16,000 (i.e., $20,000 + $14,000 − $18,000). However, the Act will reduce the PUC as follows:

ITA: 85(2.1)

(a)	Increase in legal PUC of all shares on the transfer to the corporation		$16,000 (I)
(b)	Elected amount	$18,000	
	Less: non-share consideration ("boot")	18,000	
	Excess, if any		Nil (II)
	Total PUC reduction (I − II)		$16,000

Since there is only one class of shares issued, there is no prorating of this reduction. As a result, the PUC of the share will be reduced to nil (i.e., $16,000 − $16,000) for tax purposes. The PUC is reduced to nil, because all of the tax-paid cost in UCC of $5,000 and ACB of $8,000 has been recovered through cash.

— NOTE TO SOLUTION

[1] Where the transferor and the corporation do not deal at arm's length, the legal stated capital (the initial PUC) can be less than the fair market value of the transferred assets at the discretion of the corporate directors.

Exercise 6

(A) Items not transferred under subsection 85(1):

Cash	$ 4,000	(not capital property)
Short-term investments	5,000	(capital loss denied)
Accounts receivable	9,000	(use section 22[1])
Prepaid insurance	400	(business loss of $100)
Building	60,000	(terminal loss of $2,000 denied)
Land	26,500	(capital loss denied)
Total	$104,900	(assume proprietorship debt of $74,000 and take back new debt for the balance of $30,900)

The building may not be transferred using the rules in section 85 because of the unrealized terminal loss. A stop-loss rule applies to deny the loss. The corporation will acquire the building with a UCC of $60,000 which is equal to its fair market value and the amount paid by the corporation.

ITA: 13(21.2)

If the short-term investments can be considered assets used in the active business of the corporation, they can be transferred to the corporation. However, the capital loss will be considered to be a superficial loss because the corporation is affiliated with the transferor, Mrs. Designer. Therefore, a stop-loss rule will deny the loss to Mrs. Designer. The amount of the loss will be added to the cost of the investments to the corporation, such that the corporation's ACB of the investments will be $10,000.

ITA: 54

ITA: 40(2)(*g*), 53(1)(*f*)

Section 85 need not be used when there is no accrued income to defer. If the short-term investments cannot be considered as assets used in an active business, then they should not be transferred to the corporation, because it will seriously jeopardize the qualification of the shares of the corporation as QSBCSs.

The land need not be transferred under section 85 for the same reasons as the short-term investments, because of the accrued capital loss. While the loss will be denied to Mrs. Designer, the corporation will acquire the land for $26,500 of consideration, but hold it with an ACB of $30,000 which was Mrs. Designer's tax position in the land before the transfer.

(B) and (C) Items transferred under subsection 85(1) and consideration:

	Tax value	FMV	Elected amount	Consideration Assumed debt[2]	New debt	Pref. shs.	Income
Inventory	$ 5,000	$25,000	$ 5,000	Nil	$ 5,000	$20,000	Nil
Goodwill	Nil	44,000	1	Nil	Nil	44,000	$0.50
	$ 5,000	$69,000	$ 5,001	Nil	$ 5,000	$64,000	

Since the corporation will qualify as a small business corporation, the Act will not apply to attribute income or capital gains back to Mrs. Designer.

ITA: 74.4, 248(1)

(D) Elected transfer price . . . . $ 5,001

    Allocated to debt consideration:

        debt assumed . . . . Nil

        new debt 5,000   5,000

    Allocated to ACB of preferred shares . . . . $ 1

(E) LSC before reduction $64,000

Reduction in PUC

ITA: 85(2.1)

    (i) Increase in LSC of all shares . . . . $64,000 (A)

    (ii) Elected amount . . . . $ 5,001

        Less: boot 5,000

        Excess, if any . . . . 1 (B)

        Total PUC reduction (A – B) . . . . (63,999)

    Tax PUC after reduction . . . . $ 1

The $1 of PUC after the reduction represents the amount of tax-paid cost that has not been recovered through boot received from the corporation. The $1 of income resulting from the transfer of the goodwill is a tax-paid cost. A total of $5,000 of total tax-paid cost was recovered through boot.

(F) For those assets *not* transferred under subsection 85(1) and not subject to the specific provisions discussed below, the cost for tax purposes to the corporation would be equal to the fair market value of the consideration:

Cash	$ 4,000
Prepaid insurance	400
Building	60,000
	$64,400 = debt consideration

Under section 22, the purchaser, Hi-Fashion, would record the accounts receivable at their face value of $12,000 which would be their adjusted cost base for tax purposes. Under the conditions of section 22, the corporation must include in its income the business loss of $3,000 recognized by the transferor (i.e., difference between the face value ($12,000) and the fair market value ($9,000)). Hi-Fashion is now entitled to set up a reserve to offset any potential doubtful debts (i.e., $3,000), plus an amount equal to any further decline in value. In addition, the corporation is now eligible to write off any realized bad debts since it has included an amount in income in respect of these receivables.

The ACB of the short-term investments and the land to the corporation will be their fair market value plus the denied superficial loss. Therefore, the ACB of the short-term investments will be $10,000 ($5,000 FMV + $5,000 denied loss) and that of the land will be $30,000 ($26,500 FMV + $3,500 denied loss). This puts the corporation in the same tax position on these assets as Mrs. Designer was in before the transfer.

The capital cost and, therefore, the ACB of the building in the corporation is $80,000.

For the inventory that has been transferred under subsection 85(1), the cost base would be the elected amount (i.e., inventory — $5,000). The goodwill, which is eligible capital property, would have a cost base of 75 cents (i.e., ¾ × $1.00).

— *NOTES TO SOLUTION*

[1] Reserve of $2,000 from last year must be brought into income this year. There will be a full business loss of $3,000 (i.e., face value of $12,000 less fair market value of $9,000) using section 22.

[2] The $104,900 of debt consideration for the assets not transferred under subsection 85(1) could include all assumed liabilities of $74,000, leaving none to be assumed in the subsection 85(1) transfer.

Exercise 7

An elected transfer price of $80,000 will result in the following: ITA: 85(1)

Recapture ($27,000 – $30,000)	$ 3,000
Taxable capital gain [½ ($80,000 – $30,000)]	25,000
Income	$28,000
Less: net capital loss	25,000
Incremental taxable income	$ 3,000

ACB of consideration received:

Note	$80,000
Common shares	Nil

PUC of common shares: ITA: 85(2.1)

LSC of shares issued		$20,000
Less: PUC reduction		

     ITA: 85(2.1)

(a) increase in LSC		$20,000 (A)
(b) elected amount	$80,000	
boot	80,000	
excess, if any		Nil (B)
(A – B)		$20,000
PUC for tax purposes		Nil

Capital cost of transferred property to corporation for CCA and recapture purposes is equal to the aggregate of:

(a) capital cost to transferor		$30,000
(b) proceeds of disposition to transferor	$80,000	
less: capital cost of property transferred	30,000	
excess, if any	$50,000	
½ of excess		25,000
Deemed capital cost to corporation		$55,000

     ITA: 13(7)(*e*)(i)

The capital cost used for future CCA write-offs, which shield business income from full tax, will be increased by the taxable capital gain triggered, but not, in effect, the untaxed portion of the capital gain.

Capital cost of the depreciable property for future *capital gains* purposes (equal to elected amount) is $80,000.

Exercise 8

Part (A)

Section 84.1 applies because Mr. Newberry is a Canadian resident and is not at arm's length with his brother who controls the corporation to which the Opco shares were transferred. Therefore, Mr. Newberry is not at arm's length with the corporation. In addition, Opco Ltd. is connected with Broco Ltd., since Broco owns all of its outstanding common shares.   ITA: 251(2)(*b*)(iii)
     ITA: 186(2)

PUC reduction: ITA: 84.1(1)(*a*)

    (a) Increase in LSC of brother's corporation . . . . $ 300,000 (A)

        Less:

    (b) Greater of:

        (i) PUC of operating company

            shares $75,000

        (ii) Modified ACB* of operating   } $ 75,000

            company shares $75,000

        Less: FMV of boot 500,000

        Excess, if any . . . . Nil (B)

                PUC reduction (A – B) . . . . $ 300,000

                PUC after reduction . . . . Nil

     The PUC after reduction is nil because all of the $75,000 hard cost in the operating company shares has been recovered in boot from the brother's corporation.

Deemed dividend: ITA: 84.1(1)(*b*)

    Sum of:

        (a) Increase in LSC of brother's corporation . . . . $ 300,000 (A)

        (b) FMV of boot . . . . 500,000 (D)

            (A + D) . . . . $ 800,000

    Less sum of:

        (c) Greater of:

            (i) PUC of operating

                company shares . . . . $ 75,000

                             } $ 75,000 (E)

            (ii) Modified ACB* of operating

                company shares . . . . $ 75,000

        (d) PUC reduction . . . . 300,000 (F)   ITA: 84.1(1)(*a*)

            (E + F) 375,000

      Deemed dividend (A + D) – (E + F) . . . . $ 425,000

* Adjusted actual cost.

     This deemed dividend is equal to the excess of the $500,000 in boot received from the brother's corporation over the $75,000 of hard cost in the operating company shares transferred.

    Capital gain or loss on disposition of Opco Ltd. shares:

        Elected amount and proceeds of disposition for operating

            company shares . . . . $ 500,000   ITA: 85(1)

        Less: deemed dividend 425,000   ITA: 54 "proceeds of disposition" (*k*)

        Adjusted proceeds of disposition for operating company shares . . . $ 75,000

        Less: ACB of operating company shares 75,000

        Capital gain (loss) if any, (not denied*) . . . . Nil   ITA: 40(2)(*g*)

    ACB of Broco Ltd. shares received:

        Cost of shares of Broco Ltd. after allocation of $500,000 elected

            amount to "boot" . . . . Nil   ITA: 85(1)(*g*)

* He is not affiliated with Broco Ltd. by the definition of "affiliated person" in section 251.1, since he does not control, directly or indirectly, Broco Ltd.

Part (B)

    Ultimate redemption of shares of brother's corporation

    Redemption amount . . . . $ 300,000

    Less: PUC . . . . Nil

CHAPTER 16

Deemed dividend on redemption	$ 300,000	ITA: 84(3)
Proceeds of disposition	$ 300,000	
Less: deemed dividend on redemption	300,000	ITA: 84(3)
Adjusted proceeds of disposition	Nil	ITA: 54 "proceeds of disposition" (*j*)
Less: adjusted cost base	Nil	
Capital gain (loss)	Nil	

Summary of income effects:

Sec. 84.1 deemed dividend	$ 425,000	
Redemption deemed dividend	300,000	ITA: 84(3)
Capital gain (loss) on transfer	Nil	ITA: 85(1)
Capital gain (loss) on redemption	Nil	
Net economic effect	$ 725,000	

Note that $725,000 represents the accrued gain on the Opco Ltd. shares at the time of the transfer.

Part (C)

Ultimate arm's length sale of shares of brother's corporation

Proceeds of disposition	$ 300,000
Less: adjusted cost base	Nil
Capital gain	$ 300,000

Summary of income effects:

Sec. 84.1 deemed dividend	$ 425,000	
Capital loss on transfer	Nil	ITA: 85(1)
Capital gain on arm's length sale	300,000	
Net economic effect	725,000	

Again, the $725,000 represents the accrued gain in the Opco Ltd. shares at the time of the transfer.

Exercise 9

For either alternative involving the sale of the Davpet Ltd. shares, the conditions of section 84.1 are met. Davpet Ltd. is a corporation resident in Canada and its shares are held as capital property by Ms. Erin, a Canadian resident. These shares are sold to a non-arm's length corporation, Lenmeag Ltd., since Ms. Erin is related to her father who controls Lenmeag Ltd. The two corporations are connected, since all of the shares of Davpet Ltd. are owned by Lenmeag Ltd. after the sale.

(A) Since no new shares of Lenmeag Ltd. were issued in this alternative, there is no PUC reduction. However, there will be an immediate deemed dividend computed as follows:

Deemed dividend: ITA: 84.1(1)(*b*)

Sum of:

(a) Increase in LSC of Lenmeag Ltd. shares	Nil	(A)
(b) FMV of "boot"	$300,000	(D)
(A + D)	$300,000	

Less sum of:

(c) Greater of:

(i) PUC of Davpet Ltd. shares	$1,000		
		$1,000 (E)	
(ii) Modified ACB of Davpet Ltd. shares	$1,000		

(d) PUC reduction	Nil (F)		ITA: 84.1(1)(*a*)
(E + F)		1,000	

Deemed dividend (A + D) – (E + F) $299,000

This deemed dividend represents the excess of the $300,000 in boot received from Lenmeag Ltd. over the $1,000 in PUC of the Davpet Ltd. shares.

Proceeds of disposition for the Davpet Ltd. shares will be reduced so that there will be no capital gain against which to offset the QSBC share capital gains deduction, as follows:

ITA: 54 "proceeds of disposition" (k)

Consideration in debt received on sale	$300,000
Less: sec. 84.1 deemed dividend	299,000
Adjusted proceeds of disposition.	$ 1,000
ACB of Davpet Ltd. shares	(1,000)
Capital gain	Nil

ITA: 54 "proceeds of disposition"(k)

When the $300,000 debt is repaid by Lenmeag Ltd., there will be no further tax consequences. However, the plan is ineffective, because Ms. Erin will have to pay tax on a deemed dividend of $299,000 at the time of the sale of her shares instead of the intended capital gains.

(B) In this alternative, there will be a PUC reduction, computed as follows:

PUC reduction:

ITA: 84.1(1)(a)

(a) Increase in LSC of Lenmeag Ltd. . . . . $300,000 (A)

Less:

(b) Greater of:

    (i) PUC of Davpet Ltd. shares $1,000

                               $ 1,000

    (ii) Modified ACB of Davpet Ltd. shares . . . $1,000

    Less: FMV of "boot" . . . .   Nil

    Excess, if any . . . .   1,000 (B)

           PUC reduction (A – B) $299,000

           PUC of new Lenmeag Ltd. shares after reduction
               ($300,000 – $299,000) . . . . $ 1,000

The PUC of $1,000 after reduction represents the $1,000 of hard cost in the Davpet Ltd. shares transferred. None of that $1,000 of cost was recovered through boot on this transfer.

Since no "boot" was received, there will be no deemed dividend. As a result, proceeds of disposition for the Davpet Ltd. shares are equal to the $300,000 common share consideration received from Lenmeag Ltd. The result is the following:

Proceeds of disposition for Davpet Ltd. shares.	$300,000
ACB	1,000
Capital gain	$299,000
Taxable capital gain (½ × $299,000)	$149,500
Less: Capital gains deduction for QSBCS	149,500
Effect on taxable income of Ms. Erin.	Nil

The ACB of the Lenmeag Ltd. shares acquired by Ms. Erin will be equal to the $300,000 fair market value of the shares in Davpet Ltd. given up. As a result, when the shares of Lenmeag Ltd. are either sold or redeemed the $300,000 ACB of the shares will shield an equal amount from being taxed as a capital gain and the objective of crystallizing the QSBC share capital gains exemption will be accomplished without an immediate capital gain or deemed dividend on the sale of the Davpet Ltd. shares.

Exercise 10

Of the $900,000 dividend received by Vendco, $700,000 can be attributed to post-1971 earnings of Preyco and, therefore, can be received by Vendco without tax consequences under Part I and Part IV of the Act. The other $200,000 of the total dividend received will be deemed not to be a dividend received and will be deemed to be part of the proceeds of disposition of the shares sold to Purchco. As a result, the following capital gain on the disposition of the shares would be computed:

Actual proceeds on the disposition of the shares to Purchco	$100,000
Deemed proceeds of disposition ($900,000 – $700,000)	200,000
Total proceeds of disposition	$300,000
ACB	100,000
Capital gain	$200,000

ITA: 55(2)(*b*)

These results are equivalent to Vendco's receiving a dividend from Preyco, of $700,000 without tax consequences and then selling the shares of Preyco to Purchco for their fair market value of $300,000 (i.e., $1,000,000 – $700,000). With an adjusted cost base of $100,000 for the shares, a capital gain of $200,000 would result.

Chapter 17

Income Deferral: Other Rollovers and Use of Rollovers in Estate Planning

LEARNING GOALS

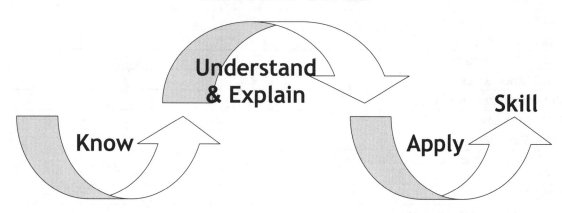

Know

By the end of this chapter you should know the basic provisions of the *Income Tax Act* pertaining to various corporate rollovers that are useful in many planning situations. Completing the Review Questions (¶17,800) and Multiple Choice Questions (¶17,825) is a good way to learn the technical provisions.

Understand and Explain

You should understand and be able to explain the tax consequences of:
- the various rollovers discussed,
- their use in various planning situations, and
- applying some of them in the estate freeze planning opportunity.

Completing the Exercises (¶17,850) is a good way to deepen your understanding of the material.

Apply

You should be able to apply your knowledge and understanding of the key elements of corporate rollovers to implement:
- a basic corporate capital reorganization, amalgamation, or winding-up of subsidiary into a parent; and
- a basic estate freeze in a way that accomplishes a client's goals.

The Assignment Problems (¶17,875) are an excellent way to develop your ability to apply the material in increasingly complex situations.

Chapter 17 — Learning Chart

Topic	Example Problem (✓)	Review Questions (¶17,800)	Multiple Choice (¶17,825)	Exercises (¶17,850)	Assignment Problems (¶17,875)
¶17,000 ROLLOVERS INVOLVING CORPORATIONS AND THEIR SHAREHOLDERS					
¶17,010 Share for Share Exchange					
¶17,015 The concept					
¶17,020 The conditions					
¶17,025 The consequences			4	1	1
¶17,030 Other issues	✓				
¶17,040 Reorganization of Capital					
¶17,045 Overview		2			
¶17,050 Conditions		1			
¶17,055 A conceptual view of the rollover for a reorganization of capital	✓	3	3	2	2
¶17,060 Benefit rule	✓			3	3
¶17,070 Statutory Amalgamations					
¶17,075 Overview		4			
¶17,080 Conditions					
¶17,085 Two levels of rollover					
¶17,090 Income tax consequences		5	1		5
¶17,095 Availability of a "bump" on vertical amalgamation				4	4, 5
¶17,100 Planning opportunities		6			
¶17,105 Effects of the rollover at the shareholder level					
¶17,110 Winding Up a Subsidiary					
¶17,115 Overview		7			
¶17,120 Availability of a "bump" and other effects on the parent			2	4	4, 5
¶17,125 Illustration					
¶17,130 Loss utilization			1		5
¶17,135 Planning opportunities					
¶17,140 Disposition by parent of subsidiary's shares					4
¶17,200 ROLLOVERS INVOLVING SHARES OR CORPORATE SECURITIES					
¶17,210 Convertible Properties		8		5	
¶17,220 Interspousal Transfers					
¶17,250 Summary of Rollovers Covered					
¶17,300 USE OF ROLLOVERS IN ESTATE FREEZING					
¶17,310 Objectives		9, 10			
¶17,320 Holdco Freeze		11, 12, 13	5, 6		6
¶17,330 Internal Freeze		11, 13	6		6
¶17,340 Reverse or Asset Freeze		11, 14	6		

Topic	Example Problem (✓)	Review Questions (¶17,800)	Multiple Choice (¶17,825)	Exercises (¶17,850)	Assignment Problems (¶17,875)
¶17,900 SUPPLEMENTAL NOTES					
¶17,910 GST/HST Consequences of Rollovers Involving Corporations and Their Securities					
¶17,915 Share for share exchange					
¶17,920 Reorganizations					
¶17,925 Statutory amalgamations					
¶17,930 Winding-Up a subsidiary					
¶17,935 Convertible properties					

Study Notes

Chapter 17 —
Discussion Notes for Review Questions

(1) Either articles of amendment or supplementary letters patent need to be filed with the incorporating jurisdiction in order to reorganize the capital of the corporation. Nothing needs to be filed with the CRA.

(2) Some of the uses of a reorganization of capital rollover include: ITA: 86

  (a) an estate freeze to allow the children to benefit from future capital appreciation;

  (b) a reduction in the value of the common shares to allow a purchaser to buy common shares for a nominal amount; and

  (c) a reduction in the value of the common shares to allow employees to buy shares at a reduced value.

(3) A deemed dividend may arise under the reorganization of capital rollover where the redemption proceeds (the reduced PUC of the new shares plus the non-share consideration) exceeds the paid-up capital of the old shares. The deemed dividend results in an adjustment to the proceeds of disposition. As a result, the proceeds will be reduced by any deemed dividend.

ITA: 54 "proceeds of disposition" (*j*), 84(3), 86
ITA: 84(3)
ITA: 84(3), 86(1)(*c*)

(4) For corporate law purposes, the two predecessor corporations are deemed to continue to exist as an amalgamated corporation. The amalgamated corporation is deemed to have existed previously as the predecessor corporations. Property owned by the predecessor corporations continues to be the property of the new amalgamated corporation. Liabilities enforceable against the predecessor corporations are now enforceable against the new amalgamated corporation.

(5) The deemed year-end as a result of an amalgamation has an impact on:

  (a) unpaid amounts — the deemed year-end will count for purposes of section 78;

  (b) CCA will have to be prorated;   ITR: 1100(3)

  (c) the small business deduction business limit ($400,000) will have to be prorated for a short taxation year; and   ITA: 125(5)

  (d) the short taxation year will count as one of the carryforward years available.   ITA: 111

(6) The CRA has indicated that, if an amalgamation is undertaken with a shell corporation solely to effect a year-end change, the GAAR would be applied. Therefore, this is considered to be an offensive transaction as far as the CRA is concerned.

IC 88-2
ITA: 245

(7) In order for the rollover on winding up a subsidiary to apply, not less than 90% of the issued shares of each class of the capital stock of the subsidiary need to be owned by the parent, which is a taxable Canadian corporation, and all of the shares of the subsidiary that were not owned by the parent immediately before the winding-up were owned at that time by persons with whom the parent was dealing at arm's length.

ITA: 88(1)

(8) Her new ACB is the total ACB she had on her preferred shares divided by the total number of new common shares. In this case her new ACB on the common shares would be $10,000 divided by 2,000 or $5 per share.

ITA: 51

(9) The primary purpose of estate freezing is to freeze all or part of the value of growing assets at their current fair market value, such that future growth in these assets accrues to someone else, usually the next generation of family members. The result will be that this future growth will not be taxed in the hands of the taxpayer on a disposition or at his or her death.

(10) Some secondary objectives of an estate freeze would be to:

  (a) defer any immediate tax cost on the freeze transaction and establish the amount of the tax liability on death;

  (b) maintain control over the asset that has been frozen;

  (c) maintain a source of income from the asset being frozen;

  (d) split income with low tax-rate family members; and

  (e) use up the QSBC share capital gains exemption on the asset being frozen, if possible.

(11) The three principal methods of freezing the value of growth assets are:

(a) holdco freeze;   ITA: 85

(b) internal freeze; and   ITA: 86

(c) reverse or asset freeze between corporations.   ITA: 85

Refer to the text for details of these methods.

(12) The basic steps involved in a Holdco freeze are:

(a) incorporate the holding company;

(b) transfer the shares of an operating corporation to the holding corporation using section 85 to avoid incurring an immediate tax cost; and

(c) have the transferor take back, as consideration for the growth asset, debt and preferred shares of the holding company. The preferred shares will have certain characteristics to achieve the freezor's objectives including a fixed retraction value which will freeze the value. Other features would revolve around desired voting control, income and security.

(13) One of the biggest dangers of doing an estate freeze on the shares of an SBC in favour of a spouse or minor children is that the corporation will subsequently lose its SBC status and the corporate attribution rules will apply to deem an interest benefit on the transferor. Remember that the corporation only has to accumulate over approximately 10% of the FMV of its assets in non-active business assets in order to fall offside. This may be done easily if the company is generating excess cash and invests it. Keep in mind that the corporate attribution rules only apply if "one of the main purposes of the transfer or loan may reasonably be considered to be to reduce the income of the individual and to benefit, either directly or indirectly, by means of a trust or by any other means whatever, a person who is a designated person in respect of the individual". Thus, before the corporate attribution rule applies, this purpose test must be met.   ITA: 74.4(2)   ITA: 74.4(2)

(14) A "reverse or asset freeze" would be used to transfer some or all of the growth assets of a corporation in which the taxpayer owns common shares to a new corporation owned by family members who will benefit from the future growth through their ownership of the new corporation's common shares. The consideration taken back on the transfer will usually consist of non-growth assets such as debt and preferred shares with a fixed retraction value. For example, an operating company owns land and building that are used in the business and the present shareholders want the increase in value of the land and building to go to their adult children.

The steps that would be taken are as follows:

(a) a new company would be incorporated with the adult children subscribing for the common shares usually for a nominal amount;

(b) the existing corporation would then transfer the growth assets to the new corporation using section 85 to defer any tax; and

(c) the transferor corporation will take back, as consideration for the growth assets, debt and preferred shares of the new corporation. The preferred shares will have certain characteristics to achieve the freezor's objectives including a fixed retraction value which will freeze the value. Other features would revolve around desired voting control, income and security.

Chapter 17 —
Solutions to Multiple Choice Questions

Question 1

(C) is correct. On winding-up, the losses of the subsidiary are not available to the parent, until the parent's taxation year commencing after the commencement of the winding-up. Thus, the losses of L Ltd. would first be available to P Ltd. in its taxation year commencing January 1, 2014.   ITA: 88(1.1)

(A) is incorrect. The predecessor corporations are deemed to have a year end immediately before the amalgamation, October 31, 2013. The amalgamated corporation first exists on November 1, 2013.

(B) is incorrect. The amalgamated corporation can utilize the losses in its first taxation year commencing November 1, 2013.   ITA: 87(2.1)

(D) is incorrect for the reasons (C) is correct.

Question 2

(B) is correct.

X Ltd's adjusted cost base of the shares of Y Ltd.	$500,000
Less: Cost amount of Y Ltd.'s assets	(420,000)
Dividends paid to X Ltd.	(15,000)
Potential bump	$ 65,000

ITA: 88(1)(*d*)

The ACB of the land can be bumped by $30,000, up to its FMV at the time X Ltd. acquired control of Y Ltd., $130,000.   ITA: 88(1)(*d*)

(A) is incorrect. The bump available on a winding-up has not been applied.   ITA: 88(1)(*d*)

(C) is incorrect. The full amount of the bump available has been allocated to the land. The ACB of the land cannot be bumped above the FMV of the land when X Ltd. acquired control of Y Ltd.   ITA: 88(1)(*d*)

(D) is incorrect for the same reason as (C). In addition, the potential bump has not been reduced by the dividends received from X Ltd.

Question 3

(B) is correct. Since Chris exchanged all his common shares as part of a reorganization of capital, the rollover applies automatically. The cost of the preferred shares is equal to the cost of his common shares, less the non-share consideration: $2,000 – $135 = $1,865. For purposes of calculating the capital gain on the disposal of the common shares, proceeds are defined as the cost of the new shares, plus non-share consideration received: $1,865 + $135 = $2,000. As the proceeds equal his ACB, there is no capital gain.   ITA: 86(1)(*b*)   ITA: 86(1)(*c*)

(A) is incorrect. The ACB of the preferred shares has not been reduced by the non-share consideration received.

(C) is incorrect. The tax-deferral provisions have been ignored.

(D) is incorrect. A capital gain equal to the non-share consideration has been recognized.

Question 4

(D) is correct as it is false. The provision specifically states that subsection 85.1(1) does not apply where consideration other than shares of the particular class of the purchaser was received by the vendor. Therefore, in the absence of any other election being made, Shelly would have a capital gain of $5,000 on the exchange if she received any non-share consideration.   ITA: 85.1(2)

(A) is incorrect as it is true. Section 85.1 is automatic; no election is required.

(B) is incorrect as it is true.   ITA: 85.1(1)(*a*)

(C) is incorrect as it is true.   ITA: 85.1(1)(*b*)

Question 5

(A) is the correct answer because this plan will freeze the value of his interest in ABC for tax purposes (since preferred shares don't grow in value) and transfer future growth to his children (because common shares do grow in value) without giving up control (because the preferred shares are voting). There will be no tax on the transfer since he will be electing at tax cost.

(B) is incorrect because changing his will to leave his shares of ABC to his children does not achieve his objective of freezing the value of his interest and having no tax on the transfer.

(C) is incorrect because gifting the ABC shares to his children results in the loss of control and immediate tax on the accrued capital gain because the gift results in a deemed disposition at fair market value.   ITA: 69

(D) is incorrect because, although a sale at fair market value taking back debt as consideration will defer tax somewhat because of the 10-year reserve available for such transfers, there will be tax on the accrued gain payable over the 10-year period and there is a loss of control.   ITA: 40

Question 6

(C) is correct, assuming an election is made at $750,001. The boot must be limited to $1 because the Act will cause any boot in excess of this amount to be a deemed dividend not a capital gain. That is why (D) is incorrect.   ITA: 84.1(1)

(A) is incorrect because a reverse asset freeze involves a transfer by a company rather than an individual. Hence, the $750,000 capital gains exemption cannot be used.

(B) is incorrect because an internal freeze using section 86 involves an automatic rollover. Hence, the $750,000 capital gains exemption cannot be used. However, while it is possible to accomplish an internal freeze with the crystallization of his capital gains exemption using section 85 as discussed in the textbook, that was not a choice offered in this question.   ITA: 86

Chapter 17 – Solutions to Exercises

Exercise 1

Section 85.1 applies because shares of a Canadian corporation (Magnanimous, the purchaser) are being issued to a taxpayer (Mr. Stewart, the vendor) in exchange for capital property (shares of Targetco) of Mr. Stewart. Since Mr. Stewart wishes to fully defer the accrued gains in his shares he should not include any amount in his income on the disposition of his Targetco shares as a result of the exchange. Mr. Stewart and Magnanimous are at arm's length before the exchange. Furthermore, Mr. Stewart will neither control nor own more than 50% of the fair market value of all of the outstanding shares of Magnanimous after the exchange.

The tax consequences to Mr. Stewart will be as follows:

Proceeds of disposition for Targetco shares ($1.25 × 1,000)	$1,250
ACB of Targetco shares	(1,250)
Capital gain	Nil
ACB of Magnanimous shares received by Mr. Stewart in exchange	$1,250

As a result, the ACB of the 1,000 shares of Targetco given up by Mr. Stewart becomes the ACB of the 500 shares acquired in the exchange and the accrued capital gain on the Targetco shares is deferred. The ACB per share of the Magnanimous shares held by Mr. Stewart will be $2.50 (i.e., $1,250/500).

Magnanimous will have acquired the 1,000 Targetco shares from Mr. Stewart at an ACB equal to the lesser of:

FMV of Targetco shares before exchange (1,000 × $2.35)	$2,350
PUC of Targetco shares before exchange (1,000 × $1.00)	$1,000

The provision will apply to limit the addition to the PUC of Magnanimous shares on their issue in exchange to the amount of the PUC of the Targetco shares received (i.e., $1.00 per share).   ITA: 85.1(2.1)

Exercise 2

There is no deemed dividend, because the redemption amount paid, consisting of cash for $675 and total reduced PUC of the new shares for $1,325, does not exceed the PUC of the old shares of $2,000. (See calculations (4) and (5) below.)   ITA: 84(3)

Issuance of New Shares

(1) Reduced PUC: ITA: 86(2.1)(*a*)

LSC increase for all new shares		$1,325
Less: PUC of old class A preferred shares	$2,000	
Less: boot	675	1,325
PUC reduction		Nil
Total reduced PUC (class B preferreds, $1,000; commons, $325)		$1,325

(2) Cost of class B preferred and common shares received:

Adjusted cost base of old shares	$2,000
Less: fair market value of non-share consideration	675
Cost of Class B preferred and common shares received	$1,325
Cost of non-share consideration (boot) received (equal to FMV)	$ 675

ITA: 86(1)(*c*)

Allocation of cost of new shares:

Class B preferred shares:

$$\frac{\text{FMV of class B preferred shares}}{\text{FMV of all shares}} \times \text{cost of new shares}$$

$$= \frac{\$1{,}755}{\$1{,}755 + \$570} \times \$1{,}325 = \underline{\underline{\$1{,}000}}$$

Common shares:

$$\frac{\text{FMV of common shares}}{\text{FMV of all shares}} \times \text{cost of new shares}$$

$$= \frac{\$570}{\$1{,}755 + \$570} \times \$1{,}325 = \underline{\underline{\$325}}$$

Redemption of Old Shares

(1) Proceeds on redemption of old shares:			ITA: 84(5)(*d*)
Boot or non-share consideration		$ 675	
Reduced PUC of the new shares — see above		1,325	ITA: 84(5)(*d*)
Redemption proceeds		$2,000	
Deemed dividend on redemption:			ITA: 84(3)
Redemption proceeds		$2,000	
Less: PUC of old shares		2,000	
Deemed dividend on redemption..........................		Nil	ITA: 84(3)
(2) Proceeds of disposition of old shares:			ITA: 86(1)(*c*)
Cost of all new shares (above)	$1,325		
Plus: cost of all non-share consideration (equal to FMV)	675	$2,000	
Less: deemed dividend		Nil	ITA: 84(3)
Proceeds of disposition of old shares......................		$2,000	
Capital gain or loss on disposition of old shares:			
Proceeds of disposition of old shares......................		$2,000	
Adjusted cost base of old shares		2,000	
Capital gain (loss)[(1)]		Nil	
Net economic effect:			
Deemed dividends on redemption		Nil	ITA: 84(3)
Capital gain (loss) on disposition of old shares		Nil	
Accrued capital gain on new shares:			
FMV ($1,755 + $570)	$2,325		
ACB......................................	(1,325)	$1,000	
Net economic effect		$1,000	

This $1,000 reflects the accrued gain (i.e., $3,000 – $2,000) on the old shares before the reorganization.

— *NOTE TO SOLUTION*

[(1)] Capital losses on a redemption are denied where the corporation is still affiliated with the shareholder (e.g., where the shareholder or the shareholder's spouse still controls the corporation after the exchange).

ITA: 40(3.6)

Exercise 3

The benefit rule will apply in this case because the FMV of Mrs. Janna's common shares ($450,000, i.e., 75% of $600,000) is greater than the FMV of the preferred shares received on the reorganization ($350,000) and it is reasonable to regard the $100,000 excess as a benefit that Mrs. Janna desired to have conferred on a related person, her daughter.

ITA: 86(2)

There is no deemed dividend, as shown by the following:

ITA: 84(3)

Issuance of New Shares

(1) Reduced PUC: ITA: 86(2.1)(*a*)

LSC increase for new preferred shares		$750
Less: PUC of old common shares	$750	
Less: boot	Nil	750
PUC reduction		Nil
Reduced PUC ($750 – Nil)		$750

(2) The cost of the preferred shares received will be equal to: ITA: 86(2)(*e*)

ACB of common shares	$	750
Less: cost of non-share consideration	Nil	
benefit	$100,000	100,000
Cost of preferred shares		Nil

Since no boot was taken back on the exchange the final PUC of the preferred shares will be $750.

Redemption of Old Shares

(1) Redemption amount:

Non-share consideration		Nil		
PUC of preferred shares received	$	750	$	750
Less: PUC of common shares given up				(750)
Deemed dividend on redemption				Nil	ITA: 84(3)

(2) The deemed proceeds of disposition of Mrs. Janna's common shares will be equal to the lesser of: ITA: 86(2)(*c*)

(a) Cost (equal to FMV) of non-share consideration		Nil
Plus: benefit		$100,000
		$100,000
(b) FMV of common shares given up		$450,000

There will be a capital gain on the disposition by Mrs. Janna of her common shares equal to:

Deemed proceeds of disposition (lesser of (a) and (b), above)		$100,000
ACB of common shares (75% of $1,000)		(750)
Capital gain		$ 99,250

The following net economic effect can be aggregated from the foregoing:

Deemed dividend on redemption		Nil	ITA: 84(3)
Capital gain on disposition of common shares		$ 99,250
Accrued capital gain on preferred shares:		
FMV	$350,000	
ACB	Nil	350,000
Net economic effect		$449,250

This $449,250 reflects the accrued gain (i.e., 75% of ($600,000 – $1,000)) on the common shares held by Mrs. Janna, before the reorganization. Note how $99,250 is realized immediately on the reorganization and the remainder will be realized on the disposition of the preferred shares.

Furthermore, Mrs. Janna has lost the ability to recover $100,000 in tax-paid cost, because the cost of the preferred shares is nil, having been reduced by the benefit. The $100,000 is tax-paid cost because it reflects the $750 of cost in the common shares, plus $99,250 of capital gain realized on the disposition of those shares and included in income. At the same time, Rayna has had the benefit of a $100,000 increase in the value of her shares without any increase in their adjusted cost base. Therefore, the $100,000 of gain will be taxable in her hands on the disposition of her common shares.

Exercise 4

If either section 87 or subsection 88(1) is used:

(A) Acme Limited will be deemed to have proceeds of disposition on the land of $50,000, so the capital gain will be deferred.

(B) M&M will be able to "bump" the cost base of the land on its books

— the "bump" would be computed as follows:			ITA: 88(1)(*d*)
M&M's ACB of Acme's shares			$75,000
Less the sum of:			
(I) cost amount of Acme's assets	$50,000		
(II) dividends paid by Acme to M&M	Nil	50,000	
Increase in ACB of land			$25,000

— this "bump" cannot exceed:

fair market value of the land at the time control was acquired	$90,000
less: ACB of the land	50,000
maximum "bump"	$40,000

— therefore, the ACB of the land to M&M will be $75,000 after a "bump" of $25,000.

Exercise 5

Adjusted cost base of common shares equal to adjusted cost base of the debentures at the time of conversion	$10,000

Adjusted cost base of each common share:

Number of shares received on conversion ($\frac{\$10,000}{\$100} \times 16$)	1,600
ACB of each share ($10,000/1,600)	$ 6.25

Chapter 18
Partnerships and Trusts

LEARNING GOALS

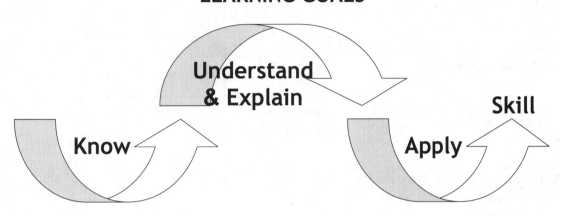

Know

By the end of this chapter you should know the basic provisions of the *Income Tax Act* that relate to partnerships and trusts. Completing the Review Questions (¶18,800) and Multiple Choice Questions (¶18,825) is a good way to learn the technical provisions.

Understand and Explain

You should understand and be able to explain how a partnership and a trust are established, how income earned within a partnership or trust is computed and how this income is taxed. Completing the Exercises (¶18,850) is a good way to deepen your understanding of the material.

Apply

You should be able to apply your knowledge and understanding of partnerships and trusts to apply them in a way that accomplishes a client's goals. Completing the Assignment Problems (¶18,875) is an excellent way to develop your ability to apply the material in increasingly complex situations.

Chapter 18 — Learning Chart

Topic	Example Problem (✓)	Review Questions (¶18,800)	Multiple Choice (¶18,825)	Exercises (¶18,850)	Assignment Problems (¶18,875)
¶18,000 PARTNERSHIPS					
¶18,010 Nature of a Partnership					
¶18,015 What is a partnership?		1			
¶18,020 Partnership versus joint venture					
¶18,030 Partnership Income					
¶18,035 General rules	✓		1	1	1, 2, 3
¶18,040 Limitation on deduction of partnership losses		2			
¶18,045 Partnership allocations: Anti-avoidance		3			
¶18,050 Computation of taxable income				1	1, 2, 3
¶18,055 Personal tax credits generated by the partnership	✓			1	1, 2, 3
¶18,060 Partnership Interest					
¶18,065 The concept					
¶18,070 Adjusted cost base (ACB)		4, 5	2	2	1, 2
¶18,080 Reorganization of Partnerships					
¶18,085 Transfer of partnership property to a corporation	✓				
¶18,090 Transfer of property to a partnership	✓	6			4
¶18,100 Fiscal Period of Terminated Partnership					
¶18,200 TRUSTS					
¶18,210 Nature of Trust					
¶18,215 General		7, 8			
¶18,220 Types of trust		9, 10	6		5, 6, 7
¶18,230 Settlement of Trust		9, 10	5		6
¶18,240 Computation of Income					
¶18,245 Income of trust			3	3	6
¶18,250 Income payable to beneficiary	✓	11, 13, 14		3	6
¶18,255 Attribution	✓				
¶18,260 Tax on split income or "kiddie tax"					6
¶18,265 Accumulating income and preferred beneficiary election					5
¶18,270 Computation of Tax					
¶18,275 Fiscal years		12	3, 4		6
¶18,280 Tax rate			3, 4	3	5, 6
¶18,285 Tax credits					
¶18,290 Minimum tax					
¶18,300 Family Planning Uses of a Trust					
¶18,305 Uses of a trust for income tax advantages		6			

Topic	Example Problem (✓)	Review Questions (¶18,800)	Multiple Choice (¶18,825)	Exercises (¶18,850)	Assignment Problems (¶18,875)
¶18,310 Uses of a trust for non-tax advantages		6			
¶18,900 SUPPLEMENTAL NOTES					
¶18,910 Partnerships					
¶18,915 Corporate partnerships	✓				
¶18,920 Transfer of property from a partnership	✓				
¶18,930 Dispositions from a Trust					
¶18,935 Disposition of capital property					
¶18,940 Disposition of income interest					
¶18,945 Disposition of capital interest					
¶18,950 GST/HST and Partnerships					
¶18,955 Treatment of partnerships under the Excise Tax Act					
¶18,960 The partnership interest					
¶18,965 Transfer of property to a partnership					
¶18,970 Transfer of property from a partnership					
¶18,975 Joint and several liability					
¶18,980 Continuation of partnership					
¶18,990 GST/HST and Trusts					
¶18,995 Treatment of trusts under the Excise Tax Act					
¶18,996 Settlement of trust					
¶18,997 Distributions of property					
¶18,998 Liability of trustees					

Study Notes

Chapter 18 —
Discussion Notes for Review Questions

(1) The term "partnership" is not defined in the *Income Tax Act*. The term "partnership" is defined in the provincial Partnership Acts. The Ontario *Partnership Act*, for example, provides that a "partnership is a relation that subsists between persons carrying on a business in common with a view to profit."

(2) False. The amount of losses a limited partner can deduct in computing income in respect of losses allocated by the limited partnership is limited. The losses can only be deducted to the extent of the limited partner's "at-risk amount" as defined. Generally, the losses may be deducted by a limited partner only to the extent that the total of his or her investment in the partnership plus his or her share of the partnership profit exceeds any amount owing to the partnership by him or her and any guaranteed return as a result of a buy-back of the partnership interest, guaranteed buy-back and so on. To the extent that limited partnership losses are restricted, they can be carried forward indefinitely and deducted under paragraph 111(1)(*e*), but only against income from the limited partnership that gave rise to the loss.

ITA: 96(2.1)
ITA: 96(2.2)

(3) Because Dadd and Ladd do not deal at arm's length, the anti-avoidance rule must be considered. The issue is whether the allocation is reasonable in the circumstances having regard to the capital invested in or work performed for the partnership by the members thereof, or such other factors as may be relevant. For example, the allocation of the capital gain to Dadd may be reasonable given that it was his property in the first place. Since Dadd is the only one with capital and cash invested in the partnership, any losses may be his losses, as the losses impair his capital in the partnership. Arguments can be made that the allocation is reasonable in the circumstances.

ITA: 103(1.1)

Because the decision has been made to allocate income on a 50/50 basis but to allocate all of the losses to Dadd, reference should also be made to another anti-avoidance rule. There should be no problem with this allocation on the basis that the principal reason for the allocation cannot reasonably be considered to be the reduction or postponement of the tax otherwise payable under the Act.

ITA: 103(1)

(4) Income is calculated at the partnership level and then allocated to the partners. A $600 taxable capital gain would be included in the income of the partnership, of which your share is $150 (25% × $600). Your adjusted cost base will be increased by $300, being your share of the taxable capital gain of $150 and your share of the non-taxable portion of $150.

ITA: 53(1)(*e*)

(5) Income is calculated at the partnership level and then allocated to the partners. A $100,000 receipt would not be included in the partnership's income, since life insurance proceeds are not taxable. The adjusted cost base of your partnership interest will be increased by your share or $25,000.

ITA: 53(1)(*e*)

(6) A rollover is available only on a transfer to a Canadian partnership. This is defined to include only those partnerships where all the members are resident in Canada at the particular time. In this case, Ms. Jones will need to determine whether the partner in the United States is still considered a resident of Canada for purposes of the Act. If not, the rollover will not be available.

ITA: 97(2)
ITA: 102

(7) A trust is a relationship whereby a person (who is called a trustee) is bound to deal with property (which is called the trust property) over which he or she has control for the benefit of persons (who are called the beneficiaries) any of whom may enforce the obligation according to the terms of the trust document. A trust is created when a person (called the settlor) transfers property to a trustee.

(8) While it is true that trusts are conduits by allowing certain types of income to flow through to the beneficiaries and retain their character for tax purposes (for example, dividends, capital gains, foreign income), the income of a trust may be subject to tax. Trusts are taxed as an individual on any income that is not paid or payable to the beneficiaries. The rate of tax paid depends on whether the trust is an *inter vivos* trust or a testamentary trust.

ITA: 104(2), 104(6)

(9) A testamentary trust is created as a consequence of the death of an individual. An *inter vivos* trust is one that is created during the lifetime of an individual. An *inter vivos* trust may also be created for tax purposes where a person other than the deceased has contributed property to a testamentary trust.

(10) A discretionary trust is a trust where the trustee is given the power of choice. The trustee may be given the power to determine the date of distribution of trust property, whether income or capital is to be paid to a beneficiary, how much is to be paid to a beneficiary and in what proportions among a group of beneficiaries it is to be paid. This feature gives the trust a great deal of flexibility and is a very useful planning tool for income splitting and estate equalization purposes.

CHAPTER 18

(11) The special treatment applies to the following types of income:

    (a) taxable dividends from a Canadian corporation which allows the beneficiary to use the dividend gross-up and tax credit;

    ITA: 104(19)

    (b) net taxable capital gains which are eligible for the capital gains deduction available in respect of qualified shares of a small business corporation and qualified farm property (note that net capital losses do not flow through to the beneficiary);

    ITA: 104(21)–(21.3)

    (c) non-taxable dividends which are excluded from the computation of taxable income;

    ITA: 104(20)

    (d) foreign income and related foreign tax paid to allow the beneficiary to claim the foreign tax credit; and

    ITA: 104(22)

    (e) superannuation and pension benefits.

    ITA: 104(27), 104(28)

(12) The trust would file a tax return for the fiscal period ending on March 15, 2013 on or before June 13, 2013 (that is, 90 days after the end of the trust's year). She would report the income in the calendar year in which the fiscal year end of the trust fell. For example, in 2013 Ms. Betty would report the income that is allocated to her out of the trust for the period ended March 15, 2013.

    ITA: 104(13), 104(14)

Chapter 18 —
Solutions to Multiple Choice Questions

Question 1

(C) $167,500 is correct.

Net income per financial statement		$ 365,000
Add: Donations		20,000
Sale of shares — Taxable capital gain	$ 60,000	
— Accounting gain	(120,000)	(60,000)
		$ 325,000
Bert's share		× ½
		$ 162,500
Dividend gross-up: $20,000 × ¼ [18% for dividends received in 2014]		5,000
Taxable income		$ 167,500

(A) $182,500 is incorrect. All of the adjustments have been ignored: donations, net accounting/tax gain, and the dividend gross-up.

(B) $187,500 is incorrect. The only adjustment that was made was for the dividend gross-up.

(D) $171,500 is incorrect. All adjustments were made except for the dividend gross-up, which, at 45%, was incorrect on dividends from a CCPC out of its LRIP.

Question 2

(C) $63,000 is correct.

Contributions — initial	$ 5,000
— additional	14,000
Share of profit	100,000
Share of non-taxable portion of capital gain	20,000
Share of charitable donations	(6,000)
Drawings	(70,000)
ACB	$ 63,000

(A) $33,000 is incorrect. The capital gain has been excluded completely.

(B) $43,000 is incorrect. The non-taxable portion of the capital gain has not been included.

(D) $69,000 is incorrect. The ACB has not been reduced by Ann's share of the charitable donations.

Question 3

(A) is true. The tax return is due 90 days after the year-end of the trust. *Inter vivos* trusts are taxed on a calendar year basis.   ITA: 150(1)(*c*), 249(1)(*b*)

(B) is true. The trust is entitled to the deduction.   ITA: 104(6)

(C) is true. The tax rate is 29%.   ITA: 122(1)

(D) is false. Al is deemed to have received proceeds equal to the fair market value of the marketable securities transferred to the trust. Therefore, Al is required to recognize the $30,000 capital gain.   ITA: 69(1)(*b*)

Question 4

(B) is true. Testamentary trusts are taxed as individuals.   ITA: 104(2)

(A) is false. The taxation year of a testamentary trust does not have to be on a calendar year basis.   ITA: 104(23)

(C) is false. The trust return is due 90 days after the end of the fiscal period of the trust.   ITA: 150(1)(*c*)

(D) is false. The trust is entitled to claim a dividend tax credit for dividends received from taxable Canadian corporations.   ITA: 104(2), 121

Question 5

(C) is correct. An alter ego trust has a deemed disposition on the settlor's death.   ITA: 248(1)

(A) is incorrect. An *inter vivos* trust generally has a deemed disposition at fair market value at the end of 21 years, unless it is a joint partner trust (described in (B)), in which case the deemed disposition takes place on the partner (i.e., spouse or common-law partner) beneficiary's death.

(D) is incorrect. A discretionary trust would always have a deemed disposition at fair market value at the end of 21 years, since it cannot be a joint partner trust (which, by definition, must pay the income out to the beneficiary and, therefore, cannot be discretionary).

Question 6

(C) Avoiding the deemed disposition is not an advantage. You cannot avoid the deemed disposition at FMV if the beneficiaries of the testamentary trust are your children.   ITA: 104(4)

(A) is incorrect because income-splitting using the available designations is an advantage.   ITA: 104(13.1), 104(13.2)

(B) is incorrect, because avoiding the deemed disposition on the child's death is an advantage.

(D) is incorrect, because providing your children with beneficial ownership but not control over their inheritance is an advantage.

Chapter 18 — Solutions to Exercises

Exercise 1

Partnership's net income for financial accounting purposes		$304,280
Deduct: Capital gain		5,000
		$299,280
Add: Amortization on office furniture	$ 3,750	
Donations	5,500	
Membership in fitness club	1,250	
Taxable capital gain (½ × $5,000)	2,500	13,000
		$312,280
Deduct: Capital cost allowance		4,300
Income to be allocated (Division B)		$307,980
Bob's share of income from partnership		$153,990
Add: Gross-up of Bob's share of partnership dividends		
(¼ × $4,000 × ½) [18% gross-up for dividends received in 2014]	$ 500	
Grossed-up personal dividends	4,375	
Personal interest income	1,200	6,075
Bob's net income (Division B) and taxable income		$160,065

Analysis of Bob's income:

	Personal	*Partnership*	*Total*
Grossed-up dividends	$4,375	$ 2,500	$ 6,875
Interest	1,200	—	1,200
Taxable capital gains	—	1,250	1,250
Business income		150,740	150,740
Total	$5,575	$154,490*	$160,065

* $153,990 + $500 gross-up

Notes:

(1) Drawings taken by the members of a partnership do not constitute a business expense but are a method of distributing partnership income to members of the partnership.

(2) Charitable donations are not deductions in computing the income of a partnership but are used as the basis for computing the charitable donations tax credit for an individual partner.

(3) Fees paid to a fitness club are non-deductible expenses.   ITA: 18(1)(*l*)

(4) Bob will be eligible for the following federal dividend tax credit:

— on share of partnership dividends (13⅓% of ⁵⁄₄ × ½ × $4,000)	$	333
— on personal dividends (13⅓% of ⁵⁄₄ [¹³⁄₁₈ × .18 for dividends received in 2014] × $3,500)		583
Total	$	916

Exercise 2

Adjusted cost base of Katie's partnership interest:

Contributions			$ 50,000
Add:	Share of profits excluding taxable capital gain (½ × ($450,000 – $20,000))	$215,000	
	Share of full capital gain (½ × $20,000 × ²⁄₁)	20,000	
	Share of capital dividends (½ × $4,000)	2,000	237,000
			$287,000

Deduct:	Share of losses (½ × $15,000)	$ 7,500	
	Drawings (½ × $176,000)	88,000	
	Share of donations (½ × $27,000)	13,500	109,000
ACB of partnership interest			$178,000

Capital gain on disposition of partnership interest:

Proceeds of disposition	$250,000
ACB	178,000
Capital gain	$ 72,000
Taxable capital gain (½ of $72,000)	$ 36,000

Exercise 3

	Trust	Rebecca	Robert
Income			
Interest	$ 4,500	$ 5,500	$ 1,500
Taxable capital gain	1,500	1,500	1,500
Taxable dividends	4,140	4,140	4,140
Net income/taxable income	$10,140	$11,140	$ 7,140
Federal tax (@ 29% for trust and 15% for individuals)	$ 2,941	$ 1,671	$ 1,071
Personal tax credit @ 15% of $11,038	—	(1,656)	(1,656)
Tuition credit and education credit	—	—	Nil
Dividend tax credit @ 6/11 of $3,000 × .38	(622)	(622)	(622)
Total tax	$ 2,319	$　Nil	Nil

Note: None of the tuition and education tax credits were claimed by Robert. Federal tuition and education tax credits of $750[1] are transferable to a parent, or the unused amount of $1,083 less any amount transferred to a supporting person may be carried forward. The definition of tax payable and the ordering rules require that the personal, tuition and education tax credits be deducted before the dividend tax credit which is lost in this case.

ITA: 118.9(1)
ITA: 118.61
ITA: 118.81, 118.92

— *NOTE TO SOLUTION*

[1] Lesser of:
(a) $750 (federal) = $750

(b) (15% × $3,500) + (15% of (($400 + 65) × 8)) = $1,083 ⎫
　　　　　　　　　　　　　　　　　　　　　　　　　　⎬　 $ 750
Minus ($1,013 – $1,656) ⎭ Nil

| Net amount transferred to parent | $ 750 |

Chapter 19
International Taxation in Canada

LEARNING GOALS

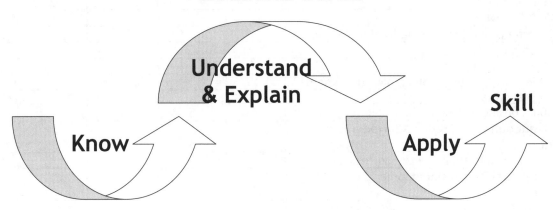

Know

By the end of this chapter you should know the basics of Canadian taxation of non-residents, the basics of Canadian tax law applicable to crossborder transactions, and Canadian taxation of residents with foreign investments. Completing the Review Questions (¶19,800) and Multiple Choice Questions (¶19,825) is a good way to learn the technical provisions.

Understand and Explain

You should have a basic understanding and be able to explain:

- The taxation of non-residents with Canadian investments or business dealings.
- The tax treatment of crossborder transactions between Canadian residents and foreign persons.
- The taxation of Canadian residents earning income from foreign investments.
- The basic application of tax treaties.

Completing the Exercises (¶19,850) is a good way to deepen your understanding of the material.

Apply

You should be able to apply your knowledge and understanding of the key provisions in the Act applicable to non-residents, crossborder transactions, and foreign income earned by Canadian residents to determine:

- Tax compliance requirements for a non-resident with Canadian investments or business dealings.
- The application and impact of a tax treaty on the taxation of various sources of income earned by non-residents in Canada.
- The Canadian taxation of crossborder loans and transactions
- The Canadian taxation of foreign investment by Canadian residents.

Completing the Assignment Problems (¶19,875) is an excellent way to develop your ability to apply the material in increasingly complex situations.

Chapter 19 – Learning Chart

Topic	Example Problem (✓)	Review Questions (¶19,800)	Multiple Choice (¶19,825)	Exercises (¶19,850)	Assignment Problems (¶19,875)
¶19,000 LIABILITY FOR CANADIAN TAX					
¶19,010 Residents			3		
¶19,020 Non-Residents				2	4
¶19,100 NON-RESIDENTS					
¶19,110 Income Earned in Canada by Non-Residents					
¶19,115 Employment income					1
¶19,120 Business income	✓			3	3
¶19,123 Regulation 105 withholding requirements					
¶19,125 Branch tax	✓				3
¶19,130 Disposing of taxable Canadian property	✓	5	1	7	2, 4
¶19,140 Deductions and Credits Allowed a Non-Resident					1
¶19,145 Tax credits available to non-residents					
¶19,150 Provincial/Territorial Income Tax Obligation					
¶19,160 Withholding Taxes on Canadian-Source Income – Part XIII Tax	✓	8,9	4	7	4
¶19,165 Rental income alternative – Section 216 elections	✓				2
¶19,170 Canadian benefits alternative – Section 217 election		10			
¶19,200 PART-YEAR RESIDENTS		2			
¶19,210 Income, Deductions, and Credits	✓	6,13	2	5	
¶19,220 Deemed Acquisition on Entering Canada	✓	7,12			
¶19,230 Deemed Disposition on Leaving Canada	✓	7		1	5
¶19,300 IMPACT OF CANADA-FOREIGN COUNTRY TAX TREATIES					
¶19,310 Application of the treaties		1			
¶19,400 CROSS-BORDER TRANSACTIONS AND LOANS					
¶19,410 Transfer Pricing	✓	3			6, 7
¶19,420 Thin Capitalization – Inbound Loans	✓	4			8
¶19,430 Corporate Debt Owed by a Non-Resident – Outbound Loans	✓	11		4	9
¶19,435 Cross-border shareholder loans/balances					
¶19,440 Low interest cross-border loans/balances	✓				
¶19,500 TAXATION OF CANADIAN RESIDENTS WITH FOREIGN INVESTMENTS					
¶19,510 Active Business Income Earned in a Foreign Jurisdiction		14	5	6	10
¶19,515 Unincorporated foreign branch operations					
¶19,520 Individuals receiving dividends from foreign corporations					
¶19,525 Corporations receiving dividends from non-foreign affiliates	✓	16			
¶19,530 Corporations receiving dividends from foreign affiliates	✓				
¶19,540 Passive Income Earned in a Foreign Jurisdiction		15	7	6	12
¶19,545 Controlled foreign affiliates	✓				
¶19,600 INFORMATION REPORTING			6		

Study Notes

Chapter 19 —
Discussion Notes for Review Questions

(1) One objective of international tax treaties is to eliminate double taxation. This is accomplished by ensuring that income is not taxed in more than one country or by providing a foreign tax credit for the taxes paid in the other country. The second objective of the treaties is to prevent tax evasion. This is accomplished through "sharing of information" provisions in the treaties. Treaties facilitate information exchange and promote resolution of disputes related to domestic tax laws of the two countries.

(2) A part-year resident is a taxpayer who either becomes a permanent resident of Canada or relinquishes permanent resident status at some point in the year. This taxpayer is taxable in Canada on worldwide income only during the period of residency. Non-Canadian source pre/post-residency income is not taxable in Canada. A non-resident is a person who is resident somewhere other than Canada and is taxable in Canada only on Canadian employment or business income, or taxable capital gains on taxable Canadian property. Part XIII withholding tax may apply to certain other types of Canadian-source income earned by a non-resident.
ITA: 2(3)
ITA: 114

(3) The transfer pricing rules are intended to ensure that transactions with a related non-resident entity occur at an arm's length price, i.e., the price that would be used between unrelated persons. In that way, profits cannot be exported beyond the Canadian tax authorities.
ITA: 247(1)

(4) The thin capitalization rules are designed to prevent the erosion of Canada's tax base by transferring profits to a non-resident through deductible interest payments. By under-capitalizing a Canadian subsidiary, a foreign parent could "force" the subsidiary to pay interest that would otherwise be taxable profits in the subsidiary instead of repatriating profits through dividends.
ITA: 18(4)

(5) A non-resident is taxable on the disposition of taxable Canadian property (TCP). TCP is defined in the Act and includes shares of an unlisted corporation resident in Canada, if more than 50% of the fair market value of the share was derived from real or immovable property situated in Canada, or Canadian or timber resource properties at any time in the prior five years. Listed shares of a Canadian resident corporation are TCP only if, at any time in the prior five years, the non-resident and non-arm's length persons owned not less than 25% of the shares of the corporation and more than 50% of the fair market value of the shares were derived from real or immovable property situated in Canada, or Canadian or timber resource properties. The relevant tax treaty would need to be considered to determine whether a treaty article overrides the domestic law. Unless the shares are treaty-protected property, the purchaser of the shares is required to withhold and remit 25% of the purchase price unless the non-resident obtains a certificate of compliance and remits a tax payment of 25% of the gain on the property to the CRA no later than 10 days after the disposition.
ITA: 248(1)

(6) Some personal tax credits are prorated for the portion of the year the individual is resident in Canada, for example, basic personal tax credit, age credit, etc. Other credits can be claimed in full, for example, donation credit, medical expense credit, etc.

(7) The individual would be taxable only on the gain from the time he or she moved to Canada. The cost base used to calculate the gain would be the fair market value of the property at the date of the move to Canada.
ITA: 128.1(1)(c)

(8) A non-resident employer is required to withhold and remit tax from remuneration paid to an employee related to duties performed in Canada. The employee will file a Canadian tax return to include the Canadian employment income less any income exempt from tax under the relevant Canadian tax treaty. The tax withholdings will be applied against any taxes payable on the return. Employers resident in countries that have a tax treaty with Canada which exempts the employment income from Canadian tax can apply for a withholding tax waiver.
ITA: 153(1); ITR: 102

(9) The withholding tax rate is 25%. However, under the Canada–U.S. Income Tax Convention this rate is reduced to 5% if the shareholder owns at least 10% of the voting stock of the corporation and 15% in all other cases.
ITA: 212(1)
Article X Canada–U.S. Tax
Convention

(10) There would only be a benefit to a section 217 election where the individual's tax calculated under Part I on those benefits would be less than the 25% withholding tax rate (or the reduced rate under the relevant tax treaty).
ITA: 212(1)(n), 217

(11) If the loan is not repaid within one year of the end of the taxation year in which the loan was made, Part XIII tax will apply to a deemed dividend to the shareholder equal to the loan balance. Subsection 17(1) will not apply where Part XIII tax is paid (and not refunded on a repayment of the balance). A refund of the Part XIII tax may be requested within two years of the calendar year in which a repayment of the balance occurs (in which case, subsection 17(1) could apply).
ITA: 15(2), 214(3)(a)

(12) The purpose of the deemed disposition/acquisition rule is to provide a tax cost base from which future income/gains are determined for Canadian income tax purposes.
ITA: 128.1(1)

(13) Non-residents who are filing a Canadian income tax return for employment income, business income, or because they have disposed of taxable Canadian property, are entitled to claim the same personal tax credits available to a resident where their Canadian-source income represents 90% or more of their world income.

ITA: 118.94

(14) A Canadian resident individual may reduce Part I taxes payable by a foreign tax credit for tax withholdings up to a rate of 15%. Withholding taxes in excess of 15% are deductible in computing Division B income. A Canadian resident corporation may claim a foreign tax credit for withholdings (without limit) unless the dividends are received from a foreign affiliate, in which case Division C deductions apply.

ITA: 113(1), 126(1)
ITA: 20(11)

(15) The FAPI rules prevent a Canadian resident from deferring tax on investment income by holding investments offshore in controlled foreign affiliates. The rules require the Canadian investor to pay tax on the foreign investment income as it is earned each year instead of when it is received as a dividend.

ITA: 91(1)

(16) Exempt surplus of a foreign affiliate represents income or gains for which Canada relinquishes its right to tax. Active business income earned in countries with which Canada has a treaty or tax information exchange agreement as well as the non-taxable portion of capital gains become exempt surplus of a foreign affiliate [other than the non-taxable portion of gains included in hybrid surplus related to dispositions of shares in foreign affiliates]. The taxable portion of gains on the disposition of properties used principally to gain or produce active business income in a designated treaty country is also included in exempt surplus.

ITR: 5907, "exempt earnings"

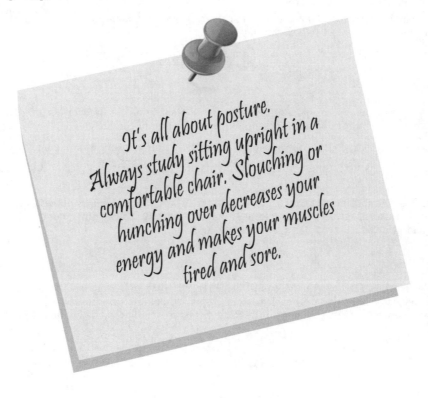

It's all about posture. Always study sitting upright in a comfortable chair. Slouching or hunching over decreases your energy and makes your muscles tired and sore.

CHAPTER 19

Chapter 19 —
Solutions to Multiple Choice Questions

Question 1

(B) is correct. Jari is taxed as a non-resident on the disposition of taxable Canadian property. The tax is federal tax on the rate schedule plus 48% of tax otherwise payable.

ITA: 2(3), 115, 120(1)

(A) is not correct. Income earned in a particular province for a non-resident includes only employment income and income from carrying on business.

ITR: 2602(1)

(C) and (D) are not correct. Non-residents are taxable on gains from the disposition of taxable Canadian property under Part I of the ITA. Withholding tax is exigible under Part XIII.

ITA: 2(3), 115(1)

Question 2

(B) is correct. The interest was earned while Mai was a non-resident, before she became a resident of Canada. Withholding tax does not apply to interest paid by a Canadian resident bank to unrelated non-residents.

ITA: 2(3), 212(1)(b)

(A) is incorrect. Only interest that is not fully exempt interest paid to a non-arm's length person and participating debt interest is subject to 25% withholding tax.

ITA: 212(1)(b)

(C) and (D) are incorrect. The interest was not earned during her period of residency.

Question 3

(D) is correct. As a resident of Canada, Antonio is taxed in Canada on his worldwide income. Canada provides a foreign tax credit to alleviate potential double taxation of the income.

ITA: 126(2)

(A) is incorrect. As a resident of Canada, Antonio is subject to tax on his worldwide income.

(B) is incorrect. Deductions for business foreign tax credits are not available in Division B of the ITA.

(C) is incorrect. Business income is sourced to the country in which the business activities are carried on (or where a permanent establishment is located under treaty). Brazil has jurisdiction to tax the income, and Canada provides a foreign tax credit for the Brazilian tax.

Question 4

(C) is correct. There are no tax consequences until Betty receives payments from her RRSP/RRIF, at which time, the payer will withhold tax on each payment. The withholding tax rate is 25%, but is reduced to 15% under treaty for annuity payments if the RRSP is matured and converted to an annuity.

212(1)(l)
Article XVIII

(A) is not correct. Taxable Canadian property, as defined, does not include RRSPs.

ITA: 248(1)

(B) is not correct. Excluded rights or interests are exempt from deemed disposition at the time of emigration.

ITA: 128.1(10)

(D) is not correct. Only payments out of an RRSP are subject to withholding tax.

ITA: 212(1)(l)

Question 5

(B) is correct. The exempt surplus balance of Maxwell Rock Ltd. will be $100,000 at the end of the year. The business income earned in Michigan is the net earnings for the year from an active business carried on by it in a designated treaty country and would be exempt surplus of the U.S. company. The business income earned in Paraguay is included in taxable surplus because the income is being earned in a country that is not a designated treaty country. Of the $150,000 dividend paid to Maxwell, $100,000 will be considered to have been paid from exempt surplus and $50,000 will be considered to have been paid from taxable surplus. The exempt surplus portion of the dividend is fully deductible in computing taxable income.

ITR: 5901
ITA: 113(1)(a)

(A) is incorrect. Dividends received by a corporation from a foreign affiliate are not eligible for a foreign tax credit.

ITA: 126(1)

(C) is incorrect. Only $100,000 of the dividend is paid from exempt surplus.

(D) Is incorrect. A deduction will be available in computing taxable income for the underlying tax paid associated with the dividend paid by the U.S. company from business income earned in Paraguay but not from business income earned in the United States. The business income earned in the United States is exempt surplus and is fully exempt from tax in Canada when paid as a dividend.

ITA: 113(1)(*b*)

Question 6

(B) is correct, for the reason stated in the question.

(A) and (C) are incorrect for the reason stated in (B).

(D) is incorrect. Bob would only need to file a U.S. form 1040NR in relation to an income producing property.

Question 7

(D) is correct. The company will be a controlled foreign affiliate of each of the Canadian shareholders because (i) it is a foreign affiliate (each Canadian shareholder owns not less than 1% of the shares and not less than 10% of the shares with related persons) of the company, and (ii) it is a controlled foreign affiliate because it is controlled by less than five unrelated Canadian residents. The income of the corporation will be FAPI because it will be considered income from property. The shareholder's participating percentage of the income as of the end of the affiliate's taxation year will be included in Division B income. A deduction for the related U.S. tax paid on the income calculated using the relevant tax factor will also be available.

ITA: 95(1)

ITA: 91(1)
ITA: 91(4)

(A) is incorrect. The income will be taxed annually. Dividends paid to the Canadian shareholders will be included in Division B income. Foreign tax credits will be available against Part I tax for U.S. tax withholdings. An offsetting deduction will be available for the lesser of the amount of the dividend and the cumulative total of prior year's net income inclusions for FAPI.

ITA: 12(1)

ITA: 126(1)
ITA: 91(5)

(B) is incorrect. The income will be taxed annually. An offsetting deduction for a dividend is not available under Division C because the dividend is not received by a corporation. Division C deductions are only available to Canadian resident corporations.

ITA: 113(1)

(C) is incorrect. The income will be taxed annually. An offsetting deduction for a dividend is not available under Division C because the dividend is not received by a corporation.

ITA: 113(1)

Chapter 19 — Solutions to Exercises

Exercise 1

Alan is deemed to have disposed of the shares on emigration at their fair market value of $40,000. Given his ACB of $28,000, he will have a capital gain of $12,000, and a taxable capital gain of $6,000.

Alan can elect to defer paying the tax that results from the deemed disposition rule. The election must be made on or before the balance due date for the year in which emigration takes place. If the election is made, the payment of the tax can be deferred without interest until the properties are actually sold. Since security is not required for up to $100,000 of capital gains resulting from the deemed disposition rule, Alan will not be required to post security with the CRA.

ITA: 220(4.5), (4.51)

Exercise 2

No, a foreign tax credit is not claimed in both countries. To do so would eliminate the taxes on the income altogether. The country where the income is sourced has the first right of taxation and consequently, a foreign tax credit is allowed only in the other country (the residence country).

A non-resident will pay the Canadian income taxes on income from duties of offices and employment performed in Canada, income from business carried on in Canada, and on taxable capital gains on taxable Canadian property. These taxes will then be used as a foreign tax credit in the country of residence. Note that some countries will recognize CPP/QPP contributions as taxes, in addition to any income taxes paid to Canada. Note that treaties can limit or eliminate a country's jurisdiction to tax source income. The country of residence will provide a tax credit only if taxes are paid.

ITA: 2(3)

Exercise 3

Canada levies tax on non-residents who carry on business in Canada. Carrying on business in Canada is distinguishable from carrying on business with Canada. While Sam-son solicits sales from Canadians, it does not solicit sales in Canada through an agent or servant. Given these facts, Sam-son is not carrying on business in Canada and is not liable for Canadian income taxes on the $76,000 profit originating from within Canada.

ITA: 2(3)

Exercise 4

The two corporations are considered associated (section 256) for Canadian tax purposes. Generally, under subsection 129(6), interest income received from an associated corporation that is deductible in computing that corporation's active business income would be considered active business income. However, as the interest is U.S.-sourced, and not from a "source in Canada", and is not deductible in computing active business income in Canada, it will be considered investment income to the Canadian corporation and not income from an active business. Hence, the small business deduction will not be available for the interest income.

The interest will be subject to the full corporate tax rate, including the $6\frac{2}{3}\%$ additional refundable tax on investment income. The addition to RDTOH ($26\frac{2}{3}\%$) will also apply.

The second issue is whether any imputed interest income arises under subsection 17(1). That subsection requires an interest income inclusion equal to interest computed using the prescribed rate less the actual interest included in income on the loan. If the interest paid is considered to be computed at a reasonable rate, an income inclusion is not required. Imputed income will not arise if the 1% rate being paid is comparable to the U.S. borrowing rate.

The foreign affiliate dumping provision does not apply because Johnson & Co. Ltd. is not controlled by a non-resident corporation.

ITA: 212.3(1)

Exercise 5

The Act defines "moving expenses" as including any expenses incurred as, or on account of, travel costs in the course of moving the taxpayer from the old residence to the new residence, cost of transporting or storing household effects, cost of meals and lodging, etc. It appears Mary Jane's expenses would qualify under this definition; however, the move must be an eligible relocation as defined by the Act. The definition of "eligible relocation" only includes relocations that are both from and to a residence in Canada unless the person is a student or person absent from but a resident of Canada.

ITA: 62(3)

ITA: 62(1); 248(1)
ITA: 62(2)

Exercise 6

Dutchco is a foreign affiliate of Canco as Canco owns not less than 10% of the shares of the company. Dutchco is a controlled foreign affiliate of Canco as it is controlled by a Canadian resident.

Dutchco is earning income from an active business in a country with which Canada has a tax convention. This income would be treated as exempt surplus. The company is also earning income from property. This income would be treated as FAPI and would become part of Dutchco's taxable surplus.

For 2012 and 2013, Canco must include, in respect of each share it owns in Dutchco, the share's participating percentage of FAPI less a deduction for the foreign accrual tax applicable to the FAPI income inclusion.

Income Inclusion	$ 9,600	80% of $12,000	ITA: 91(1)
Deduction	$(7,680)	20% of $9,600 multiplied by the relevant tax factor of 1/(38% − 13%)	ITA: 91(4)
2012 Income Inclusion	$ 1,920		

The net income inclusion is added to the adjusted cost base of the shares of Dutchco held by Canco, i.e., $500,000 + $1,920 = $501,920.

Income Inclusion	$ 9,600	80% of $12,000	ITA: 91(1)
Deduction	$(7,680)	20% of $9,600 multiplied by the relevant tax factor of 1/(38% − 13%)	ITA: 91(4)
2013 Income Inclusion	$ 1,920		

The net income inclusion is added to the adjusted cost base of the shares of Dutchco held by Canco, i.e., $501,920 + $1,920 = $503,840.

When the dividend is paid in 2013, it will be included in Canco's Division B income. A deduction is available for the portion of the dividend prescribed to have been paid from exempt surplus. Exempt surplus includes exempt earnings for any taxation year ending in the period that starts with the first day of the taxation year in which Dutchco became a foreign affiliate and ends at the time the dividend is paid. FAPI is included in taxable surplus in a similar manner. The exempt surplus and taxable surplus balances of Dutchco at the time of the dividend would be as follows: *(ITA: 12(1), 90(1))*

	Exempt Surplus	Taxable Surplus	
Income for December 31, 2012 taxation year end of the affiliate	$30,000	$12,000	ITR: 5907(1)
Income/profits tax paid to Netherlands tax authorities	($ 6,000)	($ 2,400)	
Balance February 2013	$24,000	$ 9,600	

The portion of the whole dividend of $50,000 deemed to have been paid out of exempt surplus would be $24,000. The portion of the whole dividend deemed to have been paid out of taxable surplus would be $9,600. The remainder, of $16,400, would be considered to have been paid from pre-acquisition surplus.

The 2013 income inclusions less deductions for Canco related to the dividend would be as follows:

Dividend Income	$ 40,000	$50,000 × 80%	ITA: 12(1), 90(1)
Deduction	$(19,200)	$24,000 × 80%	ITA: 113(1)(a)
Deduction	$ (5,760)	Lesser of: (1) $7,680 [$9,600 × 80%], and (2) $5,760 [$2,400 × 80% × (1/(38% − 13%) − 1]	ITA: 113(1)(b)
Deduction	$ (1,536)	Lesser of: (1) $1,536 [$9,600 × 80% × 5% × 1/(38% − 13%)], and (2) $1,920 [$9,600 × 80% less: paragraph 113(1)(b) deduction of $5,760]	ITA: 113(1)(c)
Deduction	$ (1,920)	Lesser of: (1) $1,920 [$9,600 × 80% − paragraph 113(1)(b) deduction of $5,760], and (2) 2012 net FAPI inclusion of $1,920	ITA: 91(5)
Deduction	$(13,120)	$16,400 × 80%	ITA: 113(1)(d)
Net Inclusion (Deduction)	$ (1,536)		

The subsection 91(5) deduction reduces the adjusted cost base of the shares of Dutchco held by Canco. The adjusted cost base of shares after the February 2013 dividend is $501,920.

The portion of the dividend paid from exempt surplus, i.e., $19,200, and pre-acquisition surplus, i.e., $13,120, is not taxed in Canada. The portion of the dividend paid from FAPI, i.e., $7,680 ($40,000 – $19,200 – $13,120), is taxed in Canada less a deduction for the underlying foreign tax, i.e., $5,760, and for the withholding tax, i.e., $1,536. There is a further deduction of $1,920 to reverse the prior year's FAPI inclusion (preventing double taxation of the passive income earned in the CFA), limited to the total amount of the taxable surplus dividend, net of the deduction for underlying tax.

Exercise 7

(A) The rents paid by Sam and Harry to Joe's parents are subject to a 25% withholding tax. Joe appears to be acting as an agent for his parents in collecting the rents and would be required to deduct and withhold the tax from the rents received and submit it to the Receiver General. Failure to withhold can result in interest charges and a penalty of 10% to 20% of unremitted withholdings.

ITA: 212(1)(*d*), 215(3), 227(8), 227(8.3)

Joe's parents can file a Canadian tax return within two years of the end of the year to obtain a refund of any Part XIII tax paid in excess of the tax payable (using graduated tax rates) on the net rental income (rents less mortgage interest, CCA, utilities, and property taxes).

ITA: 216(1)

Alternatively, an undertaking (NR6) to file an income tax return can be filed prior to the first rental payment for the year indicating Joe's parents' intent to file a Canadian tax return within six months of the end of the year. In that case, withholding tax can be reduced to 25% of the net rents received (i.e., rents less mortgage interest, utilities, and property taxes). The return must be filed within six months of the end of the year or Joe will become liable for the excess of 25% of the rents received less the withholdings remitted to CRA.

ITA: 216(4)

(B) If the condominium is sold in the future, Joe's parents will have disposed of taxable Canadian property. They will be required to file a personal tax return to report the taxable capital gain on the disposition of the property. They will also be required to file a separate personal tax return to report any recapture on the disposition of the property. The Canada–China Tax Convention would need to be reviewed to determine if the taxable capital gain on the disposition of the property is treaty exempt. Assuming not, the purchaser would be required to withhold 25% of the proceeds paid for the land and 50% of the proceeds paid for the building within 30 days of the end of the month of the purchase, unless Mr. and Mrs. Doe have obtained a clearance certificate and paid 25% of the estimated (or actual) capital gain on the disposition of the property plus an estimate of the tax on the recapture related to the disposition of the property.

ITA: 248(1)

ITA: 116(1), (5)

(C) It appears that Joe will become a resident of Canada under common law and will be taxed on his worldwide income. If Joe were to own the condominium, it may be possible for him to treat the property as his principal residence. He would need to be able to argue that the income-producing use is ancillary to the main use of the property as a principal residence, and he would not be able to claim CCA on the property. The rents paid to him by the roommates would not be subject to withholding tax. If Joe's parents were to loan him the funds to purchase the property, the attribution rules would not apply, as the rules only apply to individuals who are residents of Canada. Any interest Joe were to pay on loans from his parents would be subject to withholding tax, as the interest would be paid to a non-arm's length person. The Canada–China Tax Convention may reduce the rate to 10%.

ITA: 212(1)(*b*)

Study Notes

Study Notes

Study Notes

Study Notes

Study Notes

Study Notes